CW01024533

Africa Series

DEALING WITH GOVERNMENT IN SOUTH SUDAN

Eastern Africa Series

Women's Land Rights & Privatization in Eastern Africa
BIRGIT ENGLERT & ELIZABETH DALEY (EDS)

War & the Politics of Identity in Ethiopia
KJETIL TRONVOLL

Moving People in Ethiopia
ALULA PANKHURST & FRANÇOIS PIGUET (EDS)

Living Terraces in Ethiopia
ELIZABETH E. WATSON

Eritrea
GAIM KIBREAB

Borders & Borderlands as Resources in the Horn of Africa
DEREJE FEYISSA & MARKUS VIRGIL HOEHNE (EDS)

After the Comprehensive Peace Agreement in Sudan
ELKE GRAWERT (ED.)

Land, Governance, Conflict & the Nuba of Sudan
GUMA KUNDA KOMEY

Ethiopia
JOHN MARKAKIS

Resurrecting Cannibals
HEIKE BEHREND

Pastoralism & Politics in Northern Kenya & Southern Ethiopia
GŨNTHER SCHLEE & ABDULLAHI A. SHONGOLO

Islam & Ethnicity in Northern Kenya & Southern Ethiopia
GŨNTHER SCHLEE with ABDULLAHI A. SHONGOLO

Foundations of an African Civilisation
DAVID W. PHILLIPSON

Regional Integration, Identity & Citizenship in the Greater Horn of Africa
KIDANE MENGISTEAB & REDIE BEREKETEAB (EDS)

Dealing with the Government in South Sudan
CHERRY LEONARDI

The Quest for Socialist Utopia
BAHRU ZEWDE

Disrupting Territories
JÖRG GERTEL, RICHARD ROTTENBURG & SANDRA CALKINS (EDS)

The African Garrison State
KJETIL TRONVOLL & DANIEL R. MEKONNEN

The State of Post-conflict Reconstruction
NASEEM BADIEY

Gender, Home & Identity
KATARZYNA GRABSKA

Women, Land & Justice in Tanzania
HELEN DANCER

Remaking Mutirikwi
JOOST FONTEIN

Darfur*
CHRIS VAUGHAN

Lost Nationalism*
ELENA VEZZADINI

The Oromo & the Christian Kingdom of Ethiopia*
MOHAMMED HASSEN

**forthcoming*

Dealing with Government in South Sudan

Histories of chiefship, community & state

CHERRY LEONARDI
Senior Lecturer in History
Durham University

JAMES CURREY

James Currey
is an imprint of Boydell & Brewer Ltd
PO Box 9, Woodbridge, Suffolk IP12 3DF (GB)
www.jamescurrey.com

and of Boydell & Brewer Inc.
668 Mt Hope Avenue, Rochester, NY 14620-2731 (US)
www.boydellandbrewer.com

First published in hardback 2013
First published in paperback 2015

The publisher would like to acknowledge the assistance of the
British Institute in Eastern Africa in the publication of this book.

British Library Cataloguing in Publication Data
is available on request from the British Library

ISBN 978-1-84701- 114-5 (James Currey Paper)

This publication printed on acid-free paper

Typeset by the British Institute in Eastern Africa

Dedication

For my mother, Jean Leonardi

Contents

List of Illustrations

Acknowledgements

This book has been a long time in the making, and thanking the many people and institutions that have supported me in the process is a story in itself. Firstly, it could not have happened at all without the financial support of several donors: the Arts and Humanities Research Council, the Leverhulme Trust, the British Institute in Eastern Africa (BIEA) and the British Academy. The BIEA also provided an invaluable institutional base in Nairobi; I am very grateful to Paul Lane, Humphrey Mathenge and the other Nairobi staff, and particularly to Stephanie Wynne-Jones, who provided generous hospitality and friendship. An internship on the first Rift Valley Institute (RVI) Sudan field course in 2004 opened the door to a series of opportunities, sources of knowledge and helpful contacts; I will always be immensely grateful to John Ryle, Philip Winter, Dan Large, Kit Kidner and the RVI staff. Through the RVI, I also benefited from US Institute of Peace (USIP) funding for research on local justice in South Sudan in 2009–10. I am grateful to Deborah Isser, then at USIP, and Tim Luccaro, and to my co-researchers on that project, Leben Nelson Moro and Martina Santschi, for the many discussions we have had before, during and since the project on traditional authority and justice. Justice Deng Biong Mijak has also greatly assisted my research on customary law and justice in South Sudan.

Fieldwork in South Sudan was made possible through the generous help of the individuals and organisations who provided hospitality, friendship, assistance or translation – in Yei: Rainer Holstein, Skye Hughes and the Malteser team, General Malual Ayom Dor, Harriet Kuyang Logo, Jackline Nasiwa, Neha Erasmus, the Christian Women's Empowerment Programme, Mr Guya and Sunday Dickson; in Juba: Tom Rhodes, all the staff at the Juba Post newspaper, Skye Wheeler, Naseem Badiey, Jimmy Lokiling, Alfred Sebit Lokuji and Daniel Gak; in Rumbek: Abraham Mayen Kuc, Kacuol Makuer; Moses Mapuor Maker Deng, Tinda Akot, Awac Maguen Yuol, Carol Berger, Abraham Makoi Bol, Pur Buornyang, Manyang Mayom and Adak Costa; and in Wau: Fergus Boyle, Clement Morba, Silverio Abdallah, Kon Mawien and Malual Ring. I am particularly grateful to the two research assistants with whom I worked most closely: in Rumbek, John Deng Mabor Mayath, who worked tirelessly and welcomed me into his family; in Yei and Juba, Emmanuel Gonda: his contribution to this book really is immeasurable.

My deepest gratitude is to the many people who gave their time and knowledge to me in interviews and conversations; I thank by name those who helped me the most at the end of the book. The research would not have been possible without the support and tolerance of Sudan People's Liberation Movement/Army and Government of Southern Sudan officials and security officers, and I thank them for permitting me such freedom to conduct unsupervised research.

The research was equally reliant on access to archival material, and I would like to thank the staff of the National Records Office in Khartoum for all their help and support in 2002–3 and 2009. In Khartoum I am very grateful for the generous assistance and hospitality I received from Yusuf Fadl Hassan and the University of Khartoum, Babiker Badri, Rita Poni Loteka, Badreldin El Haj Musa and the other members of the Sudanese Association for Archiving Knowledge, Khalid Alamin Bakheit, Dina and Dahlia Idris, Hind Abukana, Asma Abu Niab and Rose Lisok Paulino; I am also glad to have shared my first period of research in Khartoum with Anna Clarkson. I would like to thank the National Archives in London; Chris Morton and Jeremy Coote at the Pitt Rivers Museum in Oxford; the Rhodes House Library in Oxford; the Church Missionary Society Archive in Birmingham; the Shetland Archive in Lerwick and, above all, the staff of the Sudan Archive in Durham, especially Jane Hogan. I am grateful to the Sudan Archive for the photographs in the book and to the cartography unit in the geography department at Durham for drawing the map. The Durham history department has been a most supportive base throughout this research, and I thank my colleagues, particularly Philip Williamson and David Moon, as well as the undergraduate students who have taken my courses and asked good questions. I have been privileged to supervise the PhDs of Will Berridge, Chris Vaughan, Tamador Khalid-Abdalla and Zoe Cormack, all of whom have taught me at least as much as I them. This book has also benefited from the interdepartmental research group on frontiers led by Richard Hingley and supported by the Durham Institute for Advanced Study.

Many other colleagues in African and Sudanese studies have informed and supported the process of research and writing with their good questions, discussion and friendship. I particularly thank Wendy James, Peter Woodward, Matt Davies, Laura Mann, Moritz Mihatsch, Irene Panozzoi, Munzoul Assal, Musa Adam Abdul-Jalil, Paul Nugent, Wolfgang Zeller and the African Borderlands Research Network, Mareike Schomerus, Tim Allen, Lotje de Vries, David Deng, Noah Salomon, Aly Verjee, Eddie Thomas, Joanna Oyediran, Jok Madut Jok, Luka Biong Deng, Rob Blunt, Dave Eaton, Naomi Pendle, Mary Davies; also the convenors and members of the African history/studies seminars at Cambridge, SOAS and Edinburgh. JoAnn McGregor and Mark Leopold organised their panel on 'the African Frontier' at the Edinburgh Centre for African Studies 2012 conference with fortuitous timing for me. Richard Reid never failed to make me feel that it all mattered. David Anderson led me to the PhD in the first place and provided very useful comments on the thesis. Øystein Rolandsen has been a most generous and collegial fellow historian of South Sudan. I am also very grateful to him and to Unn Målfrid Rolandsen, Naseem Badiey and Nicki Kindersley for comments and corrections on the book draft, to Charles Ambler for a most generous and helpful review of the manuscript, to Jaqueline Mitchell for being a patient and supportive commissioning editor, and to Rohan Bolton for producing the index.

My last and greatest thanks are to the people who have contributed most to this book, and much else besides. Justin Willis has been an exceptional supervisor, mentor and colleague, and I am deeply grateful for his time, support, advice and critical engagement throughout this research project; it really would not have happened without him. Both he and Douglas Johnson read drafts of the manuscript and made very useful suggestions. Douglas has generously supported and informed my research from the earliest days. My friend and colleague Chris Vaughan read the sprawling first drafts of chapters and provided much-needed encouragement and perceptive comments. My ideas, approach and arguments have developed in dialogue with Justin and Chris, and I owe them both a great intellectual and personal debt. In spite of these multiple sources of help and advice, the failings of this book are of course entirely my own.

Finally I thank the family and friends who have supported me with love, inspiration and good sense throughout the research and writing, above all my parents Jeff and Jean, my sister Rebecca and my friend Alona Armstrong. I also wish to thank the gifted teachers who led me to the beginning of this research, particularly Sarah Bedford and John MacKenzie. The book is dedicated to the first of these teachers, my mother Jean, in deep gratitude for her endless care and encouragement of me, and in honour of her skill in teaching me and so many other children to read and to love stories. The story of this book began with her.

Abbreviations

Ar.	Arabic
BLC	Boma Liberation Council(s)
CID	Criminal Investigation Department; commonly used to mean government and military intelligence services and their informers
CMS	Church Missionary Society
CoTAL	Council(s) of Traditional Authority Leaders
DC	District Commissioner (British colonial official)
GGR	Governor-General's *Reports on the Finances, Administration and Condition of the Sudan*
GoSS	Government of Southern Sudan (2005–11)
HMSO	Her Majesty's Stationery Office
LA	Legislative Assembly
MI	Military Intelligence
NCP	National Congress Party
NGO	Non-Government Organisation (local or international)
NIF	National Islamic Front
NRO	National Records Office, Khartoum
OAU	Organisation of African Unity
SAD	Sudan Archive, Durham
SAF	Sudan Armed Forces (the national army of Sudan)
SANU	Sudan African National Union (southern Sudanese political party)
SIR	*Sudan Intelligence Report*
SPLM/A	Sudan People's Liberation Movement/Army
SRO	Southern Records Office, Juba
SRRA, SRRC	Sudan Relief and Rehabilitation Association, later Commission (the relief wing of the SPLM/A)
SSU	Sudan Socialist Union (under President Numayri)
TNA	The National Archives, Kew, London
UNDP	United Nations Development Programme
USAID	United States Agency for International Development

Glossary

There is considerable variation in the names and spellings of places, ethnic groups and other terms in South Sudan; I have adopted those that are most commonly used, and/or follow the simplest orthography. Similarly transliteration of Arabic words follows their colloquial pronunciation in South Sudan.

agamlong	(Dinka) accepter/repeater of speech; formal interlocutor in courts and ceremonies
baai	(Dinka) village or homestead; the country in the sense of a community
bazingari/bazingers	slave-soldiers in private armies of ivory and slave traders in nineteenth-century southern Sudan; still used in some areas for chief's retainers
beny (pl. *baany*)	(Dinka) chief; person with spiritual and/or political power
beny alath	(Dinka) chief of the cloth: government chief
beny baai	(Dinka) chief of the village/country; government chief
beny bith	(Dinka) master/chief of the fishing spear; 'spear-master': spiritual leader
beny riel	(Agar Dinka) chief of power/strength: chiefs' court retainer/bailiff
boma	Term for lowest-level unit of local government in the SPLM and GoSS administrations; village
bunit (pl. *bonok*)	(Bari) practitioner of indigenous medicine, healing or divination
'dupi (pl. *'dupet*)	(Bari) dependents/clients (sometimes translated as 'slaves')
effendiya	(Turkish) educated bureaucrats; civil servants during the Condominium
feddan	(Ar.) measurement of land: 1.038 acres
ganun	(Ar.) laws
gela	(Bari) government; also foreigners, white people
gol (pl. *gal*)	(Dinka) cattle camp hearth: any group defined by agnatic descent
hakuma	(Ar.) government or state
hukm/hukum	(Ar.) court judgment, penalty or fine
Jehadiah	(archaic) see *jihadiya*
Jieng	(Dinka) the people; the Dinka people
jihadiya (or *jihādī*)	(Ar.) slave-soldiers in Egyptian or Mahdist armies; native police in early Condominium southern Sudan
jur	(Dinka) foreigners; other tribes
kaiyo	(Bari) first-born; senior lineage
khawajat	(Ar.) foreigners; white people
koc peen/bec	(Dinka) people of the town/rural areas
kujur	(Ar.) general, often pejorative, term for experts in indigenous

	spiritual, supernatural and medical practices
long	(Dinka) speech, e.g. in a court case (see *agamlong*)
luak	(Dinka) cattle-byre (can be a ceremonial building)
luk	(Dinka) court or gathering to resolve disputes
mac	(Dinka) to tether/constrain/imprison
makama	[Ar.] court
malakiya	South Sudanese urban residential area, originally inhabited by retired soldiers of the Egyptian army (from Ottoman Turkish)
Malakiyan	Persons descended from the original inhabitants of the *malakiya* areas, usually preserving aspects of military and Islamic cultures and creole Arabic or Nubi language (also known as Nubians)
mamur	(Ar.) junior administrative officer
matat lo lori	(Bari) chief of the iron rod i.e. rain chief
medina (pl. *medinat*)	(Ar.) town
mejlis	(Ar.) council
merkaz	(Ar.) district administrative headquarters
miri	(Ottoman Turkish) term for Egyptian ruler in nineteenth century; still used by Bari-speakers to mean 'government' (from *amir*, governor)
monyekak	(Bari) owner/lord/chief of the land
muk	(Dinka) to hold, bring up, protect
nutu or *ngutu*	(Bari/Mundari) people
nutu lo miri	(Bari/Mundari) government people
payam	SPLM and GoSS intermediate unit of local government, between the county and the *boma*
peen	(Agar Dinka) town
putet	(Bari) council or meeting of elders
razzia	(Ar.) raid
riel	(Dinka) power/strength
shari'a	(Ar.) Islamic law and its sources
sheikh	(Ar.) religious leader; chief or other notable
spear-master	See *beny bith*
Sudd	Vast swamps on the Nile in the northern part of South Sudan
tueny (dit)	(Dinka) (senior) officer; literate person; town-dweller
tukl	(Ar.) Traditional thatched house
tukutuku	Expression used in southern Equatoria for soldiers of either the Turco-Egyptian army, the Mahdist army or the Belgian Congo forces
vekil/wakil	(Ar.) agent or deputy
waraga	(Ar.) paper
wut (pl. *wuot*)	(Dinka) cattle camp; cattle herd; co-herding group, tribe or section
yic	(Dinka) right or truth
zariba (pl. *zara'ib*)	(Ar) thorn-fenced enclosure; fortified military camp or station

Introduction: The making of chiefship, state and community in South Sudan

In May 2009, fourteen hundred chiefs or 'traditional leaders' were transported by the Government of Southern Sudan (GoSS) to a conference in the town of Bentiu. The semi-autonomous GoSS had been created by the 2005 Comprehensive Peace Agreement, which ended the war of the Sudan People's Liberation Movement/Army (SPLM/A) against the Sudanese government (1983–2004). The Bentiu conference was called to mobilise the chiefs' support for internal conflict resolution, elections and the national peace process, in the lead-up to a referendum on South Sudanese secession in 2011. The GoSS President and SPLA commander-in-chief, General Salva Kiir Mayardit, opened proceedings with a public thanks and apology to the assembled chiefs for their role in the war:

> It was you the paramount chiefs who ensured that the social fabric of our people was not disturbed by the war. You organized our people to support the liberation struggle, you mobilized and recruited the youth to join the ranks of the liberation struggle, you organized your people to provide food for the army. It was your bull, your goat, your chicken, your fish and your dura [sorghum] and cassava that fed us, it is you who carried the war materials on your heads and shoulders... During our liberation struggle you proved so essential to our survival as water is essential to the survival of fish.
>
> I know as much as you do, that in spite of your major contributions to the liberation struggle, our relations were not milk and honey. Some of you were manhandled and treated badly by some of our soldiers... My dear paramount chiefs and traditional leaders, I apologize to you on my own behalf as leader, and on behalf of the SPLA and on behalf of your government for all those bad things we did to you as individuals during the course of our liberation struggle and even during peace times. I ask you as victims and as leaders to forgive ourselves.[1]

Such rhetoric was not new: even before the 2005 peace, SPLM/A leaders had been conciliatory and appreciative towards the traditional authorities, and the GoSS was now emphasising a prominent role for chiefs in local government legislation. But the President's 2009 speech represented a conspicuous rebuttal of widespread national and international commentary, which stressed the destruction of traditional authority and 'social fabric' by decades of war. According to a USAID report in 2005, customary law and chiefly authority had become 'a victim of the war', as 'the demands of war overshadowed traditional practices', resulting in the 'loss of authority of traditional chiefs over their youth'.[2] And this was a continuing process, according to another analyst:

1 Speech by the President of the Government of Southern Sudan, H.E. Gen. Salva Kiir Mayardit, to the conference of kings, queens, paramount chiefs and traditional leaders, Bentiu, Unity State, 17 May 2009 (Juba: Office of the President, GoSS, 2009).

2 Sudan Peace Fund Final Report, October 2002–December 2005 (USAID/Pact Sudan, consulted in Pact Juba offices on 25 July 2006), p. 257.

traditional values and community structure were 'under siege in post-conflict Sudan'.[3]

In a context categorised as a 'post-conflict' or 'fragile' state, institutional resilience and historical continuity are all too easily overlooked in the urgent work of state-building. Alternatively, when tradition and custom are invoked as a perceived source of legitimacy for 'new' institutions of government, it is usually with an assumption of age-old origins and automatic communal identification.[4] Yet the President's speech reflected particular patterns of relations between the state and the chiefs that had developed over a century and a half. His description of chiefs as both victims and leaders chimed with local narratives of their history at the frontline of encounters with the recurring violence and predation of successive states. It was not only in the recent war that chiefship could be seen as 'essential to the survival' of an emerging state power; the local histories of chiefship traced in this book reveal in turn how state and local community have been mutually constituted in South Sudan since the nineteenth century. These processes of state-making and the construction of traditional orders have been belied both by the prevalent view of state failure in the history of Sudan, and by the established scholarly analyses of South Sudanese societies as inherently stateless, anti-state or excluded from the state.

Since the colonial rule of the Anglo-Egyptian Condominium of Sudan, tradition and history have been employed as discursive resources by chiefs and their supporters, reworked in the face of modernising nationalism and liberation war to emerge resurgent in the twenty-first century. Yet histories of chiefship – even those told by chiefs themselves – do not root them in the 'time immemorial' of common contemporary assumption. They do not even necessarily or straightforwardly root chiefs in the local genealogies of founding fathers and ancestral first-comers, which so often provide a narrative for the political structures of rural economy and society. Instead these histories locate chiefship firmly in the encounters of rural people with the forces of state power, dated to quite specific moments in the nineteenth and early twentieth centuries. Chiefship, unlike other forms of authority, represents not the first-coming of clan and lineage ancestors,[5] but the first-coming of the state, the *hakuma* (Ar.: government).

Chiefs have not been a distinct category or class of South Sudanese society; chiefship has been held by a variety of individuals in diverse contexts. But their success has rested primarily upon their claims to plural forms of knowledge and their ability to assemble a repertoire of discursive resources.[6] Individuals have been recognised or selected as chiefs because they were seen to know how to deal with government, both in the sense of developing strategies for coping with its threats and demands, and in the related sense of brokering deals with it. Through such interpreters and interlocutors, people have sought to 'contract' government, in Rafael's 'double sense of circumscribing its reach and regular-

[3] Tiernan Mennen, *Adapting Restorative Justice Principles to Reform Customary Courts in Dealing with Gender-Based Violence in Southern Sudan* (San Francisco, CA, 2008), p. 3.

[4] It is common for both South Sudanese and international commentators and analysts to assert that tradition and custom are of 'immemorial antiquity' and that each tribe or clan has its own discrete body of customs: e.g. Aleu Akechak Jok, Robert A. Leitch and Carrie Vandewint, *A Study of Customary Law in Contemporary Southern Sudan* (Monrovia, CA, 2004), pp. 12–13. Such discourse is discussed further in Chapters 9 and 10.

[5] Unlike chiefs elsewhere in Africa who have held greater authority over land and claimed descent from pre-colonial rulers: e.g. Paul Richards, 'To fight or to farm? Agrarian dimensions of the Mano River conflicts (Liberia and Sierra Leone)', *African Affairs* 104:417 (2005), pp. 571–90; Sara Berry, *Chiefs Know their Boundaries: essays on property, power and the past in Asante, 1896–1996* (Oxford, 2001).

[6] Cf. Tobias Hagmann and Didier Péclard, 'Negotiating statehood: dynamics of power and domination in Africa', *Development and Change* 41:4 (2010), pp. 539–62.

izing one's dealings with it'.[7] The most consistent basis for chiefship has been the capacity to render the government more predictable, the claim that a chief knows how to turn the arbitrary forces of state power into a source of protection for persons and property. In the process, chiefs have helped to broker new regulatory orders, new rights and resources, and ultimately the making of the state itself.

This book is concerned then with what local histories of chiefship reveal about broader relationships with the state before South Sudanese independence in 2011. At the outset of the fieldwork in 2005, the intention of my research was not to focus on the state, but rather to develop the arguments of my doctoral thesis that chiefship had been appropriated and domesticated as part of local resistance *against* the colonial state. After all, it has not been difficult to see the Sudanese state as the enemy in the history of South Sudan; many people here have sought to evade and resist the intrusion of predatory, extractive government forces. But in the end the fieldwork produced rather different perspectives. I was based primarily in the towns of Yei, Juba and Rumbek, and conducted research mostly within a ten-mile radius of these towns. Towns are still seen as the loci of the state in South Sudan, and it soon became apparent that these urban and peri-urban zones were not places in which to live if one wanted to avoid government. Instead a whole range of inhabitants were making claims on the state and seeking resources associated with it, and were even drawing ideas of legal rights and the symbols and practices of bureaucratic government deep into family relations. The documentary records from the colonial period and earlier suggest that there had always been strong demand in these areas for the regulatory orders of the state, as well as for its protection and material resources. The towns have acted as a kind of frontier, attracting heterogeneous settlers around the nodes of the state. In turn, aspects of this urban frontier have been replicated in the constitution of communities around chiefs, as points of articulation with the state.

This book therefore traces two different trajectories. One follows continuities in the role of chiefs since the mid-nineteenth century and in their relation to the urban frontier itself. This narrative oscillates between the risks and the opportunities of chiefship, between a role of defensive gatekeeper or even scapegoat victim, and a more profitable role of negotiator, interpreter and broker. Through this trajectory, we can see the recurrence and reprising of historical themes in the contemporary discourse epitomised by the 2009 presidential address. The second trajectory, however, is one of change. This is the story of how men with often marginal origins and scant legitimate authority, who were defined by their relationship with a predatory state, came to be increasingly central to definitions of community, law and tradition; and why the latest generations of chiefs would be flown to Bentiu to contribute to the process of building the first new African state of the twenty-first century.

MAKING CHIEFSHIP: IMAGINING TRADITION AND STATE

Three years before the Bentiu chiefs' meeting, fourteen chiefs and kings from across South Sudan were taken on a Swiss-sponsored 'tour' of South Africa, Botswana and Ghana, to meet and learn about traditional leadership in these countries.[8] They returned impressed by the status of traditional authority

[7] Vicente L. Rafael, *Contracting Colonialism: translation and Christian conversion in Tagalog society under early Spanish rule* (Ithaca, NY, 1988), p. 121.

[8] Gurtong, 'UNDP: traditional leaders return from tour with call for peace', *Gurtong*, 11 September 2006, last accessed 21 January 2013, www.gurtong.net/ECM/Editorial/tabid/124/ctl/ArticleView/mid/519/articleId/2561/UNDP-Traditional-leaders-return-from-tour-with-call-for-peace.aspx.

institutions and their recognition by 'modern' governments, and dreaming of obtaining grand buildings, cars and uniforms for themselves. It was clear that they perceived the chiefs' authority in these other countries – and indeed their own potentially enhanced authority – to be derived directly from government.[9] Indeed the enduring terms for these chiefs still described them in the Bari language as 'chiefs of the *miri* or *gela*', chiefs of/for the government or the white people, while in Dinka areas they were 'chiefs of the cloth', *bany alath*, in reference to colonial chiefs' uniforms and sashes. The vernacular nomenclature was clear: these were government chiefs, distinct from other kinds of authority and power. The origin of chiefs was commonly traced to the early days of colonial rule, even by their descendants and supporters. The colonial sources too contain frequent admission by officials that they or their predecessors were engaged in the creation of new kinds of authority, and that their notion of chiefship was alien to the people on whom it had been imposed. After all, these were among the most famous 'stateless societies' of early political anthropology; the notion of a single chiefly authority was inherently at odds with political tradition here.

Why then has chiefship not only survived but come to be accorded the status of 'Traditional Authority' in South Sudan? In seeking to answer this question in other African contexts, scholars have increasingly argued for the adaptability and enduring value of chiefship as an intermediary institution.[10] Such analyses have been an important counterweight to those which exaggerated the capacity of colonial states to invent traditions or to impose new forms of authority.[11] But the emphasis on chiefs as interstitial actors nevertheless tends to perpetuate dichotomies between local society and the state, when the state-society boundary in

[9] Interview 37R/JC.

[10] Olufemi Vaughan, *Nigerian Chiefs: traditional power in modern politics 1890s–1990s* (Rochester, NY, 2000), p. 12; Ruth Watson, *'Civil Disorder is the Disease of Ibadan': chieftaincy and civic culture in a Yoruba city* (Oxford, 2003); Trutz von Trotha, 'From administrative to civil chieftaincy: some problems and prospects of African chieftaincy', *Journal of Legal Pluralism and Unofficial Law* 37–8 (1996), pp. 79–107; Harry G West and Scott Kloeck-Jenson, 'Betwixt and between: 'traditional authority' and democratic decentralisation in post-war Mozambique', *African Affairs* 98:393 (1999), pp. 475–6; J Michael Williams, 'Leading from behind: democratic consolidation and the chieftaincy in South Africa', *Journal of Modern African Studies* 42 (2004), pp. 121–2; E Adriaan B Van Rouveroy van Nieuwaal and Rijk Van Dijk (eds), *African Chieftaincy in a New Socio-Political Landscape* (Leiden, 1999).

[11] E.g. Terence Ranger, 'The invention of tradition in colonial Africa', in E. Hobsbawm and Terence Ranger (eds), *The Invention of Tradition* (Cambridge, 1983), pp. 211–62. Mamdani takes this line of interpretation much further, depicting colonial chiefship as 'decentralized despotism' and the 'clenched fist' of state power: Mahmood Mamdani, *Citizen and Subject: contemporary Africa and the legacy of late colonialism* (Princeton, 1996). The force of the colonial state is similarly emphasised by Crawford Young, *The African Colonial State in Comparative Perspective* (New Haven, CT, 1994). Many other scholars have also highlighted the novel, unprecedented role and power of colonial chiefs: Bruce Berman and John Lonsdale, 'Coping with the contradictions: the development of the colonial state 1895–1914', in Bruce Berman and John Lonsdale, *Unhappy Valley: conflict in Kenya and Africa*, Vol. 1, (London, 1992), p. 87; Justin Willis, 'Violence, authority and the state in the Nuba Mountains of Condominium Sudan', *The Historical Journal* 46:1 (2003), p. 114; Pierre Englebert, *State Legitimacy and Development in Africa* (Boulder, CO, 2000); Jan Vansina, *Paths in the Rainforests: towards a history of political tradition in Equatorial Africa* (Madison, WI, 1990), pp. 245–8; Jan-Bart Gewald, 'Making tribes: social engineering in the Western Province of British administered Eritrea, 1941–1952', *Journal of Colonialism and Colonial History* 1:2 (2000); John Tosh, *Clan Leaders and Colonial Chiefs in Lango: the political history of an East African stateless society c.1800–1939* (Oxford, 1978), pp. 182, 248; Holly E Hanson, *Landed Obligation: the practice of power in Buganda* (Portsmouth, NH, 2003), pp. 17–18; Michael Crowder and Obaro Ikime, 'Introduction', in Michael Crowder and Obaro Ikime (eds), *West African Chiefs: their changing status under colonial rule and independence* (Ife-Ife, 1970), pp. vii–xxix. See the comprehensive review by Thomas Spear, 'Neo-traditionalism and the limits of invention in British colonial Africa,' *Journal of African History* 44 (2003), pp. 3–27.

reality proves elusive.[12] As other scholars have argued, African states may in fact be deeply embedded in local society; some even depict the state as 'no more than a décor, a pseudo-Western façade masking the realities of deeply personalised political realities'.[13] Yet the idea of an abstract, bounded state should not be dismissed as a mere façade. Lund juxtaposes the obvious 'theoretical fragility of clear separation between state and society' with the evidence from research in Africa of 'the tenacity of the *idea* of a clear separation between the two'. Rather than refraining from studying such paradoxes, 'we should pay careful attention to *how* concepts and distinctions are produced, instrumentalized and contested'.[14] Such analyses build on Timothy Mitchell's earlier argument that the impression of a state-society boundary is a structural *effect*, generating the idea of an abstract and integral state.[15] Similarly, while some argue that the very terminology of traditional authority is misleading,[16] the inaccuracies or misconceptions around the use of the term only make it more important to understand how and why it is used. Willis argues that tradition is primarily a discourse, which enables a morally advantageous distance from the state to be preserved, even by those whose authority derives from the state.[17]

The approach taken in this book is thus to examine both state and tradition not as fixed entities but as ideas, discourses and imaginaries, as well as institutions, actors and processes. As such, both state and tradition have been produced as much at the local level as at the centre. This is a particularly novel approach in the context of South Sudanese history, however, where the notion of state-society separation and alienation has gone largely unquestioned. Sudan's post-colonial civil wars and crises have been attributed to instabilities at the heart of the state, and to a predatory model of centre-periphery relations.[18] Collins argues most categorically for intractable 'estrangement', 'antagonisms' and 'hostility' between centre and periphery, resulting in nothing more than a 'facade of authority' in the 'remote provinces'. Holt and Daly, on the other hand, question the 'ability of peripheral peoples to withstand the onslaught' of northern riverain culture.[19] Other historians and anthropologists have recorded

[12] Boone also criticises the 'state versus society' literature for depicting the state simply as a 'predatory Leviathan'; Catherine Boone, *Political Topographies of the African State: territorial authority and institutional choice* (Cambridge, 2003), pp. 5–6. Similarly in the Sudan context: Chris Vaughan, 'Negotiating the State at its Margins: colonial authority in Condominium Darfur, 1916–1956' (PhD, Durham University, 2011), pp. 30–1.

[13] Patrick Chabal and Jean-Pascal Daloz, *Africa Works: disorder as political instrument* (Oxford, 1999), pp. 15–16.

[14] Christian Lund, 'Twilight institutions: an introduction', *Development and Change* 37:4 (2006), pp. 678–9; also Hagmann and Péclard, 'Negotiating statehood', pp. 542–4.

[15] Timothy Mitchell, 'The limits of the state: beyond statist approaches and their critics,' *American Political Science Review* 85:1 (1991), pp. 77–96.

[16] West and Kloeck-Jenson, 'Betwixt and between', p. 457.

[17] Justin Willis, 'Chieftaincy', in John Parker and Richard Reid (eds), *Oxford Handbook of Modern African History* (Oxford: forthcoming). Traditional authority thus appears as what Bayart would term 'a discursive genre' of politics: Jean-François Bayart, *The Illusion of Cultural Identity* (London, 2005), pp. 109–21.

[18] Peter Woodward, *Sudan 1898–1989: the unstable state* (Boulder, CO, 1990); Alex de Waal, 'Sudan: the turbulent state', in Alex de Waal (ed.), *War in Darfur and the Search for Peace* (London, 2007), pp. 1–38; Douglas H Johnson, *The Root Causes of Sudan's Civil Wars* (Oxford, 2003). On the violent predation of the Turco-Egyptian state, see also Shamil Jeppie, 'Constructing a Colony on the Nile, c. 1820–1870' (PhD, Princeton University, 1996); Anders Bjorkelo, *Prelude to the Mahdiyya: peasants and traders in the Shendi region, 1821–1885* (Cambridge, 1989).

[19] Robert O Collins, *A History of Modern Sudan* (Cambridge, 2008), p. 300; Peter M Holt and Martin W Daly, *A History of the Sudan: from the coming of Islam to the present day* (Harlow, 2000), p. 194.

widespread southern Sudanese perceptions of the state as a primarily alien, dangerous and extractive entity, located in the foreign space, culture and practices of its towns, and in the distant metropole of Khartoum.[20] Towns have been 'a government place' and 'a military place', as a retired soldier put it in the 1980s. The small urban centres in South Sudan have thus been inextricably associated with a government of external, alien origin, in common with prevailing depictions of 'small-town alienation' across eastern Africa, in which towns appear as 'sites where rural people are exploited by larger economic forces'.[21]

Earlier pioneers of political anthropology had simply assumed the state to be irrelevant to the political cultures of the southern Sudanese 'segmentary lineage systems' in which they were interested. Evans-Pritchard's famous study of Nuer political organisation was prefaced with an account of the challenges he encountered in trying to study the Nuer immediately after 'their recent defeat by Government forces' and the 'deep resentment' provoked by the subsequent Nuer Settlement with its intrusive reorganisation of local administration, courts and chiefship. Yet his study epitomises a timeless ethnography, in which the colonial state was almost entirely invisible: 'the Nuer have no government, and their state might be described as an ordered anarchy'.[22] The later volume edited by Middleton and Tait, *Tribes without Rulers,* hinted only briefly at the effects of late-colonial rule: the Dinka, Mundari and Lugbara were here deliberately considered 'as indigenous systems, unaffected by European contact'.[23]

Of course these early phases of political anthropology have been extensively revised and critiqued, not only for their ahistorical approach but also for their problematic definitions of political systems.[24] But it has still frequently been assumed that such political cultures were fundamentally at odds with the modern state systems imposed through colonialism. Hutchinson's extensive and deservedly influential critical revision of Evans-Pritchard demonstrates the complex, varied and changing engagement of Nuer communities with the Sudanese state and the money economy, between the 1930s and the 1980s. She records the intense political engagement among her informants, their demand for state resources and their attempts to use paper as the medium through

[20] Sharon Hutchinson, *Nuer Dilemmas: coping with money, war and the state* (Berkeley, CA, 1996); Andrew NM Mawson, 'The Triumph of Life: political dispute and religious ceremonial among the Agar Dinka of the Southern Sudan' (PhD, Cambridge University, 1989); Godfrey Lienhardt, 'The Sudan: aspects of the south government among some of the Nilotic peoples, 1947–52', *British Journal of Middle Eastern Studies* 9:1 (1982), pp. 22–34, especially p. 27; GO Huby, 'Big men and old men – and women: social organization and urban adaptation of the Bari, Southern Sudan' (Magistergrad thesis, University of Trondheim, 1981); John W Burton, 'When the north winds blow: a note on small towns and social transformation in the Nilotic Sudan', *African Studies Review* 31:3 (1988), pp. 49–60. Cf. Kurt Beck, 'Tribesmen, townsmen and the struggle over a proper lifestyle in northern Kordofan', in Endre Stiansen and Michael Kevane (eds), *Kordofan Invaded: peripheral incorporation and social transformation in Islamic Africa* (Leiden, 1998), pp. 254–79.

[21] Douglas H Johnson, 'The Structure of a legacy: military slavery in Northeast Africa', *Ethnohistory* 36:1 (1989), p. 83; James Giblin, 'History, imagination and remapping space in a small urban centre: Makambako, Iringa Region, Tanzania', in Andrew Burton (ed.), *The Urban Experience in Eastern Africa c. 1750–2000* (Nairobi, 2002), p. 189.

[22] EE Evans-Pritchard, *The Nuer: a description of the modes of livelihood and political institutions of a Nilotic people* (Oxford, 1940), pp. 5–12.

[23] John Middleton and David Tait, 'Introduction', in John Middleton and David Tait (eds), *Tribes Without Rulers: studies in African segmentary systems* (London, 1958), p. 1.

[24] Tosh, for instance, rejects Southall's negative 1968 definition of stateless societies as lacking 'political institutions or roles', adopting instead a definition of societies in which 'political authority is widely diffused': Tosh, *Clan Leaders*, pp. 1–3, citing AW Southall, 'Stateless Societies', in *International Encyclopedia of the Social Sciences*, Vol. 15 (New York, 1968), p. 157. See also Hutchinson, *Nuer Dilemmas*, pp. 21–45; Peter Geschiere, 'Chiefs and colonial rule in Cameroon: inventing chieftaincy, French and British Style', *Africa* 63:2 (1993), p. 151.

which 'to tap the powers of government'. But, unsurprisingly in the context of the outbreak of the SPLA war, she also asserts that 'the gun had dominated the entire fitful history of Nuer accommodation and resistance' to the state. And she frequently emphasises the alien, remote loci of state power in the towns, and her impression that 'the literate elite was, on the whole, physically and ideologically isolated from the bulk of the Nuer population'.[25]

This sense of alienation from government has thus been prevalent in southern Sudanese and scholarly discourse. But rather than accepting the idea of state power as an alien imposition, I argue in this book that the history of town and state formation should also be understood in terms of local relations and long-term political cultures. The urban government centres have become incorporated into local geographical and historical narratives, in which chiefship plays a mediating role. Certain people have claimed precedence in relations with the state, on the basis that their ancestors gave land to the government in return for its protection and recognition. Chiefs and their supporters, relatives and dependants argue that the first chiefs mediated the coming of government, a highly ambiguous process since government was violently coercive, but one which is nevertheless depicted as productive of political and social order. Such discourse has sought to legitimise the close relations that certain groups developed with government, and in the process it has contributed to legitimising the state itself.

From the earliest establishment of fortified trading stations in the nineteenth century, military, commercial and government centres acted as a kind of magnet, attracting adherents to settle on a new frontier around them. By exploring the history of these emerging small towns, we see not so much an expansion of a centrifugal state frontier, but rather the production of a centripetal internal frontier, as people invaded the urban nodes of the state *from* the rural areas.[26] There are parallels with the idea of the pre-colonial internal African frontier as the site of new institutional formation, a trope which appears in many oral histories across Africa. As Kopytoff emphasises, such histories justify the political dominance of chiefs or other rulers on the grounds that they brought political order and peace to previously 'uncouth' people – a kind of 'conquest-by-invitation'. Moreover, such relations imposed 'an implicit contract' on rulers to bring protection and order.[27] What is striking in South Sudan is that this kind of rhetoric is often applied to the arrival of the state itself; the urban frontier appears in oral histories as the site of new institutional formation, including chiefship.[28]

The idea of the towns as a frontier towards which some people might be impelled enables us to both explore and depart from the prevalent dichotomy

[25] Hutchinson, *Nuer Dilemmas*, pp. 103, 281, 284.

[26] Chris Vaughan makes a similar point regarding the centripetal construction of the central state from peripheries like Darfur: 'Negotiating the State', p. 17.

[27] Igor Kopytoff, 'The internal African frontier: the making of African political culture', in Igor Kopytoff (ed.), *The African Frontier: the reproduction of traditional African societies* (Bloomington, IN, 1987), pp. 3–84, especially pp. 65–6.

[28] Le Meur argues the continuing relevance of Kopytoff's thesis to colonial and post-colonial African history, including in terms of the political frontier as a metaphorical and heuristic device 'to capture the logic of state-making': Pierre-Yves Le Meur, 'State making and the politics of the frontier in Central Benin', *Development and Change* 37:4 (2006), p. 873. See Igor Kopytoff, 'The political dynamics of the urban frontier', in Kopytoff, *The African Frontier*, pp. 255–6; Sandra T Barnes, 'The urban frontier in West Africa: Mushin, Nigeria', in Kopytoff, *The African Frontier*, pp. 261–2.

drawn between government towns and rural society in South Sudan, and in Africa more widely.[29] As Poole so eloquently asks:

> What happens if, instead of locating the margin of the state somewhere between the urban and rural spaces in which peasants live, we look for it in that odd – and highly mobile – space between threat and guarantee that surfaces every time and every place a peasant hands either legal papers or documents to an agent of the state?[30]

In South Sudan, the site of this 'slippage between threat and guarantee' was nevertheless often located spatially in the towns or on the roads, where papers were most likely to be produced or demanded. But another such site was a more mobile, institutional or personal one, consisting of chiefship in itself. Rather than embodying the political tension between the antagonistic forces of state and society,[31] chiefs have embodied the simultaneous potential for both threat and guarantee that the state was seen to offer.

Coercion was at the heart of state-making and chiefship, but it does not explain the survival of either. Instead a whole range of people in and around the towns have made claims upon the state and/or their chief, often employing notions of a contract, transaction or reciprocal deal to demand guarantees of their rights in property or persons. In its most basic expression – a kind of baseline to which chiefship recurred – this was a bargain of protection from the threat of the same state from which the guarantee was obtained; chiefs were said to have 'bought' protection for their people by working with colonial forces.[32] This evokes the idea of a coercive state-society contract akin to a protection racket, as recently articulated by Nugent:

> A coercive social contract is one in which the right to govern is predicated on the capacity of the rulers to render intolerable the lives of their subjects. In extreme cases, the contract may look more like a statist version of a protection racket in which people surrender their political voice in return for being spared from predatory acts. The mode of extraction is typically some form of tribute levied in a manner that is personalized rather than routinized.[33]

However, chiefs' ability to buy protection was rather more complicated than this. Their legitimacy has rested on their claim to transform extractive relations *into* 'routinized' arrangements. This was an ongoing, uncertain, risky process of contracting government, rather than the production of a stable social contract. It would be apparent not only in the colonial period when bureaucratic regulation became a new resource, but also through the recurrent periods of armed conflict since Sudan's independence in 1956. The role of the chiefs during war centred on their capacity to make agreements with the dangerously unpredict-

[29] Theodore Trefon, 'Hinges and fringes: conceptualising the peri-urban in central Africa', in Francesca Locatelli and Paul Nugent (eds), *African Cities: competing claims on urban spaces* (Leiden, 2009), pp. 15–35; Kopytoff, 'The political dynamics', p. 255; W Arens, 'Mto wa Mbu: a rural polyethnic community in Tanzania', in Kopytoff, *The African Frontier*, pp. 242–54.

[30] Deborah Poole, 'Between threat and guarantee: justice and community in the margins of the Peruvian state', in Veena Das and Deborah Poole (eds), *Anthropology in the Margins of the State* (Oxford, 2007), p. 38.

[31] As argued by West and Kloeck-Jenson, 'Betwixt and between'; von Trotha, 'From administrative to civil chieftaincy'.

[32] For pre-colonial chiefship as simultaneously embodying threat and guarantee, refuge and danger, see Steven Feierman, *Peasant Intellectuals: anthropology and history in Tanzania* (Madison, WI, 1990), pp. 53, 112–3.

[33] Paul Nugent, 'States and social contracts in Africa', *New Left Review* 63 (2010), p. 43.

able military forces, by which the latter's extraction of people and property might at least be regularised and routinised.[34]

The state has thus become an *idea* of regulatory order to which people have appealed, often in the face of abuses by the very agents of the state. Of course rights in property and people are notoriously contested and difficult to define, and so the legal, judicial and regulatory orders of the state became an added resource or obstacle in ongoing debates. But increasingly scholars are recognising that it is in the struggles and debates of local politics and property regimes that states are made, not simply in the projection of power outwards or downwards by the central state.[35] As Lund argues:

> [O]ne of the ways in which public authority is established is by its successful exercise as a result of struggle. When an institution authorizes, sanctions or validates certain rights, the respect or observance of these rights by people, powerful in clout or numbers, simultaneously constitutes recognition of the authority of that particular institution.[36]

By such processes, the chiefs' courts became firmly established as enduring judicial institutions in South Sudan, and in turn played a key part in constituting the local state.

The heterogeneous settlements that developed on the urban frontier were to some extent replicated around the loci of chiefship, as the latter became recognised as a means of access to the state and the associated market economy. At times this would be a fulcrum of force, through which the state extracted labour and taxes. But it might also be a potential pivot on which to make claims to state resources and protection. As one elderly man in Rumbek remarked quite dismissively, 'a chief is just there to give you your right'.[37] This is the paradox of chiefship: it has been a crucial point for the articulation of rights and relations with government, for contracting state power. Yet chiefs have often been accorded limited status or authority, particularly by people claiming greater seniority in local political structures of kinship and precedence. Chiefs have not controlled the discourse of lineage seniority; instead they were frequently depicted as junior or marginal in such structures.[38] Yet chiefship would nevertheless produce chiefdom – a loosely territorial basis for definitions of community, and one which had little basis in genealogical political discourse. Instead this was a unit defined principally by its relationship to the state.

Chiefship and 'community' have been imagined and enacted as a means by which state and society might access and know each other. But these constructs disguise another reality in which multiple local elites operate *both* as the local state and as community leaders. They have often played a key part

[34] Cf. Timothy Raeymakers, 'Protection for sale? War and the transformation of regulation on the Congo-Ugandan border', *Development and Change* 41:4 (2010), pp. 563–587.

[35] Boone, *Political Topographies*; Jocelyn Alexander, 'The local state in post-war Mozambique: political practice and ideas about authority', *Africa* 67:1 (1997), pp. 1–26; Jocelyn Alexander, *The Unsettled Land: state-making and the politics of land in Zimbabwe 1893–2003* (Oxford, 2006), esp. p. 5; Naseem Badiey, 'The State Within: the local dynamics of "post-conflict reconstruction" in Juba, Southern Sudan (2005–2008)' (DPhil, University of Oxford, 2010); Vaughan, 'Negotiating the State'.

[36] Lund, 'Twilight institutions', p. 675. Kasfir similarly defines institutionalisation as 'the process through which most active participants in a polity come to value highly a set of basic procedures for solving disputes': Nelson Kasfir, 'Southern Sudanese politics since the Addis Ababa Agreement', *African Affairs* 76:303 (1977), pp. 143–66.

[37] Interview 1bN/RC.

[38] Unlike, for example, in Giblin's analysis of Tanzanian communities: John L Giblin, *A History of the Excluded: making family a refuge from state in twentieth-century Tanzania* (Oxford, 2005).

in defining the state as bureaucratic order and modern government, distinct from the kinship order of traditional communities. Yet chiefship itself embodies the mutual constitution of these discursive orders; struggles over genealogical precedence are very often also struggles over the local state. Chiefs claim particular knowledge and skills of intermediation, but they also belong to broader local political elites who derive power and wealth from operating on the multiple manifestations of the urban state frontier. It is from such local elites that my most vocal informants came.

MAKING HISTORIES

The book makes extensive use of oral testimonies recorded in and around Yei, Juba and Rumbek, mainly between 2004 and 2008. This fieldwork relied upon interpreters and translators to provide both on-the-spot interpretation into spoken English of vernacular interviews and conversations, and to produce written English translations of interview transcripts. Two principal vernacular languages feature: Dinka (Agar dialect) in Rumbek County, and the various dialects of the Bari language (particularly Kakwa, Pojelu, Mundari and Bari) in Yei and Juba counties. I worked intensively with various assistants and translators – and my limited knowledge of vernacular vocabulary – to verify the written transcriptions and translations, and to ensure the retention of as much original idiom as possible. But it remains the case that every quoted or paraphrased interview cited in translation has passed through a considerable interpretative process, with the associated drawbacks of potential loss or shift of meaning. Hundreds more conversations and interviews were not taped but recorded as field notes, which were also extensively discussed each day with assistants to check and explore particular points. This source material was thus fundamentally mediated by research assistants, just as the government documentary sources would have been similarly mediated by the clerks, interpreters and primary informants of government officials. As Peterson argues, archives should be seen not simply as source material for historians, but as creative and significant processes and products in themselves; the missionary documentation he discusses was a new resource for and product of litigation by Africans who very much understood the significance of recording and being recorded. 'Archives inspired action, oriented behaviour, and opened up channels for claim-making.'[39]

My research was also mediated by the particular individuals in each area who were most welcoming and eager to engage with me. My arrival with pen, paper and recorder was mostly greeted with little surprise by these interlocutors; instead they set about directing and shaping my research in the apparent sense that I was a tool by which to record and gain recognition of their political and historical narratives. As Ewald stresses, the historical accounts produced from fieldwork reflect the specific moment when the research was conducted.[40] And this was a period in South Sudan – immediately before and after the 2005 Peace Agreement – in which everyone had high expectations of the *hakuma*, and of its international auxiliaries. The 'interview', 'questionnaire' and 'focus group' were becoming familiar rituals, particularly for these people close to the towns and main roads. My questions about history were often disappointing to those who hoped I would bring some form of practical aid, assuming that I was part

[39] Derek R Peterson, 'Morality plays: marriage, church courts and colonial agency in colonial Tanganyika, c. 1876–1928', *American Historical Review* 111:4 (2006), pp. 983–1010.

[40] Janet Ewald, 'A moment in the middle: fieldwork in the Nuba hills', in C Keyes Adenaike and Jan Vansina (eds), *In Pursuit of History: fieldwork in Africa* (Oxford, 1997), pp. 94–5.

of the 'UN' and hence of the *hakuma* itself. But others – particularly those with the status of 'elders' – welcomed the opportunity to discuss their recognised area of expertise and to demonstrate its value even in the world of the *khawajat* [Arabic: foreigners, white people]. There was a sense that I might be a means to convert the privileged knowledge of (usually) illiterate elders into material value: perhaps in political contests over historical precedence among or within the various local communities; or in the allocation of resources and services by international agencies; or simply in the political competition among senior men. But people were also wary and worried by the power of pen and paper – let alone a voice recorder – to incriminate them, and they produced their own guarantees and witnesses by refusing to speak to me alone, or sometimes at all. Many people were determined that their names or the names of their clans, chiefdoms or villages should be included, but sometimes people instead feared to have their names written, in case I was there to 'report' them to the government.

The research process – and we, the researchers – were thus part of the histories told in this book: histories of knowledge and power, of entrepreneurial interlocution and interpretation, of the threat and guarantee simultaneously promised by the written record, of the hopes and hesitancies in dealing with government. The field research not only influenced my reading of the archives: it also made apparent that all these archives were in themselves the result of such historical interactions. This book is thus a product of precisely the kind of interfaces and conversations between people and government on which it focuses. It is also a version of history produced in the particular context of three towns and their surroundings in the period between peace and independence in early twenty-first century South Sudan.

There were two broad features of this period which influenced the interpretations of history among my informants, and hence my own. Firstly, in the immediate aftermath of the long SPLA war, both government and people were employing notions of a social contract in their discussions of the new government, and of the anticipated new state. SPLM politicians and others were referring to their social contract with the people forged through the liberation struggle;[41] and people were asserting the debt of the new government to them, citing the SPLM/A leader John Garang's promises of a 'peace dividend'.[42] Secondly, the new government was made of 'our sons': this represented on the one hand a victorious appropriation of government by Southerners, but on the other hand it raised new issues. The less that government was alien, the less it was also neutral;[43] indigenous political and judicial cultures, together with ideas of the state, had contributed to the ideal of a source of mediation and government that would stand outside lineage and locality. People were therefore worried that government had instead become drawn into – and was even instigating – local political and military conflicts.

[41] E.g. 'the people of Southern Sudan will be the last arbitrators of their government [*sic*] performance. The social contract bestowed on SPLM by the masses during the war still continues.' Majok Yak Majok, Under Secretary of the Ministry of Health, GoSS, 'SPLM must respond to popular aspirations', *Sudan Tribune,* 30 January 2008: accessed 21 January 2013, www.sudantribune.com/SPLM-must-respond-to-popular,25805. The notion of a social contract is also explored by Øystein Rolandsen in 'To mend the broken contract: legitimacy and local government in South Sudan during the CPA-period', paper presented at the Symposium on Government and Governance in South Sudan, Oxford University, 9 June 2011, and at the ECAS4 Conference, Uppsala, 17 June 2011.

[42] Øystein Rolandsen, 'In search of the peace dividend: the Southern Sudan one year after the signatures', paper presented at the 7th International Sudan Studies Conference, Bergen, 7 April 2006, last accessed 21 January 2013 at: www.prio.no/Publications/Publication/?x=3417.

[43] Cf. Robert J Gordon and Mervyn J Meggitt, *Law and Order in the New Guinea Highlands: encounters with Enga* (Hanover, NH, 1985).

For both reasons then, people were asserting – often angrily and bitterly – their notions of an ideal state and of their claim upon it, and emphasising a history of contracting government. They were in a sense using me to stake and record their claims to the 'peace dividend', and appealing to the idea of the state in order to hold it to account. But while the political discourse and new media of the twenty-first century may have given them a particular language of contractual obligations in which to argue their claims on the state, the documentary record of the last century and a half revealed a deeper history of contracting, bargaining and dealing with government.

SITES AND STRUCTURE

The three fieldwork sites of Yei, Juba and Rumbek were focal points in a wider area of documentary research. The book makes use of archival sources on several districts or counties in a region from the Lyria and Luluba Hills on the east bank of the Nile to the Western Equatorian town of Maridi and from the southern borders with Uganda and Congo to the northern part of Lakes State. In the colonial period these were the districts with the sometimes changing names of: Yei or Yei River District; Kajo Kaji or Opari Sub-district; Meridi, Amadi or Moru District; Juba, Central, Mongalla or Rejaf District (all in Equatoria Province); and Rumbek, Lakes or Eastern District (in the Bahr el Ghazal Province). In 2005 these areas made up Central Equatoria State, and parts of Lakes and Western Equatoria States.

These areas encompass many different ethnic groups, whose languages belong to three different subfamilies of the Nilo-Saharan linguistic family. In Lakes State, the Dinka language belongs to the Western Nilotic subfamily, as does that of the Pari of Lafon Hill in Eastern Equatoria. In Central Equatoria, the Lokoya and the Bari-speakers (including Kakwa, Kuku, Nyangwara, Mundari and Pojelu) belong to the Eastern Nilotic branch of the Eastern Sudanic subfamily; while the Moru, Madi, Luluba, Kaliko, Avukaya and Baka languages are classed as part of the Central Sudanic subfamily. The western edges of the research area also touch on the Zande, whose language belongs to an entirely different family (the Adamawa-Eastern sub-family, part of the Niger-Congo branch of the Congo-Kordofanian family).[44] As we shall see, people frequently moved, interacted and intermarried between and among these linguistic categories; pre-colonial ethnic identity appears more fluid in oral histories than in contemporary political discourse, in which ethnicity has become a particularly potent political register.

The research region is bordered to the south and west by denser Equatorial forests, to the east by the more arid plains of Eastern Equatoria, and to the north by the clay plains and Sudd marshes of the Bahr el Ghazal. The research region itself declines in elevation, vegetation density and rainfall from its southwest corner towards the north and east, where the ironstone plateau drops off to the plains. The declining elevation from southwest to northeast is paralleled by an increasing cattle population; the dense vegetation of south and west Equatoria has been a habitat for tsetse fly, limiting cattle herds. It has been argued that the whole area was once densely populated by cattle and that the slave-raiding and displacements of the late nineteenth century and subsequent colonial sleeping sickness resettlement campaigns allowed areas of dense bush to expand, undermining existing ecological control and destroying cattle herds.[45] Certainly

[44] See Robert O Collins, *Land Beyond the Rivers: the Southern Sudan, 1898–1918* (New Haven, CT, 1971), pp. 49–51.

[45] Kjell Hodnebo, *Cattle and Flies: a study of cattle keeping in Equatoria Province, the southern Sudan, 1850–1950* (Bergen, 1981).

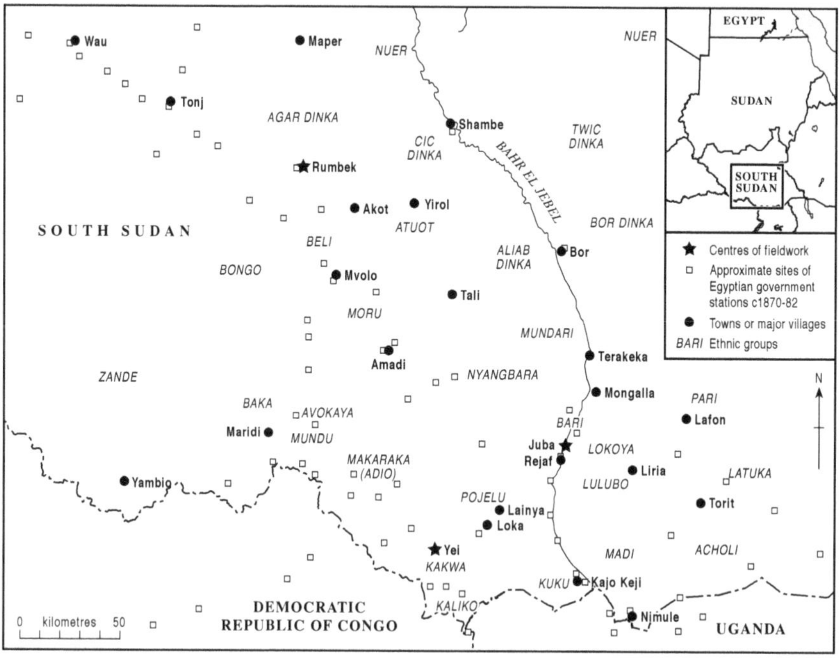

Map 0.1 Research areas, showing main towns and villages, ethnic groups and the approximate locations of Egyptian government stations, c. 1870–1882. (From the map accompanying *Emin Pasha in Central Africa: being a collection of his letters and journals*, ed. and annotated by G. Schweinfurth et al.; translated by R.W. Felkin; London: Philip, 1888)

all the people of Central Equatoria claimed to have had more cattle in the past, and records from the nineteenth and early twentieth century suggest that herds were being wiped out in some areas by the raiding of military and commercial forces or neighbouring groups. The evidence for such a major decline is not conclusive. But it is significant that almost all the ethnic groups of the region have – or claim to have – possessed cattle in the past, if not now. The boundaries between pastoralist and agriculturalist zones have therefore been blurred, as most people have combined these activities to varying degrees, and as cattle-less people have sought to acquire cattle. As in other parts of eastern Africa, herders and farmers have also traded and intermarried.[46] While cattle wealth is frequently associated with political power, the localised and diffuse nature of such power has not led to the kind of distinction between ruling pastoralists and subordinate agriculturalists that developed in the Great Lakes region.[47] Nor did the region see the development of the more intensive agriculture that was crucial to the formation of a state like Buganda to the south.[48]

Nevertheless, there is a significant – if graduated – contrast across the

[46] See e.g. Thomas Spear and Richard Waller (eds), *Being Maasai: ethnicity & identity in East Africa* (Oxford, 1993).

[47] Jean-Pierre Chrétien, *The Great Lakes of Africa: two thousand years of history*, trans. Scott Straus (New York, 2003).

[48] Richard Reid, *Political Power in Pre-Colonial Buganda: economy, society & warfare in the nineteenth century* (Oxford, 2002).

research region between the northeastern areas of highest cattle numbers (particularly among the Dinka, Mundari and northern Bari) and the south-western areas of more intensive agriculture in Equatoria. To some extent this contrast shaped relations with the state from the very beginning. People without cattle, or with very few cattle, tended to be more willing to enter into the economies of government, money and markets; more people from these areas would be drawn into the armies and employment of the state, particularly during the colonial period. Those wealthy in cattle tended to see waged employment or manual labour as menial, low-status work; in cattle-rich areas, it was generally only the poor and cattle-less who took up such employment, often in the hope of acquiring cattle. Cattle thus in one sense kept people away from towns and government, contributing to the preservation of distinct value regimes and hence the constitution of difference between state and society. Yet the cattle economy also impelled people to seek guarantees of property rights in state institutions; the chiefs' courts would always attract the greatest numbers of litigants in the cattle-keeping areas.

As this indicates, the rich diversity in livelihood, social structure and political culture across the research areas does not fundamentally affect the overall arguments of this study. The urban frontier on which the book focuses has been a particularly intense site of interaction and cultural heterogeneity, in which common strategies and institutions have emerged for dealing with government. My choice of research sites reflected my interest in questioning the stark urban-rural, state-society dichotomies that previous ethnographic studies located in the rural areas had tended to produce. I therefore based myself in the towns and spent most of my time in particular villages outside or on the edge of the towns that could be reached easily by bicycle (or sometimes motorcycle). In a sense these peri-urban sites represent the opposite extreme from the kind of state-resistant or state-avoiding societies examined by James Scott's influential study of upland southeast Asia.[49] Other regions of South Sudan and Sudan have been described as more akin to the 'shatter zones' on which he focuses, in which people have sought refuge from the state in hills, forests and ungoverned borderlands.[50]

Yet the urban frontier in South Sudan has acted as a converse kind of shatter zone, attracting heterogeneous populations in search of refuge and protection. The difference is that these people saw the opportunity for protection in the resources and idea of the state itself. This did not mean that they bought into notions of centralised or hierarchical power; local political cultures have remained pluralising and in some respects anarchic, as well as vociferously critical of governments. But such people have nevertheless discerned opportunity as well as risk on the urban frontier, or decided that the state could not be avoided and that they might better obtain protection from it by appropriating its own regulatory resources. I am not claiming that these research sites are necessarily representative of South Sudan as a whole; indeed one of the arguments of the book is that chiefship is highly varied and contingent according to locality, circumstances and individual ability. But the research sites do represent a rapidly enlarging zone of political and economic interaction, into which most people – or their relatives and acquaintances – have been drawn at one time or

[49] James Scott, *The Art of Not Being Governed: an anarchist history of upland Southeast Asia* (New Haven, CT, 2009).

[50] Wendy James, *'Kwanim Pa: the making of the Uduk people: an ethnographic study of survival in the Sudan-Ethiopian borderlands* (Oxford, 1979); Janet Ewald, *Soldiers, Traders, and Slaves: state formation and economic transformation in the Greater Nile Valley, 1700–1885* (Madison, 1990); Edward Thomas, *The Kafia Kingi Enclave: people, politics and history in the north–south boundary zone of western Sudan* (London, 2010).

another; and they reveal processes of local institutionalisation and state formation which are of much wider significance.

The book is structured in three main chronological parts, distinguished by important shifts both in the nature of the state and the character of its urban centres, and in the body of source material used in the chapters. Part I covers a long period from the first Egyptian government expedition to reach the region in 1840–41, up to around 1920, when the British colonial administration was shifting from a predominantly military to an ever-more-bureaucratic character. It uses oral histories and the scant documentary record to trace enduring features of society and polity in the region, and their intersection with encroaching imperial and commercial forces after 1840. It details the establishment of military and commercial stations in the region and their transfer to state control. By c. 1920 administrative centres had been firmly established as the nuclei of the small towns of southern Sudan; and the institution of chiefship had emerged out of the trade and warfare of the nineteenth century to be strengthened and given an enduring place in the bureaucratic records of the early colonial governments.

Up to around 1920, however, that bureaucracy was limited and the military forces of the state remained dangerously unpredictable. From the 1920s, the colonial government adopted a much greater degree of the bureaucratic regulation that has been seen as the major innovation of the colonial period in Africa. This also ensured a substantial documentary record for this period, which is the basis for Part II, together with interview material. These chapters examine the simultaneous constraint and opportunity that the new regulatory order presented after 1920, from the establishment of formal chiefs' courts, through to the formation of local government councils in the 1940s and 1950s. This was also a period in which the urban frontier was consolidated around the small towns, maintained by the tension between the colonial attempts to exclude 'rural' people from town, and the converse attractions of town and state represented by these centres.

In the 1950s, the greater sense of predictability and routine that had come to characterise relations with government was suddenly undermined and eroded by wider political change and a return to more militarised and threatening practices of governance. Part Three discusses the role of chiefs in trying to manage this dangerous unpredictability during the periods of war that dominated the subsequent history of the region. But it also explores the converse expansion of the urban frontier and of wider participation in realms of bureaucracy and governance, which would give people an increasing sense of a claim on the state, despite their experiences of its repression, exclusion and violence. As well as drawing on the scattered documentary evidence for the 1956–2011 period, Part III makes most extensive use of the oral testimonies collected in the research areas to explore the ways in which chiefs and people have sought to deal with the state. Yet even as the state was increasingly appropriated into local settings, so state and chiefship were being reproduced through the constitution of mutual difference, a paradox generated and epitomised by the tensions, uncertainties and opportunities of the urban frontier.

Part One

From *Zariba* to *Merkaz*: The Creation of the Nodal State Frontier, c. 1840–1920

Before 1840, the region that would become southern Sudan lay at the furthest limits of any long-distance commerce and beyond the reach of any state powers. Only its northernmost areas were already being raided for slaves for the markets and trade roads further north, while to the east were the distant frontiers of the Ethiopian kingdom, and to the south the kingdoms of Buganda and Bunyoro. The earliest documentary evidence is suggestive of some possible long-distance commercial linkages, notably demonstrated by the blue cloth worn by Bari rain chiefs on the Nile, which was said to have come from the east via Lafon hill.[1] But such limited connections would be dramatically overtaken by the sudden advance of new imperial and commercial frontiers after 1840. This region became the southern frontier of Turco-Egyptian expansion under the Ottoman ruler of Egypt, Mohamed ‘Ali, and his grandson, Khedive Ismail. At the same time, East African trading networks were reaching the lacustrine kingdoms to the south, spreading the hunt for ivory and slaves northwards.[2] European investment in Egypt would ultimately heighten British strategic concerns with the upper Nile, supported by the growing British public interest in the region generated by explorers and Christian missionaries and further stimulated by French and Belgian competition. By the end of the nineteenth century, it was European imperial frontiers that were colliding on the upper Nile, and by 1910 the southern Sudan was firmly incorporated into the British colonial sphere, as part of the Anglo-Egyptian Condominium of Sudan.[3]

South Sudanese are deeply aware of this history of their incorporation and exploitation by global imperial and commercial forces. In much political discourse and popular memory, the nineteenth-century slave trade has epitomised their oppression by northern Sudanese specifically, and has become a powerful ideological tool in the ‘liberation’ war against Khartoum governments. As a new state sought to generate national identity in 2011, the history of the ‘struggle’ from which it had emerged was being dated all the way back to the invasion of northern Sudan by Egyptian forces in 1820, which stimulated the southward expansion of slave-raiding and state penetration.[4] But many South Sudanese also refer to the wider international slave trade, believing that their people were taken to be sold in America or Europe. The enduring term in many areas for people working in the government has been ‘Turuk’, or ‘Turk’, memorialising the earliest imperial frontiers in the region: those of the Ottoman Empire. It was, after all, a Turk who led the first expedition to break through the vegetation in the Sudd marshes on the Nile in 1840–41, opening the way for the subsequent incursions.

South Sudanese nowadays may be well aware of these global dynamics in the nineteenth century history. But their ancestors experienced the arrival of the ‘Turk’ in more local contexts, in the form of raiding parties consisting of southern slave-soldiers and local auxiliaries and allies, and in the establishment of fortified trading stations, known as *zara’ib* (sing. *zariba*), the Arabic term for

[1] See Simon Simonse, *Kings of Disaster: dualism, centralism, and the scapegoat king in south-eastern Sudan* (Leiden, 1992), pp. 44–5.

[2] See also Mark Leopold, *Inside West Nile: violence, history & representation on an African frontier* (Oxford, 2005).

[3] For detailed accounts of the nineteenth-century history, see Richard Hill, *Egypt and the Sudan 1820–1881* (London, 1959); Richard Gray, *A History of the Southern Sudan 1839–1889* (Oxford, 1961); Robert O Collins, *The Southern Sudan, 1883–1898: a struggle for control* (New Haven, CT, 1962); John Udal, *The Nile in Darkness* Vol. 1: *conquest and exploration 1504–1862* (Norwich, 1998) and Vol. 2: *A flawed unity 1863–1899* (Norwich, 2005).

[4] ‘South Sudan officially recognises 191 years of struggle for freedom’, *Sudan Tribune,* 1 May 2011, last accessed on 21 January 2013, www.sudantribune.com/South-Sudan-officially-recognises,38743 .

thorn-fenced enclosures. Many of the *zara'ib* were subsequently taken over as Egyptian government forts in the 1870s, when various European officers were sent to formally annex and govern the region on behalf of the Egyptian Khedive. When Turco-Egyptian control was ended by the Mahdist rebellion in northern Sudan in the 1880s, these stations were abandoned by all but an occasional remnant of their garrisons, the southern slave-soldiers of the Egyptian army. When British and Belgian colonial officers arrived in the late 1890s and early 1900s, they often employed such former soldiers, and built their new stations on or near the old Egyptian forts and *zara'ib*.

By 1920 these nodes of colonial state power were established as the *merkaz* or district offices, and the militaristic cultures and practices inherited from their nineteenth century predecessors were beginning to be questioned by British colonial officials and masked by an increasingly bureaucratic administration. The previous eighty years would leave an enduring legacy for local relations with the state, but this legacy was more complex and ambiguous than might be assumed from the violent history of early imperialism in southern Sudan. Part I therefore examines not only the documentary record from 1840 onwards, but also the ways in which South Sudanese in the twenty-first century were explaining the history of their ancestors' encounters with state power.

*

1

Frontier societies and the political economy of knowledge in the nineteenth century

Based on the availability of written sources, histories of South Sudan have tended to begin from the coming of the 'Turk': the incursions up the Nile from 1840 onwards by ivory and slave traders and Turco-Egyptian government forces. The subsequent decades of the nineteenth century have been characterised as a time of violent disruption and predation, epitomised by the slave trade itself. Gray and Collins depict the people of the region as 'ill-prepared' for these foreign incursions, having been 'isolated' from any external contact prior to 1840.[1] In the early 1980s, an anthropologist contrasted the history of the Bari on the Nile with West African societies, where commercial middlemen had dealt with foreign traders, protecting their societies and generating major socio-economic change and class formation. The Bari, Huby argued, were instead 'passive bystanders forced into a political and economic game which was directed from elsewhere'; no group or class 'emerged among the Southerners with some degree of power to influence the course of events.'[2]

Certainly the violent depredations of the nineteenth century had a devastating impact on many parts of the region and established an enduring awareness of the extractive, brutal potential of the forces of the *hakuma* [government]. But relations were more complex than the histories of passive victimhood have suggested. From the outset, certain individuals and groups entered into dialogue with these foreign forces, and some succeeded in negotiating more positive relations of exchange and interaction, even if temporarily. This established enduring patterns of relations with the state, in which certain localities became more closely identified with government and long-distance commerce, and were likely to attract settlers seeking resources and relations with nascent state forces.

According to Gray, the commercial inexperience and parochialism of southern Sudanese was evident in their insistence on receiving cattle in any commercial exchanges, which generated cattle-raiding by the traders, often pursued through destructive local military alliances.[3] But the fact that the traders were forced to use cattle in their exchanges with local people also demonstrates the strongly-guarded social and economic value of cattle; successive governments too would be forced to recognise livestock as property and wealth.[4] This preservation of indigenous value regimes also differs from prevailing analyses of the contemporaneous eastern African caravan trade and its impact on local political economies.

Brokers of the new forms of commodity trade were therefore also negoti-

1 Gray, *A History*; Collins, *The Southern Sudan*; Collins, *Land Beyond the Rivers*.

2 Huby, 'Big men', p. 34.

3 Gray, *A History*, pp. 40–50.

4 E.g. Sudan Government Intelligence Department, *The Bahr el Ghazal Province* (London, 1911), p. 68.

ating the recognition of indigenous property rights in livestock and persons by the foreign and state forces. As Simonse has argued, contra Huby, individual middlemen *did* emerge along the Nile, as they would further inland as well, to act as intermediaries and agents of the traders. The linguistic knowledge, entrepreneurial brokerage and diplomatic abilities of these men (and sometimes women) represent the foundation of later government chiefship. But this was in turn rooted in an existing economy of knowledge, in which political authority derived from monopolising or multiplying skills and expertise. Far from being isolated and ill-prepared for external contact, the people of this region had always actively sought out knowledge, skills and resources from as far afield as possible. Some now extended this to contracting with the foreign forces. Such deals would increasingly break down by the 1880s and 1890s, to be replaced by more defensive, militaristic leadership. But this too reflected long-term survival strategies: people diversified their options, their social and economic relations, their leadership and their knowledge resources in preparation for just such times of danger and dispersal.

FRONTIERS OF KNOWLEDGE IN ORAL HISTORIES

South Sudanese oral histories focus on migrations: people claim descent from an ancestral migration leader, who came from a spiritual plane in the sky, or from somewhere to the east, or across rivers. In the grasslands of the Bahr el Ghazal region, Dinka oral histories and origin myths represent crossing rivers to find new pastures for cattle as vital to life.[5] To the south in Central Equatoria, people tell miraculous stories of their ancestors crossing the Nile from the east and settling on fertile soils around the distinctive hills and mountains of this region.[6] Such migrations are commonly attributed to a split within families or clans in their original homeland. South Sudanese oral histories thus correspond to the wider African narrative tropes analysed most famously by Kopytoff, in which segmentation and fission produces migrations to new frontiers on which communities and political institutions are recreated.[7]

These histories usually centre on clan or lineage rather than ethnic origins; in fact ethnicity seems to have been linked to place rather than to descent, with stories of people moving from Lugbara to Nyangwara to Mundari, so that a 'tribe' like the Mundari was made up of various groups of immigrants to a particular territory.[8] As in pre-colonial Tanzania, in 'a place of uncertain environments and uneven opportunities', people were 'entrepreneurial about their social relationships and ethnic identities'.[9] The enduring ethnic nomenclature in South Sudan was largely produced and established in the nineteenth century by the responses of informants to the questioning, categorising and recording of Europeans, whose books would inform subsequent colonial administrators. There

5 Mawson, 'The Triumph of Life', p. 114; Godfrey Lienhardt, *Divinity and Experience: the religion of the Dinka* (Oxford, 1961), pp. 171–206. Cf. JoAnn McGregor, *Crossing the Zambezi: the politics of landscape on a Central African frontier* (Woodbridge, 2009), pp. 22–40.

6 See also Scopas Poggo, 'The origins and culture of blacksmiths in Kuku society of the Sudan, 1797–1955', *Journal of African Cultural Studies*, 18:2 (2006), p. 173.

7 Kopytoff, 'The internal African frontier'; Paul Nugent, *Smugglers, Secessionists & Loyal Citizens on the Ghana-Togo Frontier* (Oxford, 2002), p. 16; Godfrey Lienhardt, 'Getting your own back: themes in Nilotic myth,' in John HM Beattie and Godfrey Lienhardt, *Studies in Social Anthropology: essays in memory of E. E. Evans-Pritchard* (Oxford, 1975), pp. 213–37.

8 See Jean Buxton, *Chiefs and Strangers: a study of political assimilation among the Mandari* (Oxford, 1963), pp. 18–19, 32–3.

9 Peterson, 'Morality plays', para. 11.

are familiar instances of derogatory names for neighbouring groups 'sticking' as ethnic labels. Most vernacular discourse simply refers to 'us', 'the people' or 'the country' in self-reference, rather than to an ethnic name.[10] Whatever the meaning of the names that were told to outsiders and attached to tribes in the nineteenth century, it is clear that people could shift between groups and adopt or acquire new identifications with relative ease, as oral histories of migration and adhesion make clear.

There are differences across the research sites in terms of how such migration, fusion and assimilation is explained in oral narratives or evident in social structures. The Agar Dinka of Rumbek straddle the edge of the ironstone plateau, which marks the frontier of the predominantly agriculturalist regions of Western Equatoria and Western Bahr el Ghazal. Below this plateau to the north and east are the grasslands of the seasonally-flooded clay plains, across which Dinka cattle-herders migrate annually to find dry-season grazing. The Dinka depict this as a frontier between the cattle-less *Jur*, 'foreigners', and themselves, *Jieng*, 'the people'. While the Agar also have farms and homesteads on the higher savannah scrublands around Rumbek, they define their society by cattle and structure it in terms of cattle-owning lineages and co-herding sections, which share seasonal cattle camps on the grazing plains. *Jur* are depicted as having been either assimilated into this society or driven out by the pastoralist advance.[11] Yet Agar Dinka histories of Rumbek emphasise a historic agreement between *Jieng* and *Jur*, rather than a process of conquest. They claim that their ancestors advanced into this area but were unable to live together with the existing agriculturalist inhabitants, the Beli, because the Beli could not abide the sound of the Agar cattle lowing. The Agar claim that an agreement was therefore reached for the Beli to vacate the area and leave it to them, in return for the Beli chief marrying Akon Buoi, the daughter of the Agar leader Buoi. In the twentieth century, Rumbek was described in local songs as 'the sand of Akon Buoi';[12] and in the early twenty-first century new wooden statues of Akon were erected in the centre of Rumbek town, demonstrating her enduring association with the coming of the Agar to the area. According to one Dinka judge writing in the 1990s, Akon's marriage represents a 'sacrifice', in return for which the Agar gained their land.[13] Such tropes of individual sacrifice would also play a significant part in oral histories from other areas concerning later agreements with state forces.

To the southeast of Rumbek, the plains around the Nile support the cattle herds of the Mundari and Bari, with a similar agropastoralist economy to the Agar Dinka; but this is an area in which cattle populations are said to have declined over the last two centuries, making access to farming land, particularly near the fertile Nile banks and islands, more valued and contested.[14] Further south and west, as the rainfall and vegetation density increases and the cattle population decreases, control of cultivable land becomes even more crucial to the production of status, authority and wealth-in-people. Successive waves of migration are narrated to explain hierarchies and relations among different sections of territorial communities. While the Agar 'bargain' entailed the exodus of the previous occupants of the land, Bari and Bari-speaking groups tend to

[10] Cf. Tim Allen, 'Ethnicity & tribalism on the Sudan-Uganda border', in Katsuyoshi Fukui and John Markakis (eds), *Ethnicity & Conflict in the Horn of Africa* (London, 1994), pp. 112–39.

[11] Cf. Kopytoff, 'The internal African frontier', p. 31.

[12] GK Hebbert, DC Yirrol, to Governor Upper Nile, 'Song of Gol Mayen', 23 Dec 1931, NRO CivSec 36/4/15, Lienhardt Papers 1/9, Pitt Rivers Museum, Oxford.

[13] Monyluak Alor Kuol, *Administration of Justice in the (SPLA/M) Liberated Areas: court cases in war-torn Southern Sudan* (Oxford, 1997), p. 27.

[14] See for example Buxton, *Chiefs and Strangers*.

affirm the political primacy of first-comers to a territory. In the southwest around Yei, Kakwa oral histories depict long-distance migrations from the Bari homeland across the Nile to new frontiers of settlement; Kakwa clans here are locally co-residential, and identified with particular territories to which they claim first-comer rights. But in other areas, people narrate historic agreements to explain why in some cases later-comers became politically dominant. Often the latter are said to have brought cattle and the spiritual power of rain chiefship, while the existing inhabitants retained authority over the land as its original occupants and owners; idioms of contract and reciprocity are thus prominent in these histories. Even in this more settled farming region of Central Equatoria, people were always highly mobile, practising shifting cultivation and clearing the dense bush to establish new settlements; often the clan 'owners' of particular lands no longer inhabited their original areas, but continued to be recognised and called upon to bless and protect the land.

In all the research areas, spiritual and political leadership has frequently been explained in terms of hereditary descent from ancestral migration leaders. But such leadership has not produced centralised polities. Across the region, people have lived in dispersed and largely autonomous territorial or herding sections, governed by family heads and senior elders; cross-cut by lineage and clan affiliations; connected to wider forms of religious and spiritual authority; and capable of mobilising more fluid networks of kinship and alliance to overcome crises or undertake military action. Oral histories of migration often serve to explain relations between multiple forms of authority, and to support social hierarchies in which control of land and/or cattle has produced control over people. These might have been stateless societies, but they did not lack hierarchies and patrimonial structures.

The idiom of kinship has served to both disguise and preserve these hierarchies, enabling the attachment of new adherents to dominant lineages or individual patrons whilst frequently preserving a degree of ambiguity about their status and relations. The prevailing idiom of patrilineal social structure can easily obscure the importance of maternal relations and the flexible and pragmatic realities of kinship and adhesion. An elderly Kakwa politician near Yei explained the transethnic connections of marriage and patrimonialism in the area:

> There were networks of relations – it was a system like a net, and it stretched across what is now the Congo border. Nephews [maternal] are very important. The people living in a clan area are not necessarily all blood relatives. The nephews sometimes choose to come and live with their uncles. And even non-nephews may come and ask to live here and they can be welcomed and given a piece of land to cultivate. My grandmother on my mother's side was a Kaliko, and we are still close to those uncles of Kaliko.[15]

Clans or communities that appear to be structured along patrilineal kinship lines were thus in reality of heterogeneous origins, their aggregation explained by discourses of kinship, marriage and patrimonialism.[16] As many oral histories indicate, women were often revered as a means of political agreement and peace, and in their marriage they established a whole new set of vitally-important relations. The role of women often appears to mediate the tensions between agnatic and affinal relations, and between patrilineal structure and the historical and contemporary reality of migration and assimilation. Dinka

[15] Interview 2aN/YC.

[16] See also the critique of Evans-Pritchard for ignoring the political importance of affinal and matrilateral relations among the Nuer, in Susan McKinnon, 'Domestic exceptions: Evans-Pritchard and the creation of Nuer patrilineality and equality', *Cultural Anthropology* 15:1 (2000), pp. 35–83.

wuot, sections that herded their cattle together, tended to be structured around two lineages, related through marriage: one of spiritual leaders known as spear-masters, and one of war chiefs, 'thus creating a strong nucleus of two descent-groups related through women'.[17]

Building wealth-in-people and political power *depended* on attracting non-agnatic followers, most obviously from maternal kin, as the use of the term 'nephew' to describe dependents in general reveals. Across the region, destitute or defeated people from other linguistic and ethnic groups are also said to have been incorporated through patrimonial relations, generating political authority and wealth for their patrons.[18] In 2006, a Bari chief asserted that such dependents were like adopted sons or daughters, but added that their original status was never entirely forgotten: a newcomer 'surrendered himself to the chief's hands and it was the chief to marry a girl for him: he had put a rope on his neck; he was now like a child of the chief'.[19] This expresses very well the simultaneous gain and constraint of entering such relations of dependence. In Central Equatoria, such hierarchies have continued to be made visible at social events and ceremonies, such as through strict conventions for eating and drinking.[20] In the colonial period, British officials would employ terms like 'commoner' to try to translate these hierarchical and patrimonial relations into more familiar class structures. But such relations were more fluid and contested than categories of class, serfdom or slavery.[21]

The migration, relations of dependency and maternal ties that feature in oral histories were all part of strategies to mitigate conflict and to insure against the risks of drought, disease and other dangers. People were often compelled to exchange status and autonomy for security and assistance. As Johnson and Anderson argue for the wider northeast Africa region, it was also vital to build up reciprocal relations with groups pursuing different livelihood strategies or controlling particular resources.[22] There is certainly evidence of such trade and relations across considerable distances in the nineteenth century, as people exchanged grain, livestock and specialist or scarce items like iron, salt and tobacco.[23] These exchanges also crossed linguistic divides, including between distinct language families, suggesting that linguistic knowledge would always have been a significant asset.

[17] Lienhardt, *Divinity and Experience*, pp. 9, 198–204; 'Nilotic kings and their mother's kin', *Africa* 25:1 (1955), pp. 29–42; and 'The Western Dinka', in Middleton and Tait, *Tribes Without Rulers*, pp. 97–135; Mawson, 'The Triumph of Life', p. 65; Douglas H Johnson, *Nuer Prophets: a history of prophecy from the Upper Nile in the nineteenth and twentieth centuries* (Oxford, 1994), pp. 57, 60, 70, 79, 184–5.

[18] George WB Huntingford, *Ethnographic Survey of Africa, East Central Africa, Part VI: The Northern Nilo-Hamites,* edited by Daryll Forde (London, 1953), p. 63; Conrad C Reining, *The Zande Scheme: an anthropological case study of economic development in Africa* (Evanston, 1966), p. 15; GO Whitehead, 'Suppressed Classes among the Bari and Bari-speaking Tribes', *Sudan Notes and Records* 34:2 (1953), p. 268.

[19] Interview 41R/JC.

[20] Interview 2bN/YC.

[21] See the wider perspectives on African slavery and clientage in Suzanne Miers and Igor Kopytoff (eds), *Slavery in Africa: historical and anthropological perspectives* (Madison, 1977).

[22] Douglas H Johnson and David M Anderson, 'Introduction', to Johnson and Anderson (eds), *The Ecology of Survival: case studies from Northeast African history* (London, 1988), pp. 1–24.

[23] Mawson, 'The Triumph of Life', p. 163; Gaetano Casati, *Ten Years in Equatoria* (Pop. ed., London and New York, 1898), p. 209; Ferdinand Werne, *Expedition to Discover the Sources of the White Nile, in the Years 1840, 1841*, Vol. 2, (London, 1849), p. 56; E Pedemonte, 'A report on the voyage of 1849–1850', in Elia Toniolo and Richard Hill (eds), *The Opening of the Nile Basin: writings by members of the Catholic Mission to Central Africa on the geography and ethnography of the Sudan, 1842–1881* (New York, 1975), pp. 65–6.

Indeed, as well as pursuing material resources and insurance strategies beyond their immediate localities, people also sought out new and distant sources of knowledge. In a capricious climate and environment, the most valuable skills were those that could predict and influence forces of nature, spirit and divinity to ensure reproduction and production; skills that enabled effective communication with God, ancestors and spirits in order to avert harm and sickness, and to bring clement weather and the fertility of people, animals and land. Some of these forms of specialist knowledge might be characterised as practical, such as skills of iron-working, hunting, fishing, healing, midwifery, poison. Others appear more esoteric, such as the capacity to bring rain, protect from disease and pests, bless and curse, or communicate with ancestral and ultra-human forces. But such distinctions have generally been irrelevant in South Sudanese epistemologies: all those possessing specialist knowledge are simultaneously revered and feared, needed and mistrusted, and exist on a spectrum from the highly moral and spiritual, to the outright immoral and antisocial. Specialist clans of iron-smiths, hunters and fishers have had a marginal and yet highly respected status. Spiritual leaders like Dinka spear-masters might be as 'unpredictable' as changing weather and capricious environments.[24] Medicines, poisons and occult powers are a source of fear and loathing and yet also highly in demand. For all the ambivalence and mistrust towards specialists, people have always travelled long distances to consult them or to acquire such knowledge for themselves. Communities or their leaders have also sought to attract such knowledge resources into their areas: 'Before the British came, the hunters, blacksmiths and so on were very important. To have a clan you must have these people... attackers will try to capture them to work in their villages.'[25]

Poggo describes Kuku blacksmiths, fishers, hunters and canoe-makers as a single category of people with the 'unique technical skills' required for 'innovation'.[26] As Guyer and Belinga argue, African communities or their leaders did not simply seek to attract and accumulate undifferentiated human capital; rather they sought to attract new members and dependents with new forms of expertise and knowledge. It was the differentiated composition of 'wealth in knowledge' that mattered even more than 'wealth in people'.[27]

Knowledge is also held up in oral histories as integral to political authority and as a factor in the political arrangements between successive immigrants. This is particularly apparent in relation to 'rain-making', which English-speaking informants often suggest is the wrong term. Rain chiefs do not 'make' rain but rather intercede with divine powers to influence when and where it falls by a variety of means, including the use of rain stones and gourds. This is explicitly described as a form of expert knowledge: according to later colonial officials, all members of Bari rain-chief clans were described as those 'who know rain'.[28]

In Central Equatoria, oral histories frequently tell of incoming migrants bringing knowledge of rain and therefore being welcomed and given land by the existing inhabitants. But this rain knowledge was also bound up with a new political economy; immigrant rain clans are commonly said to have brought

[24] Mawson, 'The Triumph of Life', p. 117

[25] Interview 3N/YC.

[26] Poggo, 'Origins and culture', p. 173.

[27] Jane I Guyer and Samuel ME Belinga, 'Wealth in people as wealth in knowledge: accumulation and composition in Equatorial Africa', *Journal of African History* 36 (1995), pp. 91–120.

[28] AC Beaton, 'The Bari: clan and age-class systems', *Sudan Notes and Records* 19:1 (1936), p. 110; AC Beaton, 'A Chapter in Bari History: the history of Sindiru, Bilinian and Mogiri', *Sudan Notes and Records* 17:2 (1934), p. 170; Ernest B Haddon, 'System of chieftainship amongst the Bari of Uganda', *Journal of the Royal African Society* 10:40 (1911), pp. 467–72; Huntingford, *Ethnographic Survey*, p. 29; Simonse, *Kings of Disaster*, pp. 106–7. Cf. Johnson, *Nuer Prophets*, p. 35.

cattle and acquired political authority, while the earlier inhabitants retained authority over the land, headed by the *monyekak*, the 'owner', 'father' or 'chief' of the land.[29] Wealth-in-people, wealth-in-knowledge and wealth-in-cattle often overlap in oral histories in this region as both the source and product of military and political dominance, and all depended ultimately on mobility and migration. Women also frequently moved through their marriage, and were therefore particularly associated with access to outside skills and expertise: rain knowledge is said to have been brought by women to their husband's clan in Kakwa oral histories. Women would also be prominent in trade and negotiation with foreigners in the nineteenth century.[30]

People sought to contract the most important holders of knowledge through relations of exchange and tribute in ways that prepared the way for later – albeit very different – relations with the state. For example, the British explorer Samuel Baker described a successful 'rain-maker and sorcerer' in southern Equatoria in the early 1860s: the Madi chief 'Katchiba', who had established so great a reputation 'that distant tribes frequently consult him, and beg his assistance as a magician'. In return for blessings, medicine and rain, or by threatening to curse or withhold rain, Katchiba had, according to Baker, been able to extract goats, grain and wives from the people: '"No goats, no rain; that's our contract, my friends", says Katchiba.'[31]

This evocation of a 'contract' is significant, even if Baker put it in rather pantomime-like terms. Similarly Dinka diviners were given payments of spears or other items in return for finding the cause of sickness, while spear-masters and prophets were given cattle 'in supplication for favours' and in return for their prayers for rain or fertility.[32] Even a powerful spear-master could be replaced for failing to manage his responsibilities.[33] The anthropologist Simonse similarly analyses relations with the most powerful Bari rain chiefs, termed by him 'kings', in terms of debt and obligation:

> By his gift of rain the King puts the whole community in debt. This debt was paid back through the many forms of tribute and corvée that existed. Rain, tribute, trade goods, matrimonial goods and the harvests resulting from corvée for the King entered one economic cycle which sustained the power of the King.[34]

The relations between powerful experts and the people who recognised and sought their expertise were thus based on exchange and economic transaction, which established mutual obligation.

The Bari rain 'kings' were rather unusual in that they appear for a time to have centralised and unified power and control of resources; we also know more about them because they were encountered by the first expeditions up the Nile in the nineteenth century. Benefiting from the hills to the east of the

[29] Beaton, 'A Chapter in Bari history', p. 183; AC Beaton, 'A short history of the Luluba Hills', NRO JD 1/1/2 and 'A short history of Liria', NRO JD 1/1/2; Stigand, Inspector Rejaf, to Governor, 6 March 1911, NRO Intel 2/29/239; Interview 1R/K. Cf. the idea of 'conquest by invitation' discussed by Kopytoff, using Southall's study of Alur chiefs as an example: Kopytoff, 'The internal African frontier', pp. 55, 65–66.

[30] E.g. Samuel W Baker, *Ismailia: a narrative of the expedition to Central Africa for the suppression of the slave trade, organized by Ismail, Khedive of Egypt*, Vol. 1 (London, 1874), pp. 276–7, 331; cf. Claire C Robertson, 'Gender and trade relations in central Kenya in the late nineteenth century', *International Journal of African Historical Studies* 30:1 (1997), pp. 23–47.

[31] Samuel White Baker, *The Albert N'yanza: great basin of the Nile* (London, 1867), pp. 126–9.

[32] Lienhardt, *Divinity and Experience*, pp. 71, 78–9.

[33] Mawson, 'The Triumph of Life', pp. 176–7, 193.

[34] Simonse, *Kings of Disaster*, p. 40.

Nile which contained iron ore, they had gained command of both rain and the iron trade. They also benefited from river transport: the rain chief ruling in 1840, Logunu, reportedly travelled annually by boat to the Mundari areas downstream, exchanging his iron for 'slaves' to work the iron in the Bari hills. The iron was then traded across long distances, exchanged with the Pari of Lafon Hill for copper, tobacco and cloth; iron rings functioned as currency.[35] The connections between iron and rain knowledge were so close that even today rain chiefs are called *matat lo lori* in the wider Bari-speaking areas: 'chief of the iron rod'; such rods were used in rain rituals.[36]

The authority of these rain chiefs was clearly based on individual ability: the earliest European account by Werne recorded Logunu's skills of diplomacy and rhetoric, as well as his judicial role in producing a 'unanimous will' among a council or assembly, based on 'innate respect' towards him, rather than any automatic 'royal power'.[37] Simonse asserts that the rain 'king' was responsible for arbitration and peace-making, 'foreign affairs' and war, as well as for ritual and cosmological functions.[38] This is perhaps not surprising – the skills and expertise required to mediate with the forces controlling the rain could also be applied to mediating social relations within and between communities. Rain chiefs and similar figures were after all 'entrepreneurs' just as later trading agents and government chiefs would be.[39]

But there has also been an enduring aversion in local political culture to the centralisation and monopolisation of knowledge and power by any individual or even one lineage, as demonstrated by the distinct, parallel authority of Dinka spear-masters and war chiefs, or of rain and land chiefs in Central Equatoria.[40] Local discourse frequently explains the multiplicity of authority and expertise in terms of successive waves of migration, or in terms of the need to protect experts from the risks of interlocutory or military roles, since their knowledge was so vital to the safety and fertility of the wider community. This was an economic and ecological context that encouraged diversification rather than agricultural intensification and political centralisation. But we might also see this political pluralism as the product of tensions and rivalry, and of the jealous safeguarding of specialist areas of expertise, in a political economy of knowledge. In the mid-nineteenth century, however, the arrival of new imperial and commercial forces in the region would create the need and opportunities for a new area of specialist expertise, and one which conveyed even more risks.

FRONTIERS OF EMPIRE: THE NILE EXPEDITIONS

In 1839, an expedition led by the Turkish naval officer, Salim Qapudan, was launched from Khartoum to penetrate the marshy vegetation blockages on the upper Nile, at the orders of the ruler of Egypt, Muhammad 'Ali. Since the Turco-Egyptian invasion of Sudan in 1820–21, government-sponsored raiding for slaves for the Egyptian army had been pushing ever further south into Shilluk

[35] Werne, *Expedition*, Vol. 2, pp. 27, 37, 68, 123.

[36] F Spire, 'Rain-making in Equatorial Africa', *Journal of the Royal African Society* 5:17 (1905), pp. 15–21.

[37] Werne, *Expedition*, Vol. 2, p. 67.

[38] Simonse, *Kings of Disaster*, p. 79.

[39] Cf. Peterson, 'Morality plays', para. 44.

[40] Even in a centralised state, Hanson similarly emphasises 'the Ganda inclination to diffuse power' and 'to avoid conflict by creating multiple avenues of power': Hanson, *Landed Obligation*, pp. 143–4.

and Dinka areas; the expedition was also motivated by hopes of minerals and ivory. Its slow but successful penetration to what is now the Juba area in Central Equatoria opened the way for annual government expeditions to the trading station established at Gondokoro; the expeditions subsequently enlarged to as many as 120 boats per year by 1863.[41] European traders based in Khartoum played a prominent role in the ivory trade in the 1850s, and European missionaries also established a Catholic mission station at Gondokoro. The ending of the government monopoly on trade and slave-raiding in the 1850s then prompted the spread of private military and commercial stations, the *zara'ib*, across the Bahr el Ghazal region west of the Nile, by merchants from Europe, the Middle East and northern Sudan.

The primary objective of the earliest government expeditions and of the subsequent traders on the Nile was to obtain ivory, or anticipated valuable minerals; slaves were only a secondary objective. But the existing patterns of enslavement, particularly the military slavery of the Egyptian army, would profoundly shape these early encounters. This is because the river expeditions took with them slaves or slave-soldiers to act as interpreters, or 'dragomans', initially from the northernmost Dinka and Shilluk areas already being raided for slaves. These were not merely linguistic interpreters but exercised immense influence as guides to the region, and as cultural interlocutors and economic brokers.[42] Over the next decade, other local interpreters emerged to ply their trade along the Nile; and by the early 1860s, 'many of the natives in the vicinity of Gondokoro [had] learnt a little Arabic from the traders'.[43] According to Gray, 'the Turks became dependent on these riverain Bari to act as middlemen in the search for and purchase of further supplies'.[44] The opportunities for profit are obvious, but such a brokerage role was not without risk too; several Bari interpreters were killed, for example, when a merchant military force was defeated by the Lokoya east of the Nile in 1860.[45]

One interpreter later employed by Nuqud, the agent of the Coptic Egyptian trader Shenuda, was described as a powerful *bunit*, a diviner or other expert, and as 'a renowned traveller'.[46] As we have seen, the kind of individuals who had gained specialist knowledge of rain-control, iron-working, magic and medicine were by definition entrepreneurial and acquisitive of new skills and expertise. They were also likely to be referred to by their people when foreigners asked to speak to the 'chief' or 'sheikh'. In some cases they naturally took on the role of mediating with the new commercial forces. The powerful Bari rain chief, King Logunu immediately saw the potential of the first expedition in 1841, and sought to enlist its aid to reassert his authority over the opposite bank of the Nile and to make war on his enemies inland to the east, described by him as cannibals.[47] From the outset, the Bari of this area thus benefited from their proximity to the river to influence the first impressions of the foreigners regarding the wider

[41] Gray, *A History*, p. 31; Paul J Lane and Douglas Johnson, 'The archaeology and history of slavery in South Sudan in the nineteenth century', in Andrew CS Peacock (ed.), *The Frontiers of the Ottoman World* (Oxford, 2009), p. 515.

[42] Werne, *Expedition*, Vol. 2, p. 133, also pp. 46, 56.

[43] Baker, *The Albert N'yanza*, pp. 105, 177–8; Pedemonte, 'A report on the voyage', pp. 62, 70–71; Ignaz Knoblecher, 'The official journal of the missionary expedition, 1849–1850', in Toniolo and Hill, *The Opening of the Nile Basin*, pp. 52–3.

[44] Gray, *A History*, p. 35.

[45] Gray, *A History*, p. 56.

[46] Franz Morlang, 'The journeys of Franz Morlang east and west of Gondokoro in 1859', in Toniolo and Hill, *The Opening of the Nile Basin*, pp. 120–26.

[47] Werne, *Expedition*, Vol. 2, pp. 69–70.

region. Following Logunu's death, his son Nyigilo dominated relations with the merchants, building on his family's prominence in the iron trade to expand into the new ivory trade. He was taken to Khartoum in 1844 by the European trader, Brun-Rollet, and subsequently travelled widely, exchanging trade goods for ivory and livestock east of the Nile as far as the Pari and Lotuko.[48] When the European missionaries arrived in 1850, they reported that Nyigilo 'was busy trading ivory throughout the day', having accumulated ivory stocks throughout the year in anticipation of the annual expedition, and enjoying a 'long-standing friendship' with the commanders of the boats.[49] As well as learning some Arabic, Nyigilo's experience of trade and travel may have uniquely equipped him to deal with the foreigners: 'he knew how to win favour by flattering strangers'.[50] Like his father Logunu, he sought assistance against his enemies, and was promised a shipment of guns by the missionaries.

However, this kind of engagement with merchants and missionaries remained risky. In the Gondokoro area a famine in the later 1850s brought matters to a crisis point at a time when relations between traders and Bari were becoming increasingly hostile; people blamed the traders, the mission and eventually Nyigilo himself, who took refuge briefly in Khartoum with Brun-Rollet, but was killed by a group of young men when he returned home.[51] His death may, as Simonse argues, reflect a longer tradition of violent tensions with the rain 'kings', but it may also suggest an emerging concern that working with the 'Turks' might undermine or distract from the vital role of the rain chief in preventing famine. An alternative local history later suggested that Nyigilo was accused of taking cattle as dues but failing to provide the rain in return, with the implication that he had broken a contract.[52]

New kinds of contract, and new intermediaries and leaders were emerging at this time. In the early 1870s, Samuel Baker – now an officer in the Egyptian army, sent to formally annex the region – made explicit his attempts to enter into 'contracts' with the Bari leader at Gondokoro, whom Baker called 'Allorron', by promising protection in return for food and labour.[53] Allorron's Bari name was Loro Lako, and he had become a local agent for the leading trading company in the area, the Egyptian Aqqad firm. Baker was told by Gondokoro elders 'that although Allorron had been the ostensible sheik [chief] for a great length of time', he was not '*the true sheik by actual descent*' (my emphasis).[54] This is a striking illustration of the way in which new kinds of leadership were competing with structures of kinship and lineage primacy. Various oral histories recorded in the twentieth century claimed that Loro Lako had usurped the dominance of the landowning Panigelo clan, having made himself useful to the most senior member of this clan by speaking Arabic with the traders.[55] This is a common

48 Gray, *A History*, p. 35; Werne, *Expedition*, Vol. 2, p. 22. According to Simonse, Nyigilo was the biological son of Logunu, but born in the posthumous name of Logunu's father; he is therefore described sometimes as Logunu's brother and sometimes as his son. Simonse, *Kings of Disaster*, p. 89, fn 30.

49 Pedemonte, 'A Report on the voyage', pp. 64, 67.

50 A Kaufmann, 'The White Nile Valley and its inhabitants', in Toniolo and Hill, *The Opening of the Nile Basin*, p. 194; Angelo Vinco, 'First Christian to live among the Bari: his journeys 1851–1852', in Toniolo and Hill, *The Opening of the Nile Basin*, p. 77; Pedemonte, 'A report on the voyage', pp. 72–3; Simonse, *Kings of Disaster*, p. 92.

51 Morlang, 'The journeys of Franz Morlang', p. 111; Kaufmann, 'White Nile Valley', pp. 194–5.

52 Beaton, 'A Chapter in Bari History', p. 189.

53 Baker, *Ismailia*, Vol. 1, pp. 220–8, 259; Simonse, *Kings of Disaster*, pp. 94–5.

54 Baker, *Ismailia*, Vol. 1, p. 257.

 55 Huby, 'Big men', p. 69.

trope in oral histories: achievement enables individuals to advance beyond their inherited status, but this is often depicted as a patrimonial reward for their good service to a senior lineage head. The rise of new men is thus disguised in idioms of kinship and patronage, which attempt to draw new political authorities into relations of subordination to senior lineages.

Far from lacking middlemen or avoiding social change then, the Bari people who had earliest and longest relations with the Nile expeditions were experiencing the rise of new men who had learned Arabic and demonstrated diplomatic and entrepreneurial skills in dealing with the military commercial forces, and whose newfound influence set up lasting tensions with other forms of authority. This pattern would be replicated in other areas as the trading forces began to penetrate further inland to the west of the Nile and into the Bahr el Ghazal region by the 1850s and 1860s, following the removal of the government monopoly on slave-raiding in 1853.[56] Interpreters continued to play a vital role in local relations. In the region around modern-day Rumbek, for example, the French trader Vayssière recorded that slave-boys were taught Arabic and became 'interpreters and commercial agents' rather than simply slaves.[57] The people who came into first contact with the new forces had the greatest opportunity to benefit from learning their languages, and to influence subsequent relations with other groups, as Schweinfurth would later observe:

> On first landing from the rivers, the Khartoomers [*sic*] opened up an intercourse with the Dinka, who did not refuse to furnish them with bearers and interpreters for their further progress into the interior, and it was from them that they learnt the names of the different tribes... In this way the Nubians have adopted the Dinka appellations of Dyoor [Jur] for Lwoh [Luo], Niam-niam for Zandey [Zande], and Dohr for Bongo.[58]

From the 1860s, the traders established a network of stations, or *zara'ib*, in the Bahr el Ghazal region.[59] Although ivory remained the focus of this trade, increasingly it was accompanied by the raiding and capture of slaves, either for export to the Khartoum slave markets and Egyptian army, or for use as servants, porters, wives and soldiers within the *zara'ib*. Demand for slaves, ivory and provisions fuelled an escalating pattern of raiding by the *zariba* forces. In some cases the vicinity became depopulated as people fled the depredations of raids and enslavement. But others would seize the opportunity to make bargains with the *zariba* leaders and deflect their predation to more distant areas.

BROKERING EXCHANGE AND PROTECTION

The period of the *zara'ib* and subsequent Egyptian government stations was foundational and formative in the history and memory of relations with the state in South Sudan, as Johnson has argued.[60] It also established a tendency for people to contract with external forces to try to secure protection and property

56 Lane and Johnson, 'The archaeology and history of slavery', p. 518.

57 Gray, *A History*, p. 45, citing Vay. MS. 20/III/54.

58 Georg Schweinfurth, *The Heart of Africa: three years' travels and adventures in the unexplored regions of Central Africa. From 1868 to 1871*, Vol. 1, trans. EE Frewer (New York, 1874), pp. 260–61.

59 Mawson, 'The Triumph of Life', p. 70.

60 Johnson, 'Structure of a legacy'; Douglas H Johnson, 'Recruitment and entrapment in private slave armies: the structure of the *zara'ib* in the southern Sudan', in Elizabeth Savage (ed.), *The Human Commodity: perspectives on the trans-Saharan slave trade* (London, 1992), pp.162–73.

rights, thus ensuring the resilience of political economies and value regimes, rather than the disruption that has been attributed to similar new commerce elsewhere in eastern Africa.

The *zara'ib* were concentrated in confined spaces, defended by trenches, earthen embankments and thorn fences or palisades, and often densely packed with huts.[61] In this sense, the antecedents or earliest constructions of the nodes of state power in the region were always clearly demarcated and exclusionary; only the trading agents, itinerant traders and holy men and soldiers and their slaves, servants and families lived inside the *zariba*. But beyond the trenches and fences, wider concentric circles of settlement developed, inhabited by a much larger slave or subject population who cultivated the land around the *zariba* to supply it with food, and who were drawn upon for raiding and to act as porters and labourers. Schweinfurth categorised the population within the *zariba* as 'consumers' and those outside it as 'producers'.[62] Johnson suggests that people had often been 'forcibly resettled around the *zariba* to provide labour and food', but that the *zariba* governors could do little to prevent these people from simply decamping to more remote areas.[63] In general most people had sought refuge by moving into 'inaccessible jungles away from the settlements'.[64]

The satellite populations around the *zara'ib* therefore represent a particular category of people willing to enter into relations with the stations, including former slaves. And these relations were mediated by individual interpreters and trading agents. The men described as 'chiefs' in the nineteenth century records were clearly very often such brokers. One of the early annual government expeditions had 'installed' a Cic Dinka chief who was subsequently observed trading ivory: 'he himself took part in the bartering'.[65] Similarly Casati later reported that chiefs had entered into 'contracts' with the slave traders.[66] As Simonse argues, for the remainder of the nineteenth century: 'In exchange for privileged access to trade goods, these chiefs offered their subjects limited protection against the depredation caused by the troops'.[67]

The rise of trading chiefs as 'new men' in the nineteenth century is a familiar pattern in the literature on eastern Africa more widely. Historians have analysed the effects of the Zanzibari long-distance ivory and slave trade in terms of its disruption of former 'social contracts' based on reciprocal obligations between kings or chiefs and their followers and dependents. Freed of the constraints of such contractual relations by their access to external wealth, weapons and allies, trading chiefs now sold off their own people and transformed former guarantees of protection into the threat of exploitation or alienation.[68] Meanwhile the influx of commodities to the region provided new opportunities for patrimonial relations. As well as the 'all-important' guns, these commodities included cloth, beads and other prestige items. In the coastal hinterlands, Glassman argues that the effects were pervasive, leading ultimately to the 'commodification of social

61 Lane and Johnson, 'The archaeology and history of slavery', p. 519.

62 Schweinfurth, *The Heart of Africa*, Vol. 2, p. 427; Johnson, 'Recruitment and entrapment', p. 170; Gray, *A History*, p. 59; Ushari A Mahmud, *Arabic in the Southern Sudan: history and spread of a pidgin-creole* (Khartoum, 1983), p. 18.

63 Johnson, 'Recruitment and entrapment', p. 170.

64 Mahmud, *Arabic in the Southern Sudan*, p. 25; Gray, *A History*, p. 61.

65 Pedemonte, 'A report on the voyage', pp. 59–60.

66 Casati, *Ten Years in Equatoria*, p. 191.

67 Simonse, *Kings of Disaster*, p. 96.

68 Feierman, *Peasant Intellectuals*, pp. 112–9; and Steven Feierman, 'A century of ironies in East Africa (c. 1780–1890)', in Philip Curtin et al, *African History: from earliest times to independence* (London, 1995), p. 364; Hanson, *Landed Obligation*.

relations'.[69] According to Feierman, 'a shift from livestock to trade goods as the most important form of chiefly wealth' constituted a 'political transformation' in the Shambaa kingdom.[70]

Yet Glassman also hints at the continuing domination of the hinterland 'by values associated with village agriculture', requiring brokers who could mediate between these and the new forms of value in the coastal towns. He mentions, almost in passing, the importance of the large cattle herds controlled by one broker chief, who was exchanging cattle for ivory.[71] In fact as Anderson shows, among the Il Chamus of northern Kenya, people were using the caravan trade to invest directly in cattle and accumulate large herds; by the 1870s they were 'only prepared to accept cattle in exchange for ivory'.[72]

In southern Sudan, it is even more evident that processes of commodification were highly constrained by the resilience of existing value-regimes, and that this in turn limited and shaped the role of new brokers. Here cloth and beads were initially seized upon eagerly as messages of individual prestige,[73] but people were not willing to trade their property (in livestock and persons) for such commodities. Cloth was a marker of relations with the foreign commercial forces: it was reported that only 'sheikhs' [a widely-used Arabic term for individuals with particular status or power] could wear cloth, and this they only did in front of the foreigners.[74] Commodities demonstrated individual knowledge, roles and prestige, but this did not fundamentally alter value regimes in which the social value of people and cattle took primacy over material possessions.[75]

Instead of using commodities to establish new relations of patronage, the trading chiefs therefore helped to establish trade on their own terms in order to accumulate resources that were of greatest value in local economies. Principally this meant cattle. Mahmud claims that 'the indigenous tribal chiefs insisted on changing the exchange currency from beads to cattle'.[76] Early expeditions found the Dinka resolute in their demand for cattle and rejection of any other goods offered to them in payment for carrying or supplies. Nor would they sell cattle.[77] The same resistance to trading their cattle led Allorron and the Bari and Lokoya into conflict with Samuel Baker.[78] The only means by which the traders could acquire this vital means of exchange was thus to raid and steal, and to enlist the support of one group against another. Gray asserts that 'raided cattle soon became the universal and indispensable medium of exchange', used to purchase

[69] Jonathon Glassman, *Feasts and Riot: revelry, rebellion and popular consciousness on the Swahili coast, 1856–1888* (Portsmouth, NH, 1995), pp. 48, 25, 36–8.

[70] Steven Feierman, *The Shambaa Kingdom: a history* (Madison, 1974), p. 172.

[71] Glassman, *Feasts and Riot*, pp. 65, 69.

[72] David M Anderson, 'Cultivating pastoralists: ecology and economy among the Il Chamus of Baringo, 1840–1980', in Johnson and Anderson, *The Ecology of Survival*, p. 251. See also Isaria N Kimambo, *Penetration and Protest in Tanzania: the impact of the world economy on the Pare 1860–1960* (London, 1991), p. 42; CH Ambler, *Kenyan Communities in the Age of Imperialism: the central region in the late nineteenth century* (New Haven, CT, 1988), pp. 26–9, 69, 103.

[73] Glassman, *Feasts and Riot*, p. 37.

[74] Werne, *Expedition*, Vol. 2, p. 140. Cf. Willis, 'Violence, authority', p. 102.

[75] Godfrey Lienhardt, 'Getting your own back: themes in Nilotic myth', in John HM Beattie and Godfrey Lienhardt, *Studies in Social Anthropology: essays in memory of E. E. Evans-Pritchard* (Oxford, 1975), pp. 217–8, 228–9, 234–5.

[76] Mahmud, *Arabic in the Southern Sudan*, p. 24.

[77] John Petherick and Katherine Petherick, *Travels in Central Africa, and Explorations of the Western Nile Tributaries* (London, 1869), p. 228.

[78] Baker, *Ismailia*, Vol. 1, pp. 221–62.

ivory and food and to reward fighters and allies. Even in the western areas around modern-day Yei, in which cattle nowadays are scarce, Kakwa and Kaliko chiefs were trading ivory for cattle, or guiding government forces to raid other cattle-rich chiefs.[79] Nearer the Nile, the rain chief Legge of Lyria became a powerful middleman, trading iron hoes for ivory, which he then exchanged with the traders for cattle at the rate of twenty cows for a large tusk.[80] Far from the people of this region being entirely ignorant of commercial cultures, they actually drew the Khartoumers into their own economy and value regime. The resulting accumulation of cattle would have been vital to the establishment or consolidation of brokers as powerful patrons, attracting further wealth-in-people.

The resolute preservation of the cattle economy would also open further interesting (and often enduring) disparities in the relations of different people and regions with the commercial and government forces. Schweinfurth suggested that agricultural groups like the Bongo in the Western Bahr el Ghazal region were more amenable to trade and employment from the outset: 'It is to their indifference to cattle-breeding, which is practised so extensively by the Dinka, that the Bongo owe their comparatively peaceful relations with the so-called "Turks."'[81] There would be an enduring tendency for cattle-less or cattle-poor people – whether individuals or wider groups – to be attracted to trade and labour as alternative means of acquiring wealth and status, though very often they used any income to acquire cattle themselves.

The system of raiding, or *razzia*, also increasingly used to acquire slaves, offered further opportunity and attraction for individuals and groups to ally with the firepower of the merchants, before their neighbours did so. People actively contracted with the military forces of the traders to pursue local warfare; in 1860, 'chiefs' from the Cic and Agar Dinka came to greet the new European owner of the Ronga *zariba* (near modern-day Rumbek), and to invoke 'the trader's alliance' to fight their enemies, as Gray puts it.[82] Such individuals were already being described as 'chiefs', and are remembered locally for having struck bargains with the traders. An oral history from the Kakwa near Yei explains that the first 'chief' was a man whose daughter was seized by the slave traders. He had the courage to approach the *zariba*, and its leader offered to return his daughter if he could persuade his people to come and live close to the camp and provide it with food. Having succeeded, he was recognised by the 'Arabs' as chief and his people were no longer raided.[83] This story evokes the notion of protection rackets, and indeed reflects the very real extent of coercion employed by the *zariba* forces; Junker reported raids on the Kaliko in which women were seized as a means of forcing their husbands to 'ransom' them with ivory.[84] But the rescuing of a wife or female relative, which forms a frequent theme in oral histories, also represents the obtaining of recognition and protection for rights in persons and property, by the interlocutors brave enough to deal with the *zariba*.

The *zara'ib* became a new kind of frontier, attracting heterogeneous settlers willing to risk its dangers and demands in order to acquire protection and

[79] Gray, *A History*, p. 49; see also Wilhelm Junker, *Travels in Africa During the Years 1875–1878* (London, 1890), pp. 451, 459.

[80] Baker, *The Albert N'yanza*, pp. 126–9.

[81] Schweinfurth, *The Heart of Africa*, Vol. 1 p. 270.

[82] Gray, *A History*, p. 48.

[83] Interview 2aN/YC.

[84] Junker, *Travels in Africa*, p. 468. Cf. Leopold, *Inside West Nile*, p. 128; Feierman, 'A century of ironies', p. 365; Feierman, *Peasant Intellectuals*, p. 117.

resources.[85] This was also a frontier of knowledge. Spoken Arabic and the cultures and practices of the military, Muslim inhabitants of the stations were important acquisitions for the leading intermediaries and brokers, but they also spread outwards into surrounding areas. In the southwest, *zariba*-trained Zande spearmen were becoming chiefs, having 'learnt to speak Arabic fluently'.[86] Slave-soldiers were also able to accumulate cattle and slaves themselves, which would have enabled them to act as powerful patrons in the local area. Such individuals moved in and out of the *zara'ib*, transporting new languages and cultures and acting as a mobile frontier upon which new settlements were forming. They may also have drawn upon experience of the *zara'ib* to articulate new kinds of contractual relations: on occasion the soldiers from northern riverain Sudan employed by the trading companies 'would invoke their contracts and refuse to fight'.[87]

From the 1860s and 1870s, the Turco-Egyptian government began to establish its own stations, often taking over the existing *zara'ib*. This administration would reach its height under Gordon, when 'in three years a network of stations was established all over the Provinces, no station being more than three days' post from another'.[88] But the government stations continued many of the same patterns as the *zara'ib*; when the European officers Gessi, Casati and Emin Pasha visited Rumbek in the late 1870s and early 1880s, they described it as a densely-populated, filthy village with a slave population in the thousands, which was still an important headquarters for slave-raiding to the south.[89] The relations between government and private traders were increasingly fraught. Gessi complained bitterly that the '*vekils*', or *zariba* managers, many of whom ended up as wealthy landowners in Khartoum, were posing as legal representatives of the *Miri* – an Ottoman term used to refer to the 'Viceroy' or Khedive of Egypt: '[they] make one believe that the exportation of ivory, slaves and cattle is done by order and at the charge of the Miri'. Not without reason, the *vekil*s he admonished retorted that there was little difference anyway between the government stations and their own: 'the Miri also does as we do'.[90] Strikingly in the various dialects of the Bari language, government chiefs continue to be named *matat lo miri*, and *miri* has retained a similar range of meanings to *hakuma*: a soldier putting on his uniform can say he is putting on his '*miri*'.[91]

The government appointed its own agents, still known as dragomans (interpreters), in the villages around the government stations to supervise taxation and porterage, a role similar to that of the later colonial chiefs:

> These men were originally slaves of the old slave-dealers. They all speak Arabic and were trained first as gun-boys, and now are employed as a kind of native police. Each native village is required to support one or more of these men, who are responsible for the peace of the place, and also superintend the payment of the grain tax to the government. Some twenty or thirty of them live near a fort

[85] Junker reported 'heterogeneous colonies' around the later government stations in the Makaraka region, where '[s]uch a confusion of different races is scarcely elsewhere to be found in a relatively so limited space in the known parts of the African continent': *Travels in Africa*, p. 286. Gordon reported a whole village, many of whose inhabitants were Arabic speaking, moving into the vicinity of a station: Gordon to Augusta, 23 February 1876, cited in Gray, *A History*, p. 113.

[86] Schweinfurth, *The Heart of Africa*, Vol. 1, pp. 226, 465, 473.

[87] Johnson, 'Recruitment and entrapment', pp. 168–9.

[88] Charles T Wilson and Robert W Felkin, *Uganda and the Egyptian Soudan*, Vol. 2 (London, 1882), p. 99.

[89] Lane and Johnson, 'The archaeology and history of slavery', pp. 522–3; Mawson, 'The Triumph of Life', pp. 70–75.

[90] Romolo Gessi, *Seven Years in the Soudan: being a record of explorations, adventures, and campaigns against the Arab slave hunters* (London, 1892), pp. 51–4.

[91] Emmanuel Gonda, personal communication, 2005.

> and when porters are wanted, or natives required for work at the station, they are commissioned to collect the requisite number.[92]

The dragomans offered their communities a degree of protection from raiding, and so Gray perceptively describes their growing prominence as 'indispensable intermediaries'.[93] The Bari around Gondokoro had retained their privileged position as interpreters; in the late 1870s Junker described them as much friendlier than the Bari around Lado to the north, who had not learned Arabic: 'Since the occupation of the former trading zeribas by the Egyptian Government and the foundation of additional military posts by Gordon, the Arab-speaking Baris had found employment about the station as interpreters, translators and inspectors.'[94]

By this time, according to Gordon's successor as Governor, Emin Pasha, relations between government stations and local people in Equatoria had become increasingly positive, and there was evidence of intermingling cultures and practices, including the spread of clothing, furnishings and coffee-drinking, and participation by local 'chiefs' in Muslim feast-days in the stations.[95] Relations were much less harmonious, however, in the Bahr el Ghazal regions and a 'deputation of Agar chiefs' came to Lado to complain to Emin about the abduction of their children by the *zariba* forces, prompting Emin's visit to Rumbek. Gray describes the long journey by these 'chiefs' as a striking sign of Emin's 'prestige',[96] but it is also an early indication of the way that such interlocutors would come to make claims and demands upon state power in the twentieth century, often travelling long distances to do so.

BROKEN DEALS

The success of the bargains struck between *zara'ib* and surrounding people depended on the maintenance of the productivity of the latter and their protection by the former, as well as on the shared rewards to be gained from directing violent predation against other groups. However, by the late 1870s, the violence of the soldiers was becoming more indiscriminate and the bargains forged with local people were breaking down. Johnson suggests that cultivation for the stations had proven too onerous and disruptive of the subsistence economy, leading people to desert the *zariba* environs.[97] The wider context was also affecting the behaviour of the traders and soldiers, encouraging short-term rapaciousness rather than the cultivation of sustainable relations, particularly in the Bahr el Ghazal where powerful traders waged war with government forces seeking to combat the overland slave trade. Gessi reported that local inhabitants were deserting the *zarai'b* and government stations, and some areas were depopulated by slaving by the early 1880s.[98] The effects of the collapsing Egyp-

[92] Wilson and Felkin, *Uganda and the Egyptian Soudan*, Vol. 2, p. 104, 107–9: dragomen also acted as guides for caravans and as postal carriers. See also Mahmud, *Arabic in the Southern Sudan*, p. 29; Baker, *Ismailia*, Vol. 2, p. 48.

[93] Gray, *A History*, pp. 100–1, 114, 142–3.

[94] Junker, *Travels in Africa*, p. 236.

[95] See Gray, *A History*, pp. 142–3; Emin Pasha, *Emin Pasha in Central Africa: being a collection of his letters and journals*, edited by Georg Schweinfurth (London, 1888), p. 382.

[96] Gray, *A History*, pp. 149–50.

[97] Johnson, 'Recruitment and entrapment', p. 170.

[98] Gessi, *Seven Years*, pp. 203–5; Wilson and Felkin, *Uganda and the Egyptian Soudan*, Vol. 2, p. 126.

tian government finances and the revolt of the Mahdi in northern Sudan were also beginning to be felt in the distant government posts in Equatoria and Bahr el Ghazal, and the regrowth of the vegetation blockages downstream on the Nile further hindered communication and commerce. Casati reported that former slaves and slave traders alike pillaged the country, 'sure of the impending anarchy', as the Mahdist forces invaded in the mid-1880s.[99] In the southwest, the advancing frontier of conquest by the powerful Avungara chiefs of the Zande was also producing conflicts or military alliances with the Egyptian and then Mahdist armies, and causing further population displacement.

The collapse of the bargains between the stations and the local people was particularly notable in the Rumbek area, which had been the site of one of the earliest *zara'ib* and subsequently became province headquarters for the Egyptian government. Casati described the breakdown of the 'friendly relations' and 'truce' that had existed between the Agar Dinka and a particular governor, whom they called 'our man', and who had 'been clever enough to make his influence felt, by inducing them to carry out the principles of mutual exchange, by fixing taxes; and by a tolerable system of justice'. It was this degree of regularity and predictability that people would always seek in their relations with government; the withdrawal of this particular governor signalled its demise in the early 1880s in Rumbek.[100] Agar oral histories suggest that by the early 1880s, grain requisitions were leaving the local population hungry, and then a spear-master was killed by the *zariba* forces. In 1883, a war leader from the northern Agar section of Pakam, Wol Athiang, succeeded in uniting with Nuer and other Agar forces to defeat a raiding force from Rumbek and then to attack and destroy the station itself.[101] Rumbek was briefly reoccupied, but Agar hostility reportedly prevented communications between the area and Equatoria, and the garrisons were withdrawn altogether in 1884.[102]

Wol Athiang would be seen later as a particularly combative chief who maintained a distance from the colonial government, but even his more militaristic leadership and protection had relied on a certain knowledge of and interaction with the Rumbek garrison. Johnson's research among both the Agar Dinka and the neighbouring Nuer revealed that Wol's sister had been married or owned by the Egyptian commander of the Rumbek garrison; 'According to the Nuer, it was the Egyptians who made Wol a chief of the Agar'.[103] As the *zara'ib* ceased to offer any protection or profitable bargains, people turned to the protection of strong military leaders like Wol. Similarly around Amadi, the risks of mediating with the traders and soldiers had rendered recognition as a 'chief' a dangerous business: several chiefs here had reportedly been castrated and buried alive by slave traders. By 1879, a strong man named 'Tak Farre' was reported to have 5000 men from various tribes under his authority, and large areas of cultivation, 'for anyone who is discontented with his chief or other circumstances comes to

[99] Casati, *Ten Years in Equatoria*, p. 198. This is supported by the memories of an elderly man who claimed to have been born in Jur Ghattas *zariba* near Tonj, interviewed by a colonial official: 'Tonj', entry in the Eastern District Notebook, 31 December 1933, NRO BGP 1/7/38.

[100] Casati, *Ten Years in Equatoria*, pp. 52–4.

[101] Douglas H Johnson, 'Prophecy and Mahdism in the Upper Nile: an examination of local experiences of the Mahdiyya in the southern Sudan', *British Journal of Middle Eastern Studies* 20:1 (1993), p. 48.

[102] Gray, *A History*, p. 158; Mawson, 'The Triumph of Life', pp. 70–78; Casati, *Ten Years in Equatoria*, p. 195.

[103] Lane and Johnson, 'The archaeology and history of slavery', p. 523; Johnson, 'Prophecy and Mahdism', p. 48.

Tak Farre and receives a welcome from him'.[104] However, Takfara was in fact the name of a government station near Amadi, suggesting either that an individual bearing this name had entered into relations with the government, or more likely that Wilson and Felkin misunderstood references to the station itself as a site of refuge and patronage. Or perhaps the individual they heard of had originated in the station; according to Collins, by the late 1880s it is impossible to distinguish between 'tribal leaders' and 'local potentates' who were 'Turk, Arab or former *jihādī*' – the latter being the irregular locally-recruited soldiers or slave-soldiers of the Egyptian army.[105]

Even in the Bari area, where chiefs like Loro Lako (Allorron) and Abu Kuka had successfully established themselves as trading agents in the 1860s and 1870s, the relationship between the government stations and the Bari deteriorated rapidly by the 1880s. Loro himself was reportedly killed on Emin Pasha's orders in 1884 for conspiring to attack Lado station; though according to Casati he was killed 'as a malefactor not as a rebel', a striking reminder of the economic relations and brokerage role that had determined his position. His death was followed by the collapse of the relations he had brokered, and the 'seizure of 3000 oxen, the devastation of the country, and the alienation of the Bari people's affection'.[106] A similar indication of the collapse of any social and economic deals between the garrisons and the Bari was preserved in an oral history recorded later, which claimed that a rain chief was attracted to a cattle auction in Emin's camp, where he was captured and executed for having previously ambushed a patrol.[107] The promise of acquiring cattle, which had been the basis of so many of the local contracts and alliances in preceding decades, was now the focus of betrayal and the collapse of those alliances.

Simonse describes the subsequent rise of Bari 'warlords', whose power depended on guns and who gained power after the collapse of the Nile trade and withdrawal of government forces. But, like Wol Athiang in the Rumbek area, these were not necessarily entirely distinct from the preceding brokers and trading chiefs. Nyigilo's successor as rain chief at Belinian, Bepo, had worked with the commercial and government forces before turning to fighting against them.[108] Similarly the rain chief Legge of Lyria was remembered as a strong military leader who helped protect the Lokoya from government attack, but he had previously also controlled the trade in ivory.[109] As Willis argues, there was very often a direct linkage between 'organizing violence and organizing trade' among such gatekeepers – and 'enthusiasm for seeking external alliance'.[110]

In 1885, after Emin had withdrawn southwards, an alliance of Bari and Dinka forces led by Bepo attacked the remaining garrisons at Lado, Gondokoro and Rejaf, but was defeated by the residual government troops.[111] The invading Mahdist forces incorporated many of the former Egyptian army soldiers and

104 Wilson and Felkin, *Uganda and the Egyptian Soudan*, Vol. 2, pp. 128–9; Gray, *A History*, p. 150. See also a similar patron in Emin Pasha, *Central Africa*, p. 306. Takfara was also recorded as a place or a river name: Casati, *Ten Years in Equatoria*, p. 203; *Sudan Monthly Intelligence Report* (henceforth SIR) 81, April 1901, p. 11, TNA FO 78/5167.

105 Collins, *The Southern Sudan*, p. 71.

106 Casati *Ten Years in Equatoria*, p. 195; Gray, *A History*, p. 160.

107 Beaton, 'A Chapter in Bari History'.

108 Simonse, *Kings of Disaster*, pp. 101–3.

109 See Simonse, *Kings of Disaster*, and also Gray, *A History*, p. 56, on Lokoya strength and military resistance, for instance in 1860.

110 Willis, 'Violence, authority', p. 102.

111 Casati, *Ten Years in Equatoria*, pp. 227–9.

slaves, and established a limited and violent presence at Rejaf, which they used only 'as a base for slave and ivory raids'.[112] This period is generally remembered as a time of military depredations, warfare and flight, when people took refuge on mountains and in caves, or further afield.[113]

According to Collins, the Mahdist commander at Rejaf in Equatoria, 'Umar Salih, built initially positive relations with some of the Bari by his care not to take anything from them 'without payment or exchange'.[114] While this appears rather unlikely, the emphasis that 'Umar placed on it in his reports suggests that positive relations between local leaders and state forces continued to rely on the capacity of the former to broker protection of property. Johnson highlights the irony whereby the soldiers continued to offer 'a kind of refuge' from the very violence they were generating.[115] After relations deteriorated further, a female prophet, Kiden, briefly established herself as a powerful dispenser of protective magic in the form of wooden guns which were supposed to defeat the Mahdist forces; she gathered huge stocks of ivory at her base on the Nile, revealing the wider interconnection of brokerage and protection and of spiritual and economic power.[116]

Kiden was captured and executed by the Mahdists, but some individual warlords and brokers more successfully navigated the later years of the nineteenth century and positioned themselves well when the Belgian and British colonial forces reached the region in the late 1890s. An example was Mödi Adong Lado, or 'Modi Adum' as his name was sometimes rendered, who would be appointed as chief when the first British colonial officers reached the area. Later in the 1930s, a British official, Beaton, recorded a local history in which Mödi was described as a 'buccaneer', who had started out as an interpreter at Gondokoro:

> When the Arab invaders first reached Gondokoro, Mödi, a member of the Nyori 'Dogale clan, threw in his lot with them. Owning rich herds and possessing a number of rifles presented to him by his Arab masters, he became a power in the land and sold his services to all who would employ him.

Mödi was then 'invited' to become chief at Fager by a rain chief, who 'was so struck by the prowess of Mödi that he invited him to collect the scattered peoples of Fager and Pipiri and make them one again'.[117] This story makes clear that Mödi had no hereditary claim to chiefship but had won wealth and status through relations with outside forces. But his resulting military and patrimonial capacity became an asset during times of war and insecurity. Beaton's informant(s) in the 1930s clearly wanted to assert the greater power of the rain chief who granted Mödi the chiefship; Casati had been aware in the 1880s that 'respect and veneration for the dispensers of rain are greater than those felt for the chiefs of the country'.[118] But the idea that the rain chief invited Mödi to gather together scattered people is also significant. Chiefs would become a focus of community cohesion, even though they were often depicted as marginal or subordinate to rain chiefs and other senior lineage heads.

112 Gray, *A History*, p. 163.

113 Beaton, 'A Chapter in Bari History', p. 180.

114 Collins, *The Southern Sudan*, p. 72.

115 Johnson, 'Structure of a legacy', p. 79.

116 Interview 2bR/K; Collins, *The Southern Sudan*, p. 90; Simonse, *Kings of Disaster*, p. 102.

117 Beaton, 'A Chapter in Bari History', p. 181.

118 Casati, *Ten Years in Equatoria*, p. 209.

CONCLUSION

In 1889, the Mahdist commander at Rejaf, 'Umar Salih, wrote to the ruling Khalifa in Omdurman about his difficulties in recruiting local people into his forces, attributing this to their difficulty understanding or accepting the Mahdists' customs and religion: 'nor can they practice our rules'.[119] Developing some form of shared rules had been and would be crucial to the making of deals between state forces and local people, however fragile, tenuous and short-lived. The nineteenth century has been depicted by scholars as a time when relations with external commercial and state forces were shaped in enduring ways by patterns of violence and by unequal firepower and terms of trade. Much of this depiction is indisputable, but the people of South Sudan were not always or simply victims in the multiple encounters involved, and nor were they necessarily 'ill-prepared' for or ignorant of the kinds of exchange, diplomacy and warfare that developed, however novel these may have been. The political economy of knowledge in the region already rewarded individual specialist expertise and skills of interlocution, and ensured that people were familiar with exchanging their property, products and services for expert guidance, intercession and protection. The tendency to contract with expert authorities was thus extended to relations with the state. The interpreters, entrepreneurs and brokers who traded their linguistic and diplomatic skills for wealth and power emerged from the existing political economy even if they were specialising in new forms of knowledge. Such individuals gathered new communities around them in the vicinities of the commercial and government centres; oral histories often rationalise their ascendancy in terms of the protection they 'bought' for people with both their knowledge and their personal risk-taking.

But at the same time, such people were investing not only in the new trade goods and weapons obtained from their relations with the stations, but also in the enduring forms of value in local economies, epitomised in the pre-eminence of cattle, iron and people even in the new exchange economies of the ivory trade. Chiefship was already representing the potential to obtain guarantees of rights in such property, through as yet unstable deals with the foreign forces. These early bargains have also become part of historical claims of certain communities to have a special relationship with the state. The people like the Bari on the Nile or the Agar Dinka around Rumbek or the settlers around other *zara'ib* and government stations did not simply acquire protection by their first contact and contracting of the new forces. Rather they established a lasting sense of a claim upon the state, and a lasting tendency to appropriate the resources and languages of the state as well as seeking to obtain protection from it. This would be reproduced in the oral histories told about the arrival of the European colonial forces in the 1890s and 1900s, to which we now turn.

[119] 'Umar Salih to the Khalifa, Muharram, 1307 (September 1889), NRO Mahdiya I/33/58, cited in Collins, *The Southern Sudan*, p. 77.

2

Colonial frontiers and the emergence of government chiefs, c. 1900–1920

> The average Bari or Dinka Sheikh [chief] is not a person possessed of any authority, being as a rule merely the headman of a village, whose population obey him or not as suits their individual fancy. There are a few who seem to be strong men, and the policy adopted has been to raise the status of the Sheikh as far as possible in the eyes of his people by trying to impress on them (and on him) that he is the representative in his own village of Government, and must act and be treated as such.[1]

The defeat of the Mahdist state by British and Egyptian forces in 1898 led to the establishment of the Anglo-Egyptian Condominium of the Sudan in 1899. The new government immediately sought to secure its control of the upper Nile against both a brief French incursion and the forces of the Belgian Congo already occupying Rejaf in the far south. The vegetation blockages in the Sudd region of the Nile, however, delayed effective occupation of Equatoria for several years. Sudan-Congo relations remained extremely tense, until an agreement to lease the 'Lado Enclave' to King Leopold II of Belgium during his lifetime; the southernmost Sudanese province of Mongalla was meanwhile established to the north and east of the Enclave.[2] The British report quoted above was written in 1906, well before the formulation of 'Indirect Rule' and 'Native Administration' as colonial policy. By the 1920s, administrators would avoid such open admission of colonial intervention in local authority, and would discard the northern Sudanese Arabic term 'sheikh' in favour of the English word 'chief'. But it is striking that from the very beginning of colonial administration in southern Sudan, the focus was on the construction of chiefship as the basis for local government.

Historical writing on the early Anglo-Egyptian Condominium government, c. 1898–1920, has emphasised its essentially military character, evident in its euphemistically-named, brutal 'pacification' campaigns in southern and western Sudan. More widely, early colonial administrations in Africa have been described as 'holding operations': military governments concerned primarily with preventing resistance and requisitioning taxes and labour.[3] In southern Sudan the early British and Belgian administrations certainly exhibited considerable continuity with the patterns of military power and extraction in the nineteenth century.

However, this period nevertheless marked a real moment of transition and

[1] Governor-General of the Sudan *Reports* (hereafter GGR), here, *Report on the Finances, Administration and Condition of the Sudan, 1906* (London, 1907), p. 710.

[2] For the detailed history of European competition on the upper Nile see Collins, *Land Beyond the Rivers*, and Robert O Collins, *King Leopold, England and the Upper Nile, 1899–1909* (New Haven, CT, 1968).

[3] John Iliffe, *Africans: history of a continent* (Cambridge, 1995), pp. 196–8.

change. The early twentieth century was a time of considerable migration, mobility and the making of new settlement patterns, as people either fled from the new government forces or sought refuge with powerful patrons or around the latest government stations, after the extensive displacement of the later nineteenth century. Over a century later, oral histories and genealogies tend to date the origins of chiefship and the establishment of towns and government to this period. The threat posed by the coercive forces of the colonial governments is presented in many of these histories as a pivotal event which marks the beginning of chiefship and the origin of particular political, institutional and spatial orders centring on the loci of the government stations.[4] In the early twenty-first century, people were staking claims to special relations with the government and rights to the town by asserting precedence, not in lineage order or migration, but in relations with government. Their oral histories thus detail the first deals their forefathers struck with the new governments, and depict chiefship as both the means and the product of these deals. And they situate the origins of this chiefship in the foundation of the towns. This chapter examines the establishment of the nodal colonial state as a new internal frontier, and the ongoing formation of communities, both on this spatial frontier and around chiefs with new or renewed patrimonial power and privileged government access. It then goes on to explore the resulting paradoxes and tensions that this produced, as manifest in these oral histories.

FROM *ZARIBA* TO *MERKAZ*: THE CONTINUITIES OF THE NODAL STATE

Johnson emphasises the degree of apparent continuity in the 'fabric of authority' in Southern Sudan, from the Egyptian and Mahdist governments into the colonial period, so that Europeans, Egyptians and northern Sudanese alike were classed as 'Turks' by most Southerners.[5] This continuity was apparent from the very first expeditions sent to occupy the region. The Bahr el Ghazal 'reoccupation' force led by Sparkes Bey in 1900 was made up of Egyptian and Sudanese soldiers, the great majority of whom were reportedly *jihadiya*, remnants of the Mahdist army, 'who were chiefly ex-slave natives of the Province'.[6] Not surprisingly, even a decade later a Belgian officer evacuating the Lado Enclave told the incoming British officers 'that many natives feared the coming of the Sudan Government, or the "Turk" as some called us, and feared our present Government might be like the old regime'.[7]

In many respects the new government was indeed like the old one: the Sudan administration continued to use many of the languages, practices and structures of the nineteenth-century commercial and imperial forces. Military patrols used or built *zara'ib* in which to camp, and their southern soldiers continued to be called *jihadiya* and *bazingari*, the old terms for slave-soldiers in the Egyptian army. The administration relied on Egyptian or Sudanese *mamurs* or junior administrative assistants, who, like their British superiors, were military officers.[8] The aims of government at this time were primarily to demonstrate its force and sovereignty and to extract ivory, provisions and

4 Cf. Kopytoff, 'The internal African frontier', pp. 56–7.

5 Johnson, *Root Causes*, p. 10.

6 'Tonj', entry in the Eastern District Notebook, 31 December 1933, NRO BGP 1/7/38.

7 RCR Owen, 'Occupation of the Lado Enclave', May–June 1910, NRO MP 1/8/51.

8 See Douglas H Johnson, 'From military to tribal police: policing the Upper Nile Province of the Sudan', in David M Anderson and David Killingray (eds), *Policing the Empire: government, authority and control, 1830–1940* (Manchester, 1991), pp. 151–67; and *Nuer Prophets*, pp. 8–9.

porters from the population; compliance with these demands was taken as indicative of 'submission' to government. From the local perspective there would have been little novelty in bands of soldiers seizing ivory, grain, livestock and carriers, and meeting any resistance with firepower, destruction of villages and crops, and seizure of captives. Reports suggest continuing attempts to hide women and children from such forces.[9] British officers were only too keen to report stories of atrocities in the Lado Enclave, where Belgian and Congolese soldiers were rumoured to employ cruel methods of obtaining ivory, grain and porters, including torture. But British-led 'punitive' patrols could also be brutally destructive, resulting in hundreds of deaths and the burning of houses and crops.[10] In preparing to take over the Lado Enclave in 1910 following King Leopold's death, the paramount concern for British administrators of Mongalla Province was to gain control of the ivory trade, and to demonstrate colonial military force, including artillery and mounted soldiers.[11]

The Sudan Government built its stations on or near previous *zara'ib* or government forts, such as Amadi, Meridi and Rumbek (see Map 0.1).[12] Even as late as 1936, the Rumbek *merkaz* or district headquarters was still referred to as 'the fort';[13] one District Commissioner highlighted the 'melancholy history' of this former 'slave-camp', and suggested that 'confidence in the good intentions of Government might have been obtained more rapidly' had such posts been 'quickly deserted'.[14] The stations were initially inhabited only by government employees, a few foreign or northern Sudanese traders, and local police and soldiers.

> Rumbek is a pleasant looking Gov. Station in the midst of the Agar Jieng district. There is a British Inspector usually in residence, a detachment of Sudanese troops and a considerable force of Jehadiah (native police). The Kordofan Trading Co. have established a small store, and there is a market including Syrian and Arabic traders. The population of the station apart from the Gov. employees is negligible. The Gov. are unable to persuade the Agar Jieng to act as porters and have this year decided to give up trying. Many of the youths however have been forced into the Jehadiah.[15]

Similarly the policemen in the small government post at nearby Lau were reported to be 'mostly Jieng [Dinka] who have been taken prisoner in the primitive expeditions'.[16] This was a common pattern: boys or young men captured in the early government expeditions would be conscripted into the policy or army, much as in the nineteenth century.[17]

9 BHH Spence to his mother, Yei, 31 December 1914, Shetland Archive, Lerwick D12/200/1–28.

10 Bimbashi HS Logan, Mongalla, to Assistant Director of Intelligence, Khartoum, 25 December 1905, NRO MP 1/8/50; *SIR* 117, April 1904, p. 5, TNA WO 106/226.

11 Angus Cameron, 'Notes on the Lado Enclave and points in connection with its transfer from the Belgians', 28 November 1907, NRO MP 1/8/51.

12 THB Mynors, 'Memoirs of Sudan service', 1982, SAD 778/8/4; Johnson, 'Recruitment and entrapment', p. 163; 'Structure of a legacy', p. 80.

13 Appeal by prisoner Majok Ater, Wau, 17 July 1936, Southern Records Office (SRO) EP 41.J.1.

14 Lakes District Handbook, 1940, p. 7, SRO EP 1.G.2.

15 Archibald Shaw, 'Trek No. 2 (West into Bahr El Ghazal Province and then south returning through the Lado Enclave) 4 April – 25 June', n.d., c. 1911, Church Missionary Society archives, Birmingham (CMS) Acc. 111, F1/4.

16 Archibald Shaw, Journal entry, Lau, 6 March 1912, CMS Acc. 111, F3.

17 Statement by Faragalla Gada, Rejaf Coy. Mongalla Police, 9 August 1925, enclosed in Governor Skrine to DC Rejaf, 15 August 1925, NRO Civsec 41/2/5; SF Newcombe, 'Report on the Lado Enclave', *SIR* 162, January 1908, App. F, pp. 29–54, at p. 44, TNA WO 106/231; Johnson, 'Structure of a legacy', p. 81.

Along the Nile in Equatoria, British officers from the Uganda and Sudan governments found the remnants of Egyptian army garrisons at Gondokoro and Rejaf respectively, who spoke their own colloquial, creole version of Arabic: the Nubi language.[18] The Nubi who settled in northern Uganda or even Kenya have had a more prominent profile, but a few of these ex-soldiers had also remained in Equatoria after Emin Pasha's withdrawal, and they formed the nucleus of the small urban populations along the Nile, living in the *malakiya*, or native lodging area of the towns.[19] These centres soon began to attract other people, however, seeking protection and patronage, following the warfare and disruptions of the late nineteenth century. Inland to the west in regions of more settled agriculture, new settlements were coalescing, for example, around the government station of Meridi and a '*jihadiya* post' at nearby Madebo:

> This is a practice which occurs at most posts in these parts. All these people are refugees from other districts... who for the most part have got into trouble and seek safety and protection by settling near a Government post, and by making themselves agreeable and useful to the soldiers, gain their friendship and protection. Subsequently, gaining confidence, and relying on the protection of the soldiers, they get 'above themselves', and become objectionable to the local Sheikhs, to whom some of them probably formerly belonged.[20]

Such processes were particularly apparent around the edges of the nineteenth century Zande military advance in the southwest, which was halted or pushed back in the first decade of colonial rule.[21] Government intelligence reports confirmed that tribes formerly ruled by the Avungara chiefs of the Zande were among the best and most willing recruits, which was attributed to their gratitude to the new government for freeing them from their despotic overlords. But this very often also reflected long-standing patterns of relations with government. Zande chiefs had also brought young men and boys from conquered peoples to their courts to gain military training and linguistic knowledge, a pattern now transferred to the government stations.[22] In 1908, Zande-speaking 'Makaraka' [Adio] from near Yei came to visit their relatives in Rumbek who were already in the *jihadiya*; some of these visitors then also enlisted in the force.[23] There were older Makaraka men still alive who were reported to have been employed on Gordon's Uganda expedition in 1878; this small group had been so prominent in relations with the Egyptian government that the entire district was then named after them.

The government stations in the period before about 1920 were primarily populated by soldiers and police, recruited more or less forcibly from the local populations, and absorbed into a semi-Arabicised and Islamicised military culture that had been evolving since the nineteenth century. But this

18 Rev FB Hadow, Journal for June 1906, CMS Acc. 409, F1; EJ Tickell to his mother, 'at entrance of River Kaya into Nile, 5 miles north of Kiri', 17–21 November 1898, TNA FO 2/164.

19 SF Newcombe, 'Report on the Lado Enclave', *SIR* 162, January 1908, App. F, pp. 29–54, TNA WO 106/231; Johnson, 'Structure of a legacy', pp. 80–4. On the Nubi of Uganda see Leopold, *Inside West Nile*.

20 AL Hadow, Maridi Intelligence Report, *SIR* 173, December 1908, App. C.II, p. 11, TNA WO 106/231.

21 See Collins, *Land Beyond the Rivers*, pp. 62–3, 67, 74–5, 82–7, 113–27, 163–71; EE Evans-Pritchard, *Witchcraft, Oracles and Magic among the Azande* (Oxford, 1937), pp. 166–7.

22 Reining, *The Zande Scheme*, p. 14; SF Newcombe, 'Report on the Lado Enclave', *SIR* 162, January 1908, App. F, pp. 29–54, TNA WO 106/231.

 23 *SIR* 167, June 1908, p. 3, TNA WO106/231.

population was expanding not just through capture and recruitment, but also by attracting satellite populations, just as the *zara'ib* had.[24] The new frontiers of the colonial state were thus formed as much or more by people coming towards the government as by any centrifugal state advance.

COMING TO KNOW GOVERNMENT: INTERPRETERS AND CHIEFS

From the first arrival of colonial government forces, certain individuals once again sought to contract them as patrons, allies and protectors. Oral histories often claim that a particular ancestor was the first to meet the 'English' or the 'French' (as the Belgians were also commonly called) when they arrived in the area, or even by trekking long distances to see the new government. Typically this is seen to have resulted in their receiving gifts and being recognised as chiefs. Colonial reports support the idea that such individuals could secure a favourable impression and alliance with government, by appearing 'friendly'. Other people were more forcibly contracted into government service as soldiers, police or prisoners, as we saw above. But they too might establish influential roles as interpreters with the civilian population and as government guides and interlocutors. Whoever gained earliest relations with the new governments was likely to influence the subsequent patterns of government relations with the population, as in the nineteenth century. Indeed sometimes the individuals employed as interlocutors or recognised as chiefs by the colonial governments claimed direct descent from nineteenth century brokers and interpreters, and very often they relied on similar skills and expertise.

The new government officials were often bewildered by both the human and physical geography of southern Sudan, frustrated by the challenges of mapping the terrain in the vast flood-prone clay plains and seasonally-migrant populations of the Bahr el Ghazal, or the dense wet-season vegetation of southern and western Equatoria, in which settlements were scattered and concealed amongst the tall grass and bush. Officials were therefore entirely dependent on local guides, and turned most often to soldiers with southern origins; the *jihadiya* were guides and translators as well as police and soldiers.[25] These individuals received little notice in the written records of the colonial state, but their influence would have been tremendous. The 1900 expedition for the reoccupation of the Bahr el Ghazal took eleven native officers, including Rihan Eff. Abdulla 'ex-slave native of Gogrial' to act as an interpreter, whose son later became a policeman.[26] When the Sudan Government took over the Lado Enclave, soldiers 'who belong to Enclave tribes and have a knowledge of the country and language' were seen to be 'useful and reliable' as interlocutors.[27] At the province headquarters in Mongalla, a Bari soldier who had fought in the Mahdist army, El Amin Rabeh, became a permanent interpreter, mentioned repeatedly in reports between *c.* 1904 and 1909. As a soldier he had been part of the Mahdist force which attacked Lafon Hill, and yet he was unhesitatingly used as an interlocutor with the Pari of Lafon (whose language was also unrelated to Bari). Only occasional remarks of his were recorded but are no doubt indicative of the opportunities he enjoyed to talk with British officials and influence their views. For example, when a government expedition to

[24] Johnson, 'Structure of a legacy', pp. 82–3.

[25] Johnson, 'Structure of a legacy', p. 81.

[26] 'Tonj', entry in the Eastern District Notebook, 31 December 1933, NRO BGP 1/7/38.

[27] Angus Cameron, 'Notes on the Lado Enclave and points in connection with its transfer from the Belgians', 28 November 1907, NRO MP 1/8/51.

Lafon Hill was halted in its tracks by the devastating attack of a swarm of bees, El Amin asserted that the bees must have been commanded by Sheikh Alikori of Lafon.[28] This may have reflected his own respect for the power of Alikori, but it would also have reinforced British assumptions that Alikori and his people were hostile or 'recalcitrant'.[29]

The distinction between the role of interpreters and that of chiefs frequently remained blurred by the functions of chiefs in mediating government relations with other groups. On the early government expeditions to Lafon Hill, the Bari 'sheikh' Lado and later his successor Wani of Mankara accompanied the interpreter El Amin to meet with the Pari leaders and supposedly persuade them of the merits of good relations with government. British officials claimed that the Bari of Mankara were close to the Pari and intermarried with them. But the use of Bari chiefs in this way also reflected a wider reliance on the particular groups that came into earliest and closest contact with government, and who were most likely to speak some Arabic.

Many of those recognised as chief had been soldiers or employees of previous governments, and they all tended to speak Arabic. When Colonel Martyr arrived in 1898 to establish the Nile Province of the Uganda Protectorate, he turned to men who represented a long history of mediating foreign intrusions in the Bari area. Kwajo and Boreng, descendants or relatives of the former trading chiefs Loro Lako (Allorron) and Abu Kuka, were recognised as chiefs in Gondokoro and Tokiman respectively. Boreng was among the chiefs who had declared allegiance to the Mahdist Emir Arabi Dafa'alla and been sent to Khartoum in the mid-1890s; he adopted the Muslim name Ibrahim and spoke Arabic.[30] To the west of the Nile, 'chiefs' were nearly always reported to speak Arabic, and several were also reported to have fought in the Mahdist forces and to have travelled in the north.[31]

In the Rumbek area too, chiefs were reported to be often either 'Government appointments' or the descendants of chiefs appointed by the nineteenth-century slave traders.[32] Like the Bari, the Agar Dinka of Rumbek also gained a relatively favourable position in government eyes vis-à-vis their neighbours, though their relations with government were more fraught, fluctuating and variable (as they had also been in the nineteenth century). In 1901, Sparkes Bey reported an initially favourable reception:

28 'Report by El Bimbashi Jennings Bramly on his tour of inspection to the Berri Hill and to the inland Baris, October 1908', *SIR* 172, November 1908, App. A, pp. 7–10, TNA WO 106/231; HDE O'Sullivan, 'Note IV: Historical re. the Berri and Jebel Lefon', *SIR* 134, September 1905, p. 17, TNA WO 106/227. A nineteenth-century Egyptian government patrol was similarly halted by an attack of bees in the Nuba Mountains, believed to be commanded by the local '*kujur*', or spiritual leader: Ali Effendi Gifoon, 'Memoirs of a Soudanese soldier', dictated in Arabic to and translated by Captain Percy Machell, *Cornhill Magazine* 1:2 (August 1896), pp. 181–2 (thanks to Douglas Johnson for this reference).

29 Similar patterns occurred in Nuer areas: Johnson, *Nuer Prophets*, pp. 158–61.

30 Interview 2aR/K; Simonse, *Kings of Disaster*, pp. 103–4; Lt. Col. Martyr, 'Report on the Nile District of the Uganda Protectorate', 15 April 1899, TNA FO 2/201; Beaton, 'A Chapter on Bari History', p. 181.

31 RCR Owen, 'Notes on Enclave', 1910, NRO MP 1/8/51; RCR Owen, 'Report on tour of inspection in Moru and Niambara districts', June 1911, *SIR* 205, August 1911, App. B, pp. 9–12, TNA WO 106/6224; Equatoria Province Monthly Diary, July 1941, NRO Civsec 57/14/53. Nuer chiefs were also appointed on the basis of their knowledge of Arabic and experience of government captivity or service: Johnson, 'Customary law and the Nuer', p. 70; DH Johnson (ed.), *The Upper Nile Province Handbook: a report on peoples and government in the southern Sudan, 1931*, compiled by CA Willis (Oxford, 1995), p. 414.

32 DC Yirrol to Governor Upper Nile Province, 'Handing over notes: Yirrol', 3 December 1935, NRO BGP 1/5/28. Cf. Robertson, 'Gender and trade relations', p. 39.

> The people of Agar (as Rambek is locally known) were reported to be likely to oppose the return of Government, however, on reaching the outskirts of the Agar district, the head sheikh of the Agar, named Daljan Majek of the Niang Section of the Dinkas, came out to meet the party and said the people welcomed our approach.[33]

This demonstrates the importance of chiefs' role as diplomats; the simple act of someone claiming to be a chief and approaching the government to talk rather than fighting or running away was often sufficient to convince the government that their people were 'friendly' and had 'submitted' to government.[34] It also provided the opportunity for chiefs to claim wide authority; the Agar were divided into sections and sub-sections and Daljan Majek was certainly not an overall 'head sheikh'. The Kuei section (of which the Nyaing were a part) built on their positive first impression by allying with the British officer Boulnois to fight against the Nuer; according to Mawson they were also hoping for his assistance to defend them against the Panyon Agar section. However, the following year the neighbouring Athuoi Agar section disastrously killed the British officer Scott-Barbour at Bahr Naam, provoking a devastating military expedition, which seized cattle and destroyed crops and villages, leading to widespread famine and destitution across the Agar territory. Mawson suggests, however, that the previous loyalty of the Kuei section may have enabled them to escape the worst of this destruction.[35] Even after the expedition, the 'Agar' were reported to be friendly to government and to be selling their sorghum to Rumbek, suggesting that those nearer Rumbek may indeed have escaped the worst of the attacks.[36]

Later colonial officials in the 1930s struggled to explain and justify the actions of their predecessors in appointing chiefs following this devastating 'Patrol': 'Too often the real leader had fled or had been shot, the natives were too disorganised, frightened or bewildered to speak up, and a 'friendly' had perforce to be chosen.'[37] In fact the patrol itself involved the capture of Agar youth who then became police or soldiers and might even end up as a chief, an example being chief Rok Rec. He was captured as a boy of eight, and 'handed over as reward for services rendered' to a native officer, in whose household he became a servant, learning fluent Arabic and taking the name Bakhit Reihan. As a young man he was 'favoured' by the British DC Bailey, who used him as a police interpreter, and he became a prison officer in Wau. He returned to Rumbek in the 1920s where he was appointed an assistant to the elderly chief Malok Mayen, eventually succeeding him as chief. By the 1930s he was praised as a 'government chief' for his own useful assistance on punitive patrols, reflecting the circular perpetuation of military raid and capture into government forces.[38]

[33] 'Extracts from El Miralai Sparkes Bey's diary', *SIR* 81, April 1901, App. D, p. 10, TNA FO 78/5167.

[34] Cf. John Lonsdale, 'The politics of conquest: the British in Western Kenya, 1894–1908', in Berman and Lonsdale, *Unhappy Valley*, p. 55.

[35] Mawson, 'The Triumph of Life', pp. 77–8.

[36] 'Report on patrol through Atwot and Agar districts, by El Bimbashi Ryan', *SIR* 119, 6 May 1904, App. C, pp. 10–12, TNA WO106/226.

[37] DC Tonj to Governor, 22 May 1937, NRO BGP 1/5/28.

[38] Rumbek Monthly Diary, January 1938, SRO EP 57.D.10; CW Beer, A/DC Rumbek, 'Note in [*sic*] Chief Rok Rec (Bakhit Reihan) Senior Chief of the Aliam Toc section of the Agar Dinka, Tumbek [*sic*] District', 1937, SRO TD 67 ('Undesirables'). Elsewhere too, capture and imprisonment was often a route to the acquisition of linguistic and government knowledge, leading to employment or chiefship: see, for example, Wendy James, *War and Survival in Sudan's Frontierlands: voices from the Blue Nile* (Oxford, 2007), p. 16.

By around 1911 the Agar were reported to be voluntarily seeking employment in Rumbek, and even enlisting in the *jihadiya*, according to the Dinka-speaking Rev. Shaw: 'I talked with many of the Agars and gathered that many of the families have begun to realise the benefit of having a blood-relation amongst the hitherto dreaded Jehadiah, and so certain of the youths are encouraged by their own people to enlist... Of the Jieng [Dinka] so far visited by me these Agars are certainly less aloof than the rest.'[39] In 1904 the 'friendly' Agar had been contrasted with the neighbouring Atuot, whose general disposition was interpreted as 'leave us alone and we will leave you alone'.[40] These early years of colonial rule saw such variation in attitudes and strategies as people tried to decide how best to deal with, or to keep at bay, the new government forces.[41] Some groups succeeded in remaining at a distance; throughout this period the northern Pakkam Agar section under chief Wol Athiang were 'still outside the Government sphere of influence'.[42] After a punitive police patrol, a chief nearer to Rumbek reportedly expressed his intention to move into Wol Athiang's territory, 'because (so he says) the soldiers never go there'. Yet even Wol repeatedly sent friendly messages to the government in Rumbek, as recorded in reports between 1904 and 1912.[43]

Even those who sought to remain remote from government were thus aware of the need for some careful diplomacy to achieve this. It was already apparent that knowledge of and communication with government was becoming vital to ensuring protection from it at the very least, if not to establishing a more preferential claim upon it. In 1907, for example, it was reported that Dinka from the Jur River area 'sent men' to Rumbek 'to get accurate news of what Government has been doing there'.[44] In 1905, one Dinka chief's interpreter 'brought' a number of Mundari chiefs to Mongalla for the first time: 'The translator of Sheikh Anok brought them in as *they did not know Government*' [my emphasis]. Such interpreters and interlocutors were dealing not only in linguistic knowledge but also in their familiarity with and experience of 'government'.

The colonial state and the institution of chiefship were both being established through enacting the process of 'coming in to government' in increasingly formal and theatrical ways. Chiefs were invited to attend rituals and ceremonies, such as a gathering and dance for the Province Governor at Rejaf in 1910. The following year the chiefs of Lado District returned to Rejaf to meet the Governor-General, Wingate, at a lavish ceremony in which they were presented with gifts of clothing or decorations.[45] Soon after, a group of chiefs and relatives of chiefs were taken on a visit to Khartoum, for which

[39] Archibald Shaw, 'Trek no. 2', c. 1911, CMS Acc. 111, F1/4; Sudan Government, *The Bahr el Ghazal Province*, p. 72.

[40] 'Report on patrol through Atwot and Agar districts, by El Bimbashi Ryan', 6 May 1904, *SIR* 119, June 1904, App. C, pp. 10–12, TNA WO106/226.

[41] Cf. James, *War and Survival*, pp. 14–20, 33.

[42] HR Headlam, 'A general report and description of Eastern District, Bahr el Ghazal Province', *SIR* 147, October 1906, App. B, pp. 9–12, at p. 10, TNA WO106/228.

[43] RN Feilden, 'Bahr el Ghazal Monthly Report', *SIR* 122, September 1904, App. A, pp. 4–5, TNA WO106/226; *SIR* 134, September 1905, p. 3, TNA WO106/227; *SIR* 213, April 1912, p. 6, TNA WO106/6224.

[44] *SIR* 157, August 1907, p. 4, TNA WO106/229; Collins, *The Southern Sudan*, p. 168.

[45] *SIR* 193, August 1910, p. 4, TNA WO 106/234; *SIR* 199, February 1911, p. 6, TNA WO 106/6224.

they had reportedly volunteered enthusiastically.[46] On a more routine basis chiefs had to come in to district headquarters (*merkaz*) so regularly that they were even encouraged to have 'town houses', where they could stay while on 'government business'.[47] They were demonstrating their familiarity and knowledge of government; in the former Lado Enclave, 'the local chiefs are said to copy in their courts all the procedure and formalities of a Government office'.[48] As these 'government chiefs' became increasingly established in the eyes – and records – of the colonial administration, they were also negotiating new local political relationships and positions.

FRONTIER CHIEFSHIP

> Before colonialism, we had no chiefs, only senior clan members: kaiyo, meaning first-born. Then when the Belgians came they demanded a lot of tax in kind. So a few individuals took opportunity to buy protection for their people by working with the Belgians.[49]

This statement encapsulates the uneasy overall bargain of chiefship, whereby chiefs ameliorated government depredations by 'buying' protection, a revealing indication of the economic brokerage that this entailed. The same interviewee went on to claim that the first chief in his area had gained recognition simply by providing the Belgians with food; other informants in the same area talk of a 'chiefship of food'. But of course being able to feed the demands of government required some means of commanding labour or extracting its fruits – and this in turn meant accumulating wealth-in-people. One of the striking features of the early twentieth century is the extent of mobility and migration in southern Sudan. This in turn may explain the repeated British reports that 'sheikhs' had no authority; the threat of migration to alternative patrons remained a significant limitation on chiefly power. The British occupation of the Lado Enclave in 1910, for example, appeared to offer opportunities for relationships of dependency to be renegotiated. Clan and family heads were reported to be trying to 'break away' from their sheikhs and set themselves up as independent chiefs, often by returning gifts of cattle or guns to their former patrons.[50]

But such migration and fission also provided opportunity for chiefs to build followings. Just as chiefs might have 'bought' protection from government, so they are remembered as having bought the allegiance of followers. Another of the Bari chiefs recognised and sent to Khartoum by the Mahdist officers was Kirba of Logo, who is admitted even by his descendants to have 'robbed' the chiefship from his maternal relatives. He is remembered as having exploited the 'weakness' of the people to exert power over an unusually wide area, based

46 Owen, 'Report on Tour of inspection in Moru and Niambara districts', June 1911, *SIR* 205, August 1911, pp. 9–12; *SIR* 207, October 1911, p. 2, both TNA WO 106/6224.

47 Archibald Shaw, Journal entry, Yei, 25 July 1917, CMS Acc. 111, F4.

48 J Crowfoot, Director of Education, to Governor-General, 'Education in Mongalla Province', 14 June 1915, CMS G3SO 1912–1919.

49 Interview 4N/YC.

50 CH Stigand, 'Report on Kagelu District', 3 July 1910, *SIR* 193, August 1910, App. A, pp. 10–12, TNA WO 106/234; Governor Owen to Percival, Senior Inspector Loka-Kagulu District, 1 July 1910, and Owen, 'Occupation of the Lado Enclave', May–June 1910, NRO MP 1/8/51. Similarly, LD Spencer, 'Intelligence report from Meridi', 16 October 1907, *SIR* January 1908, App. E, TNA WO 106/231.

upon his military prowess and the widespread fear of being enslaved by his raids; being 'exceptionally gifted' at dealing with the British administrators, he was subsequently recognised as chief. As even one of his descendants acknowledged, he accumulated wealth through the sale of ivory and through 'robbing' cattle: 'there was nothing very honest about the whole thing!' This wealth, together with government support, enabled some of the early colonial chiefs to establish themselves as powerful patrons, despite their often marginal origins. Kirba achieved this

> through briberies, through being very rich and generous, having a lot of cattle. Where there were any problems he would intervene and donate from his own. That made people like him, not really because he was good, but because of his bribery. And also because people are afraid of him. When they fight he will bring many people as slaves. And if he demands and people are not able to pay, they will have to give him people, and these people will be under him and he is the one to do the marriages of these people.[51]

The early colonial chiefs had considerable opportunity to expand such patronage capacity. Their prominence in relations with government enabled them to benefit from trade; 'sheikhs' were frequently reported to possess ivory for, or cattle from, trade, including with Greek merchants.[52] By 1910 the Makaraka chiefs Kapei and Abdulla both had Greek traders in their own villages.[53] There were of course wider benefits of such trade; in the early twentieth century there was high demand for cattle, increased by the cattle disease and losses of the later nineteenth century. The Kuku of Kajo Keji near the Uganda border, for example, were reported to be buying ivory from the Lugbara and Kakwa with sheep and goats and then selling the ivory to Ugandan traders for cattle.[54] In 1906 a Mundari chief, Logara, complained to British officials that the Aliab and Bari were preventing him trading his ivory for cattle by acting as middlemen, buying his ivory for sheep which they then sold on to get cattle.[55] As early as 1906, Dinka Bor sheikhs were reported to be selling sheep for cash in order to avoid having to pay tax in cattle, an obvious indication of the value of skilled brokerage in ensuring the most favourable exchanges with government.[56]

Government officers in turn were trying to use the chiefs to access ivory, grain and labour, helping to entrench them in a brokerage role; 'friendly' chiefs were given guns, or the assistance of government soldiers, to exact 'tribute' in grain or labourers from neighbouring settlements.[57] Chief Lukudu near Yei

51 Interview 3R/K; Simonse, *Kings of Disaster*, p. 104.

52 Angus Cameron, 'Inspection tour in the Southern Mandari country', *SIR* 140, March 1906, App. B, pp. 10–12, TNA WO 106/228; SF Newcombe, 'Report on the Lado Enclave', *SIR* 162, January 1908, App. F, pp. 29–54, TNA WO 106/231.

53 RCR Owen to Percival, Senior Inspector Loka-Kagulu District, 1 July 1910, NRO MP 1/8/51; Archibald Shaw, 'Trek No. 2', n.d., c. 1911, CMS Acc. 111, F1/4.

54 Joseph Vanden Plas, *Les Kuku* (Bruxelles, 1910), cited by GWB Huntingford, *Ethnographic Survey of Africa, East Central Africa, Part VI: The Northern Nilo-Hamites,* ed. Daryll Forde (London, 1953), pp. 44–5; CH Stigand, Inspector Rejaf Merkaz, to Governor, 6 March 1911, NRO Intel 2/29/239.

55 Angus Cameron, 'Inspection tour in the Southern Mandari country', *SIR* 140, March 1906, App. B, pp. 10–12, TNA WO 106/228.

56 Angus Cameron, 'Mongalla Province Diary for March 1906', *SIR* 141, April 1906, App. D, p. 8, TNA WO 106/228.

57 Dove, 'Tour of inspection through country occupied by Mandari Nyambara tribes between the Nile and the Bahr El Ghazal, December 1908', *SIR* 177, April 1909, App. D, pp. 17–19, TNA WO 106/232; RCR Owen to Percival, Senior Inspector Loka-Kagulu District, 1 July 1910, NRO MP 1/8/51.

in the Lado Enclave, for example, was reported to have been 'much used by the Belgians to raid other chiefs, and possesses a large herd of cattle (about 2000), most of which were captured by Belgian order from the Madi tribe to the south'.[58] As in the nineteenth century, it could be a sensible choice to affiliate oneself to a 'chief' who could deflect the depredations of government force onto other settlements, and in so doing gain livestock and other resources with which to reward followers and support dependents. According to British reports, by 1907, even the 'more independent tribesmen... were not slow to recognise that the Sheikh being virtually approved by Government as its agent... it was more desirable to be on good terms with him than in opposition'.[59]

Chiefly patronage and protection was producing new, often ethnically heterogeneous communities. Aluma, a Kakwa chief, had been appointed by the Belgians to administer the more resistant Kaliko south of Yei; in 1918 a British missionary reported that a headman of the Kakwa chief Wai was 'now moving his village in close to Aluma's', and that a number of 'the Lugbari tribe' were 'filtering across from the Congo' and 'attaching themselves' to this headman.[60] Political communities were thus transcending some ethnic and linguistic borders, sometimes with enduring effect: in the same district, a group of Moru were moved by the government into a Pojelu chiefdom, because their own area was believed to be infected with sleeping sickness:

> *Question:* So you were Moru before?
> *Response:* Yes, but we came under Ramadalla so we became Fajelu [Pojelu]. The older generations... still speak Moru, but our mothers were Fajelu so we only speak Fajelu. We became Fajelus under Ramadalla.[61]

The chiefship at Tonj, west of Rumbek, was clearly rooted in interlocution and patronage rather than historical 'tribal' structure. Chief Murjan Bongo (*Fig. 2.1*) reportedly gained his position by trekking all the way to greet the British at Fashoda at the end of the nineteenth century, and was then 'given powers over the local Bongos' at Tonj, to whom he was related maternally. He was then involved in the punitive patrol against the Agar after Scott-Barbour's death, and took a young Agar Dinka boy captured by the patrol as a 'son' or dependent, now named Khiir es-Seid. When Murjan was later exiled to Raga for murder around 1921, he 'designated' Khiir as his successor. Chief Khiir es-Seid would not only continue to be chief of the agriculturalist Bongo but also attracted followers both from the cattle-keeping Rek Dinka in the area, and from the Agar from whom he originated: 'the present Chief partly owing to his personality, partly owing to the prestige of his adopted father, and partly owing to Government backing, is now recognised generally as their Chief by the Raik near Tonj'.[62] By this time government officers would complain that too many 'natives from other districts' were attracted to Tonj, particularly Zande and Agar. The latter were claimed as relatives by Chief Khiir, though the DC's scepticism may accurately indicate that this was more a patronage network

[58] Archibald Shaw, 'Trek from Rejaf to Loka', March 1911, CMS Acc. 111, F3; AL Davis, 'Notes on the Lado Enclave', *SIR* 184, November 1909, App. A, pp. 6–7, TNA WO 106/232; Mongalla Province Intelligence Report, March 1904, NRO Intel 8/2/12.

[59] Mongalla Province Annual Report 1907, *GGR* 1907, p. 338.

[60] P O'B Gibson, Annual Letter, Yei, 18 December 1918, CMS G3 AL 1917–34.

[61] Interview 5N/YC. Cf. Ambler, *Kenyan Communities*, p. 32.

[62] Report on Bahr el Ghazal Province, enclosed in Governor Ingleson to Civil Secretary, 14 May 1935, Appendix Z: notes on districts, NRO UNP 1/4/22.

Fig. 2.1 Chief Murjan Bongo (right) and MA Ahmad Effendi Lebib at Tonj, Bahr el Ghazal Province, 1908. (Reproduced by permission of Durham University Library SAD.A15/87)

than a direct familial connection.[63] As Lonsdale eloquently sums up similar scenarios in western Kenya, such chiefs were operating within 'a system of social relations that translated the outward manifestations of military victory and cattle redistribution into the latent idiom of clan growth and affiliation'.[64] But this process would produce its own lasting tensions and debates between different sources of authority.

STAKING CLAIMS AND SPLITTING POWER

The early years of colonial rule saw the constitution of a specific institution, the chiefship 'of government', which was largely distinct from other forms of authority, and which resulted both from the indigenous tendency to separate institutions of power and expertise, and from the gradual colonial bureaucratisation of local administration. Colonial administrators were intervening significantly in local political relations to support the men they recognised – and recorded – as co-operative chiefs.[65] This in turn provided opportunity for chiefs to contract with government officials, sometimes quite literally on the verandah of the state, as the Mongalla Province Governor, Owen, experienced on taking over the Lado Enclave in 1910:

> While at Loka I was visited by very many of the Sheikhs… Each Chief brought his small party of followers and also his deck chair and pipe, and proceeded to make himself at home in my verandah, reposing in his chair, smoking his pipe and expectorating all over the floor, but taking great interest and joining in the conversation in a loud and boisterous manner and at times backed up by three or four of their followers, all talking loudly together. Apparently they had been accustomed to do this with the Belgians. As some had brought complaints and minor cases they wish settled, I found it necessary to very soon clear my verandah and get to work.[66]

The relationship of the chiefs to government was displayed by their motley European or Egyptian military uniforms and their 'retinues' or 'bands' with rifles or older guns, bugles, drums and formal drilling practices appropriated from government armies (*Figs. 2.2 and 2.3*).[67] Tables and chairs, tobacco pipes, papers, and even a metal boat bought with ivory from a Khartoum merchant, were exhibited conspicuously by chiefs, symbolising also the longer history of interaction with imperial and commercial forces.[68] British officers also handed out Remington rifles, describing them as 'a badge of office'.[69] Colonial officials seem to have quite accurately interpreted the symbolic power

[63] 'Tonj', entry in the Eastern District Notebook, 31 December 1933, NRO BGP 1/7/38.

[64] Lonsdale, 'The politics of conquest', p. 55.

[65] *SIR* 213, April 1912, p. 5, TNA WO 106/6224; *SIR* 238, May 1914, p. 5, TNA WO 106/6225. Vaughan argues for similar processes in Darfur, in 'Negotiating the state'.

[66] Owen, 'Occupation of the Lado Enclave', May–June 1910, NRO MP 1/8/51.

[67] Cf. 'Diary of El Miralai Sparkes Bey on Niam Niam patrol, 4 June to 27 July, 1901', *SIR* 86, September 1901, App. B, p. 11.

[68] Storrar, 'Letters from the Sudan, Vol. 5', 15 April–17 June 1917, SAD 53/1/1–536; Owen, 'Report on Tour of inspection in Moru and Niambara districts, June 1911', *SIR* 205, August 1911, App. B, pp. 9–12, TNA WO 106/6224; Owen, 'Occupation of the Lado Enclave', May–June 1910, NRO MP 1/8/51; Shaw, 'Trek No. 2', n.d., c. 1911, CMS Acc. 111, F1/4; Gwynne, 'Diary June–July 1911', CMS Acc. 18, F1/49; Spence to his mother, Yei, 15 July 1915, Shetland Archive, Lerwick, D12/202/1–19.

[69] Mongalla Province Annual Report 1907, *GGR* 1907, p. 346.

Fig. 2.2 Chief Wai (left) with his retinue holding rifles, at a village near Kagelu, Yei, Mongalla Province, 1917. (Reproduced by permission of Durham University Library SAD.53/1/148)

Fig. 2.3 Group of chiefs and notables, some wearing uniforms from various periods, Rumbek, Bahr el Ghazal Province, 1926. (Reproduced by permission of Durham University Library SAD.A82/185)

of guns in terms of their demonstration of a relationship with government. In 1908 one officer reported giving a rifle to Sheikh Kidi of Lafon because of a 'hostile faction': 'I knew the best way of strengthening his hands was a rifle from Government. Besides, I am sure he will feel himself more tied to Government while possessing it.' Kidi certainly drew on this 'tie' to the government, requesting a government post in his area the following year, and claiming that the Murle and Lafit were 'against him because he is a friend of the government'.[70] The government was responsive to notions of reciprocal obligation and patrimonial demands that had obvious parallels in indigenous social and political relations; the exchange of gifts and tribute seems to have been at least partially a mutually intelligible economy of signs through which relations and contracts were negotiated with government.

As elsewhere in southern Sudan and more widely in eastern Africa, the colonial government was drawn into protecting its allies, as well as using them in patrols and punitive expeditions against other groups.[71] One British official made explicit the government policy of supporting 'friendlies' against their enemies, describing the Shik (Cic) Dinka as the 'most amenable' tribe in the Bahr el Ghazal, providing bulls and grain for the government: 'In return the Shik *have a right to demand protection* from their enemies – a service which, I believe, the Government claims to give to its subjects' (my emphasis).[72] The Bari on the east bank of the Nile similarly utilised their connections to the government to gain protection from Pari raids, while those on the west bank were suspected of encouraging Belgian raids on the Mundari.[73] Before the British takeover of the Lado Enclave, chiefs in the area also sought quite literally to contract British protection. Several 'chiefs' approached the British authorities at Mongalla to complain at Belgian atrocities; they expressed willingness to pay tribute to the Sudan Government, and requested to move north or east of the Lado Enclave boundaries.[74]

But relations with government brought risks as well as opportunity, and set up a lasting moral ambiguity around chiefship that tended to encourage or reflect its separation from other forms of authority. The local histories of individual chiefships often seek to explain why in many cases the lineages or individuals with greatest spiritual authority did not take on the role of 'government chief'. A century later, people recalled the 'splitting' of powers in the early colonial period, as one Pojelu government officer explained in English: 'the administration was given to neutral people. They could be from the same family, so they would say so-and-so you become responsible for rain and for witchcraft, but this man we are keeping him for a special case which

[70] 'Report by El Bimbashi Jennings Bramly on his tour of inspection to the Berri Hill and to the inland Baris, October 1908', *SIR* 172, November 1908, App. A, pp. 7–10, TNA WO 106/231; AW Jennings Bramly, 'Report on a journey to Jebel Lafone (Lafole) and notes on the Berri tribe', *SIR* 185, December 1909, App. C, pp. 10–14, TNA WO 106/232.

[71] Johnson, *Nuer Prophets*, pp. 10, 116–8, 267; Anderson, *Eroding the Commons*, pp. 42–6; Lonsdale, 'The politics of conquest'; Chris Vaughan, '"Demonstrating the machine guns": rebellion, violence and state formation in early colonial Darfur', *Journal of Imperial and Commonwealth History* (forthcoming, 2013).

[72] 'Extract from report of Bimbashi Headlam, Inspector, Rumbek', *SIR* 144, July 1906, App. B, pp. 7–9, TNA WO 106/228.

[73] HDE O'Sullivan, 'Note IV: Historical re the Berri and Jebel Lefon', *SIR* 134, September 1905, p. 17, TNA WO 106/227; Angus Cameron, 'Inspection tour in the Southern Mandari country', *SIR* 140, March 1906, App. B, pp. 10–12, TNA WO 106/228.

[74] E.g. *SIR* 138, January 1906, pp. 1–3, TNA WO 106/228. See also Collins, *Land Beyond the Rivers*, p. 234: the Nuer saw tribute as protection money and viewed the state as a patron.

is administration.'[75] In some areas an explicit, deliberate separation between rain chiefship and government chiefship was being reported at the time by colonial officials. A Uganda officer, Haddon, made a study of the Bari political systems in 1909–10, and concluded that there were two kinds of chiefs: the rain chiefs, and the 'district' chiefs, who were not from the rain-chiefly lineages.[76] British reports claimed that the 'onerous' work of administration was not palatable to many rain chiefs, who were instead appointing younger relatives or dependants as government chiefs or headmen.[77] Similarly around Rumbek, government chiefs tended not to be spear-masters, though in some other Dinka areas chiefs did come from the spear-master lineages.[78]

It is difficult to know how far rain chiefs and other powerful people were indeed delegating or avoiding the risks and trouble of government chiefship, or how far this reflects a justificatory discourse developed by colonial officials and/or subsequent generations. Elsewhere in southern Sudan by the 1920s, British administrators would deliberately seek to secularise chiefship and use it to counterbalance the purported threat posed by spiritual leaders.[79] Oral histories often attribute the separation of the new chiefship from other forms of knowledge and authority to the predation of the early colonial governments, particularly in the Yei area where violence by the Congolese troops of the Belgian government was recorded in British reports as well as in local memory. The role of 'chief' was certainly a hazardous one; it placed an individual first in the firing line if the Belgian or Congolese soldiers were displeased. One Uganda official witnessed a 'sheikh' in the Enclave being beaten simply in order to find out where game was, and he was reportedly killed later for refusing to carry a soldier over a stream.[80] An elderly Mundari interviewee claimed that these dangers led to the appointment of 'slaves' or dependents as chiefs, while the 'real' chiefs had 'gone underground because of fear of being killed by the Belgians'. One Mundari community was said to have later complained to a British official about the Dinka origins of their chief, but the official supported the chief's own argument that he had earned his position by risking his life under the Belgians.[81]

Such discourse may well have developed among other senior men as a way to emphasise the subordinate lineage position of chiefs and the demeaning nature of their work, in order to counteract the increasing power of these upstart 'new men'. But there was of course truth in the depiction of their junior or marginal status, as well as of the risks of their role. In the early years of their administration, British officers expressed considerable confusion and uncertainty as to who the 'real chiefs' were. In a few cases, officials reported that 'sheikhs' turned out to be mere 'representatives' or 'interpreters' for the 'real' sheikh; many were only in their twenties, suggesting that these were indeed relatively junior men.[82] Colonial administrators would be endlessly

75 Interview 4R/K.

76 Simonse, *Kings of Disaster*, p. 107; Haddon, 'System of chieftainship', pp. 471–2.

77 Beaton, 'A Chapter in Bari History', p. 192; Simonse, *Kings of Disaster*, pp. 128–9; 'Tribal no. 20, Liria', NRO JD 1/1/2.

78 Governor Equatoria to DCs Aweil, Jur River and Lakes, 24 April 1942, NRO BGP 1/5/28.

79 See Johnson, *Nuer Prophets*, pp. 289–90

80 SF Newcombe, 'Report on the Lado Enclave', *SIR* 162, January 1908, App. F, pp. 29–54, TNA WO 106/231; Angus Cameron, 'Mongalla Intelligence Report', *SIR* 155, June 1907, App. B, pp. 7–8, TNA WO 106/229.

81 Interview 5R/K; Buxton, *Chiefs and Strangers*, p. 40, fn 1.

82 Mongalla Province Intelligence Report, March 1904, NRO Intel 8/2/12; Jennings-Bramly, A/ Governor, 'Report of a tour among the Baris of the East Bank', 27 August 1906, NRO Intel 8/2/12.

frustrated by their limited power, as described by one Anglican missionary in 1906: 'Denkas [Dinka] have sheikhs or chiefs but these have little or no power. One wonders why they are sheikhs. Sometimes even little boys laugh at them... it is difficult to know where the power lies among the Denkas.'[83] However, the genealogically junior or marginal status of some of the early chiefs and the temporal and executive nature of their work did not prevent them attracting followers and settlers. This is the enduring paradox of the history of chiefship, which oral histories seek to accommodate.[84] As chiefs gained or built upon the profits and patronage generated by their relations with government, they could be central to the formation or strengthening of new kinds of community. Oral histories have therefore sought to explain this apparent usurpation of lineage structures as the product of contingent, pragmatic bargains struck in order to ameliorate the risks of the early colonial period. In a sense this is an explanation to which everyone can subscribe: those claiming greater seniority than chiefs can use it to emphasise the latter's marginality and the temporary terms of such bargains; while chiefs and their supporters argue that these were enduring contracts, cemented by the risks endured by the early chiefs.

Chiefs and their supporters around Yei, for example, claim that their predecessors risked their lives or even shed their blood to obtain recognition from government, which in turn benefited their chiefdoms. In one Kakwa clan the story goes that the 'first-born' senior elder sent other men to deal with the 'French' [Belgians], one of whom was an adopted dependent of his from outside the clan, Lasuba. 'Lasuba was defiant; when the French came they were beating Lasuba, smearing his face with honey and burning it with fire, but still he persevered.' When the senior elder was dying he called all the clans of the area to elect a new leader, but people feared the brutal behaviour of the 'French' forces. So they selected Lasuba to be chief because he was seen as an outsider and hence more expendable than a senior clan member. Yet as time went by, it became evident that the chiefship was in fact 'a good road' for Lasuba, and rivalries emerged as members of the senior clan now tried to claim the chiefship. Later supporters of Lasuba's line therefore argued that the senior clan had given away its right to the chiefship at the time of Lasuba's selection, when the clan elders allegedly declared that he had earned the chiefship by his bravery, and cursed anyone who tried to reclaim it.[85]

An even more complex and revealing story of the founding of chiefship was told by members of a neighbouring clan, who claim that their grandfathers lived on the land where Yei town is now situated. They were attacked by *tukutuku* soldiers of the Belgian government and the wife of their rain chief was captured for resisting, and had her hands amputated. The rain chief, Göriwa, is said to have gone to the military camp to negotiate her release, and in return agreed to move his settlement to provide land for the government buildings. He was then 'given' the chiefship, and an iron pillar (most likely to have been a flagpole base) was erected near the new government *merkaz* on the land he vacated. Other ancestral Kakwa leaders are associated with particular mountains in the region; an elderly woman from this clan argued that the iron post in Yei was the equivalent of such a mountain for their line of rain chiefs, in a clear example of the way in which the establishment of the town was held up as a pivotal and

[83] Rev. FB Hadow, 'Journal for April 1906', CMS Acc. 409, F1.

[84] Very similar tensions and limitations on chiefly power are described in Bill Bravman, *Making Ethnic Ways: communities and their transformations in Taita, Kenya, 1900–1950* (Oxford, 1998), especially pp. 111–6.

[85] Interview 9R/YC; also see Cherry Leonardi, 'Violence, sacrifice and chiefship in Central Equatoria, Southern Sudan', *Africa* 77:4 (2007), p. 545.

Fig. 2.4 Iron post in Yei town, said to have been handed to a local chief by Belgian colonial forces. (Photograph © Cherry Leonardi)

foundational moment in their history. Yei town was thus incorporated into the historical geography of this clan.[86]

> So the white people asked Göriwa, 'You, do you hold the chiefship of Yei?' Göriwa answered, 'No, I have come to take my wife. My in-laws say they need the corpse, or else they will kill me'. They said, 'Your wife has her hands cut off'. 'I have to carry her like that', said Göriwa. And so the iron post was brought and put into Göriwa's hand, with this command: 'Carry this iron and peg it in Yei, and hold Yei also'. Now this means that Yei is of our clan, and the chiefship is also of our clan. This chiefship in Yei here is of our clan; this is so. The mutilation of the wife of Göriwa is the chiefship of our clan. This is how the chiefship stands; the grandsons also know it. Göriwa's wife was brought from Rejaf. Yes, and that iron post is the sign of Göriwa, and Yei is in his power, including the chiefship of the land. All this is so.[87]

The story contains similar themes to oral histories about relations with the nineteenth century stations, including the role of a woman – in this case said to be a strong, 'fierce' woman who fought the soldiers – for whom the chief was compelled to approach the government forces. But the particular result of this rescuing of a woman was not only the granting of a chiefship by the government, but also the establishment of a claim upon the town and even on the state itself. In the early twenty-first century, the iron post was still there near the centre of the town (*Fig. 2.4*), and seemed to represent and cement a particular contract which the people of this chiefdom believed they had with

[86] Unlike Lonsdale's depiction of Kenyan urban space as external and alien to Kikuyu moral geographies: John Lonsdale, 'The moral economy of Mau Mau: wealth, poverty and civic virtue in Kikuyu political thought', in Berman and Lonsdale, *Unhappy Valley* Vol. 2, pp. 315–504; Giblin, 'History, imagination'.

 [87] Interviews 22R/YC, 29R/YC.

the government in the town, including a right to urban plots of land. Local historical discourse describes chiefship as an object, a burden to be 'carried' by chiefs, rather like the burdens that porters had long been forced to carry for foreign forces. But this in turn is understood to have established a kind of debt and reciprocal obligation upon government.

CONCLUSION: COMING IN TO GOVERNMENT

The period up to about 1920 has been characterised by historians of Southern Sudan as a period of military administration.[88] By 1920, the Khartoum government was expressing concern at the extent of force being employed by the provincial administrations on a regular basis, both in terms of corporal punishment, and punitive patrols.[89] The last significant military patrols in the research areas were conducted against the Mundari and Aliab Dinka between 1919 and 1921, although in other districts resistance and counter-insurgency would continue for another decade or more.[90] Coercion had certainly been a dominant feature of early colonial administration. But the reach of this predatory force was limited and sporadic. Punitive and extractive expeditions were devastating in their effect and left enduring memories, but they were irregular and not always effective, encountering environmental barriers and potentially costly in deaths, injury and illness. Many areas remained entirely outside the 'influence' of government, while other people pursued strategies of diplomacy and tribute payment in order to deflect and ameliorate government requisitions.

But it was not simply the case that the population remained as far away from the government stations as possible, encountering the state only when it sent expeditions to demand taxes or to demonstrate its coercive capacity. In a wider context of fluid and mobile settlement patterns, some individuals or groups were drawn to live in the vicinity of the government stations, in search of profitable employment, trade, alliance or protection. Also the colonial record frequently suggests that it was not the state that penetrated rural communities, but the chiefs and other interlocutors who 'came in to government'. From the earliest arrival of the new colonial forces, individuals actively sought them out to establish privileged claims upon them and to contract their power, whether in personal disputes, inter-communal conflicts and competition, trading relationships or direct employment. From interpreters 'bringing in' chiefs to the government stations, to chiefs travelling long distances to greet the new 'Turks' or coming to discuss local politics and disputes on the government verandah, chiefship was produced through approaching the state itself. This verandah would expand over the remaining colonial period into a broader urban frontier around the government stations.[91] But very often the habitation of these zones would build upon particular relations with government forged in the earliest decades of colonial rule, brokered by the most entrepreneurial chiefs.

[88] E.g. MW Daly, *Empire on the Nile: the Anglo-Egyptian Sudan, 1898–1934* (Cambridge, 1986), pp. 396–7.

[89] Daly, *Empire on the Nile*, p. 151.

[90] Mongalla Province Intelligence Reports, May 1918–June 1920, NRO Intel 2/48/408, and October–November 1921, NRO Intel 2/30/251; Governor Willis, Upper Nile Province, to Civil Secretary, 'The Future of the Mamour', 16 March 1929, NRO Civsec 1/11/36.

[91] The spatial verandah metaphor is elaborated in Garth Andrew Myers, *Verandahs of Power: colonialism and space in urban Africa* (New York, 2003).

Part Two

From *Makama* to *Mejlis*: The Making of Chiefship and the Local State, 1920s–1950s

In Moru District in 1918, a police attack on an Atuot community was blamed on the district *mamur*, a subaltern Egyptian or Sudanese officer:

> On investigation it transpired that the police had attacked the followers of a friendly Atwot Chief called Dubbai who had lived on the Moru boundary for two years. As the attack was unexpected and came as a complete surprise about 100 Atwots were killed including women and children and their cattle captured and driven in to Amadi. The police of course were acting on the instructions of the Mamour [*mamur*].[1]

Over the next few years, British officials would use such evidence to urge the removal of Egyptian *mamurs* from the southern provinces, as part of the wider reaction in the Condominium government against educated Egyptian and northern Sudanese. The growing preference for traditional, tribal authority has generated analysis of the early 1920s as a turning-point in histories of the Condominium.[2] But in southern Sudan, this shift was largely rhetorical, as the new language of 'Indirect Rule' provided fresh justification for the existing pragmatic reliance on the local intermediaries and agents appointed as chiefs and headmen.

The more significant shift in the southern provinces after the First World War was instead in the gradual bureaucratisation and regularisation of government. As Fields writes, Indirect Rule was a legitimising theory which 'aimed to give the present and future actions of the rulers *consistency and order*' [my emphasis].[3] The reported atrocity against the Atuot in 1918 was indicative of the broader character of the preceding administration: not simply its military structures and methods, but its potential for 'unexpected', apparently arbitrary actions, and the unpredictability of its demands and depredations. Chiefs claimed privileged knowledge of how to deal with these capricious forces, much as other specialists had already been 'necessary to cope with the unpredictable cruelties of climate, disease and personal misfortune' in northeastern Africa.[4]

In the 1920s, however, 'the spectacular violence of the patrol' would largely be transformed into 'the ordinary routine' of the new chief's court, or *makama*.[5] The position of the chiefs depended on their ability to extract labour and taxes from people, and to enforce proliferating colonial orders regarding agriculture, settlement, grazing, hunting, trade, public health and migration. Unsurprisingly then, scholars have come to see the Indirect Rule rhetoric of traditional legitimacy as a cloak for the investment of chiefs with the brutal and extractive force of the colonial state.

Such analysis of colonial chiefs has been increasingly challenged by other scholars, arguing not least that the brute force of the colonial state was rather more limited in the first place, and was certainly not consistently available to chiefs. But nevertheless we still need to address the implications of arguments that the power of colonial chiefs derived from their gatekeeping position in the colonial economy: that chiefly collaboration was 'the political form of the articulation of modes of production'.[6] In southern Sudan, such articulation was

1 Mongalla Province Intelligence Report, May 1918, NRO Intel 2/48/408.

2 See e.g. Holt and Daly, *A History of the Sudan*, pp. 112–20.

3 Karen Elise Fields, *Revival and Rebellion in Colonial Central Africa* (Portsmouth, NH, 1996), p. 41.

4 John Lonsdale, 'The conquest state of Kenya, 1895–1905', in Berman and Lonsdale, *Unhappy Valley*', p. 21.

5 Willis, 'Violence, authority', p. 108.

6 Berman and Lonsdale, 'Coping with the contradictions', p. 91; Mamdani, *Citizen and Subject*, p. 23.

more limited, gradual and partial than in the settler, plantation or industrial economies in eastern and southern Africa on which these analyses have been based. Chiefs in southern Sudan were never able to monopolise the complex exchanges and negotiations produced by the introduction of money and by the limited processes of commoditisation. The position of chiefs should be explored therefore not as a gate kept between discrete economic spheres, or between a bounded state and society, but in terms of the multifaceted frontiers upon which community, state and chiefship were simultaneously forming. These frontiers took a spatial form around the government administrative centres, as these evolved into small towns in the 1920s and 1930s.

By the 1940s, the Condominium government was shifting away from its emphasis on chiefship as the lynchpin of Native Administration, and promoting more progressive visions of local government, embodied this time in the new institution of the local council, or *mejlis*.[7] This shift did not greatly alter the established structures of chiefship, though it did contribute to a widening frontier of participation in government and towns. But the political discussions and developments of the late 1940s and 1950s would also remind people of the unpredictability of government and the risks of this frontier. By the end of the Condominium in 1956, people were once again turning to chiefs to seek protection and to mitigate a capricious state. But the idea would nevertheless endure that this mitigation might be achieved by appealing to the regulatory orders of the state itself.

[7] For a thorough account of changing government policies throughout the Condominium, see Martin W Daly, *Imperial Sudan: the Anglo-Egyptian Condominium 1934–1956* (Cambridge, 1991) and *Empire on the Nile*.

*

3

Constituting the urban frontier: chiefship and the colonial labour economy, 1920s-1940s

In 2006, a very elderly Bari man, a former mechanic, recalled being moved when still a small child in the late 1920s to make way for the building of the new provincial headquarters of Juba. He stated that the chief at the time, Gaddum, had been made chief because he knew more Arabic than the rest of the people, and that he was responsible for conscripting labour for the government.

> People at that time did not know government affairs... A chief of long ago was not good: he would beat people, so the people were very much afraid of him. Now people are good; they know laws. But at that time, if you were a brave person, you were beaten for nothing; actually there was no law. And people were forced to work without being paid; working on the roads for no money.[1]

Knowledge of Arabic and 'government affairs' had often been converted into chiefship in the early years of the Condominium by individuals like Gaddum. For this interviewee, and for many others, the enduring memory of such chiefship was its coercion of labour and its arbitrary force. In general the documentary records and oral histories similarly emphasise the forced extraction of labour as the most obvious feature of colonial rule in southern Sudan, and as the primary function of chiefs, together with the often associated collection of tax. There is plenty of evidence to support Mamdani's broader analysis of colonial chiefship as 'like a clenched fist', enforcing 'a regime of extra-economic coercion, a regime that breathed life into a whole range of compulsions: forced labour, forced crops, forced sales, forced contributions, and forced removals'.[2] By the late 1930s and particularly with the added requisitioning of the Second World War years in the 1940s, even some colonial officials were becoming increasingly concerned at the extent of coercion that was embedded in the whole system of 'native' administration.

It would not be surprising then if people did not 'like' the government, as this man put it rather mildly: 'People were satisfied with cattle, goats and staying with their children; they did not need anything from the government.' The preservation of indigenous value regimes centring on 'cattle, goats and children' remained conspicuous in the colonial period, not least because the Condominium's exclusionary and conservative administration of the southern provinces rendered the cash and commodity economy perennially limited and unreliable, restricting the extent of new social and economic differentiation that occurred elsewhere in Africa in the interwar years.[3] But the colonial economy

[1] Interview 45R/JC.

[2] Mamdani, *Citizen and Subject*, p. 23.

[3] E.g. Berman and Lonsdale, *Unhappy Valley*, Vol. 1; Sara Berry, *No Condition is Permanent: the social dynamics of agrarian change in Sub-Saharan Africa* (Madison, 1993).

nevertheless generated considerable change, opportunity and constraint, producing complicated and contingent strategies and struggles. At the height of colonial Indirect Rule rhetoric in the 1920s and 1930s, both government and chiefs asserted 'custom' as the basis for chiefly requisition of labour and tax. But by the 1930s, custom was also being invoked by other people to oppose chiefly demands and coercion, and considerable doubt crept into colonial administration over the customary legitimacy of chiefs. At the same time, people were pursuing other strategies to evade the requisitioning of their labour or property, strategies which increasingly took them to the urban frontier, and to participate in the overlapping economic frontiers of commoditisation and monetisation. At these frontiers, they would obtain not just cash income, but knowledge and experience of contractual relations. Scholars have argued that Indirect Rule entrenched social status and membership of communities as determinants of access to resources in colonial Africa.[4] But at the same time, colonial government and economy provided new idioms of contract with which to claim rights and resources.[5] In southern Sudan, contractual relations were not new, but they would now be reworked in bureaucratic and legalistic languages to oppose colonial and chiefly coercion, as suggested in the elderly interviewee's emphasis on the reforming and empowering capacity of 'the law'.

However, a simple opposition between coercive colonial chiefs and their 'subjects' does not begin to explain the complexity of changing relations and rights in this period; nor does the idea of a unilinear progression from 'status' to 'contract' as the basis of rights in property and people.[6] Instead the changes and debates provoked by the colonial economy were managed in southern Sudan through the constitution of moral frontiers. A number of binary oppositions were being established, between town and village, government and society, market and non-market economies, even as people were increasingly crossing and re-crossing these apparent boundaries. Chiefship itself was located at these frontiers: it originated in encounters on the urban frontier and government verandah and, as Mamdani argues, its power and profits derived from standing at 'the intersection of the market economy and the nonmarket one'.[7] But this did not convey the extent of power and monopoly that Mamdani assumes. Instead the key to the consolidation of chiefship in this period lies in the disputes that, as Chanock argues, 'moved along the frontiers between commodity and non-commodity status': 'shifting frontiers which appear to have dragged property disputes back into the moralities of relationships'.[8] As families, households, individuals and the new administrative 'communities' struggled over their control of people and property, they would increasingly turn to the chiefs and their courts to settle disputes and to enable conversions and translations across these 'shifting' frontiers.

The next chapter will examine the role and significance of the chiefs' courts in these processes, but firstly this chapter establishes the context for the disputes that would reach the courts, and addresses the development of the frontiers on which they were situated. It begins by examining the colonial conception of rural chiefship, and the paradox of associated labour conscription

[4] Sara Berry, 'Social institutions and access to resources', *Africa* 59:1 (1989), pp. 41–55; Berry, *No Condition is Permanent.*

[5] Martin Chanock, 'A peculiar sharpness: an essay on property in the history of customary law in colonial Africa', *Journal of African History* 32 (1991), pp. 65–88; Frederick Cooper, *Decolonization and African Society: the labor question in French and British Africa* (Cambridge, 1996), p. 3.

[6] Cf. Chanock, 'A peculiar sharpness', p. 69.

[7] Mamdani, *Citizen and Subject*, p. 23.

[8] Chanock, 'A peculiar sharpness', pp. 86–7.

and road construction. It then explores the complex debates stimulated by the colonial emphasis on custom as the basis for chiefly control of labour, and the subsequent shift in policy to 'clans' and 'family groups' as supposedly more customary and corporate units. But the colonial economy was simultaneously generating opportunities and strategies by which people sought to evade the demands on their labour from either chiefs or supposed kinship units. Frontiers of labour migration and education became sites on which to avoid chiefly authority, and yet these same frontiers also remained sites for the making of chiefship. The chapter goes on to explore the production of these frontiers by multiple actors as sites of moral ambiguity, arguing that this both constituted and constrained chiefship.

THE ROAD TO RURAL CHIEFSHIP: COERCION AND CUSTOM

> I have searched in vain in the writings on N.A. [Native Administration] for some help and guidance with a people like this. All the theory tacitly assumes a background of social organisation with a hierarchy of chiefs who are chiefs and not just family headmen, and who issue orders and carry them out over units far wider than the family group.[9]

As this rather plaintive remark from a British District Commissioner (DC) in the Upper Nile Province indicates, the adoption of a formal policy of Indirect Rule – or Native Administration, as it was usually known in Sudan – posed considerable challenges for administrators in the southern provinces, despite appearing to justify their longstanding systems of chiefship. Indirect rule ideology gave impetus to the elusive colonial ideal for territory, tribe and chiefship to coincide in neat units of settlement and administration. Administrators experienced indigenous social relations as a sticky web of unseen connections and allegiances, and turned frequently to the comfortingly solid metaphors of the brick buildings and parish boundaries of their own home geography by which to imagine clarity and 'tribal' structure. The broader contradictions and fallacies of Indirect Rule[10] were epitomised in southern Sudan by the prominence of roads in the colonial vision of a supposedly 'traditional' social and administrative order. It is unsurprising then that in local memory roads often represent the coming of both government and chiefship, the associated requisitioning of labour, and even the constitution of new communities along these arteries of the colonial state.[11]

The 1921 Milner mission had led the Sudan Government to promote a 'dual policy' of education and development alongside the strengthening of traditional authority. But following the mutiny and uprising in northern towns and the assassination of Governor-General Stack in Egypt in 1924, the Condominium government turned firmly against the educated *effendiya* of Egypt and northern Sudan.[12] In 1927, Governor-General Maffey issued

[9] DC Marwood, Bor, to Governor, Upper Nile, 9 May 1938, NRO BGP 1/5/28.

[10] Pels, 'The pidginization of Luguru politics'; Berman and Lonsdale, *Unhappy Valley*, Vol. 1; Berry, *No Condition is Permanent.*

[11] Roads have had a similar significance in northwest South Sudan: see Thomas, *The Kafia Kingi Enclave*, pp. 85–101.

[12] See Civil Secretary to Governors, 20 October 1924 and 6 December 1924, NRO Civsec 50/2/10, for the removal of *mamurs* and promotion of chiefs. On the conservatism of the administration, see Daly, *Imperial Sudan*, pp. 29, 255. For relations between Egypt and Britain and the expulsion of Egyptians from Sudan, see Douglas H Johnson, 'Introduction', to *British Documents on the End of Empire Project*, Series B, Vol. 5, *Sudan* (London, 1998).

a memorandum rejecting dual policy and urging the division of Sudan into 'compartments' within which rural authority and tribal custom could be protected and utilised.[13] And the south was treated as a huge compartment in itself. The Closed District Ordinances of the 1920s imposed a strict system of permits on northern traders entering the southern provinces.[14] In 1930, the Civil Secretary, MacMichael, made explicit the 'southern policy' as the desired creation of 'self-contained racial or tribal units', from which the disruptive effects of education, urbanisation and politicisation would be excluded.[15]

Yet the colonial government continued to require literate and bi- or multi-lingual Sudanese to work in its administrative bureaucracy. In the southern provinces, it turned to the various Christian missionary societies to provide basic schooling in their own territorial 'spheres', a system that produced perennial tensions between missionaries and government officials over the appropriate form of education to be providing.[16] These tensions recurred also within the government itself, torn between the idea that education would 'spoil' the rural African, and its own need for literate junior employees.

The restrictions on educational provision in the south helped to maintain the value of linguistic and bureaucratic knowledge and experience, and its continued conversion into chiefship. Despite its ideal of rural tradition, the government was educating and selecting chiefs to implement an increasingly bureaucratic system of local government, which tied them to offices, schools, markets and towns. Government officials strongly encouraged the education of chiefs' sons, even though they would also become concerned that chiefs were becoming a 'petty bureaucracy' rather than a truly 'native', traditional institution.[17] Chiefs themselves often eagerly seized the opportunity of investing in the new knowledge resources, sending their own sons, nephews or dependants to the mission schools, supporting schools and teachers, and employing clerks.[18] The power of bureaucracy was becoming increasingly apparent as the first formal chiefs' courts were established and expected to keep records; by 1929, the Yei court president was chosen not because he was the 'bigger' chief, but because he was 'the only one that can read and write'.[19]

From the early 1920s, a poll tax to be paid in cash was imposed in place of any former arrangements to pay tribute in the form of livestock, grain or labour, accompanied by the production of tax registers: lists of taxpayers which chiefs

[13] Minute by John Maffey, 1 January 1927, NRO Civsec 1/39/104; *GGR* 1926, pp. 5–6.

[14] On Southern Policy see Johnson, 'Introduction' to the *British Documents on the End of Empire*; Robert O Collins, *Shadows in the Grass: Britain in the Southern Sudan, 1918–1956* (New Haven, CT, 1983), pp. 165–96, 249–66.

[15] Harold MacMichael, 'Memorandum on Southern Policy', enclosed in Civil Secretary to Southern Governors, 25 January 1930, appended in Muddathir 'Abd al-Rahim, *Imperialism and Nationalism in the Sudan: a study in constitutional and political development 1899–1956* (Oxford, 1969), pp. 244–9.

[16] See Lillian Passmore Sanderson, 'Education in the Southern Sudan: the impact of government-missionary-southern Sudanese relationships upon the development of education during the Condominium period, 1898–1956', *African Affairs* 79:315 (1980), pp. 157–69.

[17] DC Yirrol to Governor Upper Nile, 'Report on Yirrol District', 15 April 1934, NRO BGP 1/5/28.

[18] Interview 1R/K; Director of Education, 'Report on education in Southern Sudan', 1 May 1924, CMS G3 SO; Archibald Shaw, Yei, 25 July 1917, CMS Acc. 111, F4; F Finch, Yei, 5 May 1932, and Lea-Wilson, Juba, November 1923, CMS G3 AL; Deputy Governor Brock to Financial Secretary, 25 August 1928, NRO Civsec 1/39/104.

[19] James Barber, 'The moving frontier of British imperialism in northern Uganda, 1898–1919', *Uganda Journal* 29:1 (1965), p. 32; Governor Nalder, 'Mongalla Province Summary of Information', November 1933, NRO Civsec 57/35/131; Nigel Davidson, Legal Secretary, 'Note on Chief's Court at Yei', 15 May 1929, NRO Civsec 1/13/42.

had to submit to the *merkaz* each year. Bureaucratic ritual was promoted by government as a means of building authority and control much more than for its practical value, as one DC in Rumbek later admitted: 'The very fact of listing has impressed the Dinka with the strength of the chiefs' control, but there is no special advantage to Government from such an intensive system of taxation.'[20] By the mid-1930s, attempts at 'devolution' made chiefs responsible for paying their own clerks and police and keeping basic financial records. Chiefs' clerks were supposed to provide monthly reports on their tax registers, including 'deaths, deserters, returned absentees etc'.[21]

One DC in Yei even gave a bureaucratic heart to his vision of village community: 'if offices or registries are provided, the broken down tribal elements may well regroup themselves into a new and vital village life'.[22] In this area, a campaign against sleeping sickness from 1910 onwards provided the pretext for resettling the population away from streams and infected areas, and away from the Uganda border across which the disease was presumed to have travelled.[23] This also provided an opportunity to resettle people closer to 'prominent chiefs', and along newly-constructed roads, which the Yei DC claimed had 'introduced a new and companionate element into native life'.[24] But roads and villagisation were primarily a means of projecting state power into the countryside. Even in Rumbek District, sections of Agar Dinka were moved onto the Rumbek–Yirrol road after they had refused to pay taxes.[25] Well-kept roads were frequently cited by administrators as evidence of the character of a community or its chief: a visible sign of good administration, and 'essential for the development of the country'.[26]

Roads also feature prominently in oral histories, particularly in the resettlement areas like Yei. Here the roads came to define the communities settled along them, who even now refer to their villages by the nearest milepost, thus naming settlements by their distance from the town and making explicit their relationship to the nodes and arteries of the state. But a more widespread implication of the government roads was the associated burden of labour for their construction and maintenance. This labour was obtained

[20] DC Yirrol to Governor Upper Nile, 'Handing over notes, Yirrol', 3 December 1935, NRO BGP 1/5/28.

[21] E Liversidge, A/DC Yei, to Governor Equatoria, 28 October 1938, NRO EP 2/2/8.

[22] Christopher Tracey, 'Note on Native Administration, Yei District, Equatoria', 15 February 1939, NRO EP 2/2/8.

[23] Heather Bell, *Frontiers of Medicine in the Anglo-Egyptian Sudan, 1899–1940* (Oxford, 1999); PM Dove, 'Report on a tour through the Kakwa and Kaliko country', *SIR* 205, August 1911, App. A, pp. 8–9; *SIR* 209, December 1911, p. 5, TNA WO 106/6224; Sleeping Sickness Annual Report 1923–4, NRO MP 1/6/39; Yei District Monthly Diary, February 1945, NRO EP 2/24/87. For details of the villagisation and isolation measures see Hodnebo, *Cattle and Flies*, pp. 94–9.

[24] Christopher Tracey, 'Note on Native Administration, Yei District, Equatoria', 15 February 1939, NRO EP 2/2/8; Yei District Annual Report 1939, NRO EP 2/26/94; Leonard F Nalder, *Equatorial Province Handbook*, Vol. 1 *Mongalla* (Khartoum, 1936), p. 51; Spence to his mother, Yei, 15 December 1914 and 31 December 1914, Shetland Archive Lerwick D12/203/2 and D12/200/8; Principal Medical Officer to Civil Secretary, 28 August 1927, NRO Civsec 44/10/44.

[25] Rumbek District Monthly Report, April 1937, SRO EP 57.D.10; JD Tothill, 'Report, 1940', NRO EP 2/3/10.

[26] Moru District Annual Report 1939, NRO EP 2/26/94; Governor Mongalla to Financial Secretary and Civil Secretary, 'Report on the economic situation and possible developments of Mongalla Province', 27 March 1925, NRO EP 2/23/86. For a striking illustration of the new settlement pattern along the roads by c. 1930, see Map 4 in Hodnebo, *Cattle and Flies*, p. 98. For similar villagisation on new roads in Cameroon, see Geschiere, 'Chiefs and colonial rule', p. 153.

through the chiefs, so much that chiefship was even held by some people to have originated with the road-building:

> These first chiefs came as a result of opening of roads... So people were asked to move and settle along the roads, and then they were given assignments of building the roads. So there used to be road camps... and then in that time the British were able to pick some of the reasonable people there and give them this assignment of having control over the area. So that thing became the beginning of chieftaincy.[27]

Many people recalled the extent of coercion in the systems of road construction and maintenance, coercion that was channelled through the hierarchy of chiefs, sub-chiefs and headmen: 'I remember once the sub-chief was given fifteen strokes because he had not been forceful enough in forcing people to go out and clean the roads.' Chiefs gave out sticks representing the number of labourers required from each headman for road construction; if anyone refused, his goats would be seized and he would be lashed and forced to work for seven days.[28]

The roads were also opening the way for the introduction of further demands on labour, whether for other government construction projects or, in Equatoria, for new cash crops, particularly cotton. By 1927, side roads had been constructed in Yei District to all the villages not already relocated to the main roads, to enable lorries to collect cotton, ensuring that 'a very large part of the population of the district is within easy reach by car'.[29] Chiefs were expected to enforce the cultivation of cash crops and payment of poll tax with the proceeds. Only 'considerable administrative pressure' could persuade people to grow cotton, especially when prices dropped from 1932.[30]

The relationship between tax collection and cash crops ensured that chiefs shared something of administrators' motives for promoting the crops, since they were invariably blamed for failure to produce sufficient cash for taxation. Chiefs began to receive salaries from 1930, while sub-chiefs and headmen were entitled to a percentage of the taxes they collected.[31] But salaries were also linked to the number of taxpayers in a chiefdom. In Moru District, compulsory cotton cultivation was abandoned in 1937, but 'many cultivators did not realise they need not sow cotton and in some cases the chiefs forced them to do so, to facilitate head tax collection, for deficiency in which the chief is blamed'.[32] By 1939, reports conceded that cash crops had largely been a failure, and that cotton was seen as simply another form of government 'forced labour', 'grown purely for the hakuma and not for themselves, since in bad years at least it does little more than pay the poll-tax'.[33]

The chiefs were obviously benefiting from their middleman position in tax and labour exchanges. In the 1930s it was reported that they frequently

27 Interview 4R/K.

28 Interview 3R/K.

29 Report on CMS educational work in the southern Sudan, 3 August 1927, CMS G3SO 1912–19.

30 Governor Nalder, 'Mongalla Province Summary of Information', November 1933, NRO Civsec 57/35/131; Equatoria Province Monthly Diary, January–April, September 1937, NRO Civsec 57/4/17.

31 Governor Nalder to DCs and Civil Secretary, 'The future of Native Administration in Mongalla', 5 February 1935, NRO Civsec 1/39/105.

32 JG Myers, 'Provisional Report of the Economic Botanist on Yei, Meridi, Yambio districts', 1939, NRO Civsec 1/5/11.

33 Yei and Moru District Annual Reports 1939, NRO EP 2/26/94. Cf. Johnson, *Nuer Prophets*, p. 268.

covered tax deficits by foregoing the 5 per cent remuneration to which they were entitled, and then recovering it in 'kind' later from defaulters, raising British concern that this could lead to 'oppression'.[34] When coffee and other crops were introduced in some areas, it was reported that only the chiefs and headmen were making a profit, because only they could afford to employ labour.[35] Prison labour was also often used by the chief for either government works or his own cultivations: 'People could be ordered to dig the chief's garden for months, or build houses.'[36] A visitor to Yei District in the late 1940s would report that Chief Modi was receiving an annual government grant of 'about ten times as much as most of his subjects ever saw in a year'. The same chief jealously sought to maintain control over labour, and reportedly resorted to 'sabotaging' the labour lines of the Haggar coffee firm, 'because he fears that he will lose their services on road maintenance'.[37]

Yet just as government officials sought to justify road-building and resettlement on the grounds that they were restoring proper village life, so they sought, particularly in the early years, to justify and enforce chiefs' control of labour by reference to 'custom'. The early chiefs' court regulations in the 1920s emphasised the customary authority and rights of chiefs, including to a tusk or leg of hunted game, and to demand labour in the chief's cultivation 'to enable him to entertain guests'; '[a]ll men under a chief are to be entirely under his control'.[38] In 1924 the proceedings of the Amadi court reported that more than a third of cases related to 'tribal discipline', including refusals to perform labour or pay tax.[39]

Chiefs themselves may have sought to use 'custom' to control labour. One Anglican missionary, Whitehead, was told of a past Bari 'class' system, 'before the coming of the Turk or the European', in which servile groups, the *'dupi*, were bound to chiefs, providing labour and other service in return for the payment of their bridewealth by the chief. But the new potential to earn cash and convert it into bridewealth was undermining this basis of patrimonialism by giving former clients independent means of marrying. Whitehead suggested that Bari chiefs were therefore trying to enforce labour obligations solely through historical and genealogical claims: 'My children, although I have not assisted you in marriage, you will work for me because you are the *'dupi* of my grandfather.'[40] This was exactly the discourse that tended to win the sympathy of colonial officials, who sought to ensure that descent-based status should be the basis for chiefship: 'the respect is really due to the office because certain families by tradition are alone eligible for the office'.[41]

[34] 'Central District Information Book', 1939–40, NRO JD 1/1/5; Moru District Annual Report 1944, NRO EP 2/27/97.

[35] Christopher Tracey, 'Note on Native Administration, Yei District, Equatoria', 15 February 1939, NRO EP 2/2/8; extract from Yei District Annual Report 1940, and Governor Equatoria to DC Yei, 16 August 1939, NRO EP 2/5/18; Yei and Moru District Annual Reports 1939, NRO EP 2/26/94.

[36] Interviews 7N/YC; 1R/K; 2aR/K; 6R/K; 6N/YC.

[37] Michael Langley, *No Woman's Country: travels in the Anglo-Egyptian Sudan* (London, 1950), p. 81; Yei District Monthly Diary, January 1942, NRO EP 2/24/87.

[38] DC Maynard, Opari-Yei District, to Governor, 'Lukiko regulations', 2 January 1924, NRO MP 1/1/2; Mamour Mongalla, 'Bari-Mandaris Habits and Laws of Legislation together with adopted rules for Mongalla district chiefs court', 11 September 1924, NRO MP 1/1/2.

[39] Anonymous, 'Amadi District Notes on Chiefs Courts', 1924, NRO MP 1/1/2. Cf. Martin Chanock, *Law, Custom and Social Order: the colonial experience in Malawi and Zambia* (Portsmouth, NH, 1998), esp. pp. 113–23.

[40] GO Whitehead, 'Social change among the Bari', *Sudan Notes and Records* 12:1 (1929), p. 95.

[41] 'Note by Mr Parr for DC's meeting, Tonj', Juba, 21 March 1942, NRO BGP 1/5/28.

Such colonial ideology has led scholars to argue that Indirect Rule elsewhere in Africa entrenched social and lineage status as the basis for access to resources, particularly land, prompting ongoing debates over status and identity.[42] But land produced less conspicuous struggles in southern Sudan than did the requisition and partial commoditisation of labour, crops and livestock. This is at least in part because chiefs here rarely succeeded in asserting rights to the control of land or people on the basis of their own status in patrilineal structures. By the 1930s, even colonial administrators would become aware of chiefs' limited or contested claims to the kind of descent-based status that they assumed would define 'customary' access to resources.

FROM CUSTOM TO CONTRACT? NEW FRONTIERS OF LABOUR AND LEARNING

In the 1930s, custom was increasingly invoked to oppose chiefs as much as to justify their control of labour. By 1939, British officials were admitting that government demands for labour and for cash taxes had gone beyond any customary 'duty' that people might have performed for their chiefs.[43] At the same time, the colonial government suddenly became aware of alternative geographies than those it had constructed, and of communities and authorities other than its Native Administration units. In the midst of an extensive 'tribal survey' of Mongalla Province in the mid-1930s, Governor Nalder declared the vital and underlying importance of the real customary units: the 'clans'. This partly resulted from wider colonial concern that poll tax and resulting wage labour were having an individualising impact on African society.[44] But the increasing government receptiveness to the possibility of allegiances other than to the chiefs also opened up new areas of discourse on the ground in southern Sudan, as senior men seized the opportunity to articulate multiple claims to authority and status, often in opposition to the chiefs. Administrators therefore increasingly claimed that chiefship had been a foreign innovation, and that their predecessors had often appointed 'some complete nobody' or 'ingratiatory busybody'.[45] Clearly 'status' was increasingly invoked to diminish and contest chiefly authority, by depicting chiefs as junior in the structures of lineage and clan. At the same time, new ideas of contractual rights were being acquired on the expanding frontiers of labour commoditisation.

Having identified 'the extreme importance' of 'clans', Nalder promoted new administrative policies that would be continued after his departure across the new Equatoria Province created in 1936 (an amalgamation of the former Mongalla and Bahr el Ghazal provinces).[46] The poll tax was abolished in favour of a collective tribute payment.[47] The tribute was supposed to be allocated and

[42] Berry, *No Condition is Permanent*, pp. 16–41. Land is discussed below in Chapter 5.

[43] Christopher Tracey, 'Note on Native Administration, Yei District, Equatoria', 15 February 1939, NRO EP 2/2/8.

[44] Equatoria Province Annual Reports 1937, NRO Civsec 57/24/99, and 1938, NRO Civsec 57/25/103.

[45] LF Nalder (ed.), *A Tribal Survey of Mongalla Province, by members of the Province staff and Church Missionary Society* (London, 1937), p. 22.

[46] Governor Nalder, 'Mongalla Province Summary of Information', November 1933, NRO Civsec 57/35/131.

[47] Governor Nalder to DCs and Civil Secretary, 'The future of Native Administration in Mongalla', 5 February 1935, NRO Civsec 1/39/105; and 'Mongalla Province Summary of Information', NRO Civsec 57/35/131.

collected by the clan and lineage heads according to wealth and age within the group; the intention was to encourage a sense of 'corporate responsibility'.[48] Cash-crop cultivation was also promoted on a family or 'clan' basis: Nalder asserted that historically there had been 'no individual wealth' in the province, and he promoted the use of clans as economic units.[49]

But the new emphasis on clans swiftly mired administrators in greater confusion and uncertainty than ever, exacerbated by the tendency for vernacular languages to use the same word for different levels or sizes of social or kinship grouping.[50] Clans, it emerged, were defined by exogamy, by descent from a common founding father or migration leader, and often by totems and other ritual prohibitions or spiritual functions. But in many areas clan members were extremely dispersed, including among different tribes.[51] The new policy therefore led to further resettlement campaigns to try to turn clans into co-residential units, as a CMS missionary in Kajo Keji reported:

> Then came an experimentation in taxation when the old poll-tax discs were called in and the natives assessed by clans. This reshuffling of the clans meant that numbers of people had to move and make new homes. Those who had not moved after several warnings had their huts burned down.[52]

By 1939 the Yei DC was reporting difficulties: '[t]he collective idea has not yet been revived'.[53] Ten years later a meeting of DCs in Juba would reveal that while in theory taxation took the form of a family or clan tribute payment, in reality it had continued to be collected as an individual or household poll tax.[54] Attempts to introduce communal cultivation were similarly unpopular; people complained 'that some work hard and some don't'.[55] One Yei DC bluntly contradicted Nalder: 'These agricultural tribes have no communal property'.[56] In cattle-keeping areas there was also resistance to collective tribute. At the 1940 Appeal Court and chiefs' meeting in Rumbek District, there was 'a unanimous desire that the principle of individual tax should not be changed for the imposition of a lump sum'.[57] As Lienhardt would later emphasise, among the Dinka 'it is only in special situations unrelated to official requirements that the lineage is a corporate group, and the clan is never a corporate group'.[58]

Despite the new emphasis on descent groups, in reality the system of chiefs, sub-chiefs and headmen therefore remained the primary, pragmatic means of

48 'Central District Information Book', NRO JD 1/1/5; Governor Parr, 'Note circulated to DCs on 20 December 1938 on Taxation', NRO EP 2/2/8.

49 Governor Nalder to DCs and Civil Secretary, 'The future of Native Administration in Mongalla', 5 February 1935, NRO Civsec 1/39/105; and 'Mongalla Province Summary of Information', November 1933, NRO Civsec 57/35/131.

50 Cf. Justin Willis, 'Clan and history in western Uganda: a new perspective on the origins of pastoral dominance', *International Journal of African Historical Studies* 30:3 (1997), pp. 583–600.

51 THB Mynors, 'Notes on the Moru Tribe', 1935, SAD 777/3/1–40.

52 FJ Finch, Annual Letter, Kajo Kaji, 10 July 1935, CMS G3 AL.

53 Yei District Annual Report 1939, NRO EP 2/26/94.

54 Meeting of DCs, Juba, 5–7 December 1949, SRO MD 32.A.1.

55 Juba and Yei District Annual Reports 1939, NRO EP 2/26/94.

56 Logan Gray, DC Yei, to Governor Equatoria, 22 June 1938, NRO EP 2/2/8; Governor Parr, 'Note circulated to DCs on 20 December 1938 on Taxation', NRO EP 2/2/8.

57 Rumbek District Monthly Report, January 1940, SRO EP 57.D.10.

58 Godfrey Lienhardt, 'Dinka clans, tribes and tribal sections', in AC Beaton, *Equatoria Province Handbook*, Vol. 2 (Khartoum, 1949), pp. 45–7; Lienhardt, 'The Sudan', p. 29; also Mawson, 'The Triumph of Life', p. 46.

extracting labour and taxes and enforcing cultivation and road maintenance. But by the end of the 1930s, 'custom' could no longer be so easily invoked to justify chiefly control of labour. In 1939, the Yei DC produced a damning indictment of the extent of unpaid labour that had been obtained through the chiefs, who had to force their people to perform government services which 'they do not consider a duty but an impost' and which were 'performed by the recalcitrant at the additional cost of beatings and imprisonment'. The chief 'inevitably has to appear as a government employee and against his own side'.[59] The DC's lengthy criticism was dismissed as an exaggeration by the Province Governor. But the labour burden would only intensify during the Second World War years, as Juba became an important base on the military supply route from the Congo to Cairo. The resulting forced requisition of cattle, grain and labour across the region was deeply unpopular, and 'undermined' and 'strained the authority of chiefs severely', leading to violent resistance on occasion. Not surprisingly, the chiefs were said to be 'constantly trying to persuade one to use govt police for unpopular work which is properly the lot of their own police'.[60]

By the later 1930s, colonial officials had also become concerned at the extent of labour migration by young men to the towns or to the plantations of southern Uganda, despite having deliberately encouraged such pursuit of money earnings by imposing a cash tax. In one part of Yei District, a survey of labour in 1941 suggested that 47 per cent of adult men were employed away from their villages.[61] More than one DC blamed labour migration on government requisition of unpaid labour: 'its effect was to teach the people that it paid handsomely to be truculent and as far away as possible'.[62] One pointed out that migration enabled men to convert their own labour into 'drink and clothes', rather than having it exacted from them: 'Those who remain at home are alone available for the Chief's governmental demands.'[63]

The family-based taxation was supposed to ensure that the wages of migrant labourers would be brought back to their districts to pay taxes. But this transformed rights in people into a tax burden, and generated new tension as family and clan heads tried to avoid paying tax on behalf of absent labourers.[64] Such developments seemed to confirm the fears of colonial officials that labour migration would erode family and tribal ties. They also reported increasing complaints among chiefs that young men preferred to seek waged labour than to fulfil their obligations to assist in household cultivation or their labour duties to in-laws; Yei chiefs lamented the general decline in 'parental discipline and boys manners'.[65] Chiefs also defended rising bridewealth demands by arguing

59 Christopher Tracey, 'Note on Native Administration, Yei District, Equatoria', 15 February 1939, NRO EP 2/2/8.

60 Lakes District Handbook 1940, SRO EP 1.G.2; Lakes District Annual Reports 1944–5, Moru District Annual Report 1944, Juba District Annual Report 1945, all NRO EP 2/27/97–8; Equatoria Province Annual Report 1946, NRO Dakhlia 57/10/32; Equatoria Province Monthly Diary, August 1940, NRO Civsec 57/12/46; Yei District Monthly Diary, June 1943, NRO EP 2/24/87; Rumbek District Monthly Report, April 1941, SRO EP 57.D.10; DA Penn, A/DC Juba, cited in Beaton, *Equatoria Province Handbook* Vol. 2, p. 27.

61 Equatoria Province Monthly Diaries, August–October 1941, NRO Civsec 57/14/53.

62 Moru District Annual Report 1944, and Juba District Annual Report 1945, both NRO EP 2/27/97–8; Yei District Annual Report 1939, NRO EP 2/26/94.

63 Christopher Tracey, 'Note on Native Administration, Yei District, Equatoria', 15 February 1939, NRO EP 2/2/8; Conrad C Reining, *The Zande Scheme, an anthropological case study of economic development in Africa*. Evanston, IL, p. 28.

64 Logan Gray, DC Yei, to Governor Equatoria, 22 June 1938; Governor Parr, 'Note circulated to DCs on 20 December 1938 on Taxation', both NRO EP 2/2/8.

65 Yei District Monthly Diary, March 1945, NRO EP 2/24/87.

that 'parents-in-law expect their sons-in-law to work in their cultivations, and that if they are in work elsewhere must demand a higher bride price to compensate for the loss of their service'.[66]

Young men on the other hand were clearly trying to retain control of their own labour, particularly if they had been to school. School appealed more to boys and young men lacking other means to marry or acquire property, than to those who would inherit wealth and property in the form of cattle. Around Rumbek administrators and missionaries alike reported that boys who came to the mission schools tended to be 'from the lower strata of society', orphans and the poor, and therefore lacking sufficient cattle to marry; the hope of waged employment thus offered an alternative avenue to income and status. 'The antagonism of most Dinka to education has resulted in a preponderance of low grade pupils with a bad home background.'[67] According to one missionary, schoolboys refused to perform manual labour and 'throw in their lot' at home; instead they would 'naturally drift towards the town... wandering around, waiting, talking, hoping and perhaps agitating'.[68]

The frequent complaints by colonial officials and chiefs that schooling made boys too arrogant to undertake physical labour are indicative of the way that the experiences and knowledge gained through the mission schools might empower young men to resist demands on their labour. The experiences and indeed frustrations of the young men who sought or entered waged employment in the towns or across the border would produce important new means of arguing labour relations, not merely with their own relatives, but also with chiefs and government. Labour migration should not be understood in purely economic terms: people also migrated to new frontiers, as ever, in search of knowledge, experiences and skills: 'Juba was the place to be employed and the centre of knowledge: the place to learn Arabic and English.'[69] A British missionary in Yei claimed that young men were being attracted to Uganda not only by the demand for cash taxes, but also by 'a spirit of adventure' and the attraction of new places; another claimed that 'Uganda seems to be the "Promised Land"'.[70] Colonial officials and missionaries would deprecate the migrants' waste of their limited income on clothes and alcohol, but these men were displaying their acquisition of knowledge on the frontier just as nineteenth century chiefs and brokers had worn cloth to exhibit their relations with the traders. As Larick writes of the Kenyan Lokop, it was generally the young warrior class who acquired 'the foreign material evidence for worldliness' through rustling or warfare, and later through colonial armies, education and urban employment.[71]

One of the most important knowledge resources that money-earners were gaining was the language of contract. By the 1940s such language was being deployed to contest the coercion of unpaid labour. As the critical Yei DC put it,

[66] Equatoria Province Monthly Diary, April 1946, NRO Dakhlia 57/2/5.

[67] Lakes District Annual Report 1945, NRO EP 2/27/98; DC Yirrol to Governor Upper Nile, 'Handing over notes, Yirrol', 3 December 1935, NRO BGP 1/5/28. One elderly Bari man near Juba recalled his father removing him from school because he needed him to care for large cattle herds, while another came to Juba because he was poor and needed to earn cattle for his bride-wealth: Interviews 50R/JC; 51R/JC.

[68] LWC Sharland, Rumbek Annual Letters, 10 August 1953 and 11 September 1954, SAD 865/2/1–52.

[69] Interview 8N/JC.

[70] ABH Riley, 'Yei', reprinted from *Diocesan Review*, August 1938, CMS G3 AL 1935–9.

[71] Roy Larick, 'Warriors and blacksmiths: mediating ethnicity in East African spears', *Journal of Anthropological Archaeology* 10 (1991), p. 309. See also Leopold, *Inside West Nile*, p. 77; Reining, *The Zande Scheme*, p. 28.

it was not 'surprising that since they have been purposely taught that personal labour is a commodity, they should shirk the imposition and exaction of such labour unremunerated'.[72] As their power over clients diminished, according to Whitehead, chiefs had to provide more immediate reward for labour such as beer and food, or even payments of livestock.[73] By the 1950s, agricultural work parties were beginning to be hired and paid in cash by those who could afford it, such as government employees, and of course chiefs.[74] In 1948, the Moru were reported to refuse 'point blank' to work on dispensary buildings without payment, and a few years later the district authorities agreed 'that compulsory labour should give place to voluntary labour, and that an increase in wages should act as an incentive to this end'.[75] Labour strikes also spread, particularly in the 1940s.[76]

It was not only waged labour that took people to the urban frontier; women in particular were also making money through the sale of alcohol or crops in the towns. According to population estimates for Wau town in 1935, a male taxpaying population of 1,900 was swelled to an estimated 7,000 by 'Dinka women'.[77] The most lucrative activity in the towns was alcohol production and sale, and these were predominantly female occupations.[78] Women were the main traders in Rumbek, not only in alcohol in the town itself, but also in bringing produce like grain and sesame for sale in the market. There is evidence that women too were seeking to contract with government. During a food shortage in Rumbek in 1937, the government ordered famine reserves of grain to be distributed through the chiefs to those most in need. But 'several hundred women all bearing empty gourds and receptacles besieged Rumbek' to demand grain directly from the government. They were said to be from 'the heavy population in the immediate vicinity of Rumbek'.[79] These women living in the vicinity of the town were already operating on the urban frontier; such people were also the most likely to make claims on government.

But the history of this period is not simply one of a shift from status to contract as the means of controlling labour or dealing with government. Status and contract had always co-existed, interacted and competed as idioms in which to claim rights to people, property and protection. Chiefs deployed both idioms to assert their right to command labour for government purposes and personal profit, and both idioms were also used against chiefs. As Mading Deng writes of the Ngok Dinka, the word *kany*, 'which may be translated as "debt" or "claim", covers just about all obligations, contractual or reciprocal'.[80] While the commoditisation of labour did produce important shifts towards contractual relations, money-earners nearly always sought to convert monetary value and

[72] Christopher Tracey, 'Note on Native Administration, Yei District, Equatoria', 15 February 1939, NRO EP 2/2/8.

[73] GO Whitehead, 'Crops and cattle among the Bari and Bari-Speaking tribes', *Sudan Notes and Records* 43 (1962), p. 135.

[74] Interview 7R/K.

[75] Equatoria Province Monthly Diary, April 1948 and June 1949, NRO Dakhlia 57/5/13; and April 1952, NRO Civsec2 30/3/6.

[76] Equatoria Province Monthly Diary, February and April 1948, NRO Dakhlia 57/5/13.

[77] Report on Bahr el Ghazal Province, enclosed in Governor Ingleson to Civil Secretary, 14 May 1935, Appendix Z: notes on districts, NRO UNP 1/4/22.

[78] Cf. TFG Carless, 'Malakal Town', in Johnson, *Upper Nile Province Handbook*, pp. 319–20.

[79] Rumbek District Monthly Reports, January and July 1937, SRO EP 57.D.10.

[80] Francis Mading Deng, *Tradition and Modernization: a challenge for law among the Dinka of the Sudan* (New Haven, CT, 1971), p. 103.

valuable knowledge into social status, as we shall see below.[81] Commoditisation did not therefore erode or replace existing value regimes and moral economies. But it did produce debates and disputes over how to make these conversions, and it was into these struggles that the chiefs were able to insert themselves as continuing brokers between forms of value.

CHIEFLY BROKERAGE AND THE BENEFITS OF BUREAUCRACY

As Peterson argues, colonial government 'most often worked through routine' and 'predictable forms', stereotyping and categorising Africans through registers, identity cards or court records: 'For Africans, the bureaucratic form of power was at once a structure constraining the possible range of action and an opportunity for novel forms of discourse.'[82] Unlike in Tanganyika, where Giblin argues that family provided a refuge from the bureaucratic regulations of the labour market,[83] in southern Sudan people saw in government ideals of bureaucratic regulation the potential variously to resist or regularise the demands upon their labour from government, patrons and relatives; to convert labour into cash; and to acquire and protect their property. The most successful chiefs claimed to be negotiating new regulatory orders that would similarly protect labour and property.

Chiefs' success in this period continued to rely upon their skills of brokerage and know-how. This was epitomised by the chief of Lyria, Lolik Lado. In 1934, the DC had removed the ruling rain chief of Lyria and appointed the illiterate Lolik as chief, largely on the basis of his 'efficiency' as headman of neighbouring Langabu. According to Lolik himself, his appointment was secured by public flogging of the sub-chiefs and any objectors.[84] Government officials made no attempt to conceal this outright imposition, and by 1936 Lolik had become their model chief: 'A Government Chief! And a very great success in every way – Liria and Luluba are now excellently ruled. Since September [Lolik] rationed and paid 300 men monthly, who have been at work on the road, to everyone's entire satisfaction.'[85] Lolik continued to be handed funds with which to pay and provision the road gangs and was also praised for the rapid expansion of cash-crop cultivation in Lyria, including cotton. He began to deal directly with the Sudan Defence Force garrisoned in Juba during the Second World War to purchase their grain requirements. His role as broker was soon recognised by private traders, who handed him money with which to purchase ground-nuts and grain. By 1941 he was handling relatively vast sums of money:

> Some £1200 passed through his hand during the year. He is trusted by the District Commissioners, his people and merchants (the latter's trust is I think a very high tribute). He again purchased groundnuts (20 tons) for the army without supervision. He has done some quite remarkable road work in the Lulubo Hills, without technical or other assistance, and has shown himself a natural road engineer.[86]

[81] Cf. Derek R Peterson, *Creative Writing: translation, bookkeeping, and the work of imagination in colonial Kenya* (Portsmouth, NH, 2004), p. 17.

[82] Peterson, 'Morality plays', para. 9.

[83] Giblin, *A History of the Excluded*, pp. 107–37.

[84] Simonse, *Kings of Disaster*, pp. 135–6.

[85] RC Cooke, entry in Mongalla Province Chiefs Register, December 1936, NRO JD 1/1/2.

[86] Entry in Mongalla Province Chiefs Register, 1941, NRO JD 1/1/2.

Fig. 3.1 Chiefs (centre, in colonial uniforms) and teachers at a Church Missionary Society out-school, Rokon, Equatoria, c. 1939–41. (Reproduced by permission of Durham University Library SAD.787/3/260)

It is easy to see the parallels between Chief Lolik and the nineteenth-century 'chiefs' who were essentially trading agents and suppliers for the *zara'ib*. As government 'agents', the chiefs continued to benefit from brokering economic negotiations and bargains between government and people, including the ongoing ivory trade; hunters had to give one tusk (or the proceeds from its sale) of each elephant to their chief. Chiefs were frequently reported to be trading crops like coffee and sesame, or investing money, with the small number of town merchants, with varying degrees of government approval. Chiefs were also reported to be acting as 'bankers' in the rural areas as people began to earn little bits of cash. And by the 1940s chiefs were requesting that markets be 'laid out' at their own village centres.[87]

The close links of chiefs to the emerging cash economy and the urban frontier were particularly apparent around the expanding provincial capital of Juba. Following his successful imposition of Chief Lolik in Lyria, the Juba DC, Cooke, embarked on a determined effort to install a new generation of

87 Yei District Monthly Diary, March–April 1945, NRO EP 2/24/87; Rumbek District Monthly Reports, January and March 1937, SRO EP 57.D.10; DC Lakes to Governor, 30 September 1940, NRO EP 2/35/128; Equatoria Province Monthly Diaries, December 1948 and January 1949, NRO Dakhlia 57/5/13.

mission-educated chiefs in the district (*Fig. 3.1*). Not surprisingly, 'Captain Cooke' remains a prominent figure in oral histories:

> Cooke wanted educated people for taxes, [to keep] the registers. The graduates from the schools became teachers, road foremen, junior clerks, storekeepers and so on. Cooke revolutionised the chieftaincy by bringing them as chiefs. It was a struggle, because chiefs did not decide matters on their own but by councils of elders: the notables and family of the chief... So there were a lot of problems, but in Tokiman there were less problems.[88]

The chiefdom of Tokiman was a large territory within which Juba town itself was located. Its people had experienced 'long contact with the government and its ways'. This was reflected in the history of its chiefship, from 'Abu Kuka' (Laku Rondiang), a trading agent for the Aqqad firm in the nineteenth century, to his Muslim, Arabic-speaking nephew Boreng, or Ibrahim, who had been taken to Khartoum by the Mahdists in the 1890s. Boreng's son Gaddum Ibrahim succeeded in around 1910, and was described as an 'autocrat', concurring with the local memories of him expressed by the elderly interviewee at the beginning of this chapter. He was succeeded briefly in the 1930s by his brother, Lako Boreng, who cemented the close connections of this chiefship to the new town of Juba, including running the Juba ferry, 'one of his perquisites'.[89]

On Lako's death in 1936, his younger half-brother, Severino Swaka Boreng was appointed as chief. Severino learned to speak and write Arabic in the Mongalla *malakiya* school, before going on to learn English and take his Catholic name in the Rejaf West mission school. He was employed as a medical clerk in the 1930s when he was appointed chief.[90] Chief Severino maintained his *malakiya* connections and in 1945 he was appointed as 'the chief of Juba Town Native Lodging Area', with responsibility among other things for ensuring that all local produce was brought to the central town market.[91] He was in turn succeeded in the 1950s by another mission-educated young man, Andarea Farajalla, who had previously worked as a clerk or foreman for the government road construction gangs.[92] Andarea too acted as the unofficial chief of Juba town as well as of rural Tokiman. He had a butchers' license in the town and represented the *malakiya* on the town council.[93] By the late 1950s he was reported to be living permanently in the town, collecting poll tax and rates in Juba for the Juba Town Council, and working as president of the Juba Town Court.[94]

The chiefdom of Tokiman was unusual in its long history of relations with foreign traders and governments and in its proximity to the expanding provincial capital of Juba. But it exemplifies wider patterns, as the more entrepreneurial chiefs established themselves as powerful brokers in the intersecting economies of town and village, as well as in the coercive exchanges between government and people. There were obvious profits to be gained from

88 Interview 9N/JC.

89 HRP Harrison, A/DC Central District, to Governor Equatoria, Juba, 19 September 1936, SRO EP 66.D.8.

90 HRP Harrison, A/DC Central District, to Senior Medical Inspector Equatoria, 16 September 1936, NRO Dakhlia3 1/6/32.

91 Juba Town Council minutes, 9 May 1945, SRO EP 100.C.2.D.

92 Interview 10N/JC.

93 Juba Town Council minutes, 30 October 1951, SRO EP 100.C.2.D; Juba Town Council Executive Officer Sir El Khatim Hassan Taha to Governor, 25 July 1958, SRO EP 100.L.1.

94 Assistant Governor Clement Mboro to Governor Equatoria, 30 April 1957, SRO EP 66.D.8.

such a role. But their position also made chiefs a potential lever by which people might seek to obtain better terms for their exchanges with government.

In particular, people were seeking to protect their property. It is apparent from both records and recollections of the colonial period that the ultimate threat employed by government – and often chiefs – to compel the payment of tax was the seizure of property, notably in the form of livestock. People sought to avert this through multiple strategies, including the sale of their labour or crops, and even of livestock, as preferable to its arbitrary seizure. The principle motivation to pay the cash poll tax and to undertake unpaid labour must have been simply to avoid worse losses. Even as early as 1907, the government reported eager acceptance of a cash tribute payment in place of the cattle tribute:

> Dinkas in particular are anxious to collect any money they can so as to avoid paying away their bulls... There has also been more energy put into the preparation of ground for cultivation, at any rate near the stations, and by some of the more intelligent Dinka Sheikhs. These latter wish for grain for the same reason as they desire money – i.e., to save their cattle.[95]

As government demands became more institutionalised and regularised, people tried to work out their own strategies to meet them. If and when cash crops earned sufficient returns, people cultivated them. When cotton prices were high they were naturally more enthusiastic about the crop.[96] Some new crops were eagerly adopted; for example in Yei District, cassava and sweet potatoes were being widely grown by 1940.[97] When a free grain market was introduced in 1949, removing the low prices previously fixed by government, growers responded to the higher prices by producing more surplus for sale.[98] But there was resistance to crops and practices that did not provide sufficient returns. When cotton prices fell, the Bari were reported to be abandoning their cotton plots in favour of work in Juba, while the Kuku in Kajo Keji migrated to work in Uganda.[99] In central Africa, Vaughan suggests that people made a deliberate decision to channel family labour into cash crops,[100] but in Equatoria, labour migration often proved a more viable means of earning cash, together with informal trade in crops like tobacco.

Chiefs often reflected these household strategies in their negotiations with government over tax and labour, or their attempts to conceal from government lucrative illegal activities, such as poaching or trade in spirits, cannabis, ivory or weapons. Chiefs were under government pressure to report or suppress illegal commerce, but they were very often involved in it themselves or it

95 Mongalla Province Annual Report 1907, *GGR* 1907, pp. 337–8.

96 E.g. Equatoria Province Monthly Diary, May 1952, NRO Civsec2 30/3/6. See also John Tosh, 'Lango agriculture during the early colonial period: land and labour in a cash-crop economy', *Journal of African History* 19:3 (1978), pp. 415–39.

97 JD Tothill, 'Report, 1940', NRO EP 2/3/10.

98 Equatoria Province Monthly Diary, August 1949, NRO Dakhlia 57/5/13.

99 Equatoria Province Monthly Diary, August 1937, NRO Civsec 57/4/17; Yei and Moru District Annual Reports 1939, NRO EP 2/26/94.

100 Megan Vaughan, 'Food production and family labour in southern Malawi: the Shire highlands and upper Shire valley in the early colonial period', *Journal of African History* 23:3 (1982), pp. 351–64. See also Jens A Andersson, 'Administrators' knowledge and state control in colonial Zimbabwe: the invention of the rural-urban divide in Buhera District, 1912–80', *Journal of African History* 43 (2002), p. 128.

earned their 'obvious sympathy'.[101] The value of chiefly brokerage was increasingly recognised: in the Zande districts, people took the 'wise precaution' of giving gifts to their chiefs in the hope of obtaining 'protection against the administration'.[102] Chiefs' role as tax collectors placed them in a pivotal position in the conversions of livestock, produce and natural resources into money. This gave them considerable power and opportunity for profit, but it also enabled them to distribute and rebalance governmental demands on the population according to local understandings of the economy as well as to their own advantage. In 1937, the Rumbek chiefs urged the government to collect the new cash-tax immediately after the sesame harvest when people had cash from selling surplus sesame, rather than after the grain harvest in January when it forced people to sell their own grain, causing later food shortages. Similarly in 1947, the Yei chiefs protested that if tax was to be increased, then the government-fixed grain prices received by their people should also increase. Chiefs 'painted a gloomy picture' of the state of their crops to the government, leading one official to 'wonder how much some of these rather pessimistic reports have to do with government buying of surplus crops, which does not appear to be popular'. In 1950, the Juba District chiefs' meeting told the DC that people were reluctant to grow cotton because it was not profitable. One DC admitted that there may have been 'a disinclination on their [the chiefs'] part to make what might be unpopular decisions' regarding labour and taxation.[103]

Mamdani sees the coercion of labour from tax defaulters as an indicator of the despotism of the chiefs.[104] But people might resort to providing labour in order to avoid livestock or produce being taken to pay taxes instead, particularly during periods of shortage:

> Most of the road construction work is done by tribal labour recruited from indigent persons during the time of tax collection. During the years of economic stress the people were willing to work on the roads in order to raise the money for taxes.[105]

Families and sections sought to earn cash for taxes in order to avoid the extraction of more productive or vital resources. But the only way to avoid their livestock or produce being sold or confiscated, as we have seen, was to instead invest the labour of the young men, either in waged employment, in cash-crop cultivation or in working for chief or government in place of paying taxes. Chiefs even convinced administrators of the impossibility of commoditising cattle, defending instead their value as a highly individualised and socially-embedded form of property.[106] Chiefly coercion and extraction of labour and taxation was thus intertwined with the potential capacity of chiefs to ameliorate and regularise these demands, and to provide some flexibility as to how people met them.

[101] Christopher Tracey, 'Note on Native Administration, Yei District, Equatoria', 15 February 1939, NRO EP 2/2/8; Juba District Annual Report 1945, NRO EP 2/27/98; Yei District Monthly Diary, July 1942, NRO EP 2/24/87.

[102] Reining, *The Zande Scheme*, p. 37.

[103] Moru District Annual Report 1944, NRO EP 2/27/97; Equatoria Province Monthly Diaries, December 1940, NRO Civsec 57/12/46, and February and November 1948, NRO Dakhlia 57/5/13.

[104] Mamdani, *Citizen and Subject*, p. 56.

[105] DC Yirrol to Governor Upper Nile, 'Handing over notes Yirrol', 3 December 1935, NRO BGP 1/5/28. Cf. Hanson, *Landed Obligation*, p. 169.

[106] DC Yirrol to Governor Upper Nile, 'Handing over notes Yirrol', 3 December 1935, NRO BGP 1/5/28.

CONSTITUTING MORAL FRONTIERS

Far from guarding a traditional rural economy then, chiefs were very much operating on the urban frontier, or replicating its intersection with the state and market economy out in the rural areas. Yet they would also seek to maintain and police such frontiers in order to preserve their own privileged role as brokers upon them. In this they found ready support from the government, with its intense dislike of urbanisation, despite its converse promotion of money and markets. As Andersson argues of Zimbabwe, 'the rural-urban divide constituted another colonial invention of tradition, albeit a largely imaginary one'.[107] But this divide was not solely produced by the colonial state: for multiple reasons, others too would seek to draw moral distinctions between spheres of exchange and expertise that were in reality far from discrete.

The colonial government continually sought to exclude people from the towns and to demarcate the town boundaries. From the 1930s, they reported efforts to 'clean up' the towns by evicting inhabitants like the 'young men without jobs' who were said to 'haunt' towns like Juba and Meridi: 'they are a shifting community, containing many ex-Government servants, employees or dependants on the Mission, and the remainder seeking money and the excitements of town life'.[108] Officials were concerned that southern Sudan was 'full of a wandering type of undesirable, who has broken away from tribal and social control and has been unable to settle down to any decent mode of life', and that such people would corrupt surrounding populations, attracting 'the undesirable elements of the local tribes who tend to drift to the town, and thus become even further divorced from tribal control'.[109]

Migration to the towns in general was seen by government as an evasion of chiefly authority and rural social control, epitomised in their notion of urban 'detribalisation'.[110] Officials therefore sought to isolate and delimit the *malakiya* Native Lodging Areas and prevent their expansion or influence. In 1937, for example, the Rumbek District government decided to tackle the expanding urban population:

> At present the village is full of Dinka of both sexes, some already completely detribalised and others nearly so – some out of work Zande, ex soldiers and police of Wau, Raga and other southern districts. It will take some time to sort out, but the majority of the Dinka, fast becoming 'townees', will be sent outside to live their lives in their proper environment, and the 'strangers within the gate' will be reduced to a minimum and approval sought for the remainder to be repatriated to their homes.

The houses of police families and 'town loving Dinka' within a radius of one mile from Rumbek were demolished.[111] Such concentric patterns of settlement

[107] Andersson, 'Administrators' knowledge', p. 122.

[108] THB Mynors, A/DC Moru, to Governor Mongalla, Amadi, 24 January 1934, NRO EP 2/14/57; Juba District Monthly Diary, April 1938, NRO Civsec 57/7/29.

[109] DC Yirrol to Governor Upper Nile, 'Handing over notes Yirrol', 3 December 1935 NRO BGP 1/5/28.

[110] On the general government dislike of 'detribalised' natives, see Yoshiko Kurita, 'The role of "negroid but detribalized" people in modern Sudanese history', *Nilo-Ethiopian Studies* 8–9 (2003), p. 6; Arens, 'Mto wa Mbu', pp. 248–9.

[111] Rumbek District Monthly Reports, January–March 1937 and February 1940, SRO EP 57.D.10; Mawson, 'The Triumph of Life', pp. 82–3. Cf. TFG Carless, 'Malakal Town', in Johnson, *Upper Nile Province Handbook*, pp. 312–20.

around the town reveal the replication of the *zariba* patterns of the nineteenth century.

As we have seen, chiefs were also closely connected to the town economy and society, and needed their own 'town houses' to use on their regular visits to the *merkaz*. Even a chief from an area as remote from government as the far north of Rumbek District was building links to the town. Marial, the son of the long-lived warrior-chief Wol Athiang, was reported in 1937 to be 'married' to a woman beer-seller in the Rumbek *malakiya* who had twice previously been married to Egyptian soldiers and lived in Egypt and Khartoum. Chief Marial apparently found her house 'a pleasant lodging when he visited Rumbek'.[112]

Yet chiefs were often at the forefront of moral condemnation of the *malakiya*. In 1929, Kuku chiefs requested that women convicted of adultery be 'treated as a common prostitute and live in the mulikia [*malakiya*] quarters which is [*sic*] specially put aside for woman of this category at Kajo Kaji Merkaz'. The idea that the *malakiya* was a site of prostitution reinforces its distinction as a particular immoral space, and the association of towns with the commoditisation of rights in people.[113]

By the 1950s the chiefs' quarters in Juba had become potentially lucrative urban plots, to the dismay of a southern Bari chief, Andarea Gore who was 'much disturbed by "public nuisance" at night' while staying there. His written complaint to the district rural council is revealing of the role of chiefs in constructing and demarcating the urban-rural boundary:

> I learnt that some of the Tombur people build the *tukl*s [traditional houses] for hire and sale for those in need as their trading business to earn their living in Juba. The chief's quarter or plot does not mean it is entirely allotted for the chief's own purposes or for the townees of that chiefship to settle on it. NO. I repeat no.
>
> It was allotted to the chief as a responsible person in the name of the chiefship concerned. In other words, it is a 'villagers' rest house', and it belongs for the villagers when they come to town they go direct to their quarter for a day or more, then return to village where he comes from.[114]

The chiefs' quarters were supposed to be a space for the village inside the town, and as such meant only to be inhabited on a temporary basis. Yet as the appropriation of chief's quarters by the 'townees of that chiefship' suggests, chiefship as an institution was simultaneously mediating and brokering access to government and town.

Not only the chiefs, however, but many other people also had an interest at times in asserting a moral distinction between town and village, market and society, even if at other times they operated upon such frontiers or diversified their economic strategies and social relations across them. The towns of Juba, Yei and Rumbek are all depicted in oral histories as alien, immoral centres, which attracted only the destitute and criminal elements of society. As one current Bari chief explained, when the first towns were founded, 'the *malakiya* was connected with crookery and cheating; Malakiyans lied but children from the village told the truth'.[115] Another elder, also living permanently in Juba, claimed that the only Bari who came to live in the *malakiya* in colonial days were those without cattle, who came to earn money in order to marry, and

112 Rumbek District Monthly Report, January 1937, SRO EP 57.D.10.

113 RCR Whalley, A/DC Opari/Kajo Kaji, to Governor Mongalla, 'Resolutions from Kuku chiefs of Kajo Kaji Lukiko', 22 November 1929, NRO Civsec 1/39/104.

114 Chief Andarea Gore to Juba District Rural Council, Khartoum, 9 January 1958, SRO JD 38.G.2.14.

115 Interview 12N/JC.

were viewed with mistrust as potential thieves.[116] Malakiyans themselves now complain about these historical stereotypes associating their community with orphan or illegitimate origins, crime and prostitution.[117]

Such discourse was not simply the product of rural elites and gerontocracies, seeking to protect their wealth and status in existing value regimes.[118] It also reflected the very real risks and insecurities of the urban frontier. Even those who most actively sought out the opportunities of the frontier also encountered its vagaries and limitations, reminding them that investment in the enduring value of livestock, people and land remained a vital strategy. The cash economy frequently proved disappointing and limited, and the demands on wage-earners from their relatives and dependents would always outstrip their actual earnings, especially if they were supporting themselves in the towns where food prices were frequently very high: 'All merchants in Yei district report a greatly reduced turnover... It is thought that Government servants and full time labourers with families find that their pay packets will only meet the greatly increased cost of foodstuffs, and consequently little or no money is left for clothes and luxuries.'[119]

By the mid-1940s government officials were themselves complaining at the lack of goods to purchase with money: 'To say that our people don't want money is nonsense. They want goods (which is the same as wanting money) but the shops don't stock what they want.'[120] Increasingly people were buying grain with money during food shortages, but the grain trade was a highly exploitative system controlled by mainly northern Sudanese merchants who bought grain at low prices when people needed cash to pay taxes and then resold the grain to them during shortages at three times the original price.[121] Such terms of trade no doubt shaped local perceptions of market trade as inherently arbitrary. As people became more dependent on grain purchases, they were often forced to sell livestock to buy grain at the high prices prevailing in the market.[122] Despite officials' assertions of their efforts to ensure fairer prices, the formal markets remained closely connected to the government in popular perceptions: 'the Dinka are convinced that the merchants and the Government are two aspects of the same thing – and I have been twitted at public meetings for being very thick with the merchants'.[123]

Even money-earners therefore continued to invest in alternative forms of wealth and property and in the insurance of kin, social and patrimonial relations. In the Zande districts of southwest Equatoria, Reining shows that even by the 1950s, money was used only to purchase imported commodities in the shops, or for special social events and exchanges, not to buy subsistence items, the only exception being a tiny number of government employees or townspeople without access to the non-money subsistence economy, whose

116 Interview 13N/JC.

117 Interviews with Malakiyans in Khartoum and Juba, August 2008.

118 As argued by John Lonsdale in 'The moral economy of Mau Mau: wealth, poverty and civic virtue in Kikuyu political thought', in Berman and Lonsdale, *Unhappy Valley*, Vol. 2, pp. 315–504.

119 Equatoria Province Monthly Diary, October 1948, NRO Dakhlia 57.5.13.

120 Torit District Annual Report 1944, NRO EP 2/27/97.

121 Rumbek District Monthly Report, January 1937, SRO EP 57.D.10.

122 Equatoria Province Monthly Diary, July 1949, NRO Dakhlia 57.5.13; Lakes District Handbook 1940, pp. 29–30, SRO EP 1.G.2.

123 Lakes District Handbook 1940, p. 36, SRO EP 1.G.2. Cf. Giblin, 'History, imagination', pp. 194–5.

difficulties 'resulted not only in a poor diet but in a profound dissatisfaction with their rates of pay'. Governor Owen of Equatoria similarly reported the 'implacable conviction' among government employees that 'their pay is not enough for them to lead self-respecting lives free from the fear of poverty'.[124] The only solution, according to Reining, was to attach themselves to 'a homestead... sharing in its subsistence economy'. The limitations of the money economy thus underscored the need to build and maintain social relations, and one of the primary uses of money was for 'social purposes', including marriage.[125]

Unsurprisingly, studies of the colonial economy and small-town formation in southern Sudan have tended to emphasise inherent exploitation and inequality.[126] Yet, as Giblin writes of Tanzania, while colonial urban landscapes might have signalled 'a message of exclusion', some people, particularly younger men, nevertheless discerned 'a message of opportunity'.[127] The constitution of moral frontiers by multiple actors in this period did not by any means succeed in erecting effective barriers; for as many (and often the same) people were transgressing and taking advantage of urban, economic and educational frontiers, and making claims upon the state. But this did not mean that the moral distinctions were any less real, and they set up an enduring moral ambiguity around the towns and the money economy: ambiguity which also attached to the institution of chiefship itself.

CONCLUSION

Berman argues that the reliance of colonial governments on chiefly collaborators in Africa led ultimately to the instability of the colonial state: 'the chiefs compromised its authority as they undermined their own position', by abusing their control of land, labour and taxation.[128] Colonial administrators in southern Sudan were certainly mindful of this danger, and increasingly critical of their appointed chiefs. But chiefs' role in the colonial economy made them pivotal not only in the imposition of government demands, but also in the amelioration, regularisation and avoidance of those requisitions. Chiefs struggled to satisfy both government and people, and were constantly being reported as uncooperative or inactive as they employed passive resistance or sought to avoid antagonising powerful people. But even the most successful colonial chiefs, who became wealthy and powerful brokers on the urban frontier, might prove advantageous for people seeking better terms of taxation and protection of their property. Far from undermining or compromising the colonial government, chiefship was becoming institutionalised and in the process helping to constitute the local state, by brokering regulation and order in people's dealings with the state. The urban frontier was crucial in these processes, despite offering opportunities to evade or resist chiefly authority and government demands. The moral ambiguity of the frontier was both a

124 Governor TRH Owen, writing in 1947, unreferenced citation in Peter P Garretson, 'The Southern Sudan Welfare Committee and the 1947 strike in the southern Sudan', *Northeast African Studies* 8:2–3 (1986), p. 188.

125 Reining, *The Zande Scheme*, p. 91.

126 Burton, 'When the north wind'; Abdel Ghaffar M Ahmed and Mustafa Abdel Rahman, 'Small urban centres: vanguards of exploitation. Two cases from Sudan.' *Africa* 49:3 (1979), pp. 258–71.

127 Giblin, 'History, imagination', pp. 195–6.

128 Bruce Berman, 'Structure and process in the bureaucratic states of colonial Africa', in Berman and Lonsdale, *Unhappy Valley*, Vol. 1, p. 165.

product of – and a way of managing – debate and struggle over the changing economy. By condemning or questioning the values of town, money and market, people were able to protect the value of their social relations and rural property, even as they increasingly sought money and urban resources. The chiefs meanwhile distinguished urban and rural life in order to preserve their brokerage role between these moral economies and forms of value. This role was becoming institutionalised in their courts, to which we now turn.

4

Claiming rights and guarantees: chiefs' courts and state justice, c. 1900–1956

> I decided to go to school because people were looting my father's cattle, so I wanted to defend his property by becoming acquainted with the British rulers. When I told my father, he refused, so I ran away and joined the school. Later I wrote an appeal letter to the British DC about the person who was looting my father, and the DC called all the chiefs to hear the case. I made sure that my father got his right, so then he realised the value of school.[1]

This statement (in English) by a very elderly retired schoolteacher in Rumbek asserts the value of the new knowledge that might be acquired on the colonial urban and bureaucratic frontiers described in the previous chapter. His is a district where most people were reportedly reluctant to send their children to school, if they instead had cattle to look after. Yet while cattle-owning might have often kept young people away from the urban frontier and waged labour, cattle disputes would paradoxically bring many more people to the new institutional frontier of state justice. As a particularly movable, individualised and socially-embedded form of property, cattle were often the focus of multiple simultaneous claims, which may explain the frequently-observed litigiousness of Dinka and other cattle-owners.[2]

More generally across the research areas, the new colonial chiefs' courts established in the 1920s evolved into arenas for the deployment and debate of rival claims to property and persons. Colonial chiefs' courts were not then simply the instruments of chiefly and gerontocratic patriarchal dominance.[3] Instead these courts should be seen as a frontier institution, characterised by both replication and innovation, and playing an important role in negotiating the complex intersections of the cash economy with rural regimes of property and value. The courts did not play a predictable role in these intersections and conversions, but rather were potentially responsive to plural registers of moral and legal discourse emanating from government, from rural authorities and from fresh formulations and productions on the urban and bureaucratic frontiers. This plurality in turn reflected the ambiguous position of the chiefs themselves, as they too sought to convert bureaucratic knowledge and monetary earnings into status, property and progeny; to compete with other senior men; to assert individual achievement and expertise as the basis for political authority, and yet to build their own families and patrilines. The courts reflected local political orders and social hierarchies, but these were plural and competing orders, as the next chapter will also show. In southern Sudan the

1 Interview 14N/RC.

2 See also Mading Deng, *Tradition and Modernization*, pp. 102–3.

3 As argued, for example, in Chanock, *Law, Custom and Social Order*, and Mamdani, *Citizen and Subject*.

courts often became the focus of competition *between* chiefs and the senior lineage elders.[4]

But by drawing on 'state effects' and the regulatory orders of government, the courts nevertheless created an impression of unity, of a single order, backed up by the latent coercive force of the state. It is for this reason that many of my oldest informants associated the coming of government with the establishment of 'law and order', with the recognition of property rights and the enforcement of discipline, and why people generally have emphasised the 'oneness' of the law and of the judicial system, despite their obvious plurality and hybridity. This effect resulted from the need for chiefs to distance themselves from individual responsibility for their decisions and penalties; to abstract their justice by reference to state law and power. This in turn reflected enduring indigenous cultures of externalising or collectivising arbitration and sanction, with which this chapter begins. It goes on to show that many other people would also increasingly appropriate the abstract idea of state law and justice as a new resource in their own disputes. The courts upheld the principles of property rights and marriage exchanges that underlay the authority of lineage and generational seniority. Yet the courts simultaneously encouraged and enforced the value of money, literacy and government. The results were varying, contingent and contested. But nevertheless the multiple accommodations and appropriations of the chiefs' courts were at the centre of broader deals with government.

DEMAND FOR FOREIGN MEDIATION

Back in 1862, the wife of the British trader John Petherick reported a complaint brought to their boat by two Aliab Dinka women against their elderly husband, 'Shotbyl'. Shotbyl, who wore the leopard-skin of a spiritual chief, had come with his wives to greet Petherick. After he left, his wives returned to the boat to complain about him, and he then also returned to request Petherick's mediation:

> A kind of court was held on board, and the wives were first summoned, and they most positively swore that they had not food sufficient, and that their husband was harsh and cruel. The old chief sat silent; but the second chief spoke indignantly, 'It is not true; these women are bad. Look at them – do they appear starved? No, their hands are always in the dish with his; but they are weary of him and seek a divorce. They also teach their children to rebel against him.' Others gave testimony to the same effect; Petherick therefore decided that the women should at once return home. They refused to do so and threw themselves on the deck, screaming and kicking; two or three of our men lifted them up and carried them on shore, when immediately they ran off in an opposite direction to their village... The younger wife was soon caught by the friends: she seemed heartily pleased to have excited so much attention.[5]

The case is striking only in its date. The vociferous testimony of the women and the nature of their complaint could have come from a court case in 2006, suggesting that the marital obligations still argued in the courts nowadays draw upon deep historical cultures. The role of relatives as witnesses was

4 Cf. Brett Shadle, '"Changing traditions to meet current altering conditions": customary law, African courts and the rejection of codification in Kenya, 1930–60', *Journal of African History* 40 (1999), pp. 411–31, and 'Bridewealth and female consent: marriage disputes in African courts, Gusiiland, Kenya', *Journal of African History* 44 (2003), pp. 241–62.

5 Petherick and Petherick, *Travels in Central Africa*, pp. 122–3.

also an enduring practice. But most revealing of all is the way that the women appealed to Petherick as an outside arbiter, and that everyone involved then participated in constituting a formalised proceeding. This account shows a deep historicity to the more recent appropriation of aspects of formal orders in apparently informal arenas.

Evidence of well-established judicial cultures was also apparent to one of the first British colonial officers: in 1908, a detailed report was produced on Dinka laws by the Upper Nile Inspector, O'Sullivan:

> The tribal system of self-administration is by 'courts' of the 'old people' of each village or clan. These 'old people' are not elected but are held to be qualified merely by the fact of old age, as having the best knowledge of tribal traditions and customs and of the best way to direct matters and settle disputes. The Sheikh is not the judge or law-giver of his section. He is the leader of the warriors and acts as president and spokesman of his court of advisors composed of the 'old people'. The father or head of a family is treated with great respect by his people, but he refers even matters of 'family disputes' to the court of the old people... There is no leader who can give a death sentence nor order any tribal fine for any offence to be paid to him.[6]

Over the subsequent century, the great majority of disputes and problems would continue to be settled by family or neighbourhood elders. There has been a strong culture against any individual acting as a sole judge; family or community unanimity and order has been both a goal of such processes and often the only guarantor or sanction for enforcing the outcomes. In settling disputes, the elders have produced and reinforced social hierarchy and order, often using kinship as an idiom through which to establish and enforce duties, rights and obligations, and in the process ascribing pre-eminence to lineage and family structures. Colonial officials tended to be only dimly aware of such processes, which were largely kept private from the state or even from other families or communities. But however powerfully normative the 'court of the old people' might have been, it has always had its limitations. Individuals or parties in dispute might well refuse attempts to resolve or reconcile their conflict, or feel unfairly or harshly treated by the dominant elders. And what of disputes and conflicts between different family groups, villages or sections? Particularly if these led to killing, stealing or serious hurt, it was a great challenge to negotiate a peaceful outcome rather than a revenge attack and lasting feud.

There has then always been a great need for mediation and arbitration from outside the immediate community. In 1908 O'Sullivan emphasised the importance of the sanction of divine punishment (rather than any direct death penalty), and the resulting need for what he termed 'sacrifices of atonement' as well as for payments of cattle or women as compensation to offended parties. These sanctions and sacrifices ensured a significant role in serious cases of killing and conflict for 'inspired men': the spear-masters, prophets and earth or rain chiefs.[7] According to a DC of Tonj in the 1930s, the spear-master [*beny bith*] not only played a religious role in mediating with God and spirits, but 'in the past (and to a large extent today) he was the only mediator in the more

6 HDE O'Sullivan, 'Dinka laws and customs', *SIR* 162, January 1908, App. D, pp. 16, 25, TNA WO 106/231.

7 O'Sullivan, 'Dinka laws and customs', p. 16; Douglas H Johnson, 'Judicial regulation and administrative control: customary law and the Nuer, 1898–1954', *Journal of African History* 27 (1986), pp. 59–78; Mading Deng, *Tradition and Modernization*, pp. 69–93.

troublesome quarrels amongst members of his clan'.[8] The most important *beny bith* around Rumbek, Gol Mayen, continued to be recognised by the British as the source of powerful sanctions to uphold peace agreements.[9] The curse of rain chiefs in Equatoria functioned similarly; Simonse describes their role as a 'dam' or 'buffer' between hostile elements, 'initiating, facilitating and monitoring peace processes'.[10]

As this idea of a 'buffer' suggests, the spiritual role of spear-masters, prophets and rain or earth chiefs in mediation and peace-making conveyed a kind of neutral status.[11] The demand for a source of neutral mediation was also, however, directed towards foreign forces and powers. Poisoning or witchcraft accusations were brought to Egyptian officials in nineteenth century Equatoria, perhaps because such cases were considered dangerous by local authorities and it was normal to seek outside diviners or sources of protection.[12] In serious cases of killing, witchcraft or theft, it was dangerous for any individual member of a community to adjudicate or inflict penalties, since this might provoke revenge or supernatural consequences. Such cases necessitated either a collective response, such as the mob killings of rain chiefs analysed by Simonse,[13] or a means of abstracting judicial decisions through the use of oracles, spiritual sanctions or recourse to some distant, outside authority.[14]

Such indigenous judicial mechanisms would meet in creative and dynamic ways with colonial and post-colonial ideals of the bureaucratic state. Eckert argues that a scholarly emphasis on the allegedly alien nature of state law for ordinary people in, for example, India, misses the point that 'Indians often operate with precisely the notion of a modern bureaucratic state guided by universalist norms in mind', even if they also deviated from those norms.[15] But in southern Sudan, a similar appropriation of aspects of bureaucratic state norms should not be seen as simply the adoption – however creative – of Western models of the state. Rather the latter were interacting with deep indigenous principles and means of obtaining neutral, fair arbitration. It was for this reason that the outside origins of chiefs, or the marginality that their government relations and specialist knowledge engendered, were also an asset when it came to justice.

Initially, the British colonial authorities would be more likely to forcibly support one group against another than to mediate between them. But gradually the government was also beginning to meet indigenous demand for more peaceful resolution. In 1906 the British administrator in Rumbek reported

8 DC Tonj to Governor Equatoria, 'Further notes on the Beny Bith', 22 May 1937, NRO BGP 1/5/28.

9 Governor Equatoria to DCs Aweil, Jur River and Lakes, 'Record of Tonj discussions 29–31 March 1942', 24 April 1942, NRO BGP 1/5/28.

10 Simonse, *Kings of Disaster*, p. 218. On the curse of Nuer prophets, see also EE Evans-Pritchard, 'Preliminary draft of an account of the Moro', n.d., 1930s, NRO Dakhlia 112/14/95; and Johnson, 'Judicial regulation', pp. 61, 72.

11 Nuer 'leopard-skin priests' were also valued for their foreign/outside origins: EE Evans-Pritchard, *Nuer Religion* (Oxford, 1956), pp. 292–3. Similarly: Toru Komma, 'Peacemakers, prophets, chiefs and warriors: age-set antagonism as a factor of political change among the Kipsigis of Kenya', in Eisei Kurimoto and Simon Simonse (eds), *Conflict, Age & Power in North East Africa* (Oxford, 1998), pp. 193–4, 198.

12 Junker, *Travels in Africa,* Vol. 1, p. 333.

13 Simonse, *Kings of Disaster*; also Mading Deng, *Tradition and Modernization*, p. 91.

14 Cf. Fields, *Revival and Rebellion*, p. 264.

15 Julia Eckert, 'From subjects to citizens: legalism from below and the homogenisation of the legal sphere', *Journal of Legal Pluralism and Unofficial Law* 53:4 (2006), p. 66.

'innumerable cases' coming before him, resulting from the 1901 punitive expedition and subsequent famine, during which many Agar Dinka had to borrow food or exchange it for children with neighbouring groups.[16] These Agar were approaching the very forces responsible for the original devastation in order to settle the resulting debts and disputes, epitomising the paradox of relations with government. In 1911 a number of Atuot chiefs came to Rumbek to bring three individuals with cases of cattle theft against Agar: 'this is a new departure and very satisfactory, the more so as the stolen cattle were found and restored to their rightful owners'.[17] Chiefs were bringing people to government and thus brokering access to the force of the state. This role was strongly promoted by the government: 'The inhabitants are to understand that whenever they have trouble among themselves, which their sheikhs cannot settle for them according to tribal custom, they must come to the nearest Government post when they will receive assistance and their cases will be settled.'[18]

One very elderly man from the Amothnhom sub-section of the Agar Dinka around Rumbek explained his section's original accommodation with government primarily in terms of its judicial services. He emphasised the initially alien and unrecognisable nature of government, 'far away' in the town. But Awan Macot, the son of the leading spear-master in the area, 'managed to go to the town while a boy' and returned to persuade his uncles, the senior men, of the value of government:

> So they said, 'Yes, he [government] will stay here as our visitor so as to help us enjoy our property in our sandy place [Rumbek]. He will learn how we do our things and will teach us what is in the law. He will ask, "You, what has caused your dispute?" The other one will say "It is this man that has taken something of mine". He will then say, "Give back this man's thing". If you fail to be given it, he will help you and arrest the other man, because stealing is not good. Do you see then, this person has been castrated [brought under the law]? The government has managed to do it.'

One of Awan's uncles was less convinced, and cursed him for bringing such a foreign person 'with lower teeth' (the Agar extract their lower incisors). But Awan responded, 'My paternal uncles, don't curse me: you will see. The person who has no clan [the government] is also powerful like the one with the spear.' The interviewee concluded, 'It is this spear [of Awan Macot] that brought our present government... now nobody should take the property of someone else by force.'[19]

The fact that the government person lacked a clan is thus presented as a virtue; being outside any particular lineage, the government could theoretically offer neutral justice. Moreover the vivid expression that those who were forced to return stolen property had been 'castrated' is very revealing of the disciplinary power of government that is so often alluded to in local discourse, in all its ambivalence.[20] The Agar word for the government stations,

[16] HR Headlam, 'A general report and description of Eastern District, Bahr el Ghazal Province', October 1906, *SIR* 147, App. B, p. 11, TNA WO106/228. Cf. Johnson, *Nuer Prophets*, pp. 10–11.

[17] *SIR* 205, August 1911, p. 4, TNA WO 106/6224.

[18] 'Proclamation on reversion of Lado Enclave to Sudan Government', in Governor Owen to Percival, Senior Inspector Loka-Kagulu District, 1 July 1910, NRO MP 1/8/51.

[19] Interview 73R/RC.

[20] Cf. rumours that DC Fergusson intended to actually castrate all Nuer men in the 1920s, possibly resulting from a mistranslation of hernia operations in government hospitals: Johnson, *Nuer Prophets*, p. 269.

peen, reportedly connoted verbs like 'to prevent' or 'to prohibit'.[21] Another elderly headman from the same sub-section similarly said that the coming of government had brought fighters 'under control' by settling cases that would otherwise have required revenge.[22] The colonial government was introducing new rules to local dynamics of raiding and rights in property. Those whose property was recognised – the senior family and lineage heads like the old man quoted above – benefited from greater security. But their authority would also be challenged by new opportunities to acquire property and new arguments for individual property rights.

From the earliest years of the Condominium, certain people sought the disciplinary power of government and approached British officials with complaints and disputes. Before 1922, two to three thousand complaints a year were recorded by officials in Rumbek, brought directly to the *merkaz* to be heard by the British Inspector or a *mamur*.[23] A former DC also recalled his treks to the chiefs' centres, where 'thronged the litigants, each bent on the direct approach to the DC as the quickest means of getting what he thought was justice'.[24] Officials described people 'hawking' cases from chief to chief and inundating British administrators with unresolved disputes.[25] The demand for government justice increased in Rumbek beyond the capacity of officials to meet it or to subsequently enforce decisions, as a later DC recalled in 1927:

> The method then in vogue was that, when a decision had been arrived at by the D.C. or the Mamur, the person who had won his case was issued with a slip of paper... In theory Deng Malwal would go to Majok Banjok 'armed' with his warraga [Ar.: paper] and would at once receive the cattle awarded to him. In practice he usually received a knock on the head with a club instead. With the result that practically every human being in the district used to wave warragas in my face at all times of the day (and night, when possible). I have even had them brought to me when in bed in a rest house on the road.[26]

Waraga, or paper, would acquire a power and significance through these written judgments, as we shall see. This account suggests that it was primarily seen as a way to communicate with and contract the *hakuma*, without whose power it had little internal efficacy. But as it became 'quite impossible to hear anything like the number of complaints which reached the Merkaz',[27] colonial officials began to institute formal chiefs' courts and to try to devolve some of the power, symbolism and ritual of government office to these new arenas.

21 'Song of Gol Mayen', GK Hebbert, DC Yirrol, to Governor, Upper Nile, 23 December 1931, NRO CivSec 36/4/15, in PRM Lienhardt Papers 1/9.

22 Interview 63R/RC.

23 Report on Bahr el Ghazal Province, enclosed in Governor Ingleson, to Civil Secretary, 14 May 1935, NRO UNP 1/4/22.

24 PP Howell, 'Recollections of service in the Sudan', 1983, Howell Papers, SAD 769/5/54.

25 Reining, *The Zande Scheme*, pp. 18–19.

26 DC Eastern District to Governor Upper Nile, Lake Yirrol, 'Report on Eastern District (Atwots and Dinkas), Bahr el Ghazal Province, on the occasion of its transfer to the Upper Nile Province', 1 December 1927, NRO BGP 1/5/28.

27 Report on Bahr el Ghazal Province, enclosed in Governor Ingleson, to Civil Secretary, 14 May 1935, NRO UNP 1/4/22.

INSTITUTIONALISING STATE JUSTICE IN THE CHIEFS' COURTS

The 1920s were a high point of government efforts to concentrate power in the institution of chiefship, but by the end of the decade, there was concern that DCs and *mamurs* had been playing too direct a role in supervising the early chiefs' courts. The 1931 Chiefs' Courts Ordinance therefore gave the presidents of the 'B' Courts third-class magisterial powers. It also provided for the creation of 'A' Courts, consisting of just one chief, with headmen or elders appointed by him, which were intended to deal with the bulk of cases, so that the B courts could become more like appeal courts. Just a year after the Ordinance was passed, however, officials were expressing concern that these courts were still regarded by the people as 'purely Government institutions', characterised by 'an aping of what they thought were our ideas and our laws; and a tendency on the part of the chiefs police to push people about, make them stand at attention and so forth'.[28] By 1938 such concerns had grown: '[t]he Chiefs have been so far the mouthpiece through which government orders have been issued to the people; the courts have been regarded as the government's way of settling cases'.[29]

As the government increasingly promoted ethnographic enquiry in the 1930s, the continuing judicial or mediatory role of the 'inspired men' – spear-masters and rain and earth chiefs – began to be reported by colonial officials.[30] Bari councils, *putet*, were hearing cases, often led by a rain chief.[31] Around Rumbek, there were increasing concerns among officials that the chiefs had been a government-imposed innovation: the Agar Dinka chief Rok Rec, a former policeman, reportedly sought to monopolise court cases and to exercise his 'natural ambition to have no competitors for the favour of the government'.[32] In Upper Nile Province by this time, government officials were deliberately seeking to exclude spiritual authorities from the courts.[33] But there were instead concerted efforts in Rumbek and Yirrol in the 1930s to involve elders and spiritual leaders in the judicial system, either as members of the chiefs' courts or in village-level mediation. The Equatoria Province Governor Parr even declared in 1942 'that much harm has been done because in their early days the Dinka courts came to be regarded as Government courts on which a Bany Bith [spear-master]... would think it impossible to serve'.[34] As both Johnson and Hutchinson show, the composite justice practised in the chiefs' courts did not address the deeper spiritual effects of committing wrongs or provide the means of removing resulting pollution and reconciling blood feuds, functions which the spear-masters continued to perform.[35]

The distinctive, 'government' nature of the chiefs' courts had two important consequences. Firstly, the relationship between chiefs and senior authorities was not necessarily harmonious. The chiefs and other court personnel tended

[28] Governor Mongalla to Governor Upper Nile, 'Notes on native courts', 7 September 1932, NRO Civsec 1/13/42.

[29] Equatoria Province Annual Report 1938, NRO Civsec 57/25/103.

[30] Mongalla Province Monthly Diary, April 1931, NRO Civsec 1/39/104.

[31] Anonymous, 'Juba District Handbook', NRO JD 1/2/6.

[32] Rumbek District Monthly Report, February 1937, SRO EP 57.D.10.

[33] Douglas H Johnson, 'Colonial policy and prophets: the "Nuer settlement", 1929–30', *Journal of the Anthropological Society of Oxford* 10:1 (1979), pp. 1–20; and *Nuer Prophets*, pp. 289–90.

[34] 'Note by Mr Parr for DCs meeting, Tonj', Juba, 21 March 1942, NRO BGP 1/5/28.

[35] Johnson, 'Judicial regulation'; Hutchinson, *Nuer Dilemmas*.

to be younger men.[36] In Rumbek, 'the greybeards say that the institution of "Government" courts with uniformed members has ruined the tribal authority and discipline of the senior members of the "Gol"'.[37] Faced with the growing potential of younger family members or dependents to gain greater economic independence, senior men may have been seeking more public arenas in which to exercise their authority in dispute resolution. By the 1930s they certainly appear to have seized the opportunity presented by shifting government policy to complain about the new laws and procedures of the chiefs' courts. One DC reported in 1938 that the encouragement of a greater role in justice for the elders had simply prompted an influx to Rumbek of 'old men screaming about antique cases'.[38] By 1940 this was being reported in a more positive, but still revealing, light:

> In some areas the senior age-group, which should normally have so much influence in the community had been unable in the face of autocratic chiefship to keep its place. These elders have recently been encouraged to emerge from the shade of their huts and re-enter the world of affairs. They came with a burst into public life and at once started to upset cases that had been settled for years past.[39]

A few years earlier in the same area, a DC reported the difficulty he was encountering in finding out 'the real customary law', since the introduction of an 'Arbitrary code of laws with scales of compensation by cattle' produced by chiefs who were mostly 'a younger generation' and 'drawn from foreign tribes'. He claimed that the old men could rarely be persuaded to talk about the laws; they were 'usually very diffident, and when at last prevailed upon to speak, they do so almost defiantly, as though they were afraid of losing what little was left to them'.[40] This is revealing not just of the various versions of law over which elders and chiefs might disagree, but also of the deeper reasons why the 'old men' might have kept their distance initially from the new courts. Pels discusses similar reports of reticence and diffidence in Uluguru, Tanganyika, as indicative of an important element of 'substrate or subaltern politics', which involved keeping a 'cool heart' and avoiding contradicting another person openly.[41] In southern Sudan a similar political culture explains not only reluctance to openly oppose chiefs, but the very separation of chiefship from other kinds of authority. Spiritual leaders claimed that the work of a chief was too 'hot', because it provoked people's anger and resentment, while they needed to remain 'cool' in order to bring rain or other blessings.[42] By acting as individual judges, chiefs risked becoming a focus of ill-feeling, curses and other means of revenge.

The initial distance of senior men from the chiefs' courts also meant, however, that people may have seen these institutions as an alternative to the established sources of mediation or arbitration. According to Buxton, 'people of formerly dependent status will bring cases before them who would not have brought them previously' to councils of elders.[43] A British missionary in the Central (later Juba) District similarly suggested in 1929 that former 'servile classes' tended to 'feel that in the government they have a champion that

36 See also Buxton, *Chiefs and Strangers*, p. 129.

37 Rumbek District Monthly Reports, June–July 1937, SRO EP 57.D.10.

38 Rumbek District Monthly Report, March 1938, SRO EP 57.D.10.

39 Lakes District Handbook, 1940, p. 16, SRO EP 1.G.2.

40 DC Yirrol to Governor Upper Nile, 'Handing over notes Yirrol', 3 December 1935, NRO BGP 1/5/28.

41 Pels, 'The pidginization of Luguru politics', p. 751.

42 Interview 32R/YC.

43 Buxton, *Chiefs and Strangers*, p. 128.

fosters the spread of property'.[44] As a very elderly Bari inhabitant of the Juba Malakiya explained,

> There used to be no court; problems were just settled by the elders. Then they brought the B court... and all the chiefs had to come to the court in the Malakiya market... People were happy because they were free to speak and express; there was no pressure like there is in the community, and so the court was fairer.[45]

Colonial officials recognised that the chiefs' courts might be useful to poor people otherwise ignored by 'rich' elders, reporting in the Dinka districts 'litigation which is a nuisance to everybody but... does ensure the poor man getting his case heard'.[46] Of course, as the same official admitted, even the chiefs' courts were never blind to social status, and government law was also increasingly seen by senior, wealthy people as a means of protecting their property. But nevertheless, the courts were also open to alternative value-systems and forms of wealth, not least because they offered justice as a monetised transaction, located in 'the Malakiya market'.

'A CLAIM ON HIS CHIEF': CONTRACTING GOVERNMENT, TRANSACTING JUSTICE

The alternative, government-connected character of the chiefs' courts was underscored from the outset by their links to the urban and monetary economy. Like chiefship itself, the chiefs' courts had often originated in or maintained close connections to the government *merkaz* and to the *malakiya* and market, as a 1936 report on Moru District made clear:

> At Amadi the people are encouraged to bring in local produce at the monthly meetings of the Chiefs Court and a market has been held for several years. The conjunction of markets with court meetings seems promising and might be tried elsewhere.[47]

Markets and courts had already been held simultaneously during border meetings with neighbouring administrations. Exchanging goods and settling disputes, debts and claims were both forms of property transaction, and often the latter arose from the former. But the courts often preceded the markets, an indication of the role of the new courts in promoting the use of money. The chiefs' role as brokers was also reflected in their own continuing connection to commercial dealings: in 1944 one B court north of Juba 'passed the time by putting in a proposal that shops should pay rent to the chiefs'.[48] Officials in Dinka districts trying to stimulate the trade in cattle hides also gave up on market trade and forced a trade instead through the courts:

> After years of preaching and trying to get the merchants interested, we at last made a great advance when we ordered that no man could bring a case to Court unless at the same time he brought a properly prepared hide. That got

[44] Whitehead, 'Social change among the Bari', p. 95.

[45] Interview 15N/JC.

[46] Jur River District Annual Report 1944, NRO EP 2/27/97.

[47] Nalder, *Equatoria Province Handbook*, p. 157.

[48] JH Dick, 'Trek Diary', 16–27 October 1944, SAD 748/10/1–71.

> 'em... I have given orders that for the present no hides at all are to be sold and bought until they have been inspected and stamped at the Chiefs' Court.[49]

The courts further promoted market trade by the selling off at auction of cattle taken as fines; initially such auctions would be the only source of cattle that could be purchased with cash.[50]

The earliest court buildings were constructed within the government *merkaz*, and chiefs had to construct their own huts in which to stay while attending the monthly court.[51] The courts thus ensured that the chiefs spent regular periods staying in the towns. By the 1930s, chiefs in Tonj and Rumbek Districts had reportedly become too busy with their courts to visit the cattle camps in the grazing areas, or to manage the annual grazing migrations.[52] The courts thus tied the chiefs to the economy of government, town and market and pulled them away from 'their herds', as the British official put it.

Other people were also drawn into the town in the pursuit of dispute resolution and justice, just as they would later be drawn in to buy, sell or exchange in the markets. In what would become an enduring pattern, the government discovered in 1937 that the town court in Rumbek had been hearing local Dinka cases, to the annoyance of the rural chiefs.[53] This court was headed by a northern Sudanese (Dongolawi) merchant, with Zande and Makaraka ex-soldiers as members: in other words it represented the multi-ethnic population of the *malakiya*. Yet people brought cases to it even before they bought goods from the market. By 1947, officials in Rumbek were complaining that the Appeal Court sessions held in the town were drawing in 2000–3000 people a day (counted because of a simultaneous vaccination campaign): 'very large meetings of this kind have a disturbing influence on regular administration and are generally undesirable... it encourages all and sundry to come to the Merkaz'. In the continuing struggle to exclude rural people from the town, this DC recommended that the appeal courts be held out in the rural areas.[54] But people would always bring cases to the *merkaz* as well as to the rural chief's courts, in direct pursuit of government justice.

According to Mading Deng, the Dinka came to see litigation as 'a form of occupation and a source of wealth'.[55] Court cases also drew people into the money economy, to risk investing court fees in the hope of overall gain:

> As I see things, natives attach much more importance to anything if they have to pay for it... The introduction of a fee has not had the effect, viz, the cutting down of cases, but undoubtedly the Dinka appreciates that he now has *a claim on his Chief* to see his case through [my italics].[56]

Court cases and appeals were in themselves a kind of monetised transaction, in which people paid for the adjudication of their disputes. Court fines were

[49] Eastern District Notebook, October 1935, NRO BGP 1/7/38.

[50] Hutchinson, *Nuer Dilemmas*, pp. 66–7; Abdel Ghaffar M Ahmed and Mustafa Abdel Rahman, 'Small urban centres', p. 267.

[51] LE Holland, DC Amadi, 'Lukikos District order No. 1: The Formation of Lukikos in the Moru Aliab district', 15 September 1923, NRO MP 1/1/2.

[52] Eastern District Notebook, 1932–5, NRO BGP 1/7/38; Rumbek District Monthly Report, February 1937, SRO EP 57.D.10.

[53] Rumbek District Monthly Report, January 1937, SRO EP 57.D.10.

[54] Lakes District Handing Over Notes 1947, SRO EP 1.G.2.

[55] Mading Deng, *Tradition and Modernization*, p. 107.

[56] Eastern District Notebook, 1935, NRO BGP 1/7/38.

similarly demanded in money. As O'Sullivan's 1908 report on Dinka law and justice showed, the idea of a fine payable to the chief was a novel introduction, but it may have further contributed to the commodification of justice in the colonial courts. As one Rumbek DC complained, people seemed to regard court fees 'as perquisites of the native chiefs and District Commissioner'.[57] As such a personal payment to the chief or DC, court fees were understood as a way of establishing a personal claim upon them. Further, the idea had grown (still prevalent nowadays) that the higher the fee, the stronger the claim: some people reportedly tried to pay an appeal fee before their original cases had even been heard by the court, thinking that the higher appeal fee would 'secure success'.[58]

Despite government attempts to characterise the chiefs' courts as traditional, rural arenas, in reality many of their cases were brought by wage-earners and townspeople, seeking to convert their knowledge and earnings in the world of the *hakuma* into social status and property. Recourse to the courts increased in tandem with the spread of money and the consequent need to mediate and convert between different currencies and forms of value: 'it may even be necessary to increase the court fees, if money continues to become more plentiful and thus gives fuller rein to the Dinkas' passion for litigation'.[59] When cash did become particularly plentiful during the Second World War and there were few goods to purchase with it, people increasingly invested money in court fees: 'Civil cases show a steady increase since 1942... due to a surplus of cash in the hands of a people who treat litigation as a national pastime'. In turn, with heavy government requisitioning of cattle also going on, between 1943 and 1944 the Rumbek courts doubled the amount of cash fines while more than halving the number of cattle taken as fines.[60] This responsiveness to the changing economy contributed to the further institutionalisation of chiefs' brokerage role, as did the capacity of the courts to fix exchange rates between money and non-money economies. As early as 1923, the courts in Mongalla were establishing fixed monetary values for livestock, hoes and other objects of social and economic value, at a time when monetised market trade in such items was barely beginning.[61]

Money-earners sought to invest their cash in litigation in order to claim cattle or other non-money forms of value, and to enhance their status in social and economic structures. One government clerk was fined for adultery with a cash penalty, but when he re-offended and defaulted on payment of this fine, one of his cows was seized. He claimed that he had tried to redeem the cow by paying its value in money, but had not been given opportunity to do so (a claim denied by the DC):

> Supposing I have not money and my cow goes through lack of money I should never grumble but so far there was the money and it was return and the cow taken whereas I was fine with money and not cows this I cannot understand. Also when a prisoner punished for fine of cows or money the punishment does

[57] Rumbek District Monthly Report, December 1937, SRO EP 57.D.10.

[58] Rumbek District Monthly Report, September 1937, SRO EP 57.D.10.

[59] DC Yirrol to Governor Upper Nile, 'Handing over notes Yirrol', 3 December 1935, NRO BGP 1/5/28.

[60] Lakes and Aweil Districts Annual Reports 1944, NRO EP 2/27/97.

[61] E.g. *Mamur* Mongalla, 'Bari-Mandaris habits and laws of legislation together with adopted rules for Mongalla district chiefs court', 11 September 1924 NRO MP 1/1/2. See also DC Wordsworth, Torit, to DC Tonj, 6 September 1946, NRO EP 2/2/9.

> not change from money to cows, this is quite different thing altogether except that I am being cheated... [*sic*][62]

Although in this case the separation had been contravened, the fact that the appellant was arguing for it suggests that it may indeed have been the norm for penalties to be given specifically as either cattle or money. The courts were making decisions as to the form of fines and compensation, and in so doing were enabling different currencies and value-systems to exist in parallel. The transactions in the courts interacted with those in the market to establish rates of exchange between these parallel systems; this appellant also complained at the monetary valuation of his cow by the court. Yet however dissatisfied this writer was, his very use of a letter to make his complaint reveals his advantageous position in a judicial system that gave increasing weight to *waraga*, written papers.

PAPER AND POWER: ABSTRACTING CHIEFLY JUSTICE

An obvious aspect of the innovatory nature of the colonial courts was their emphasis on adjudicating a decisive verdict and their individualising procedures; however numerous the parties, cases required individual plaintiffs and defendants. While chiefs relied on their court panels, they were clearly also known for their individual judicial ability. In the Bari area, the death in 1939 of Chief Lukak Leggi Logo, President of the Juba B Court, was reported as a great loss, 'as he was looked on by the Bari as a "Cutter" of cases'. Reports also highlighted the tendency of people to vote with their feet to express their opinion of individual chiefs and courts:

> It has been interesting to watch how the number of cases increase in the A courts with the better chiefs. A bad chief has a bad court and few cases appear. A good chief replaces him and cases immediately increase as the litigants find they can now get satisfaction.[63]

But individual reputation and the responsibility for 'cutting cases' also conveyed risks and potential blame. Chiefs therefore sought to both sanction and abstract their decisions by reference to state law and procedures. Dinka courts employed an *agamlong*, literally an 'accepter' or 'repeater' of speech, to amplify and regulate the speeches of litigants and court members. Some of my informants suggested that the *agamlong* originated in the use of interpreters by colonial officials; certainly in multilingual areas or cases, courts have used interpreters more generally. But others explained that spear-masters had always had their own *agamlong* to repeat their speeches, so that people had confidence because the spear-master 'did not work alone'.[64] Similarly the court *agamlong* was explained to me in English as making things 'official': 'he repeats what is said so that it becomes law'.[65] In marriage negotiations, a maternal relative would also be chosen to act as an *agamlong*, and would be the principal witness in case of future problems.

As Peterson argues, even before literacy, Africans had thus sought their own means of permanently recording human decisions, but now '[r]ecords were helpful because they interposed a third element – the archive – between

[62] John Majok to Governor Equatoria, Wau, 11 March 1944, SRO EP 41.J.1.

[63] Juba District Annual Reports 1939 and 1944, NRO EP 2/26/94 and EP 2/27/97.

[64] Interview 71R/RC.

[65] Interview 16N/RC.

human co-participants in an argument'.[66] Similarly in southern Sudan, the role of the *agamlong* in interposing, mediating, formalising and witnessing the speeches of different parties was increasingly paralleled by the possibilities of the written court record. One Rumbek DC noted in 1940 'a growing desire for the written record of a court' and attributed this to the involvement of British administrators in courts, so that 'it was observed that a man who could point to a recorded court judgment was much more likely to obtain his cattle'.[67] In light of the tendency to call in debts decades after they were first incurred, it is not surprising that people quickly saw the practical advantage in paper records.[68]

> People realised that if the case is written, it could be referred to again in the future. Your right is recorded, so if someone appeals in another court, that court will ask for the papers, and if something has not been written, you might not get your right again. Writing prevents confusion, so people like it.[69]

Court papers functioned as a means of direct appeal to the government, and with the potential efficacy to ensure execution of judgments and debts. A CMS missionary in Rumbek in the colonial period recalled how 'in colloquial speech we used to be told again and again by Dinkas who wanted a paper from us... "You have power"', which he defined as 'material influence or authority'.[70] The Dinka word for 'power' was likely to have been *riel*: the court bailiffs in Rumbek are still known as *beny riel*, 'chiefs of power/strength'.[71] The word *riel* is also indicative of a collective delegation and abstraction of executive force:

> *Beny riel* is the one given instructions and power by the *hakuma*; it is not his own power. Like if a group sit like this and decide something and then ask one of the group to carry out that thing, he is *beny riel*. We have authorised him to have that power so we have to accept it.[72]

One colonial chief is remembered to have been removed by popular complaints and cursed by his people because he went by himself to enforce a court decision by seizing cattle, rather than sending the *beny riel* or police to the cattle camp.[73] Chiefs were supposed to delegate court authority to institutionalised forms of force (court bailiffs and police), rather than exercising executive power single-handedly. Court judgments and penalties are commonly called by the Arabic word *hukum*, a term which Willis defines in a northern Sudanese context as 'the ability to punish through a government-recognised court'.[74] The coercive, disciplinary power of the colonial courts was part of the broader assertion of a monopoly on violent force by the colonial state, however incomplete; the government was also seeking to suppress the 'revenge' attacks that

66 Peterson, 'Morality plays', paras 36–7.

67 Lakes District Handbook 1940, p. 52, SRO EP 1.G.2.

68 Cf Sally Falk Moore, 'Treating law as knowledge: telling colonial officers what to say to Africans about running "their own" native courts', *Law and Society Review* 26:1 (1992), p. 30.

69 Interview 1bN/RC.

70 LWC Sharland, Annual Letter, Rumbek, August 1955, SAD 865/2/40.

71 Interview 54R/RC. In Bor, the official chiefs' court was known as the court of *riel*, translated as 'strength' by SM Zanen and AW van den Hoek, 'Dinka dualism and the Nilotic hierarchy of values', in PE de Josselin de Jong, R. de Ridder and Jan A. J. Karremans, *The Leiden Tradition in Structural Anthropology* (Leiden, 1987), p. 173.

72 Interview 1bN/RC.

73 Interview 1cN/RC.

74 Justin Willis, '*Hukm*: the creolization of authority in Condominium Sudan', *Journal of African History* 46 (2005), p. 30.

Fig. 4.1 Bari chief and elders hearing a case at a court in Juba District, with the speaker holding a forked 'talking stick' (between 1949 and 1959). (Reproduced by permission of Durham University Library SAD.835/4/29)

had been the obvious precursor or alternative to *hukum*. But it might also be the abstract, punitive force of the state that people sought out in the chiefs' courts.

The collective appearance of the chiefs' courts was another important factor in their gradual acceptance, as another elderly man declared: 'You go to the court where all the chiefs are together, because a court where cases are to be written is not to be judged by one chief alone.'[75] Both the written record and the collective court panels contributed to the development of the chiefs' courts as a particular public space. There were reported 'signs that taking cases to a court might become a cheap recreation akin [to] free cinemas in England'; 'all and sundry' were said to be attending the A courts.[76] Mundari courts by the 1950s were 'crowded with ordinary people', and according to Buxton, Mundari expressed 'disapproval of the present amount of litigation although they continue to indulge in it', seeing it as frivolous or demeaning to take small disputes to the chief.[77] By the 1940s there was even some government concern that the courts were becoming too popular and that cases were being brought

[75] Interview 14N/RC.

[76] Equatoria Province Annual Report 1937, NRO Civsec 57/24/99; anonymous, 'Juba District Handbook', NRO JD 1/2/6.

[77] Buxton, *Chiefs and Strangers*, pp. 128–9.

'which would otherwise have been settled informally out of court... Where people only go to court to get public sanction, when issue has already been decided, then it is better to avoid bringing disputes to court.'[78]

In fact this notion of 'public sanction' is probably crucial to understanding the role of the chiefs' courts. Public assemblies of elders had always been held to settle major disputes, but the chiefs' courts were a particular, formal public space, whose invasion by crowds of 'ordinary people' represented an unusual opportunity to enter a government arena. Bari courts used a forked stick, or 'talking stick' (*Fig. 4.1*), to regulate proceedings and to convey formality; only a person holding the stick was allowed to speak, thus making their speech official much as the *agamlong* did in Dinka areas. Every victorious litigant who used his receipt from the court to assert his or her right was helping to gain recognition of the chiefs' courts as institutions as well as of their definitions of rights.[79] The formalities of the colonial chiefs' courts and the potential power of their papers produced a new kind of judicial abstraction and institutionalisation. This opened new possibilities to make claims and argue rights through a variety of registers.

CLAIMING ONE'S RIGHT

> As the country is subject to Union Jack I expect my right to be given in this case if found.[80]

This statement comes from another letter written in English by a government employee – Daniel Kweirot, a medical assistant in Akot, near Rumbek – to the province governor to complain that the chiefs' courts had awarded him a number of cows but had failed to execute these decisions and actually obtain the cows for him. His complaint and case are very revealing of the multiple definitions of 'rights' that might have been argued in and beyond the courts in the 1930s and 1940s. Daniel had already successfully argued for his private, individual property rights in the chiefs' courts: rights to cattle that he had purchased with his government wages and then 'lent' to people to care for, while still providing milk for his own children; but these herders had then used his cows to pay their own debts to other people. The chiefs had apparently recognised Daniel's right to his cows. But they had not enforced their return to him. The Lakes DC, Nightingale, admitted that the courts were 'extremely bad' at enforcing their judgments.[81]

Daniel interpreted this failure as a denial of his 'right'. This English word, which was already being deployed in the colonial period by more educated people like Daniel, has acted as a creolised and multivalent term, an interpretation both of Western notions of legal rights and of vernacular concepts like *yic* in Dinka. According to Lienhardt, *yic* means 'truth which is arrived at and stated by a *communal* intention', an objective truth which transcends the subjective truths of disputants.[82] The Agar have a saying that '*yic* cannot be

[78] Margery Perham, 'Sudan VI: native administration book – draft chapter on the South', 1946, Rhodes House Library, Oxford, MSS Perham 542/5.

[79] Lund, 'Twilight institutions', p. 675.

[80] Daniel Kweirot, Medical Assistant Akot Dispensary, to Governor Equatoria, 28 September 1946, SRO EP 41.J.1.

[81] JF Tiernay, Governor Equatoria, to DC Lakes, Juba, 18 December 1946, SRO EP 41.J.1.

[82] Lienhardt, *Divinity and Experience*, pp. 139, 247–8. On the Nuer concept of 'moral right', also see Johnson, 'Judicial regulation', p. 59.

covered'; the purpose of courts is to uncover and reveal *yic*.[83] Yet Lienhardt's account also represents a rather idealised notion of the possibility of achieving an objective and consensual 'truth', which perhaps disguises the extent of struggle and contest in such mediation. He also suggested rather critically that although the 'government courts' in the 1940s were following the same process as a traditional *luk*, 'now the conclusion to which the gathering comes is partly governed by foreign rules of procedure and the admissibility of evidence, and is formulated as a decision which can be imposed upon the disputants'.[84] The decisions made by gatherings of senior men might always have been 'imposed' to some extent, though perhaps in more subtle ways than by the chiefs' courts. But the 'foreign' rules and procedures of the chiefs' courts were nevertheless bringing changes, exemplified in Daniel's written appeal to the 'Union Jack'. In particular, the courts may have introduced a new dynamic into the existing tension between subjective and objective truth. For 'right' or *yic* was also referred to both in the colonial period and since in terms of recognition of *individual* rights, of 'my right' as Daniel put it. As a Dinka lay magistrate put it in 2006: 'When you have a right, you claim your right and nothing can cover it'.[85]

The courts may indeed have transformed dispute resolution into a greater contest, a struggle to have one's *yic* recognised. In the case of a different pastoralist society in the northern Kordofan Province of Sudan, Willis argues that struggles to control resources were 'matters of honour', and it was 'honourable to assert rights – a woman's right to be clothed, or not to have to move endlessly with the animals; a man's right to water his stock; a husband's exclusive rights over his wife's sexuality'. Also, as Willis shows, a sense of 'honour impugned' was likely to lead to violence.[86] In pastoralist societies, warfare and raiding has acted as both a means to acquire and assert honour and rights – individual as well as collective – and as a means by which young men might acquire material resources. As such conflicts were partially suppressed during the colonial period,[87] the courts were growing in significance as an alternative arena in which to achieve the same goals. According to Mading Deng: 'The hardships of litigation, such as walking long distances to the chief's headquarters and sometimes going hungry in the course of these journeys, have assumed an adventurousness now taken as evidence of masculinity in Dinka youth.'[88]

Johnson argues that the colonial courts introduced a novel emphasis on the immediate payment of debts and compensation, whereas local society operated on the basis of long-term debts and duties, which bound people in relations of obligation: 'The courts' insistence on a precise and punctual repayment of obligations seems to have emphasised, in practice, what was owed the individual rather than the community.'[89] But people may well have therefore used the new courts in quite specific ways, when they were determined to call in a debt, or to label borrowing or reclamation as theft, even at the risk of breaking relations. Colonial officials came to realise that in cases of cattle theft it was often 'simply that the offender considers he has right to a cow and finds the stealthy

[83] Cf. Paul Bohannan, *Justice and Judgement among the Tiv* (London, 1957), cited in Mading Deng, *Tradition and Modernization*, p. 50.

[84] Lienhardt, *Divinity and Experience*, p. 248.

[85] Interview 17N/RC.

[86] Willis, '*Hukm*', p. 47.

[87] E.g. Lakes District Annual Report 1944, NRO EP 2/27/97.

[88] Mading Deng, *Tradition and Modernization*, p. 106.

[89] Johnson, 'Judicial regulation', p. 74.

removal of it simpler than its recovery through legal channels'.[90] But the courts' frequent failure to implement decisions, as Daniel's complaint reveals, may also have been a way to retain flexibility and delay in practice, as well as a sign of their reluctance to provoke the fights and complaints that frequently resulted from implementation.[91] Sometimes litigants wanted to have their right recognised, established and recorded, but not necessarily to have it executed immediately. Colonial officials would always be irritated by the revival of 'old' cases years or even decades after they were first heard, but this resulted from the changing circumstances of the litigants, who might wait until a debtor could afford to pay before calling in the debt.[92]

We thus see glimpses of the continuing complexity of litigation and judicial outcomes, as litigants and court members deployed multiple notions of rights and acted upon these in variable ways. It is clear that as people like Daniel appropriated colonial law and the British flag to argue their cases, and as the appeal system was promoted more by the government, litigants were increasingly gaining knowledge of government law and judicial procedure, and using these to hold chiefs to account. In 1938 a man appealed to his B court, because the chief in the A court had sentenced him to more lashes than the court warrant allowed. Many chiefs and policemen were prosecuted in the B courts for unfair or illegal activities.[93] People understood the appeal hierarchy, and the link to the state that it represented: 'The village chiefs [*bany baai*] were working with the whites. If the chief did not give you your right, you went to the white man in charge of the court [*luk*] until you got your right, even though the village chief had denied it.'[94] The practice of 'complaining' to British officials when they toured the district was also another means of appeal. Around Rumbek, DCs reported 'the restless clamouring of Agar litigants' – mostly about delays in hearing cases or executing judgments – and the 'startling amount of cases and complaints waiting to be dealt with'.[95] In 1938 it was also reported that '[s]everal cases of orphans being gravely oppressed in their claims to cattle have recently come to light' and were investigated in a special meeting of the Appeal Court of chiefs and DC.[96]

The chiefs' courts with their government-influenced, bureaucratic procedures were an arena in which literate money-earners could often show off their knowledge and understanding of government. But such individuals also sought to enlist more directly the support of government officials against or above the chiefs. A file of appeals, mainly from convicts in Juba prison, to the Equatoria Province Governor between 1936 and 1952 suggests that government employees in particular sought to exploit their privileged access to British officials. One retired policeman in Kajokeji reportedly appealed a number of old cases each time a new DC arrived in the district, occasionally with success.[97]

As well as producing cases specifically about property rights, the economic

[90] Lakes District Monthly Report, December 1940, SRO EP 57.D.10; Johnson, 'Judicial regulation', p. 66

[91] Lakes District Monthly Report, October 1940, SRO EP 57.D.10.

[92] Cf. Moore, 'Treating law as knowledge', pp. 29–30.

[93] Equatoria Province Monthly Diaries, November 1938, NRO Civsec 57/7/29, and February 1939, NRO Civsec 57/11/42; Yei District Monthly Diaries, March 1942, September 1942, March 1945 and December 1945, NRO EP 2/24/87; Yei District Annual Report 1939, NRO EP 2/26/94.

[94] Interview 56R/RC.

[95] Lakes District Monthly Reports, February–March 1937, SRO EP 57.D.10.

[96] Lakes District Monthly Report, February 1938, SRO EP 57.D.10.

[97] WBH Duke, A/DC Yei, to Governor Equatoria, 19 November 1946, SRO EP 41.J.1.

and social changes of the colonial period also led to particular disputes and debates over marriage, bridewealth and divorce; most court cases were about women, as British officials liked to point out derisorily. Young men earning wages might be able to pay their own bridewealth in cash and hence gain greater independence from senior male relatives or patrons who would previously have controlled the resources required for marriage. But on the other hand, wage-earners often struggled to find sufficient resources to pay the bridewealth alone, particularly if their bride's parents demanded payment in cattle. If their relatives were too poor or refused to help, expecting them to be self-sufficient, young men might instigate a situation whereby they would be taken to court by the girl's family, in which case their own relatives would likely be summoned to court and ordered to assume collective responsibility for a compensation or marriage payment: 'It is not uncommon for a young man to force the issue by making the girl pregnant and coming to terms with her angry and reluctant parents.'[98] One DC noted an increase in pre-marital intercourse, because 'lack of cash for dowry leaves present-day youth with little alternative'.[99] Government officials keen to prevent the escalation of such cases even encouraged their employees to invest in cattle in order to marry properly. The police were a particular problem, according to a Tonj DC:

> They are very keen on marrying without meeting their tribal dues – pinching girls, and that creates great trouble. Make them save so much a month, if unmarried, to buy cattle, and watch their 'marriages' closely. Most of them are of the 'aboor' (cattleless) class, and join up with the idea of getting a wife.[100]

As this suggests, colonial employment – and either the coercive power or material resources it might bring – had always offered new opportunities to those who were poor or marginal in rural society. While on the one hand the chief's courts were upholding the marriage systems of the rural economy, on the other hand they might be manipulated by young men seeking to pay their bridewealth in cash. Chiefs were also reportedly sensitive to the consequences of high bridewealth, citing parental greed as the cause of later 'unfaithfulness and troubles', and recommending a fixed limit even in 1924.[101] By the 1940s chiefs were expressing concern at high inflation: 'many girls are staying unmarried in their fathers' homes because the average young man cannot afford to pay the bride price demanded'. Across the Equatorian districts, courts therefore imposed maximum limits on the bridewealth.[102] This would of course only be effective if marriage disputes reached the courts, ensuring that parents would prefer to settle marriages out of court, where they could negotiate a higher bridewealth, while the young men might prefer to end up in court and pay the restricted amount.

The chiefs' courts might then be useful to young men seeking to marry, despite their apparent support of parental rights and gerontocratic privilege. Similarly women and girls also found ways to influence the courts in their favour, despite the misogynistic imprint of colonial officials upon the early

98 LWC Sharland, Annual Letter, Rumbek, 1946, SAD 865/2/1–52. See also Mawson, 'The Triumph of Life', p. 119.

99 THB Mynors, 'Notes on the Moru Tribe', 1935, SAD 777/3/1–40.

100 Eastern District Notebook, 28 August 1935, NRO BGP 1/7/38.

101 Mamour Mongalla, 'Bari-Mandaris Habits and Laws of Legislation together with adopted rules for Mongalla district chiefs court', 11 September 1924, NRO MP 1/1/2.

102 Equatoria Province Monthly Diaries, August–September 1946, November 1946 and December 1947, NRO Dakhlia 57/2/5; Interview 8R/K.

courts.[103] They cited ill-treatment by husbands as grounds for leaving them, and they also increasingly used the issue of original consent to claim divorce. This was the one justification that won some support from administrators, who were concerned about child betrothals. In one court in 1940, chiefs proposed that '[a]ny girl who refused her parents choice should have the opportunity of saying so before a native court which would point out to her parents the dangers of a forced marriage'.[104] Women also used the B courts to appeal sentences of adultery, and in areas of heavy labour migration, they used the courts to divorce absent husbands, 'refusing to be left as grass widows and claiming their freedom to remarry'.[105] By the 1940s, courts were granting remarriages in such cases. In addition, 'many cases have been seen in native courts connected with complaints by wives against husbands for failure to cultivate'; 'idleness' was reported to be a legitimate reason for divorcing husbands.[106] Women were thus using the courts to define and enforce their rights in relation to the labour and other duties of their husbands. In so doing, they were reinforcing the role of the chiefs' courts in mediating the changing relations and ideas of rights generated by the colonial economy.

CONCLUSION

Many of my oldest informants presented the coming of government in idealistic terms of the constitution of new legal and judicial orders and the protection of property: 'If there was no court case, people could not live together: people who were many would rob all the property of those who were few, and small children would be robbed and carried away.'[107] But there were also significant indigenous precedents for the colonial chiefs' courts, and the latter were increasingly shaped by existing judicial cultures. In the 1940s, Lienhardt found important parallels between the work of spear-masters and chiefs. Through the speeches of spear-masters during sacrificial ceremonies, the disparate lineages and individuals became aggregated into a larger community. The same Dinka word, *long*, was used for these sacred speeches as for the speeches during court cases. 'Quarrels weaken and divide the community', and both sacrifices and court hearings were therefore vital to reunite and strengthen the community.[108] The role of spear-masters, rain chiefs and other spiritual authorities in bringing peace – often expressed in terms of bringing rain and 'cooling' the land – was beginning to be shared with or paralleled by

[103] Holland, 'Lukiko District order no. 3', 30 September 1923, NRO MP 1/1/2; Governor Mongalla to Governor Upper Nile, 'Notes on native courts', 7 September 1932, NRO Civsec 1/13/42; Brock, Governor Bahr el Ghazal, to Civil Secretary, 4 July 1929, NRO CS 1/13/43. On Brock's 'extreme moral zeal' see Douglas H. Johnson, 'Criminal secrecy: the case of the Zande "secret societies"', *Past and Present* 130 (1991), p. 180.

[104] Nigel Davidson, Legal Secretary, 'Note on Chief's Court at Yei', 15 May 1929, NRO Civsec 1/13/42; Equatoria Province Monthly Diary, September 1946, NRO Civsec 57/12/46. See also Kristin Mann and Richard Roberts (eds), *Law in Colonial Africa* (London, 1991), p. 41, and Shadle, 'Bridewealth', p. 255, on the wider colonial emphasis on bridal consent.

[105] Equatoria Province Monthly Diaries, October 1947, NRO Dakhlia 57/2/5, and October 1937, NRO Civsec 57/4/17.

[106] Yei District Monthly Diaries, April 1942 and September 1944, NRO EP 2/24/87; 'Application of the Southern Sudan Teachers and Dressers to Governor and Bishop of Southern Sudan', 29 May 1944, NRO EP 1/4/17.

[107] Interview 45R/JC.

[108] Lienhardt, *Divinity and Experience*, pp. 241–9. Cf. Wendy James, *The Listening Ebony: moral knowledge, religion, and power among the Uduk of Sudan* (Oxford, 1988), pp. 179–81.

the role of the chiefs, who were increasingly playing a role in ending conflicts and negotiating settlements and compensation.[109] Dinka chiefs at the time were reportedly arguing for the complementary role of 'spiritual and temporal Dinka chiefs', and emphasising that this 'division of functions was not introduced by Government', but was their 'own indigenous system'.[110]

In the Dinka language, chiefs, like spear-masters and war chiefs, were said to *muk baai*. The word *muk* had multiple meanings, often related to parenting, including holding, protecting, feeding, caring and instructing. The *baai* was the village, settlement or country – a co-residential community bound by social and marital ties.[111] Through the judicial and disciplinary role of their courts and police, the chiefs became associated with the potential to bring order and cohesion to this community. Ironically the senior people who produced such discourses were seeking to use chiefship to protect their property and resources from the effects of the very economy that the chiefs had long brokered. These paradoxes generated considerable litigation and debate, but the litigation increasingly came into chiefs' courts; and the debate was taking place within communities increasingly defined by their chief.

109 EE Evans-Pritchard, 'Preliminary Draft of an account of the Moro', NRO Dakhlia 112/14/95; Beaton to Governor, 'History of the Nyori district', 2 November 1932, NRO EP 2/34/127; Mynors, 'Notes on the Moru', 1935, SAD 777/3/1–40; Johnson, 'Judicial regulation', p. 72; Equatoria Province Monthly Diaries, January 1940, NRO Civsec 57/12/46, February to March 1946, NRO Dakhlia 57/2/5, and July, September, and November 1950, NRO Dakhlia 57/9/24; Nalder, *A Tribal Survey of Mongalla*, pp. 44–5.

110 Governor Equatoria to DCs Aweil, Jur River and Lakes, 'Record of Tonj discussions, 29–31 March 1942', 24 April 1942, NRO BGP 1/5/28.

111 Mawson, 'The Triumph of Life', p. 59.

5

Containing the frontier: the tensions of territorial chiefdoms, 1930s–1950s

> It is hoped that in these more peaceful times a purely territorial unit (comparable to a small English village) may come to be accepted in native eyes as a genuine coherent group. [1938][1]

The ideal of the village community as a territorial, social and administrative unit was imported by colonial officials from their British homeland, and in some areas imposed forcibly upon the indigenous geography of southern Sudan. During the 1920s and 1930s, such visions had interacted in tension with the emphasis of Indirect Rule on tribal units of Native Administration, culminating in the mid–late 1930s in the Equatoria Province policy of harnessing units of descent and kinship, in the hope ultimately of building tribes. By this time, however, the Condominium government was already moving away from Indirect Rule ideologies and beginning to promote territorial 'Local Government' on the model of English counties and parishes, governed by local councils. In the southern provinces this was expected to be a very gradual process, and administrators tended to modify the terminology rather than the basis of Native Administration, turning the existing chiefs' B courts into councils. But they did adopt the new policy with some relief, as justification for their previously pragmatic efforts to create territorial units of administration. Largely abandoning their quest for the elusive 'tribe', they concentrated now on the further 'amalgamation' of chiefships into larger territorial chiefdoms.

It has been argued that the most important administrative innovation wrought by colonial rule elsewhere in Africa was the territorialisation of authority and community: 'a colonial chief defined his sphere of rule by control over a bounded territory and not a kin group, which was the most prevalent – but not exclusive – form of pre-colonial governance'.[2] The creation of territorial chiefdoms in southern Sudan was indeed a significant transformation of the indigenous geography, and had major implications for community formation. But this territorialisation was not an entirely novel imposition, replacing kinship as the basis for community. Pre-colonial polities were not actually defined strictly by kinship, though their structures might be articulated in a kinship idiom. Instead political authority was acquired through specialist knowledge and the cultivation of heterogeneous followings through the resources and ability to offer protection that this expertise afforded. Kinship and marriage helped to maintain relations across long distances, but relations with non-kin neighbours and protective patrons could be equally important. People had always needed

[1] Equatoria Province Annual Report 1938, NRO Civsec 57/25/103.

[2] David Gordon, 'Owners of the land and Lunda lords: colonial chiefs in the borderlands of Northern Rhodesia and the Belgian Congo', *International Journal of African Historical Studies* 34:2 (2001), p. 318. See also Bill Bravman, *Making Ethnic Ways: communities and their transformations in Taita, Kenya, 1800–1950* (Portsmouth, 1998), pp. 108–16.

to come together in co-residential (or co-herding) groups larger than their own extended family, in order to secure resources, defend themselves and their property, maximise their sources of expertise, and create relatively stable units within which exogamous marriage, economic exchange and general social interaction could take place.[3] The pragmatic, quotidian realities of settlement and social relations therefore belied the rhetorical structure of strict patrilineal orders.

The (equally pragmatic) colonial emphasis on territoriality was therefore not an entirely alien basis for community; even the goal of large amalgamated chiefdoms intersected in dynamic ways with indigenous recognition of the advantages of wealth-in-people and strength in numbers. What was more novel though was the attempt to prevent migration between territories and chiefs through the bureaucratic regulation of tax registers. Such measures were never very effective, particularly in relation to individual migration: chiefs and landowning patrons still sought to attract newcomer clients, and the tax registers were subject to considerable manipulation and limited supervision. But it did become more difficult for entire groups or sections to split off from chiefs, with the effect that chiefdoms increasingly contained the tendencies to fission which might previously have found their outlet in migration.[4] Instead these tensions were channelled into the internal politics and disputes of chiefship, which were intensified by the later colonial period as chiefdoms became points of access to limited government resources. Chiefdoms were being produced through discursive struggles and colonial misinterpretations as a new 'form of locality',[5] linked to the state by roads, registers and courts. Chiefship was a potential entry-point *to* the state from the village, as well as vice versa; as such it was becoming a frontier in itself, akin to – and in places overlapping with – the urban frontier.

This in turn meant that discourses of familial fission and lineage rivalry were now focused onto chiefship, encouraged by the enduring government interest in genealogical descent, history and hierarchy, as Berry has argued more widely.[6] This chapter begins by examining the distinctive outcome of such discourse in southern Sudan; unlike in other parts of colonial Africa, the chiefs here did not succeed in controlling the production of lineage histories to their own advantage.[7] Discourses of agnatic seniority and primacy within families, lineages or chiefdoms frequently depicted chiefs as junior men and reminded them that they had to earn their authority and defer to their seniors. This is perhaps also though why chiefship increasingly became a basis for identification and community, because it produced alternative and potentially more inclusive discourses of political authority than those of lineage seniority. The chapter goes on to discuss the implications of territorial chiefdoms for the tensions between fission and fusion, to argue that territorial chiefdoms were nevertheless being produced *through* these very political tensions.

LAND, LINEAGE AND TERRITORIALITY

In the first half of the colonial period, substrate political debate over chiefship and genealogy remained largely unnoticed by colonial officials, or at least did

3 Cf. Ambler, *Kenyan Communities*, pp. 17–19.

4 Kopytoff, 'The internal African frontier'.

5 Le Meur, 'State making', p. 874.

6 Berry, *Chiefs Know their Boundaries*.

 7 E.g. Giblin, *History of the Excluded*; Lonsdale, 'The politics of conquest', p. 55.

not often enter their documentary records. But in the 1930s, the new focus of administrators on kinship and descent groups contributed to the bubbling up of local politics into government awareness and public arenas. As Pels argues, the 'superstrate political discourse of tribal representation' within British indirect rule doctrine encouraged the vocalisation of certain elements of local, substrate political discourse in particular settings of government contact. As in Uluguru, this substrate discourse was also divided between representations of 'stable' lineage politics and 'a more fluid negotiation of "big man" positions', which complicated and confused the colonial interpretations of it. Kinship and history were already discursive resources in local political struggles, but now they were also gaining currency with colonial administrators and entering the realm of bureaucracy. While in Uluguru the 'paradoxes and contradictions of indirect rule' ultimately led to political crisis and attacks on chiefs,[8] in southern Sudan the internal tensions of chiefship instead contributed to its consolidation as the focus and field of local politics.[9]

From the outset of colonial rule, administrators sought to 'amalgamate' small, scattered communities into large chiefdoms, as among the Bari of Rejaf District: '[i]t has been the endeavour of the Sudan Government to amalgamate these small communities under a few recognised chiefs, by finding out who were the most important in former times and actively supporting their present representatives'.[10] Even before the formal articulation of Indirect Rule, colonial officials had thus made their own historical imaginaries the basis for building the authority of chiefs.

Yet history and genealogy would also be a tool of opposition to chiefs, whose own origins could be accused of lying outside the descent-based claims to which colonial officials were always most receptive. By 1935, such claims were becoming more prominent: a 'sense of solidarity derived from their family and clan ties' was being 'emphasised by all authorities'.[11] Government officials performed a kind of sleight of hand, by which chiefs – whose junior, marginal or outside origins they had frequently admitted – were now reported to have genuine 'hereditary or tribal claims' to their position.[12] This slippage in turn revealed interaction with local political discourse as well as with wider colonial doctrines. As chiefship had clearly become more lucrative and influential, and as administrators demanded heredity, considerable jostling was going on around chiefly positions and units. Some chiefs had established themselves as lineage leaders by investing the earnings of their position in marriages and patrimonial followings. In other cases chiefs were claimed as junior members of a lineage which asserted dominance and spiritual power through genealogical precedence and seniority. But the more that chiefship became hereditary, the more it was subject to competing discourses of lineage seniority and other genealogies of authority.[13]

The ethnographic enquiries of the 1930s thus made clearer than ever the continuing multiplicity of authority within and across chiefdoms. Chiefship and chiefdom appeared as merely the latest layer of political and social geography:

[8] Pels, 'The pidginisation of Luguru politics', pp. 740, 755.

[9] Berry, *Chiefs Know their Boundaries*, especially pp. 36–55, 196.

[10] Chauncey H. Stigand, *Equatoria: the Lado Enclave* (London, 1923), p. 42.

[11] Governor Nalder to DCs and Civil Secretary, 'The future of Native Administration in Mongalla', 5 February 1935, NRO Civsec 1/39/105.

[12] Governor Nalder, 'Mongalla Province Summary of Information', November 1933, NRO Civsec 57/35/131.

[13] For the wider British rhetoric from the 1930s emphasising 'public opinion' and the danger of autocratic chiefs, see Shadle, '"Changing traditions"', p. 428; Tosh, *Clan Leaders*, p. 143.

> In considering the history of the peoples found in Amadi District, the original disposition of the local groups must be kept in mind, before their artificial regimentation by Government... Recollection of this original tribal map is often invaluable as a guide to local 'politics'.[14]

> The golden rule is to see how the cattle are herded, for in the cattle camps one will find a compact and exact replica of the actual tribal organisation.[15]

There were at least three kinds of land rights underlying or cross-cutting the new administrative geography. Firstly, there were communal rights to areas of cultivable land – often expressed as ownership of the 'soil' – claimed on the basis of descent from the first-comers to this land. Such 'clan' or 'gol' cultivation lands were reported to have clearly established boundaries in the colonial period, indicating that such rights *mattered*. Associated with this kind of land right were spiritual and ritual functions to ensure fertility, performed by the 'first-born' clan leaders, which also acted as a powerful sanction to enforce clan rights. Secondly, within these clan lands individual usufruct rights to particular plots were allocated or inherited. Thirdly, groups of different descent herding their cattle together (*wuot*, in Dinka) might claim primary rights to grazing territories or to particular resource points such as water sources, salt licks or fishing sites. These rights tended to be non-exclusive and 'not strictly enforced', but there were also more conflicts over this type of land right, when there was pressure on particular grazing or water.[16]

There was considerable variation, however, in the nature and exercise of these rights, according to population density, soil fertility, general security and modes of livelihood. In the western Mundari area around Tali in Equatoria, according to Buxton's interpretations in the early 1950s, the most important land rights were of the first kind; she terms the territories held by each landowning clan as 'the indigenous chiefdoms', which she claims used to be independent political units. Some were large areas containing several villages, but most were 'little more than a dispersed village with its surrounding woodland and grazing'. Each of the landowning clans was segmented into lineages (of between about fifteen and fifty adult men) living in straggling chains of family hamlets; both hamlets and the overall lineage villages were separated by border zones of bush and grass or crops. Many lineages and families within a chiefdom had come from outside the landowning clan and been absorbed as kin or affiliated dependents; the same vernacular term could be used to refer to a family, lineage or clan, but also to the inhabitants of a chiefdom 'many of whom are unrelated'.

Buxton stresses that the land used by each lineage or family was not particularly significant, since cultivable land was generally plentiful, and migration and shifting cultivation practices meant the frequent abandonment of former village or hamlet sites. It was the overall clan territory in which rights were more intensely invested, and which the clan might unite to defend. Individual or family landholdings were not viewed as property: 'fields are only soil, they are not like cattle', as Buxton quoted her informants.[17] Nalder had similarly emphasised that cattle were 'regarded as the one and only measure

14 THB Mynors, 'Notes on the Moru Tribe', 1935, SAD 777/3/1–40.

15 DC Aweil to Governor Equatoria, 19 January 1938, NRO BGP 1/5/28.

16 Lakes District Handbook, 1940, p. 69, SRO EP 1.G.2. 'Kraal sites are not necessarily occupied nowadays by the original owners,' Rumbek District Monthly Reports, January–February 1939, SRO EP 57.D.10. For colonial accounts of land tenure see Nalder, *Tribal Survey*, pp. 138–9, 176–7; Beaton, *Equatoria Province Handbook*, pp. 52–5.

17 Buxton, *Chiefs and Strangers*, pp. 36–43,

of wealth' in Equatoria, while Stigand claimed that cattle were the only form of property and inheritance among the Kuku.[18]

Buxton contrasted the low population density of her research area with the Nile banks where fertile soil attracted more concentrated settlements, more immigrants and more competition and conflict over land. One Juba DC, Beaton, reported clear boundaries between clan lands along the river and the inheritance of individual plots, indicating the greater value of land here.[19] Bari informants tend to support this view, emphasising the greater individualisation of land rights on the fertile islands and riverbanks near Juba:

> Each village, the land on which they have their settlements is supposed to belong to a certain group of people, collectively and individually. This land is a lifetime property; it's supposed to be passed from son to son. Especially the island lands which are supposed to be very fertile, each community member is supposed to have a particular piece of land which is his own exclusively. The case of my mother, for instance: when she got married, because my father was able to satisfy my [maternal] uncles and pay twelve heads of cattle, so as a reward for that they gave my mother a piece of land as a gift. Until today it still belongs to us, from my mother's side.[20]

A missionary in this area, Whitehead, also emphasised the strength of usage rights to land held by wives, which passed to their own sons on their death, rather than to their husbands; land was thus not controlled exclusively by patrilineal structure.[21] And land was also used to attract maternal relatives, dependents and immigrants *into* a patrilineal clan:

> The headman is responsible for the clan land – he knows where your grandfather lived, where his blood is, who has each plot. It is one village, but each clan has its own land. Your [maternal] nephew can come and live in the clan and has a right to inherit a wife [i.e. as would an agnatic relative], but the children would belong to this clan.[22]

Whitehead also stated that access to land was easy to obtain from the Bari land chief (*monyekak*) or clan heads.[23] The fertility and health of people, livestock and soil depended on the ritual and spiritual mediation of authorities whose vernacular names could be translated variously into English as 'owners', 'fathers', 'masters' and 'lords': however awkward these translations, they perhaps convey the idiom of patrilineal seniority, autochthony and precedence in which such claims to specialist authority were expressed. Strikingly the colonial records contain very little reference to disputes over cultivable land or between landowning clans.[24] This may reflect the plentiful land and small populations to which officials and anthropologists attributed a lack of dispute: wealth was still measured in people and livestock, not land in itself. But it may also indicate that land allocation and the resolution of any land disputes were kept away from the

[18] Nalder, *Tribal Survey*, p. 53; Stigand, *Equatoria*, p. 160.

[19] AC Beaton, 'Land Tenure among the Luluba and Oxoriok', 22 May 1934, NRO JD 1/1/2; Nalder, *Tribal Survey*, p. 138.

[20] Interview 3R/K.

[21] GO Whitehead, 'Property and inheritance among the Bari', *Sudan Notes and Records* 31:1 (1950), pp. 143–7.

[22] Interview 49R/JC.

[23] Whitehead, 'Crops and cattle'.

[24] One exception is Nalder's mention of a Mundari case in which 'complainants were definite in their refusal to accept a bull from people who had poached on their land, in order to retain their rights': *Tribal Survey*, p. 138.

chiefs' courts and government attention. Even before 1920, Stigand had written of the importance of a 'chief of the land and water' in Equatoria, who was 'often the power behind a chief':

> Although he is supposed to own all the land, by doing so he does not interfere with other people's rights. He would be applied to in the case of deciding on any movement of the people... The 'father of the land's' power is seldom noticed or heard of, and so little does he interfere, that one might remain for long in ignorance of his presence, and the 'chief of the people' would alone appear in administrative cases. However, the latter consults the 'land chief' on all important points and sometimes even takes to him cases he is unable to decide himself.[25]

The limited government awareness of the father/owner of the land, or *monyekak* in Bari, reveals the generally successful protection of the realm of land matters and fertility from government attention or interference. Beaton emphasised that the Bari *monyekak* was 'not the clan "head" in such matters as rendering labour to chief or government or the collection of tax'.[26] This no doubt contributed to the retention of greater moral authority by such figures. But by the 1930s, the more avid readers of wider ethnographic literature among British administrators were alerted to the potential power of 'the lord of the land': Nalder cited accounts of similar functionaries in West Africa.[27] Unlike in the Gold Coast, however, where land tenure was a much greater focus of the colonial government,[28] the Sudan administrators and the *monyekak* appeared largely content to ignore one another.

As discourses of history and genealogy had become productive of government recognition and rights, the interplay of discursive eloquence and political dominance that characterised local politics was increasingly being reproduced by the bureaucratic practices of government officials and anthropologists. Buxton, for example, repeatedly mentioned that the dominant landowning clans had 'a lot to say about themselves', ensuring that she recorded their detailed histories, whereas 'client lineages usually have little to say about their origins'.[29]

The tendency towards bureaucratisation of land matters provided opportunities for wider interaction with the state and for debate over historical claims. A vivid illustration of this was provided by a new British education department official on his first visit to Yei District, where the Forestry Commission's demands to reserve land had created some tensions during the 1940s. The new arrival accompanied the DC, Duke, from Loka to Yei:

> One our way, Duke had to stop and pay compensation to a tribe whose land had been encroached upon by the Forestry Commission. A long discussion ensued with the alcoholic Chief and certain raucous spokesmen of the tribe; there followed a long inspection of the boundary area, and the D.C. finally decided that the tribe preferred to keep their land rather than accept a fairly handsome compensation. This was my first practical experience of the work of a D.C.; I think I shall never in my life forget the lorry stopping and the driver automatically producing from the rear a table and chair, on which Duke placed himself au beau milieu de la route, discussing the pros and cons with a fat

25 Stigand, *Equatoria*, p. 34.

26 Nalder, *Tribal Survey*, p. 125.

27 Nalder, *Tribal Survey*, p. 26; JN Richardson, Assistant Governor Mongalla, to DC Latuka, Juba, 17 May 1930, NRO EP 2/12/46.

28 See Christian Lund, *Local Politics and the Dynamics of Property in Africa* (Cambridge, 2008), pp. 37–46.

29 Buxton, *Chiefs and Strangers*, pp. 19, 33.

> file in front of him; neither shall I forget the feverishly expectant eyes of the tribe, watching the discussion as it proceeded in Moru, Arabic and English alternately.[30]

This account is striking for its attention to the instantaneous creation of bureaucratic authority, for the prominence of the chief and 'raucous' spokesmen, and for the multiple translations that were going on. It shows how rights to land could be recognised in a brief moment like this, underscoring the vital role of interlocutors in securing communal territorial rights. As the power of the DC to record land rights in his 'fat file' was understood, the heads of landowning clans may have come into new direct contact with government bureaucracy.

Another example in the same area resulted from a protracted attempt to create a forest reserve in an area south of Yei, which the government called 'the Bala Hills', and believed was uninhabited.[31] In 1948, the Yei DC reported increasing complaints in the district at the extent of 'territorial demand' being made by the government for either forestry purposes or continuing sleeping sickness campaigns. Often it was the chiefs' B court that voiced such complaints, and, for example, demanded 'royalties' on the timber cut by the forestry department.[32] But when demarcation of the proposed Bala Hills reserve started in 1950, it was two 'elders' who 'appeared at Yei district office to lodge protests against any reservation of the area without financial recognition of their ancient rights'.[33] The government refused in this case to compensate them and the Bala Hills dispute rumbled on for several years; eventually a meeting was held in 1953 to discuss the government plans.

> The people objected very strongly to the name Bala Hills and speaker after speaker rose to prove that the name should not be Bala at all. The audience were carried back over the past, in one case as far back as the time when the Nile divided to allow the original ancestors of the Bori tribe to cross over from the East... The most dramatic bard of all was one who argued that the hill should be called Jebel Alima after a remarkable and undoubtedly fascinating woman chief of that name.[34]

'Dramatic bards' were using history not only to argue their rights in substrate political discourse but increasingly at the multiplying interfaces with government. It was therefore apparent that there were enduring layers of political and social geography beneath the more recent mangled colonial attempts to create new administrative units and to resettle people. These layers limited the power of chiefs and existed in tension with territorial definitions of chiefdoms, especially as the government sought to make people stay within the latter.

CHIEFS NEED PEOPLE: AMALGAMATION AND MIGRATION

Chiefship itself had often originated in mobility and migration, in terms of both the individual acquisition of linguistic and other foreign knowledge and the subsequent attraction of adherents. But this also gave chiefs' followers

30 HB Bullen, 'Personal diary of visit to southern Sudan, May–August 1947', SAD 864/2/16.

31 Equatoria Province Monthly Diaries, November–December 1949, NRO Dakhlia 57/5/13.

32 Equatoria Province Monthly Diaries, April, October–November 1948, and July 1949, NRO Dakhlia 57/5/13.

33 Equatoria Province Monthly Diary, January 1950, NRO Dakhlia 57/9/24.

34 Equatoria Province Monthly Diary, February 1953, NRO Civsec 2 30/3/6.

their own means of holding chiefs to account by the threat and practice of further migration to alternative patrons: 'No chief wanted his people to leave him', as Reining put it.[35] Increasingly, however, government officials sought to fix chiefship to particular territories and centres and to build 'coherent' communities by preventing migration between chiefs.[36] Throughout the colonial period, people subverted and evaded attempts to establish new communal and administrative boundaries. Because chiefs did not necessarily exercise control over land – and because land was not scarce – they could not use this as a patrimonial means of retaining people within their territories. But the introduction of salaries for chiefs by around 1930 had created incentives for both DCs and chiefs to reduce the number and enlarge the size of chiefships, because their salaries were 'computed on their number of tax payers'.[37] Together with their labour needs, chiefs had thus been given an added incentive to try to control large numbers of people, the latest manifestation of older patterns of 'wealth-in-people'.[38] But the larger the chiefship, the more difficult it also became to manage and supervise the various groups and individuals within it.

Administrators resorted to territorial units as the most practical basis of administration, and continued longer-term strategies of 'amalgamation' of smaller chiefships to create larger units. But there were continuing tensions between ideals of hereditary descent and administrative pragmatism: 'Government has already cut across any strict hereditary principle by permitting amalgamation and therefore in future we must be prepared to do the same again.'[39] In Moru District, administrators gave up on the idea of a clan-based tribute in favour of territorial headmanships.[40] Similarly in Rumbek District, the units of chiefship were based on the *wuot*, loosely territorial herding groups of multiple clans and lineages. Lienhardt explained both the reasons for and difficulties of the territorial policy in such areas:

> Both the clan and the lineage, being to differing degrees dispersed groups, were useless for administration... The Government found it necessary for administration, the collection of tribute etc., to deal with co-residential, territorial groups, though owing to the ease with which the Dinka move from one place to another to set up their homes, and the constant movement of the young men with their cattle, this was not easy.[41]

Both chiefs and administrators increasingly sought to define territorial chiefdoms and to regulate such movement. At a chiefs' meeting in Rumbek in

[35] Reining, *The Zande Scheme*, p. 25; Dove, 'Tour of inspection through country occupied by Mandari Nyambara tribes between the Nile and the Bahr El Ghazal, December 1908', April 1909, *SIR* 177, App. D, pp. 17–19, TNA WO 106/232; Keen, 'The tribes of Meridi Sub-district', 1946, NRO Dakhlia 112/14/95; Governor Nalder to DCs and Civil Secretary, 'The future of Native Administration in Mongalla', 5 February 1935, NRO Civsec 1/39/105.

[36] See also Douglas H Johnson, 'Tribal boundaries and border wars: Nuer-Dinka relations in the Sobat and Zaraf valleys, c. 1860–1976', *Journal of African History* 23:2 (1982), pp. 183–203, especially pp. 196–202.

[37] A/Governor Mongalla to Financial Secretary, 24 September 1935, NRO Civsec 1/39/105.

[38] Cf. Lonsdale, 'The conquest state', p. 15; Berry, *No Condition is Permanent*, p. 33.

[39] 'The Future: Selection of Chiefs', in Juba District Handbook, 1935, NRO JD 1/2/6; cf. Geschiere, 'Chiefs and colonial rule', pp. 160–3. On the politics of amalgamation and heredity elsewhere, see Nugent, *Smugglers, Secessionists*, pp. 126–46.

[40] Equatoria Province Monthly Diary, February 1939, NRO Civsec 57/11/42; Moru District Annual Report 1944, NRO EP 2/27/97; Interview 10K/MD; THB Mynors, 'Notes on the Moru Tribe', 1935, SAD 777/3/1–40.

[41] Godfrey Lienhardt, 'Dinka clans, tribes and tribal sections', in Beaton, *Equatoria Province Handbook*, Vol. 2, pp. 45–7.

1937, 'grazing transgressions were discussed and arrangements made to collect and return tribesmen living in an authorised areas[*sic*] beyond the control of their native authorities'.[42] Reports from across Equatoria make evident the extent of movement that was still occurring in the 1930s and 1940s, and the overlapping patterns of allegiance and jurisdiction of different chiefs:

> I think further research is needed into the territorial boundaries of Chiefs and sub-chiefs. We must have things in terms of territorial as opposed to tribal or clan administration, though of course the ideal is for the two to administer. We cannot permit persons to live in one Chiefs [*sic*] area and owe allegiance to another chief. If people want to change their chief they must also be prepared to move their villages and cultivations.[43]

However, the attempts to promote villagisation and enforce territorial chiefdoms were complicated by a growing realisation of the negative effects of the sleeping sickness and roadside resettlements detailed in Chapter 3. As early as 1933, the Director of Agriculture, Cameron, warned that the resettlement on roads could have adverse effects because it concentrated cultivation on the high ironstone ridges on which roads were constructed and where the soil was shallow.[44] By 1940, his successor Tothill was arguing that there were 'the strongest possible objections on the agricultural side' to the 'ribbon development' along the roads, and urging that the population should be moved away from the roads wherever possible.[45] Administrators therefore began to allow 'applications' to move away from the roads.[46] But during the 1940s many people moved without any official approval.[47] According to one DC, the Moru chiefs responded negatively to these autonomous resettlements: 'Die hard chiefs still pine for the rigid regimentation of the past and would like to see everyone forced to live on the roads again.'[48] They continued to push for re-concentration in the 1950s:

> The Amadi B court resolved 'That no economic progress or advance towards local government was possible for the Moru unless they abandoned their present habit of living in scattered hamlets'. To implement this resolution the Court directed that each chief, on his return to his country, should visit his sub-chiefs, collect the elders of the sub-chiefship and agree on a suitable area for concentration of the people.[49]

In the nearby Meridi area, people had always maintained their right to move between chiefs and sub-chiefs, despite government disapproval: '[i]t follows

42 'Wun Allel chiefs meeting, 26 January 1937', Rumbek District Monthly Report, January 1937, SRO EP 57.D.10.

43 BV Marwood, Governor Equatoria, to DC Juba, 29 March 1947, SRO EP 66.D.8.

44 Cameron, Director of Agriculture, in Governor Nalder, 'Mongalla Province Summary of Information', November 1933, NRO Civsec 57/35/131.

45 JD Tothill, 'Report, 1940', NRO EP 2/3/10; Rumbek District Monthly Report, April 1937, SRO EP 57.D.10.

46 Equatoria Province Monthly Diary, December 1940, NRO Civsec 57/12/46.

47 Yei District Monthly Diaries, February and April 1944, NRO EP 2/24/87; Equatoria Province Monthly Diaries, April 1940, NRO Civsec 57/12/46; March 1944, NRO Civsec 57/20/78; November 1948, NRO Dakhlia 57/5/13; Lui station newsletter 1943 and report 1944, CMS G3 Sg6; Yei central school report, 1941, CMS G3 Sg11; Lui hospital reports, 1942 and 1943, CMS G3 Sm2. According to Tosh, migration was one of the few clear acts of peasant resistance to unpopular chiefs: *Clan Leaders*, p. 212.

48 Equatoria Province Monthly Diary, April 1943, NRO Civsec 57/19/74.

49 Equatoria Province Monthly Diary, January 1950, NRO Dakhlia 57/9/24.

from this that subchiefs have little or no authority, and there is unlimited scope for playing one off against another'. Yet despite this administrator's perception of 'chaotic' organisation, he had to admit that the people seemed 'tractable and contented'.[50] In 1944, people were officially allowed to move between chiefdoms in Moru District, provided they registered the transfer: 173 were recorded as having moved between chiefs, and 258 between sub-chiefs in that year.[51] Such records indicate the growing efforts to record and control movements between chiefs; people who settled outside the territory of their own chief were now being described as 'squatters'. In 1942, a completed census was used to reorganise tax lists to try to ensure that people paid tax to the chief in whose territory they were settled, a process which 'caused some discontent to both chiefs and people'; disputes over the subjects of chiefs were still being reported in 1957.[52]

Similarly in Juba District, people moved into other chiefs' areas to escape demands for labour, grain or cotton cultivation, including across linguistic boundaries: Mundari were reportedly moving into Aliab areas, and Lokoya were 'wandering' into Bari country.[53] In some cases, people discontent with their chief were given express permission to transfer to a neighbouring chief.[54] But in 1948 the Governor of Equatoria expressed concern at the tendency to fission:

> My file on the appointments and dismissals of chiefs in Juba District presents a sorry picture of incompetence and maladministration among many of the holders of such posts, and of continuous chopping and changing over by small groups from one chiefship to another. These continuous permutations exaggerate the natural tendency of tribal groups to disintegrate and make effective administration well nigh impossible.[55]

While government and chiefs never succeeded in preventing individual or small-scale migration, it did become increasingly difficult for entire groups to relocate like this. Where the option of spatial withdrawal was curtailed, aspirations and grievances alike increasingly coalesced on the political and administrative frontier of chiefship itself.

CHIEFSHIP AS INTERNAL FRONTIER

The perennial tendency for sections or descent groups to try to gain independence from chiefdoms continued throughout and beyond the later Condominium period. Dinka chiefs from Aweil District explained that this resulted from chiefs or sub-chiefs frequently being suspected of favouring their own descent-group, provoking 'jealousy between clans' and fragmentation of chiefdoms.[56] The

[50] Keen, 'The tribes of Meridi Sub-district', 1946, NRO Dakhlia 112/14/95. See also Nalder to DCs and Civil Secretary, 'The future of Native Administration in Mongalla', 5 February 1935, NRO Civsec 1/39/105.

[51] Moru District Annual Report 1944, NRO EP 2/27/97.

[52] Moru District Monthly Diaries, January–February 1942, SRO MD 57.D.2.

[53] AC Beaton, entry in Mongalla Province Chiefs Register, January 1933, NRO JD 1/1/2; Equatoria Province Monthly Diary, January 1946, NRO Dakhlia 57/2/5.

[54] GRC Lumsden, DC Juba, to Governor Equatoria 24 April 1946; ED Arbuthnot, DC Juba, to Governor Equatoria, 4 June 1948, SRO EP 66.D.8.

[55] HA Nicholson, A/Governor Equatoria to DC Juba, 7 June 1948, SRO EP 66.D.8.

[56] Governor Equatoria to DCs Aweil, Jur River and Lakes, 'Record of Tonj discussions 29–31 March 1942', 24 April 1942, NRO BGP 1/5/28; Penn, DC Lakes, to Governor Equatoria, 8 October 1938, NRO BGP 1/5/28.

death, retirement or removal of a chief was often an occasion for the revival of claims and counter-claims to the chiefship, but this rivalry in itself reflected the enhanced status attached to chiefship by this time. Increasingly in some areas, chiefly families were being challenged by clans or families claiming a more senior position in lineage and landowning structures. The colonial government was receptive to the latter's historical and genealogical arguments. But it had also invested considerably in chiefship, and was often reluctant to risk the status quo. The outcome of disputes was hence variable, but the language in which they were argued was invariably one of history and descent, idioms in which chiefs were often far from dominant. Yet the fact that these disputes were so focused on chiefship ensured that the institution was nevertheless strengthened.

An example was Ilibari, a village near Juba that had been part of the Gondokoro chiefship of Modi Swoka, the descendant of the famous nineteenth-century chief Allorron or Loro Lako. Modi's successors were both accused of misappropriating tribute money and favouring their own relations when ordering working parties for Juba. In 1939, the DC therefore decided to put Ilibari under a neighbouring Bari chief, Melodian Logono of Belinian, provoking a letter from the current chief Lako Boreng: 'Why should an independent tribe be made compelled [*sic*] to go under another tribe against their wish?'[57] In 1946, Chief Melodian was succeeded by Loko Logono, prompting a renewed demand by the Ilibari for their own chiefdom, on the grounds of unfair treatment by Melodian; a smaller independent chiefdom was therefore created.[58] Later research in the 1970s–80s suggests that the problems in Ilibari had been caused by rivalry between Modi Swoka's Lé clan, and the senior clan in Ilibari, Panigelo.[59] DC Cooke had been receptive to complaints against Modi's son, Chief Tongun Modi, for taking livestock and beating people, on the grounds that 'his father Modi Shoka had no claim to the chiefship'.[60]

This case thus reflects two key overlapping features of complaints against chiefs: the usurpation of lineage seniority by chiefly lines; and accusations of inequitable treatment of other clans within a chiefdom, which might draw on idioms of patrimonial obligation towards subordinate clans and families. But the case of Ilibari also demonstrates the danger that internal political dispute and complaints against a chief could lead to amalgamation under a neighbouring chief, and hence to worse marginalisation in a larger chiefdom. Increasingly efforts were concentrated on maintaining independent chiefships, as for example when a Meridi chief was also imprisoned for embezzlement: 'amalgamation with a neighbouring chiefship was recommended but the people's strong desire for independence manifested itself in the collection of the money embezzled'. This action convinced the government to allow the appointment of a relative of the chief rather than amalgamating the chiefdom.[61] Interviewees elsewhere claimed that people refused to be amalgamated or were 'very bitter' if they were; they 'had the feeling that they had been deprived, robbed of what they should have'.[62]

The outcome of local political disputes and chiefship contests varied according to the context and the attitude of both the DC and any other chiefs

[57] Chief Lako Bureng to Civil Secretary, January 1940, SRO EP 66.D.8.

[58] GRC Lumsden, DC Juba, to Governor Equatoria 24 April 1946, SRO EP 66.D.8; Equatoria Province Monthly Diary, March–May 1946, NRO Dakhlia 57/2/5.

[59] Huby, 'Big men', p. 70

[60] RC Cooke, DC Central, to Governor Equatoria, 19 June 1937, SRO EP 66.D.8.

[61] Moru District Annual Report 1939, NRO EP 2/26/94.

[62] Interviews 3R/K; 6N/YC; DA Penn for DC Juba to Governor Equatoria, 3 September 1949; JF Tiernay, Governor Equatoria to DC Juba, 9 December 1950, SRO EP 66.D.8.; Equatoria Province Monthly Diary, March 1952, NRO Civsec2 30/3/6.

who were brought in to mediate. In some cases people were able to successfully complain against a chief and assert their autonomy; in other cases chiefs were supported against rebellious factions. Sometimes claims based on history and genealogy predominated; in other cases officials and chiefs asserted more pragmatic rationales for preserving the status quo, as in this example from western Rumbek District:

> A chiefs' meeting was held at Allel. The application of three sub-chiefs of the Cic Ador to split off and join the Gok was not approved. Though the Sub Chiefs concerned could produce genealogical evidence supporting their claims, the court took a realistic attitude and said that the social pattern had now crystallized for the Ador and Gok: that all kraals could show 'strangers within the gate' and that this reason alone was not sufficient to support their claim.[63]

However, even if in this case the 'genealogical evidence' was ineffective, this was clearly the language in which such disputes were being articulated. In other cases chiefs were less successful in suppressing the claims of sub-sections. In 1958, the Jebel Lado headmanship of Loro Nyijak to the north of Juba was detached from chief Mere Kiri and reincorporated into the Tokiman chiefship, necessitating the agreement of the boundary between headman and former chief. A special C chiefs' court heard the resulting dispute:

> When the public opinion was in favour of moving the boundary to River Kuda, chief Mere Kiri was very much opposed to it and insisted that the boundary shall be extended further south of River Kuda. The chief, in order to support his own case, related a big story going back to the time of Belgian occupation as to whose grandfathers owned that land. Both the people of chief Mere Kiri and of Mokongo [Headman] Loro Ngijak did not agree with chief Mere Kiri and said that their grandfathers had this river in common and there is no cause to quarrel.[64]

One chief who used history more successfully to defend the integrity and autonomy of his chiefship was the rain chief of Sindiru, Pitya Lugor, despite persistent government dissatisfaction with his and his son's administration. He declared in writing, 'my chieftaincy is not new, it is an old state. Long ago when the Govt. came in this country, all the power was in the hand of my ancestors'. But despite his success in convincing government officials that he was the only chief with 'an ancient history' in the district, he was unable to secure his son's succession in the face of opposition from both his people and the Bari Council of Chiefs; his educated nephew was chosen instead. It emerged through these discussions that Pitya had only become chief because his own nephew, who 'should' have succeeded Pitya's elder brother, was too young.[65] Even this powerful rain chief was thus subject to the prevailing discourses of patrilineal genealogy encouraged by colonial officials.

Pitya himself and other chiefs made ample use of written letters to communicate their claims to government, and more widely people were using more bureaucratic tools in their disputes over chiefship. 'Agitators' against the appointment of a new chief in Juba District 'produced lists of those reputed to want one of the Legge family as Chief'.[66] In 1946–47, a series of 'petitions'

[63] Rumbek District Monthly Report, January 1941, SRO EP 57.D.10.

[64] Juba Rural District Council Monthly Report, August and November 1958, Appendix B: SRO EP 100.B.4/7.

[65] Juba District Annual Report 1939, NRO EP 2/26/94; Chief Pitya Lugor to Governor-General, Sindiru, 4 January 1936, NRO Civsec 66/9/84; 'Juba District Handbook', 1935–9, NRO JD 1/2/6.

[66] Equatoria Province Monthly Diary, February 1949, NRO Dakhlia 57/5/13.

were sent to the government from a section under Chief Yosepa Sokiri Yokwe, complaining at their unfair treatment by the chief. Chief Sokiri then wrote a long letter to the Juba DC in his defence, claiming that the problems had arisen from his execution of unpopular government orders:

> The trouble comes from the grain of government. They complain against chiefs works, and that is to say next time I will not do the government work properly... I want my people not to go away. If they want to go away because of my work, I will stop them from my work.[67]

This was of course the perennial problem for chiefs: enforcing government demands for labour and tax placed a strain on chiefs, and could lead to people deserting them.[68] Chief Sokiri's rather plaintive wish to retain these people was not convincing enough for the government, despite some official sympathy for his position. The DC explained to the Governor that this section had originally belonged to another chiefship but had been put under Sokiri twenty years earlier; he was not their 'natural chief' therefore, and probably had treated them unfairly. In this case then, claims on the basis of history and genealogy won out and the government accepted the refusal of the section to remain under Sokiri: 'there is, I think, nothing for it but to allow those who want to to join another Chief'.[69] As well as instancing a successful appeal to government, this case also demonstrates how segmentary tendencies and sectional rivalries now focused on the politics of chiefship.

As well as producing disputes and complaints, the internal tensions within chiefdoms might also manifest in accusations of and concerns about witchcraft and poison.[70] Such concerns were intensified by the increasing territorial confinement of people: the areas that produced the most reports of witchcraft and poison cases were also those of the densest and most permanent settlement, particularly Yei and Kajo Keji.[71] Chiefs were often believed to have been targeted by witchcraft, and the threat or fear of supernatural retaliation was a form of sanction against chiefly abuses; interviewees recalled particular chiefs who had suffered infertility or early death because they had provoked people's 'hatred'.[72] When Chief Lokolong Leggi died in 1937, his brothers refused the chiefship 'as they were afraid of being killed or poisoned'.[73] The idea that chiefship could lead to mysterious deaths is a common trope in Central Equatoria, and some people explain their own family or clan's abdication of chiefship in terms of this fear.

The discourse of the dangers of chiefship had two obvious sides to it: on the one hand it was means of imposing accountability on chiefs and deterring them from making enemies within the chiefdom. But on the other hand chiefs and chiefly families have presented the dangers and deaths in the chiefly line as evidence of the burden of chiefship that they have carried, and hence their continuing right to it.[74] In a sense chiefship came to embody the tensions and dangers of membership in an enlarged territorial community. But it also came to

67 Chief Yosepa Sokiri Yokwe, Kagwada, to DC Juba, 10 January 1947, SRO EP 66.D.8.

68 Cf. Berry, *Chiefs Know their Boundaries*, p. 11.

69 ED Arbuthnot, DC Juba, to Governor Equatoria, 31 January 1947, SRO EP 66.D.8.

70 Cf. Kopytoff, 'The internal African frontier', p. 19.

71 Stigand, *Equatoria*, p. 67; FJ Finch, Kajo Kaji, 10 July 1935 and 8 November 1938, CMS G3 AL; Evans-Pritchard, *Witchcraft, Oracles*, p. 37.

72 Interview 50R/JC.

73 RC Cooke, DC Central, to Governor Equatoria, 16 July 1937, SRO EP 66.D.8.

74 See Leonardi, 'Violence, sacrifice and chiefship', p. 546.

signify the benefits of protection and external relations that such communities had always provided.

TETHERING PEOPLE TO THEIR CHIEFS: THE PRODUCTION OF LOCALITY

The more that government and chiefs attempted to keep people within particular territories, the more tense and conflicted local politics could become. But on the other hand administrative policy may have been recognising the relevance of territorial units of settlement or herding, inhabited by multiple kinship groups brought together by the need for defence and sociability. There were enduring tensions in local societies, which fed into the confusions and contradictions of government policy, between the attraction of larger group affiliation, and the desire to control resources within individual and autonomous households, families and lineages.[75] As Buxton emphasised, while agnatic kin relationships, however distant, were never entirely forgotten, it was 'situations of daily life' and 'territorial solidarity' that were often more important; Mundari history demonstrated 'desire to form separate territorial and political units even at the expense of severing kinship'.[76] Some administrators also argued that the creation of territorial units made sense because people living in the same localities interacted and co-operated with one another much more than with distant kinsmen.[77]

According to Lienhardt, the Dinka verb used in the 1940s in relation to the government was *mac*, meaning to tether or constrain. Lienhardt associated this with the government capacity to imprison, and it certainly evokes the colonial attempts to confine people to particular territories and chiefdoms. Yet he reveals the typical ambiguity of the word in his explanation that it was also used for the reservation of cattle for special and spiritual purposes, and for bridewealth.[78] In fact the notion of tethering would also be used of the chiefs, who were later said to be a 'tethering-rope' for the calf-like youths.[79] In the Dinka context, chiefdoms corresponded most closely to the socio-political organisation of the *wut*, the cattle camp or kraal, within which multiple lineage groups tethered their cattle, and which provided both a social unit within which marriage could take place between exogamous lineages, and 'a political unit large and powerful enough to defend itself against aggression'.[80] In 1938, colonial officials suggested it might be better to accept that chiefdoms were defined by cattle camp and territory, not tribe or descent, and contained a mixture of people: 'The transition from a clan organisation with leading men having jurisdiction only over members of their own clan into a territorial organisation in which the chief and elders have jurisdiction over all clans who have joined a particular cattle kraal territory has taken place in Lakes and Tonj districts.'[81]

The internal contradictions of indirect rule doctrines were once again

[75] Lienhardt, 'The Western Dinka', pp. 97–135.

[76] Buxton, *Chiefs and Strangers*, p. 51.

[77] THB Mynors, 'Notes on the Moru Tribe', 1935, SAD 777/3/1-40.

[78] Lienhardt, 'The Sudan', pp. 27–8.

[79] Minutes of the Meeting of HE the Commissioner Lakes Province with Aliamtoc Chiefs on 3 August 1984, Bahr el Ghazal Province Archive, Wau, LP 66.B.1.

[80] Lakes District Handbook, 1940, pp. 14–15, SRO EP 1.G.2.

[81] Extract from minutes of Dinka DCs' meeting held at Tonj, 21–26 January 1938, NRO BGP 1/5/28.

apparent here, as notions of political evolution ran up against the attempts of other administrators to reify patrilineal clans and tribes. Some DCs saw the strength of more territorial *wut* chiefdoms as evidence of the disintegration of 'Agar structure' and erosion of the role and authority of lineage leaders due to the power of government chiefs.[82] But there was of course truth in the suggestion that descent groups had already tended to come together in larger cattle-camp affiliations, and that these more territorial or grazing communities had been open to assimilating newcomers. The Aweil DC argued that different family groups had always occupied shared territories, and 'for self protection had combined together and herded their cattle in a common kraal'.[83]

It was this function of protection and defence that was being transferred to chiefdoms and valued in chiefs. A chief's link to the government could be an asset in protecting territorial and resource rights by negotiating favourable compensation, peace and grazing agreements. In 1958, the Mundari chiefs of Gemeiza complained to the government about Dinka bringing cattle into their grazing territory and also stealing cows from them: 'The chief [Lako Legge] was very serious over the matter and reported it to the local authorities'. A few years later it was reported that Dinka chiefs were asking permission to graze in the area of Chief Lako Legge, suggesting that he was continuing to mediate these relations.[84]

While specialist authorities like land or earth chiefs continued to play their role in securing the fertility of the land, the new rules of the government ensured that chiefs would thus become increasingly prominent in securing and defending land rights. As a rain chief near Yei later put it, the land belonged to the clan landlords, 'but the person who guards the whole of it is the chief'.[85] In 1949, for example, the Juba town council tried to persuade the Bari villagers near Juba Dairy (i.e. the Juba na Bari village, which had already moved once to make way for the town) to move to a new site near the *malakiya*. But Chief Severino of Tokiman 'pointed out the tendency of the Bari to attach themselves to the land where their fathers lived and he explained the difficulty of moving these people far away from the island situated opposite their present village'.[86]

The potential benefits of belonging to larger chiefdoms were recognised in discourses of good chiefship. In 1938, a new chief was reportedly selected by elders to the east of Rumbek:

> There is no 'beny-bith' [spear-master] or other 'ruling' family and the old men's reasons for this selection were that he was rich in cattle, was respected, and had enough character to hold the country together.[87]

The reference to 'holding the country together' is an important and revealing insight into the development of discursive ideals of chiefship. The value of cattle-rich and strong chiefs was measured in terms of their capacity to protect the key resources and property of rural households and lineages: land and/or cattle. The Pakkam Agar chief Wol Athiang, consistently reported and remembered as a strong and defiant chief, was a source of frustration for

82 E.g. Rumbek District Monthly Report, January 1939, SRO EP 57.D.10; Lakes District Handbook, 1940, pp. 14–15: SRO EP 1.G.2

83 DC Aweil to Governor Equatoria, 19 January 1938, NRO BGP 1/5/28.

84 Juba Rural District Council Monthly Report, November 1958, Appendix B, and March 1962, SRO EP 100.B.4/7.

85 Interview 9R/YC.

86 Minutes of the Juba Town Council 14th meeting, 28 June 1949, SRO EP 100.C.2.D.

87 Rumbek District Monthly Report, February 1938, SRO EP 57.D.10.

colonial officials seeking to settle conflicts, such as that between the Pakkam and the neighbouring Luac in 1939: 'settlement was, at times, made difficult by the rather unbending attitude of the Agar Chief Wol Athiang'.[88] Yet for the Pakkam section, Wol was an effective means of defending boundaries and manipulating district officials, who came into their own conflicts with neighbouring administrators through their support for him. In contrast, another Agar section complained that their chief was failing to offer such protection, and asked for his removal 'on the grounds that he was not strong enough to prevent other Chiefs of the Aliam Toc section from taking their cattle'.[89]

Strength was similarly the most important quality of a chief among the Mundari, according to Buxton: 'A good chief for the Mundari was a strong chief; a bad one was not a repressive one, though harshness was regrettable, but a weak one'. Strength was measured in the ability to retain large followings: 'numerical superiority is the basis of political power'.[90] There is a certain tautology to this discourse: a weak chief would lose support and a chief without people was a weak chief. But it is clear that indigenous ideas about strength in numbers were intersecting in dynamic ways with government policies of amalgamation.

The importance of population numbers to the status of chiefships was increasingly being emphasised by government officials. Sub-chiefs tried to claim independent status as chiefs on the basis of their population numbers in comparison to other chiefs.[91] In the late 1950s amalgamations of chiefdoms continued to be promoted on the grounds that larger populations would receive more social services:

> Chief like Lolik Lado with 2715 tax payers weighs more that [*sic*] Aznaba with 277 tax payers. If the people of Aznaba join their neighbouring chief Phulai they will be able by their joint efforts to carry more efficiently their duties and will have the right to ask for services in return.[92]

As this suggests, the idea that chiefship was a point of access to government services was increasingly promoted in the late-colonial and immediate post-colonial periods, and fed into the emphasis on numbers. Government services tended to be located at the headquarters of chiefs, as for example in Lakes District where 'density of population' was a determinant of the location of wells, contributing to the drive to concentrate population around the chiefs.[93] In Juba District in 1955 headmen in one chiefdom complained that their chief was living away from the centre of population: 'They asked that Chief Kiri should come and live in the centre of Miri and that the Dispensary should also be in the centre, so that every one should enjoy the medical facilities.'[94] Agricultural assistance was similarly channelled through the chiefs.[95]

Chiefs' role in managing external affairs in relation to government was thus gaining enhanced value as the possibility of accessing government resources gradually developed. This role was also seemingly extending to other kinds of

88 Rumbek District Monthly Report, April 1939, SRO EP 57.D.10.

89 Rumbek District Monthly Report, September 1938, SRO EP 57.D.10.

90 Buxton, *Chiefs and Strangers*, pp. 66, 70.

91 Lakes District handing over notes, 1947, SRO EP 1.G.2.

92 GMA Bakheit, 'Minutes of meeting held in Tali to discuss the future of the people of ex chief Aznaba Lokule', 2 February 1959; and 'Minutes of meeting at Sindiru on 22 January 1959 to discuss the question of Sindiru chieftainship', SRO EP 66.D.8.

93 Lakes District Handbook, 1940, p. 5, SRO EP 1.G.2.

94 Juba Rural District Council Monthly Diary, May 1955, SRO EP 100.B.4/7.

95 Equatoria Province Monthly Diary, June 1948, NRO Dakhlia 57/5/13.

external resource; for example, chiefs were increasingly expected to manage relations with specialists within and beyond their own chiefdom, such as witchcraft diviners and rain experts.[96] People complained to the chief, for example, if a rain-maker was believed to be holding up the rain, and the chief might imprison or punish him.[97] On the other hand, in 1938, the Terekeka chiefs 'presented a combined petition that an Aliab Dinka... whom they said was a noted rainmaker in his own country, should be allowed to reside among the Mandari'.[98] The chiefs' courts were increasingly claiming to address the problem of witchcraft; while this may have been a useful way for chiefs to assert their authority and even to threaten or accuse troublesome individuals, it may also have been a response to popular demand for protection from the perennial threat of witchcraft.[99]

Chiefship had become both a figurehead for community identity and autonomy, and the focus of internal rivalries. But as well as generating and reflecting the tendency to segmentation and fission, in some cases chiefships were becoming seen as a basis for unity and for the gathering of larger communities. Buxton's account of the Mundari in the 1950s sums up the tension between a fierce desire for autonomy and recognition at the level of small individual settlements or lineage groups, and an awareness that this autonomy and recognition might only be secured through strength in numbers. She explains that the thirty-plus independent 'village-chiefdoms' of the Mundari had been amalgamated under just six government-sponsored chiefs, leading to internal tensions and rivalries and the continuing importance of 'the old geo-political organisation'. Yet '[s]ome of the small groups now amalgamated, however, admit that they could not have remained independent indefinitely because of their lack of numbers and the pressure of powerful neighbours. Many of them were already in loose federations under their own leaders.'[100] The tension between amalgamation and segmentation did not go away, but it had become channelled into chiefship disputes and lineage politics rather than wholesale migration.

CONCLUSION

The colonial attempts to define the Native Administration units by territory and to restrict the option of migration had multiple effects, as well as limited effectiveness. Administrators were seeking to strengthen communal attachment to territory and to recognise history and descent as the basis for communal land rights and authority. A widening interface with government was giving elders and clan or lineage heads greater opportunity and incentive to articulate their rights, and to ensure their bureaucratic preservation and reproduction. At the same time, chiefs were becoming seen as potentially the most effective means of defining and defending territorial rights, whether against government appropriation or the encroachment of other groups. Yet if people were increasingly restricted in their movement and settlement, this could exacerbate internal tensions and suspicions of witchcraft; people might also threaten or attack chiefs by occult means. As internal tensions still

96 Cf. Lonsdale, 'The politics of conquest', p. 64.

97 Interview 4R/K; Simonse, *Kings of Disaster*, especially pp. 345–73; Spire, 'Rain-Making in Equatorial Africa', pp. 15–21.

98 Equatoria Province Monthly Diary, October 1938, NRO Civsec 57/7/29.

99 FJ Finch, Annual letter, Kajo Kaji, 8 November 1938, CMS G3 AL.

100 Buxton, *Chiefs and Strangers*, p. 35.

produced powerful tendencies to fission, migration to the internal frontier was being replaced by a focus on gaining administrative recognition and autonomy. As in Benin, local political life worked 'along (irregular) cycles of fission and fusion, as if the segmentary logic of the frontier were imprisoned in the village cage'.[101]

Indirect rule in Africa made membership in a 'community' 'the primary basis for claiming rights to productive resources'.[102] In southern Sudan, this process was hindered by the multiplicity of authorities exercising control over productive resources. But communities were nevertheless also being made here during the colonial period. The contradictions and confusions of colonial administration led to the paradox that while community was actually defined by territory, it had to be explained by reference to history and genealogy.[103] The production of such discourse more widely in colonial Africa has often been attributed to the chiefs, and the advantages of their interlocutory role with government. But in southern Sudan it instead opened up a discursive space in which chiefs might be marginalised by genealogies of autochthony and first-coming. Yet these claims to ancient land rights and precedence helped to embed communities in territories, just as disputes over chiefship helped to produce chiefdom as community. Through tension and conflict, chiefship, lineage structures and territorial chiefdoms became intertwined in an ongoing production of locality as community.

[101] Le Meur, 'State making', p. 875.

[102] Berry, *No Condition is Permanent*, p. 41.

[103] Cf. David Maxwell, *Christians and Chiefs in Zimbabwe: a social history of the Hwesa people c. 1870s–1990s* (Edinburgh, 1999), pp. 44–5.

6

Uncertainty on the urban frontier: chiefs and the politics of Sudanese independence, 1946–1958

The final decade of the Condominium heightened popular expectations of government and opened up new avenues of communication and opportunity for southern Sudanese to access the state. Burton claims that it was from the 1940s that towns were 'accepted' by local people, 'when it became clear that in order to protect their own political and economic interests, it was essential to participate in town-oriented affairs more directly'.[1] Yet the effect of an urban-rural, state-society divide was nevertheless being sharply crystallised in this period, firstly through the consolidation and political activism of an increasingly self-conscious, town-dwelling, literate 'class' (as the government increasingly termed them). By the 1950s, many of these educated men, in common with nationalist politicians in the rest of Sudan and Africa, were presenting themselves as distinctly modern in comparison to the 'traditional' chiefs, a discursive bifurcation that would endure subsequently in southern Sudan.

Secondly, wider political change and events in the 1950s also fed into the cultural and cognitive hardening of a rural-urban divide. Over the preceding decades of colonial rule, the *hakuma* had – particularly for the people living in the vicinity of the towns – acquired aspects of predictability and recognisability, whether in the person of a few long-serving, vernacular-speaking British officials, or in the wider regularisation of taxation demands, justice and policing. Much of this predictability and regularisation was seen by both government and people to be achieved by and mediated through chiefship – an effective chief 'knew the government' and hence could render it more predictable. But in the 1950s, the circulation of news and rumour about political developments, and the 'Sudanisation' of the army and administration, made the *hakuma* seem once again to be dangerously unpredictable. On the one hand this could expose the limits of chiefly knowledge and undermine the tenuous legitimacy of the chiefs. But on the other hand it reminded people of the need for skilful interlocution to avert the increasingly unwelcome or dangerous attention of the government.

In 1955, this need would be brought home in a particularly dramatic way by a mutiny of southern troops in Equatoria, and the eruption of violent rebellion in several southern towns, in which hundreds of northern Sudanese families, as well as many southerners, were killed. Northern Sudanese administrators and merchants thus became the target of southern Sudanese mistrust, fear and political resentment. But the Sudanisation of the administration did not in itself mark a dramatic change; the northern officials (and the few southern ones) had been trained by the British and their reports continued much the same styles, attitudes and policies as their predecessors. There had been continuing fear and resentment of British officials before northerners became a focus of political mistrust; it was against British paternalistic authoritarianism that educated southerners

[1] Burton, 'When the north winds blow', p. 57.

had been protesting over the previous decade.[2] Historians of Sudan have tended also to argue for the continuities of the mid-1950s, spanning the immediate pre- and post-independence periods.[3] Of course for South Sudanese, 1955 has instead been held up as the pivotal moment in their history, and as the beginning of the civil wars with Khartoum governments. A recent re-examination of this period by Rolandsen agrees with Johnson that a state of civil war did not commence until 1963. But he argues that 1955 nevertheless marked the beginning of an uneasy state of 'no peace, no war' in southern Sudan, characterised by military rule and repression, sporadic actions by the remnants of the mutineers, and the movement into exile of some of the leading southern politicians.[4]

From the perspective of the local histories we have been tracing, 1955 was certainly a sudden turning-point in relations with the towns and government. The urban frontier had been blurring and expanding in the preceding decades; now people fled its risks and exposure and sought refuge in the bush. Southerners were reminded abruptly (if they had ever forgotten) of the need for protection, concealment and defence from an increasingly intrusive and unpredictable state. In the aftermath of the mutiny, the new government blamed the literate class of government employees, teachers and politicians for the violence. From a rather different perspective, many ordinary people also interpreted the events of 1955 as confirmation of the danger of seeking to participate too closely in the government and of inviting government politics into local communities. As relations with government resumed after 1955, it was with renewed wariness and greater distance. In a sense history was coming full circle from the late nineteenth and early twentieth centuries, so that chiefs were once again necessary gatekeepers providing, above all, protection. But the 1950s were very different from the Turkiyya, Mahdiyya or early Condominium; now people were subject to a new regime of bureaucratic information and surveillance, the more frightening for its inconsistency and reliance upon individual informants. Chiefs' knowledge and interlocution held more than ever the possibility of both threat and guarantee in such uncertain times.

POLITICAL PARTICIPATION ON THE URBAN FRONTIER

The last decade of the Condominium saw a rapid, interconnected expansion of the government interface, urban frontier and public political arenas. Although chiefs continued to play a prominent role in all these sites of interaction with the state, many other people were gaining knowledge and experience of government and towns through schooling, government employment, military service, trade, labour migration, churches, court cases and so on. From the women who 'besieged'[5] the Rumbek merkaz demanding famine relief, to the 'raucous spokesmen'[6] contesting land reservations around Yei, people had been increasingly seizing or creating opportunities for discourse, demands and debates in public arenas and government offices. In the 1940s and 1950s, this was further encouraged by the creation of new local government councils and provincial and national assemblies. Their capacity and effectiveness was even more

2 See also Scopas S Poggo, *The First Sudanese Civil War* (New York, 2009), e.g. p. 24.

3 Holt and Daly, *A History of the Sudan*, p. 145.

4 Øystein H Rolandsen, 'Civil War Society? Political processes, social groups and conflict intensity in the southern Sudan, 1955–2005' (PhD, University of Oslo, 2010), and 'A false start: between war and peace in the southern Sudan, 1956–62', *Journal of African History* 52:1 (2011), pp. 105–123; Johnson, *Root Causes*, p. 31.

5 See chapter 3, footnote 79.

6 See chapter 5, footnote 30.

limited than in other parts of colonial Africa, where the role of councils in the late-colonial period has received mixed assessment. But while such analyses have focused largely on the political context and action of councils, it is also important to examine the ways in which the expanding institutions of local government gave their members a sense of participation in the state itself, even if they also continued to be frustrated by the exclusionary government reaction. Indeed the 'tantalizing mixture of opportunity and restriction' presented by such councils in Kenya[7] had always characterised southern Sudanese relations with the colonial government, and their experiences of the urban frontier.

Local government councils were created from as early as the mid-1930s in some areas, largely based on the existing chiefs' B courts, which had already functioned as arenas for discussion between chiefs and government officials. In the early 1950s, these were given new formal status as elected rural councils. The Marshall Report of 1949 on local government had suggested that, ideally or eventually, chiefs should not serve on councils but should be purely executive authorities[8]. But as one chief pointed out when this was reported to the Bahr el Ghazal Province Council in 1950, since 'the chiefs are the only educated men, they must at present be the members of the Councils'. In 1948 the Bahr el Ghazal Province had been re-separated from Equatoria Province, which established its own Province Council, elected by the B court chiefs. In Yei District, two chiefs, Tete and Modi, were chosen, but there was greater debate over this at Yei:

> The difference between rural Kajo Kaji and urban Yei was clearly reflected at these meetings. At Kajo Kaji there was no serious proposal that anyone other than Chief Tete should be chosen. At Yei however many speakers suggested that the selective net should be cast more widely, and that a local teacher might be as good a representative as a chief. The deciding factor was that only two seats had been allotted to Yei district and as one had already gone to a Kajo Kaji chief, the Yei chiefs considered themselves bound to elect a chief from amongst themselves to fill the other seat.[9]

Council politics were thus also chiefs' politics and characterised by a degree of rivalry and competitiveness between chiefdoms and even between chiefs of different districts. But the discussion also revealed the widening 'net' of political participation in the town and district arenas in Yei. In the late 1940s, a 'Yei Public Forum' was instituted as a kind of debating chamber, discussing, for example, the topic of 'Women's clothes':

> Few speakers kept to the point and the sixty or seventy people present were obliged to listen to merchants extolling the quality and cheapness of their latest 'Khartoum' or 'Congo' fashions. A cunning butcher, with his eye on the ladies, promised men who brought him their animals, good money with which to buy their wives dresses.

Seventy was not a huge number and these were probably townspeople with the money to consider women's fashions. But the fact that these were also livestock-owners is indicative of urban-rural connections, and their wives' attendance suggests growing public participation in such urban arenas. Over Christmas in 1949, large crowds 'thronged' Yei town: 'There were dances on the football pitch, a sports gathering and a cinema show at the playhouse'.[10]

7 Donald G Schilling, 'Local Native Councils and the politics of education in Kenya, 1925–1939', *International Journal of African Historical Studies* 9:2 (1976), p. 233.

8 AH Marshall, *Report on Local Government in the Sudan* (London, 1949).

9 Equatoria Province Monthly Diaries, March 1948, NRO Dakhlia 57/5/13, and June–December 1951, NRO Dakhlia 57/9/24.

10 Equatoria Province Monthly Diaries, August and December 1949, NRO Dakhlia 57/5/13.

As more people interacted with the towns and government, the value of education and bureaucratic knowledge was increasingly recognised, indicated in the more frequent writing of letters and complaints to government and the recording of court cases. This is why even the Yei chiefs wondered if a teacher might be better-equipped than them to serve on the Province Council. Elders and clan heads thought similarly, as evidenced in elections to new district education councils in 1950. In one of the Juba District elections, an ex-soldier, the only literate candidate, was elected rather than one of the three chiefs standing: '[l]iteracy won, clan heads murmuring as they cast their votes "because he reads", for fear of reprisals from their chiefs'.[11] The need to read was certainly apparent in a report of the highly bureaucratic culture and practices of the Juba Town Council in 1949:

> Juba Town Council dealt with brickmaking, town roads, times of meeting and the necessity for giving members a better idea of their duties and responsibilities. To this end a sub-committee was formed to discuss the 'literature' needed to educate the members in their job, eg copies of the warrants, the Local Government townships legislation etc.[12]

In 1951, seven policemen or soldiers, seven sub-chiefs and three teachers were elected to the Meridi Advisory Local Council. The Province Councils had also elected members to the national Legislative Assembly (LA) in 1948, including two educated chiefs with experience of mission or government employment for Moru and Juba districts, and a CMS teacher, Benjamin Lwoki, as member for Yei District. Lwoki, who would go on to become a leading politician, emphasised in a speech to the Yei B Court that he was not a chief or leader, but rather had been chosen as a 'messenger' and 'servant' of the community.[13]

Increasingly, literate and urban southerners were appropriating these new languages of representation and citizenship and deploying them in more local contexts. During the war years, the educated employees of both government and missions had begun to display a sense of identity and awareness of wider national and international political developments.[14] By 1945, the Civil Secretary was writing that:

> There is probably no class of Sudanese with whom the government is least in touch with [sic] or least knowledgeable about as the educated southern Sudanese. But there are indications – from petitions, letters and conversations with individuals – that many of them are puzzled and resentful about the backwardness of the S. Sudan.[15]

The following year, a missionary reported 'rather a 'Bolshie' element amongst the more educated', and their growing criticism of 'the white man'.[16] In 1946, southern government staff formed the Southern Sudan Welfare Committee to campaign for equal wages to their northern counterparts, and in 1947 they

[11] Equatoria Province Monthly Diary, January 1950, NRO Dakhlia 57/9/24.

[12] Equatoria Province Monthly Diary, November 1949, NRO Dakhlia 57/5/13.

[13] Equatoria Province Monthly Diaries, November 1948, NRO Dakhlia 57/5/13, and June 1951, NRO Dakhlia 57/9/24.

[14] Equatoria Grade Clerks to Civil Secretary, 20 February 1940, and BV Marwood, Governor Equatoria, to Civil Secretary, 26 April 1940, NRO Dakhlia 3 1/6/31.

[15] Civil Secretary to Council, 3 February 1945, NRO EP 1/1/2.

[16] LWC Sharland, Annual Letter Loka, August 1946, CMS AF AL. See also Justin Willis, '"The Nyamang are Hard to Touch": mission evangelism and tradition in the Nuba Mountains, Sudan, 1933–1952', *Journal of Religion in Africa* 33:1 (2003), p. 52.

joined a strike in several towns by government labourers over wages: 'the culmination of a feeling of dissatisfaction which had been growing over the past two years, in a hot house atmosphere of political propaganda and unrest, at the allegedly inferior position of the southern government servant vis a vis his northern confrere'.[17] Garretson emphasises the origins of the strike in the hardships of life for urban money-earners.[18] The result was an immediate wage increase for government employees, and the following year southern staff were transferred to the northern wage scale, though strikes over wages would continue to occur.[19] Southern officials and mission employees formed their own 'Southern Intellectuals Organisation', which became the Southern Party, and later the Liberal Party. According to Hilary Logali, the son of a leading member, Paulo Logali, the party were strongly influenced by wider African nationalism, which had been introduced to the province by demobbed soldiers after the war. They initially saw alliance with the northern Sudanese Graduates Congress as the route to gaining independence for the Sudan. But the almost total exclusion of southerners from the Sudanised administrative posts in the 1950s fuelled the growing sense of southern political identity and grievance.[20]

From 1949, party leaders and members of the National Legislative Assembly toured their districts, reportedly seeking to publicise political developments and improve their own knowledge of the districts. Growing public interest in local government and wider politics was reported. In Meridi, 'large crowds attended the council elections and everyone professed to understand what they were about'. Even in the Mundari area of Juba District, long regarded as 'backward' by the government, it was reported that there was 'an awakening interest in other than purely local affairs'. The news of the Anglo-Egyptian Agreement in 1952 furthered this 'quickening of interest', and people began to hold 'both formal and informal meetings' and 'take a lively and enthusiastic interest in the constitution and the elections'.[21] Howell is sceptical about how widespread this interest really was beyond the towns and the government employees and politicians who were holding these meetings. He favours the view of Governor Owen of Bahr el Ghazal, in 1951: 'The general political situation has been closely followed in the towns and is causing some restlessness among students, but is not understood by the bulk of the people'. By 1953 some Dinka reportedly thought that the *hakuma* was simply coming to an end.[22]

However, the urban frontier was, as ever, a vital source of information about the changing *hakuma*. The son of the first Moru government clerk claimed that his father 'had status as the first one to go to school; they listened to him, and if he visited the village many, many people would come to see him and hear

17 Equatoria Province Annual Report 1947, NRO Civsec2 30/10/32.

18 Garretson, 'The Southern Sudan Welfare Committee'. See Chapter 3 above.

19 Equatoria Province Monthly Diaries, May 1948 and July 1949, NRO Dakhlia 57/5/13; 'Application of the southern Sudan teachers and Dressers to Governor and Bishop of southern Sudan', 29 May 1944, NRO EP 1/4/17; Annual Letters: Bertram, Lui, September 1948; Crabb, Mundri Divinity school, 17 June 1949; Earl, Loka, 21 August 1947; and Guillebaud, Yei, August 1947, all CMS AF AL.

20 Hilary Paul Logali, 'Autobiography', SAD 890/1/1–80; JF Tiernay, Deputy Governor, to all DCs and heads of department, 11 July 1946, and Civil Secretary to Governor Equatoria, 24 July 1946, NRO EP 1/4/17.

21 Equatoria Province Monthly Diaries, June, July and September 1949, NRO Dakhlia 57/5/13; June and October 1951, NRO Dakhlia 57/9/24; and February, April, July and September 1952, NRO Civsec2 30/3/6.

22 John Howell, 'Political Leadership and Organisation in the Southern Sudan' (PhD, University of Reading, 1978), pp. 108–9, 113, citing Bahr el Ghazal Monthly Diary, October 1951 and March 1953.

about the developments in government'.[23] Just as people had been sent to find out about the government in the early colonial period, so people sought news from town now. The extent of communication aroused concern in government about the power of 'rumour'. In November 1952, it was reported that in Equatoria the announcement of self-determination within three years had 'caused a stir amongst the local people... the lack of good communication and the absence of any newspapers resulted in many unfounded rumours'. The following month, an 'unusually large number of political visitors to the Province' aroused excitement, apprehension and a 'sense of insecurity' throughout the Province.[24] These growing insecurities helped to preserve a role for chiefs despite the growing competition from other government interlocutors.

REPRESENTING THE COMMUNITY: CHIEFS AND LATE-COLONIAL POLITICS

The period after the Second World War was a time of new or heightened expectations of the state, and hence of its intermediaries. But it was also a time of uncertainty and fear, culminating in the violence and reprisals of 1955. Government began to seem much less predictable as it moved towards independence and as some long-serving British officials were replaced with new northern Sudanese administrators. The chiefs therefore came under renewed pressures to protect and defend local communities, and yet to simultaneously meet popular expectations of state resources and rewards. Simonse suggests that '[t]he network of government chiefs was one of the rare, if not the only, genuine southern Sudanese interlocutor with the colonial government in the preparations for Sudan's independence.[25] This rather disguises the extent of contest and complaint about the chiefs that also surfaced particularly vociferously at this time, as local political factions perhaps perceived the opportunity in changing government rhetoric, and certainly capitalised on the widespread resentment at wartime government demands channelled through the chiefs. Participation in new provincial and national political arenas also generated new tensions and challenges for the chiefs and brought them into more direct competition with alternative, literate interlocutors. Chiefs, politicians, government and mission employees were to some extent all gambling on the different possible outcomes of the political processes of this period – some gambles paid off and secured them a continuing or enhanced role in government, while others led to criticism and recrimination. The contingency of chiefship and interlocution is thus particularly apparent at this time, as are the multiple discourses which people might appropriate to argue their rights and claims.

In 1947, a conference of southern government employees, chiefs and clergy was held in Juba, to discuss southern participation in new political institutions, particularly the national Legislative Assembly in Khartoum. Although remembered as the moment when southerners acquiesced in – or were tricked or forced into – remaining part of Sudan, there was only very limited opportunity for discussion of the question of Sudan's unity.[26] The conference provides one of the few records of individual chiefs' speeches, and reveals the kind of role they presented themselves as playing and the idioms and discourses they employed. It suggests that chiefs were developing a discourse of their traditionality, drawing

[23] Interview 10R/K.

[24] Equatoria Province Monthly Diaries, November–December 1952, NRO Civsec2 30/3/6.

[25] Simonse, *Kings of Disaster*, p. 138.

 [26] Howell, 'Political Leadership', pp. 104–5.

both on colonial rhetoric, and on a more vernacular claim to 'have the people'. In the new political language of 'representation', chiefs claimed to represent more genuinely their rural communities than could literate townsmen.

The reports of the Juba conference suggested that after the first day, a 'distinct cleavage of opinion' opened up between 'tribal leaders', i.e. the chiefs, and the 'educated community', regarding if and when southern representatives should be sent to the Legislative Assembly.[27] Chiefs Lolik Lado, Gir Kiro and Cir Rehan repeatedly emphasised their need to consult further with their people in order to adequately represent their views. Chief Lolik employed local idioms, likening southerners' dilemmas to that of 'a girl who has been asked to marry a young man' and who would want 'time to hear reports of that young men from other people before consenting'. He added that '[t]he ancestors of the Northern Sudanese were not peace-loving and domesticated like cows' –a revealing metaphor of ideals of political authority – and he 'insisted on the southerners' need for protection and for further time to consider the matter in conference with the elders of the people'.[28] This is exactly the kind of interlocution and discourse that had probably won many a chief some popular approval and success in dealing with government.

Howell argues that the chiefs were being seriously diminished at this time, weakened by their lack of education: 'increasingly more villagers were being brought into contact with government in the form of schools, clinics, police posts, council officials, and so on. And it was to the educated that the villagers looked for assistance and advice in the alien and often hostile world of external authority'. There is certainly truth in the sense that new kinds of knowledge were needed to deal with a changing or unpredictable government at this time. But 'the educated' did not simply take over the chiefs' role as, in Howell's words, 'intermediaries between the government official and the locally influential'.[29] Firstly, the government officials continued to treat the chiefs as the principal intermediaries – the political activities of educated southerners ensured that British and Sudanese administrators alike would mistrust them and continue to promote the idea of traditional, rural chiefship. Secondly, the 'locally influential' were often successfully depicting the people of town and government as untrustworthy or too distant, as a northern Sudanese administrator in Bahr el Ghazal suggested in June 1955:

> The Educated Southerner continues to argue and stand for Federation thinking that it will mean more jobs and more promotions to them. The Chiefs can hardly see value or understand what the Educated mean. The Elders understand only economic or cultural development of their areas – politics or political concessions mean nothing to them.[30]

Hilary Logali admitted that the Liberal Party 'did not have a strong grassroots base, except for the town of Juba'. He also claimed that Chief Andarea Gore, who had been a member of the Legislative Assembly, quit politics because he was

[27] Equatoria Province Annual Report 1947, NRO Civsec2 30/10/32. Stanislaus Paysama suggests that chiefs nevertheless took the lead in unifying the southern delegates in favour of participation: Fr V Dellagiacoma (ed.), *How a Slave became a Minister: autobiography of Sayyed Stanislaus Abdallahi Paysama* (Khartoum, 1990), pp. 52–3 (thanks to Douglas Johnson for this reference).

[28] 'Proceedings of the Juba Conference on the Political Development of the Southern Sudan, June 1947', appended in Dunstan M Wai (ed.), *The Southern Sudan: the problem of national integration* (London, 1973), pp. 185–205.

[29] Howell, 'Political Leadership', p. 148.

[30] Bahr el Ghazal Province Intelligence Report, June 1955 (by Daud Abdel Latif), NRO UNP 1/20/168.

too 'affected by rural life' and 'became rustic and faded into political oblivion'.[31] It was the chiefs' continuing ties to 'rural life' alongside their knowledge and experience of government that helped to preserve their role as intermediaries.

But the distinction between chiefs and the educated was largely a discursive one, and the two categories remained overlapping: as we have seen, some chiefs had been to school and even worked for government before becoming chiefs; some became members of the National Legislative Assembly like Andarea Gore. But some of the educated came from chiefly families; often the bitterest political contests occurred within or between chiefly families.[32] It was competition and conflict within the emerging local political elites that frequently produced the rhetorical differentiation between their interconnected components.

The early politicians themselves traded accusations of accepting bribery,[33] and the idiom of buying and selling (out) was prominent in the political discourse of the time and in recollections more recently. According to government reports after independence in the later 1950s, Abdel Rahman Sule, a Malakiyan from Juba and one of the earliest southern politicians, used 'parables' at Liberal Party political rallies in 1957 and early 1958, not to deny that politicians were receiving money, but to emphasise that this would not make them betray the South:

> Some people accusing us of taking money from the Umma Party but if somebody gives you hundred pounds, two hundred or even five hundred and asks you to leave your house and he sleeps with your wife – Do you agree? (shouting No, No). And so if we take money from the Northerners we shall never play with our South.[34]

On another occasion he allegedly asked a Zande audience, 'Can you sell your own daughter to a man you dislike for even LS 300 [Sudanese pounds]. If not, how can you dare to sell away the South, your dear mother, to a person you dislike', adding 'I am a pure Moslem since my childhood but I shall never betray my mother "The South" politically at any one time.' This report claimed that the Umma Party had stopped 'scattering money' to the Liberal Party after realising it was being used for such 'propaganda against northerners in general'. The reported result was that the Liberal Party resorted to collecting 'money, bulls and dura' [sorghum] from people, by telling them it was a government order; the local chiefs avoided the meetings and collections, and it was they who were later instructed to oversee the return of what was taken.[35]

These intelligence reports written by government officials no doubt reflected their own views of the Liberal (or indeed Umma) Party, and a preference for chiefs over politicians that was inherited from their British predecessors. But Abdel Rahman Sule's metaphors of family relations and rights suggest a very deliberate strategy to express southern political agendas in terms of the kind of rights in persons and property that would have been immediately recognisable to his audiences. Similarly Howell cites another political leader, Stanislaus Paysama, writing in 1957 to a new Liberal Party branch at Nasir to warn of the dangers of collaborating with northern parties: 'If you tie your cow in another

[31] Logali, 'Autobiography', SAD 890/1/1–80.

[32] Howell, 'Political Leadership', pp. 166–8.

[33] E.g. 'Translation of leaflet issued from Khartoum on 24.12.57 in Moru language circulated widely in Moru area' (by or pro- Ezbon Mundari and criticising MP Timon Biro), NRO UNP 1/20/168.

[34] Abdel Rahman Sule's speech at the Wau airfield road, 2 December 1957, as allegedly quoted by Police Commandant Sayed Hassan Mohd Salih, enclosed in Allam Hassan Allam, Governor Bahr el Ghazal, to Registrar of Judiciary, Khartoum, Wau, 14 December 1957, NRO UNP 1/20/168.

[35] Equatoria Province Intelligence Reports, January 1958, NRO UNP 1/20/168.

man's cattle camp he will drink all the milk and during the epidemic he will declare that the first dead cow was yours'.[36] It was through such discourse that ideas of the state and of political rights were gradually being disseminated, and were interacting with existing notions of rights and expectations of the *hakuma*.

However, the politicians did not succeed in convincing people of their incorruptibility: according to Howell, 'resentment tended to become generalized against MPs many of whom had become relatively wealthy from the less reputable aspects of Khartoum politics, and whose expensive drinking habits and "town" ways did not go unnoticed'.[37] Since the 1953 elections, there was reported to be 'widespread apprehension' that the southern representative in the national institutions in Khartoum would be isolated from 'his people' and therefore vulnerable to corruption.[38] At the time of the 1955 mutiny, a British missionary, Rev. Allison, highlighted the 'lack of trust' in the southern politicians, 'owing to so many changing their Party to line their pockets'.[39] Even if such reports reflected the perspectives of their authors, the views of critical administrators or missionaries would have been feeding into wider public opinion in the southern towns and beyond.

One prominent political figure in Rumbek, who was remembered with particularly widespread criticism fifty years later, embodies the blurred line between chiefs and local politicians. Mangok Mabok is said to have been captured when he was a boy and taken away to Egypt and northern Sudan for many years, where he took the Muslim name Abdalla Adam. In 1937 he began to appear in Rumbek District reports, as a retired soldier who 'returned to the district a few years ago and is now living a tribal Dinka life' and had 'rendered good services as President of the Ayak Court at Akot. His general guidance and advice have prevented many irregular and illegal seizures of cattle by Chiefs who appear to have made a habit of it for several years.' He was also 'helping' in the tribute collection for the Athoi section.[40] Such a role may have placed him in direct competition with the chiefs and other senior men, but of course the chiefship itself often had similar origins in military capture and government service. In 1948, Mangok was nominated by the government to the Legislative Assembly.[41] In late 1955, he was reportedly leading Rumbek and Yirrol chiefs in opposition to federation, arguing that the South was not able to 'stand on its own feet' and that in any federal structure, the Dinka would be dominated by the Fertit of Western Bahr el Ghazal.[42] According to local memories, he was working for 'the Arabs', to whom he had promised to 'sell the whole land': 'he was the one persuading people and bribing the chiefs' to support independence for a united Sudan.[43] A very elderly man claimed that Mangok had been cursed by the last British DC and developed leprosy as a result.[44]

[36] Stanislaus Paysama to John Cuol, 11 August 1957, cited in Howell, 'Political Leadership', p. 163.

[37] Howell, 'Political Leadership', p. 163.

[38] AC Beaton, 'Report on the effects of the Anglo-Egyptian agreement on the Southern Sudan', 17 March 1953, FO 371/102753, in Johnson, *British Documents on the End of Empire*, Part II, pp. 228–33. See also Johnson, Nuer Prophets, p. 298: Southern politicians were removed from daily contact with their people by national politics.

[39] Oliver Allison, Annual Letter, Khartoum, 31 August 1955, SAD 817/6/96–102.

[40] Rumbek District Monthly Report, January 1937, SRO EP 57.D.10.

[41] Minutes of the first meeting at Wau of the Bahr el Ghazal Province Council, 12–13 November 1948, SRO EP 1.C.2.

[42] Bahr el Ghazal Province Intelligence Report, December 1955–January 1956, NRO UNP 1/20/168.

[43] Interview 19aN/RC.

[44] Interview 65R/RC.

Accounts such as this, and the criticisms of southern politicians for being bribed or tricked, resulted from rivalries among and between politicians, chiefs and senior men. But they also both reflected and contributed to an increasing atmosphere of uncertainty and insecurity. In this context, chiefs were able to present themselves as more rooted in and protective of their communities than other intermediaries. In 1948, Chief Modi Baraba, the most prominent Yei chief, exhorted Benjamin Lwoki to 'speak firmly' for his constituency in the Legislative Assembly.[45] In 1954, the same chief wrote to Lwoki, on behalf of the 'Yei citizens', an interesting new appellation in itself. He complained at the 'bullying' by northern merchants and senior officials in the town, and blamed the latter for 'secretly' planning the sudden transfer of the new southern administrative officer to Yambio: 'we should like him to work in Yei here for at least 2 years officially in order that we have to study his behaviour towards the people and watch how he carries his duty forward'.[46]

This reflects the longstanding and recently intensified demand for knowledge, to render government predictable – an increasingly difficult task when new administrators were being appointed and transferred. But Chief Modi was also claiming here to speak for the people of Yei (asserting his authority over the town in the process); as even Howell argues, chiefs 'needed to represent, and be seen to represent, parochial interests if they were to continue to have any political influence… it was as leaders of their own community – political agents in the same way as kujurs, large cattle-owners or traders could be – that chiefs influenced parliamentarians and candidates in the southern elections'.[47] Chief Modi was certainly presenting himself as a more genuine spokesperson for the people of Yei than the parliamentarian he was addressing.

If Chief Modi succeeded in distancing himself from the politicians, Chief Jambo of Moru District famously did not. In 1953 an Egyptian delegation led by Major Saleh Salem came to the region, seeking to form a southern pro-Egyptian, Unionist party. They met with Chief Jambo and convinced him and his son to sign a document allegedly giving up the idea of British safeguards for the South. This led to widespread hostility to Jambo, and the refusal of his B Court to accept his continuing presidency; he was especially criticised for failing to consult his people first.[48] According to an interviewee from his chiefdom, people were 'furious', but Jambo claimed he was convinced into signing because he wanted independence, and so 'he would appreciate anyone who could help, even if it was the devil himself!'[49] The reported effect at the time was nevertheless that, 'people were disinclined to meet any more visitors as many declared that they had been betrayed by those who had been elected to represent them'.[50] Chief Jambo survived, but he had gambled unsuccessfully in trying to contract new relations with the Egyptian and Unionist politicians.

In 1955, chiefs in the neighbouring Zande districts provoked more serious hostility when all but four of them signed a document expressing their support for the newly Sudanised administration against the southern political opposi-

45 Equatoria Province Monthly Diary, November 1948, NRO Dakhlia 57/5/13.

46 'Yei Citizens Chief Modi Baraba' to Sayed Benjamin Lwoki, Yei, 2 December 1954, SAD 761/7/1–56.

47 Howell, 'Political Leadership', p. 149.

48 Public Relations Officer to Sudan Agent London, 3 April 1953, and Samwele Kajivora, Mundri, to Governor-General, 28 January 1953, TNA FO 371/102747, Files 1051/293, 493; Equatoria Province Monthly Diary, December 1952–March 1953, NRO Civsec2 30/3/6.

49 Interview 10R/K. Jambo went on to visit Egypt repeatedly: Equatoria Province Monthly Diary, July 1953, NRO Civsec2 30/3/6; Collins, Shadows in the Grass, pp. 445–6.

50 Equatoria Province Monthly Diary, December 1952, NRO Civsec2 30/3/6.

tion. Reining argues that the resulting threats and attacks on the chiefs were also a culmination of increasing resentment at their enforcement of the resettlement and cotton cultivation required by the ambitious colonial Zande Development Scheme. Certainly this provided particular ammunition for the educated politicians like MP Elia Kuze to attack the prestigious chiefly families descended from the pre-colonial Avungara kings. But even here, the traditional-modern dichotomy was more a political strategy than a real divide; Reining reveals that in the 1954 parliamentary elections in Zande West, both candidates were equally educated, but one was from the chiefly family, while his victorious opponent was a 'commoner': 'The main theme of the commoners' campaign was opposition to the ruling clan.'[51]

Reining also stresses the atmosphere of 'uncertainty' at the time of his research in the 1950s: 'No Zande, whether chief or commoner, felt that he had control over the behaviour of those who influenced him politically, and no one could predict what would happen next.'[52] On the one hand, this period generated opportunity and intense competition among and between chiefs and other political leaders to present themselves as the most trustworthy and accountable interlocutors – now termed 'representatives'. But on the other hand, all the different intermediaries were facing similar challenges in trying to negotiate with a government that appeared less known and predictable than the colonial one had become. In much of the contemporary and subsequent discourse, the central issue was a perceived lack of knowledge, whether in terms of southerners needing more knowledge and education to catch up with their 'elder brothers' in the north, or in terms of the enduring claim that politicians practised cunning and trickery. The belief that ordinary people could easily be 'tricked' by the educated and town people was an expression of vulnerability in the politics of knowledge, as well as a moral criticism. Such perceived vulnerability would impel people both towards and away from the source of this specialist knowledge in the towns.

TROUBLE IN THE TOWNS: AUGUST 1955

By the 1940s and 1950s, the chiefs around Yei, Juba, Rumbek and other smaller towns were spending more time than ever in town and the people of their chiefdoms were similarly engaging in urban employment and trade, if not dwelling in or on the edge of town. For such people in particular, the national political developments in the decade before Sudan's independence had raised expectations, tensions and insecurities, disseminated swiftly and easily through the enhanced avenues of communication between town and the immediate vicinity. Unsurprisingly, it was in and through the towns that the tensions exploded in 1955: it is telling that the first sign of trouble in the town of Terakeka on the day of the Torit mutiny was that 'the Sultan [chief] did not come to town and the Court did not function'.[53] The Torit mutiny and its spread would reveal the continuing close association of towns and army, and set a precedent for rebellion by a combination of soldiers, police, students and civil servants. The frustrated ambi-

[51] Reining, *The Zande Scheme*, p. 29; TS Cotran, *Report of the Commission of Inquiry into the Disturbances in the Southern Sudan during August 1955* (Khartoum, 1956); Howell, 'Political Leadership', p. 132.

[52] Reining, *The Zande Scheme*, p. 12.

[53] Cotran, *Report of the Commission*, p. 53. See also Rolandsen, 'A false start', p. 110.

tions of students and government employees have been a major driving force for political opposition and armed resistance in South Sudan since that time.[54]

Such frustrations were mounting in the years before 1955. A few months before the August mutiny and rebellion swept through the towns of Equatoria, the Bahr el Ghazal Governor had warned: 'The largest single factor for the deterioration of security in this peaceful province is the behavior of the police which is so alien to the people'.[55] A further problem reported by the subsequent commission of enquiry was the close relationship between the northern Sudanese merchants in the towns and the new northern officials: the former 'seem to be trusted to act as informants to the administration more than other inhabitants with the result that to the ordinary southerner long meetings between say a District Commissioner and a Gallabi [northern Sudanese trader] in the Merkaz sometimes lasting for hours whilst a southern Chief is patiently waiting his turn inevitably gives an impression of favouritism, whether real or imaginary'.[56]

In 1955, the 'trouble' started in the recently developed small textile production town of Nzara in the Zande Scheme of western Equatoria, following the chiefs' unpopular expression of support for the government, and the subsequent arrest of MP Elia Kuze and the four chiefs who had refused to sign the pro-government document. A protest by textile workers against mass redundancies at the Nzara factory in late July 1955 was met with military force and six people were shot dead. A fortnight later, two government clerks, an army officer and several soldiers were arrested in Juba on suspicion of plotting a mutiny of southern soldiers. Protests at the arrests led the government to call in northern troops; according to the official report into the subsequent disturbances, '[m]any civilians took their families and left Juba as they thought Northern troops were coming to kill them'. On 18 August southern soldiers in Torit mutinied and fired on their northern officers after receiving orders that their company was to be transferred to the north. The unrest spread to other towns in Equatoria, and hundreds of northern officials and merchants and their families were killed. Howell argues that the violence may have reflected some 'personal grievances against predatory merchants' among townspeople, but that it was not directed or controlled by the southern MPs or senior officials; rather it was primarily led by low-ranking soldiers, police sergeants, prison warders, junior clerks and teachers.[57]

The civilian population fled the Equatorian towns, as British missionaries in Yei reported a few weeks after the mutiny:

> The local situation has reached something of a stale-mate. A military column of Northern Sudanese troops arrived last Sunday. The local people however have all disappeared and show no signs of being co-operative. The officers in charge have tried to establish contact with local chiefs and leaders but have so far failed. This means that Yei town is now very orderly, but quite devoid of its local population.[58]

Even in Rumbek, where there were no killings, after some shooting by police and prison warders, 'the civilian natives left the town in panic'.[59] An elderly teacher remembers that day as a pivotal moment of transition, conflating it with subsequent independence:

54 Howell, 'Political Leadership', pp. 140, 309–18.

55 Bahr el Ghazal Province Intelligence Report, May 1955, NRO UNP 1/20/168.

56 Cotran, *Report of the Commission*, p. 125. Paysama also recalled judicial favouritism by DCs towards northern merchants: Dellagiacoma, *How a Slave became a Minister*, p. 58.

57 Howell, 'Political Leadership', pp. 133–5; Cotran, *Report of the Commission*; Reining, *The Zande Scheme*, p. 34.

58 Steven and Anne Car to their parents, Yei, 10 September 1955, SAD 817/7/1–154.

59 Cotran, *Report of the Commission*, p. 77.

> Many were shot here; some police and others joined the mutiny. Then the government closed the schools. The British Governor-General was forced to hand over the flag and leave us to solve our own problems. People ran into the bush, because the police and army were catching people, searching them and beating them.[60]

By the time the government forces entered the towns of Equatoria, they found them deserted. Not for the last time, the towns had suddenly become the most dangerous place to be, and the gradual accommodation with towns and government over preceding decades had been brutally disrupted. But this would be the beginning of an oscillating, confusing and unpredictable relationship between town and bush – at times the towns were the focus for rebel attacks or government recriminations, and people sought refuge in the bush; at other times or places the military conflict and the rebel or government forces penetrated the bush to an unprecedented extent, driving people to seek refuge in towns or abroad. The risky relationship with the towns thus continued, albeit in fluctuating and ever more dangerous ways.

In the immediate post-1955 period, the bush remained a refuge for mutineers and for other people seeking to evade the government or even their own chiefs, as one Moru chief reported in 1959:

> The under mentioned people... have been ordered by the Government to build their home with me behind Yei river. Now they have refused and have returned all to Bibe across Yei river, and have refused the work of Government, and they are staying in the forest like wild animals.[61]

The chief's derisory complaint that his people were living 'like wild animals' is very revealing of wider ideas about space and community. Chiefs had become seen both by government and perhaps by people too as a focus for community and as a means of 'tethering' otherwise scattered populations. This would become a more prevalent idea over the course of the post-1955 period; as people experienced forced displacement and 'scattering', so the idea of a unifying and cohesive chiefship became increasingly appealing. Belonging to a chiefdom has come to be presented as a signifier of humanity, society and domesticity, distinguishing people from wild animals – 'If there were no chiefs, there would be no community; people would wander about like animals'.[62] During war and insecurity, chiefs are presented as having been – ideally – a means of regrouping and a source of defence and protection. In reality of course, this gatekeeping would become ever more dangerous and ambiguous. The chiefs' authority had more links to the town than to the bush, but increasingly they would be required not only to temporarily reconstitute their authority beyond the sphere of the hakuma, but also to mediate with new forces emerging from or operating in the bush.

'CO-OPERATING WITH THE MOUTH': CHIEFS AND THE AFTERMATH OF MUTINY

> Practically all Chiefs were tested during the recent events: some proved to be very loyal; others took part in the riots and the looting or even the killing, while

60 Interview 14N/RC.

61 Chief Ngere Abuh, Kariba village, to General Service Officer, Amadi, 14 February 1959, SRO MD 66.D.1.

62 Member of a youth group, Raja County, 2 February 2005, cited in Frederick Golooba-Mutebi and Adak Costa Mapuor, 'Traditional Authorities in South Sudan: chieftainship in the Bahr el Ghazal region' (Nairobi: UNDP unpublished report, 2005).

> a third category took a passive attitude. Our policy must aim at strengthening their position and prestige without spoiling them.[63]

This statement by the Governor of Equatoria, Abdel Aziz Omer El Amin, in December 1955 makes clear the Sudanised administration's continuing commitment to the institution of chiefship – the final sentence could have been written by a British official at almost any time in the previous fifty years, wrestling with the perennial internal contradictions of Indirect Rule. From 1955 both the power and the fragility of the chiefs' interstitial position would be particularly evident, as they increasingly struggled to predict government actions. For ordinary people, the chiefs' embodiment of the potential for both threat and guarantee became more crucial than ever.

As the Governor was well aware, the position of chiefs during the mutiny and uprising had actually varied considerably. Some were reported to have tried to disperse mobs and prevent northerners being killed, while others participated in the violence. In Yambio District, four of the Zande chiefs who had signed the pro-government document had their houses burned down during the uprising.[64] Afterwards, chiefs were appointed to the courts that tried the hundreds of people arrested as 'mutineers', 121 of whom were executed, and hundreds more imprisoned. Chiefs might have seen benefits in the removal or imprisonment of rival government interlocutors, as the 'educated' southerners were principally blamed for the trouble by the government and reportedly by many other people. Chiefs' salaries were meanwhile raised in 1952, 1954 and 1956.[65] But they had also been reminded of the risks of their own position, and the potential threats from both government and people. A British missionary reported the continuing strain on the chiefs in November 1955:

> It seems reasonably certain that the chiefs are 'cooperating' with the Administration. They are running the Tribal Courts, bringing in mutineers and guns, looters and loot. But from the difference in behaviour of the chiefs when they talk to me in front of the officials, and when they are alone with me, their cooperation is with the mouth rather than with the heart. They have been badly frightened. They have been made personally responsible for producing the mutineers coming originally from their area. To some extent therefore their cooperation is obtained by duress... Probably a dozen chiefs and sub-chiefs are in prison on various charges ranging from murder to looting. Four from the Yei–Torit area have de-camped.[66]

The strategy of 'co-operating with the mouth' only was a longstanding one employed by chiefs to deflect the worst depredations of government. But in the atmosphere of increasing suspicion and fear it was an ever more delicate balancing act. In 1957 a southern politician expressed concern that administrators were threatening chiefs and that this would drive a wedge between the latter and 'the educated class'.[67] The sporadic activities of a few soldiers who remained at large after 1955 were used as a pretext for the government to maintain military rule in Equatoria Province. Government spending in the south was

63 Minutes of the District Commissioners Meeting held in Juba on 6–9 December 1955, SRO MD 32.A.1.

64 Cotran, *Report of the Commission*, p. 114.

65 Minutes of the Southern Provinces Governors meeting held at Juba on 28 October 1956, SRO MD 32.A.1.

66 Colin Legum, 'Report on Southern Sudan', November 1955, SAD 817/8/1–119; Reining, *The Zande Scheme*, p. 34.

67 Howell attributes this to Buth Diu but cites Stanislaus Paysama to John Cuol, Khartoum, 11 August 1957: Howell, 'Political Leadership', p. 163.

cut except for security purposes and schools were closed completely for a year. The Torit district officials did not move back to the town from the army barracks until November 1956. In Juba the military presence remained particularly overt: 'Some of the MPs are going to raise in parliament the question of the armed police and army within Juba Town. They say that the show of arms caused much alarm and fear to the citizens and is unnecessary.'[68]

A year after the mutiny, 700 huts were burned down in villages around Yei suspected to be helping fugitive mutineers, reinforcing once again the risks of inhabiting the towns and their vicinities. Chiefs in the district were 'fully instructed that any infringement of peace or security shall be their sole responsibility in their areas together with their sub-chiefs and head-men'. Some chiefs received government praise for arresting suspected mutineers while others were reported to be hiding and assisting outlaws.[69] A number of chiefs had escaped across the Uganda or Belgian Congo borders, including Chief Abina Yenge of Kajo Keji.[70] Some chiefs reported being threatened or attacked by alleged mutineers. In other cases mutineers made threats in defence of chiefs, such as the Belinian chief whose son (later known as David Dada) had joined the mutiny:

> Late reports reveal that the 3 mutineers (including son of Sultan Lako Lagona of Juba District now in custody) have moved from Bilimang area to a place lying between Gondokoro and Juba... It is reported that the Sultan's son threatened that if his father now in custody for screening him is dismissed as a result and anyone other than one of his brothers is appointed in his stead as Sultan, he would kill such successor.[71]

Apart from the sporadic military activities of fugitives and the reprisals by government, chiefs were also ordered to report any suspected subversive political activities. In 1958 the Equatoria Province Governor made a speech in Terekeka and 'made it clear that chiefs as the direct administrative and judicial bodies in their respective areas who are supposed to stop and report activities leading to breaches of the peace, are not as such allowed to indulge in politics'.[72] Chiefs in Bahr el Ghazal Province were similarly ordered to prevent unlicensed political meetings and any other potentially subversive activities.[73] In 1956, one northern official had reported that the Equatorian chiefs were trying to maintain good relations with both the government and the southern politicians calling for federalism:

> The general position of the Chiefs is not yet clear. They appear to be holding the stick in the middle. They do not want to show hostility either to the Government, in case that Federation is not granted they should not lose their jobs;

[68] Equatoria Province Intelligence Reports, April–May and November 1956, NRO UNP 1/20/168.

[69] Equatoria Province Intelligence Reports, February, June–July and July–August 1956, NRO UNP 1/20/168; Sudan African National Union (SANU), *Memorandum presented to the Commission of the Organisation of African Unity for Refugees* (Kampala, November 1964), p. 19; Howell, 'Political Leadership', p. 187; Rolandsen, 'A false start', pp. 112–3.

[70] P O'B Gibson, statement for the African Secretary, CMS, 1 November 1955, SAD 817/8/1–119; Equatoria Province Intelligence Report, 16 April–5 June 1957, NRO UNP 1/20/168.

[71] Equatoria Province Intelligence Report, 21–28 September 1956, NRO UNP 1/20/168. Threatening assassination letters were reportedly sent to government officials from 'AVO' warning them not to 'give order to the chiefs to kill the Mutineers': Equatoria Province Intelligence Report, March 1957, NRO UNP 1/20/168.

[72] Minutes of the District Commissioners Meeting held on 29 March 1958 at Governor's Residence, SRO MD 32.A.1.

[73] Notice posted by DC Jur River District, AM el Amin, 26 December 1957, Bahr El Ghazal Province Archives, Wau, BGP 36.H.1.

> visa-vis [sic] to the educated class in case Federation is achieved when they would get sacked.[74]

'Holding the stick in the middle' was an apt expression of the ambiguous, interstitial position and role of the chiefs. The government reports from the late 1950s certainly suggest that the majority of chiefs were at least maintaining the appearance of co-operating with government and informing on any potential resistance.

In Yei District chiefs were also once again expected to provide labour for the new government and private coffee and tobacco plantations established in 1958–59. A report by an academic visitor to the south in 1960 suggests that in such areas chiefs were continuing to broker local commercial and labour relations: northern merchants were 'once more living in distant villages under the protection of co-operative chiefs'; some 'well-disposed chiefs' were pushing coffee production, together with the government and mainly northern plantation owners; and 'in the last two years a British-American firm has made impressive progress in popularising tobacco as a peasant crop capable of bringing real riches (as much as £60 profit per feddan)'.[75] An elderly politician, whose home village was one of the centres for coffee-growing, and whose house was still surrounded by rusting farm machinery in 2005, suggested that this crop had enabled the brief emergence of a small class of coffee-growers after 1956, who became wealthy enough to purchase bicycles and vehicles and to build large houses. He added that cotton and coffee were always grown through the chiefs, but that the lack of 'consistent markets' prevented chiefs ever becoming really rich.[76] The southern political movement, the Sudan African National Union, later complained that both government and private coffee plantations established here in 1958–59 had relied on forced low-paid labour conscripted through local chiefs.[77] In a sense the involvement of some Equatorian chiefs in both private cash-cropping and the provision of labour for plantations was simply a continuation of their long-standing commercial brokerage role. But this role obviously held new risks in this period.

The report by an academic observer in 1960 depicted a revival of confidence on the part of the administration in the south, 'supported by strong military detachments at strategic centres'. Since 1958, General Abboud's government had naturally continued the predominantly military administration of the southern provinces, particularly Equatoria.

> But at present the recovery is based largely on force and fear; the consent of the South has yet to be gained. One evening I saw the Police in Juba 'native area' beating up terrified young boys and was told by southerners that I had seen nothing as yet and that the Police were loathed in a way inconceivable six or seven years previously; and the Governor of Equatoria recently explained at length to a University wife the force necessary to keep the native in his place. Memories of the repression which followed the Mutiny still determine the attitude of many southerners.[78]

In this atmosphere of suspicion and fear, chiefs' role as interlocutors and informants further gained both power and danger, as they were forced to make continuing calculations as to what information to report to whom in return for

74 Equatoria Province Intelligence Reports, June–August 1956, NRO UNP 1/20/168.

75 Anonymous. enclosure in Roland Oliver to MW Parr, 12 October 1960, CMS Acc. 469/04.

76 Interviews 2aN/YC; 2bN/YC.

77 SANU, *Memorandum presented to the Commission*, p. 45.

78 Anonymous. enclosure in Roland Oliver to MW Parr, 12 October 1960, CMS Acc. 469/04.

(unreliable) protection. One example suggests that chiefs were careful to report any potentially subversive activity to government. A local shopkeeper in Lainya reported a newly-released mutineer speaking against the government. The shopkeeper claimed to have repeatedly refused to talk with the former soldier and wrote that 'our Chief Timon Bero said his people are not to speak politics again, and according his orders we obey his rules'. The letter from the shopkeeper was passed through Chief Timon, ultimately to the DC. Yet while chiefs and people might be involved in informing to the government, this was clearly selective; when a police investigator visited Chief Timon on another occasion to find two students, the chief successfully convinced him that they were not to be found in Lui.[79] The chief's order not to 'speak politics' probably also reflected his own bitter experience of parliamentary politics; like Chief Jambo he had taken a pro-Egyptian position in the early 1950s and in the campaign for the 1958 elections he was heavily criticised by his opponents for his previous parliamentary performance.[80]

A similar concern with the dangers and unpredictability of politics was expressed by a very elderly Zande chief, another area where chiefs had been particularly criticised and even attacked in 1955:

> In Zande District, Chief Ukuo Bari sent his son to tell the Asst Governor that he has heard registration was taking place for a new Parliament. He said that they had voted in the last election for a candidate to go to Parliament and this resulted in the disturbances. Now he thinks that the Government should nominate the candidates to go and that he and his people are not willing to vote for the coming elections.[81]

Under government projects of Islamisation and Arabicisation after 1956, chiefs were forced to make their connections to government ever more explicit. According to reports from missionary and church sources, chiefs in the Amadi-Meridi area 'were told they had better "embrace Islam" or they would not remain chiefs much longer', and Islamic schools and even mosques were constructed in chiefs' centres. In 1960 more than twenty Zande chiefs and several Moru chiefs were reported to have formally converted to Islam, and in 1961 lists of Meridi District chiefs showed all but one with Arabic names.[82] Most people nowadays would say that these names and nominal conversion were forced upon the chiefs. The son of Chief Lupai Longaju of Limbe in central Equatoria recalls that his father had to change his Christian name of Onesimus to Omer, and was 'arrested and told to build a mosque'; later however the chief would join 'Joseph Lagu's camp' on the Uganda border and act as a judge for the rebel Anyanya forces. The adoption of Muslim or Arabic names by chiefs should certainly not be read as an indication of political sentiment or affiliation – many such chiefs would simultaneously or subsequently support the rebel forces in the 1960s. Rather it reflected a much longer history of chiefship as an institution based on mediating government and marked out by the symbols and languages of the *hakuma*; many chiefs in the nineteenth century had similarly adopted Islamic names and cultures.

[79] 'Security report', 12 May 1960; Chief Timon Bero to DC Maridi, 13 May 1960; 'Amorama', merchant Lainya bush shop to DC, c/o Chief Timon, 25 September 1960, all SRO MD 41.A.1.

[80] Equatoria Province Monthly Intelligence Reports, December 1957–January 1958, NRO UNP 1/20/168.

[81] Equatoria Province Intelligence Reports, September–October 1957, NRO UNP 1/20/168.

[82] KM Saeed for Inspector Local Government, Maridi Rural Council, to Commandant of Police, Juba, 26 December 1961, SRO MD 14.A.1; Brian de Saram to Rev. JV Taylor, 'Impressions of the Sudan gained from Stanley Toward', 2 December 1960, and George Bennett to his mother, Lui, 3 September 1961, CMS Acc 469/04.

But part of the purpose of their mediation had always been to hide and conceal local politics and activities from state scrutiny, whilst giving the impression of providing information to government. This task became increasingly important and ever more risky over subsequent decades.

CONCLUSION

The coming of national politics and independent government in the mid-1950s was experienced by most people in the south in terms of greater uncertainty, insecurity, violence and a heightened government military and security presence. Unsurprisingly people in more remote rural areas did not exactly welcome the supposed opportunities for greater participation in government. In 1951, 'Juba district Mandari tribesmen attribute the lack of rain during the last few years to the greater interest taken in their affairs by the government'.[83] By 1958, people in the same area refused to vote in the elections:

> At first the people were not keen on election and consequently we had difficult time to convince them to come and cast their votes. Some of the people seemed to have no confidence in any candidate standing for Parliamentary election... At Tali the armed Forces from Bahr el Ghazal passed through the country few days prior to Election. This manoever [sic] created fear in the Mundari and as result Tali has the lowest percentage in the whole of the constituency.

This was reported by a Bari administrative officer from Juba District, and perhaps therefore with greater understanding of local perceptions of the elections. He went on to identify another problem in the area:

> Another factor which has also affected polling is the combination of chiefships into one polling station. I gathered from the people of Tali that such compilation of Election Rolls might be a propaganda to amalgamate the chiefships into one... If it will not be very expensive, every chiefships [sic] should have its polling station and should not be put together with other chiefship. In the tribal organization in such occassion [sic] where people and the chiefs have to move to another soil they feel their integrity affected.[84]

Even at a time of such insecurity, people continued to contest and resist the amalgamation of chiefships that caused so much internal political dispute in preceding decades. The politics of chiefship would always intersect with the wider political context. Chiefdoms might be a source of refuge and protection from government, yet they were also the focus of state penetration and attention. The ambivalent position of chiefs would be ever more apparent in subsequent decades, as they dealt with the military forces of governments and rebels. Their knowledge and interlocution with government could represent either the guarantee of protection and regularisation, or the threat of betrayal. But often, as in the 1950s, the chiefs themselves were caught between different pressures and threats, left uncertainly 'holding the stick in the middle', rather than – as perhaps Mamdani would have it – wielding it in their clenched fist.[85]

[83] Equatoria Province Monthly Diary, January 1951, NRO Dakhlia 57/9/24. At a political meeting held at Thiet on 10 April 1958, a 'madman' also said 'it is the "Turuk" who spoilt the rain'; NRO UNP 1/20/168.

[84] Venanzio Loro, Returning Officer, Juba West Constituency no. 75, report on polling, 7 April 1958, SRO CEOE 1.A.5.

[85] Mamdani, *Citizen and Subject*, p. 23: 'The authority of the chief... was like a clenched fist'.

Part Three

From *Malakiya* to *Medina*: The Fluctuating Expansion of the Urban Frontier, c. 1956–2010

The historiography of the period between Sudanese independence in 1956 and South Sudanese independence in 2011 has been dominated by the two lengthy periods of civil war, c. 1963–72 and 1983–2004. Most scholars have concentrated on explaining these conflicts, detailing the suffering and coping of southern Sudanese, and emphasising their alienation from a series of authoritarian regimes and brief unsatisfactory parliamentary governments in Khartoum.[1] The first parliamentary period straddled the declaration of independence in 1956 and established a pattern of sectarian politics and unstable coalition governments, in which the dominant northern Sudanese political parties were united only in opposing the federal structures demanded by Southern politicians and other emerging regional parties. The promotion of Islamisation and Arabicisation in the south by these parliamentary governments and by the subsequent regime of General Abboud (1958–64) demonstrated the centralising, authoritarian tendencies of the northern riverain political elite. The mounting armed rebellion in the south was an initial focus for criticism of Abboud's military government, feeding into the discontent which drove the October Revolution of 1964. Yet it was another military ruler, General Numayri, who would succeed in negotiating a settlement with the leader of the southern Anyanya rebels, Joseph Lagu, in 1972. Numayri in turn provoked the outbreak of the second period of civil war in 1983 by increasing interference in the Southern Regional Government, culminating in the abrogation of the 1972 agreement and the breakup of the Southern Region. Both periods of parliamentary government in the 1960s and 1980s saw an escalation of the conflicts in the south, as political agendas and divisions among northern politicians hindered any settlement. The National Islamic Front (NIF) regime (now the National Congress Party), which seized power through the military coup of 1989, provoked new or escalating conflicts on numerous peripheries. But for pragmatic reasons under international pressure, it also negotiated the Comprehensive Peace Agreement with the SPLM/A, signed in 2005, which made possible South Sudan's secession in 2011.

The history of this period can however be told in ways other than simply as a series of authoritarian regimes and civil wars. In the research areas, people told personal histories of war, loss and displacement, but these were intertwined with struggles to find schooling, get married, earn money, protect families and property, deal with difficult neighbours and relatives, redress and revenge grievances, and gain status or power. War appears as a context for people's life stories, rather than as the focus in itself of their narratives. In fact my informants frequently set the recent conflicts in the longer history of encounters with state violence going back to the nineteenth century.[2] Chiefs (and others who supported chiefship) particularly emphasised a history of suffering and sacrifice, in order to assert claims to chiefly authority and to state recognition, resources and rights.

In many other African states in the decades after independence, nationalist politicians were often eager to overturn the old colonial structures of administration, and to depict chiefs as either colonial collaborators or outdated obstacles to modernisation. Sudanese politicians similarly sought to contrast their own modernity and advancement with supposedly backward traditional authorities, contributing to the ongoing discursive production of dichotomies between an urbanised, literate intelligentsia and rural society. This culminated in the formal 'liquidation' of the Native Administration by Numayri's revolutionary government, and the subsequent establishment of a new system of councils by

1 See in particular Johnson, *Root Causes;* Woodward, *Sudan 1898–1989;* Collins, *A History;* Hutchinson, *Nuer Dilemmas.*

2 Alexander makes a similar point regarding Mozambique: 'The local state', p. 9.

the 1971 Local Government Act. Chiefship never really disappeared, however: members of the chiefly families and former Native Administration continued to play a prominent role in the new councils across Sudan, and local government officers soon started to call for a reinstatement of such personnel, particularly in their roles of conflict prevention and resolution. Especially in the southern provinces, administrators were unwilling or unable to 'liquidate' chiefs, whose courts remained 'a vital administrative prop'.[3] The subsequent revival of traditional authority would reach its height in the 1990s under the NIF regime, which has been criticised for 're-tribalising' local administration.[4] In both periods of civil war, the southern rebel movements sometimes targeted individual chiefs for collaborating with government. In other recent civil wars in Africa, chiefship has been analysed as a factor in provoking rebellion in the first place, particularly by marginalised youth or landless poor.[5] But both the Anyanya One and the SPLM/A instead more often sought to incorporate or appoint chiefs in their own administrative structures, ensuring that the institution of chiefship would if anything be strengthened by the history of the wars.

The history of the post-1956 period has also been a story of urbanisation, albeit frequently interrupted by the flight or expulsion of people from the towns during the wars. Government centres have been transformed over this period from the heavily restricted settlements of the colonial period – centring on the *merkaz* offices, the small markets of northern or Greek traders and the 'native lodging area' or *malakiya* – into the small but nowadays rapidly expanding towns, or *medinat* [sing.: *medina*] in Arabic. Part III traces the history and consequences of this urbanisation, and it argues that the continuing moral and discursive production of the urban frontier has been a vital means of managing the economic, social and political changes wrought by decades of war, and by the ultimate South Sudanese capture of the state.

[3] John Howell, 'The reform of local government, 1971', and 'Councils and councillors, 1969–72', in John Howell (ed.), *Local Government and Politics in the Sudan* (Khartoum, 1974), pp. 65–75, 89–106, at p. 66.

[4] Most vociferously by Mahmood Mamdani in *Saviors and Survivors: Darfur, politics and the war on terror* (New York, 2009).

[5] Richards, 'To fight or to farm?'; Richard Fanthorpe, 'Neither citizen nor subject? 'Lumpen' agency and the legacy of native administration in Sierra Leone', *African Affairs* 100:400 (2001), pp. 363–386.

*

7

Trading knowledge: chiefship, local elites and the urban frontier, c. 1956–2010

During the most intense periods of civil war or uprising since 1955, most people took refuge in more remote parts of 'the bush' or across southern Sudan's borders. A much smaller proportion sought safety in the government-held towns, despite their repressive security regimes. But whenever there has been sufficient peace or stability, people have swiftly returned to – or relocated to – the small towns, in search of employment, enterprise and education. The edges of the town might be seen as the frontiers and limits of state power, as in much wider analysis of post-colonial African states; as such, the towns have often been analysed as a space of threatening, external power.[1] Indeed, the appearance of a stark urban-rural dichotomy prevails in much moral commentary among South Sudanese themselves, who frequently depict the town as an alien, immoral world of money and antisocial behaviour. In part this reflects – and acts as a warning against – the continuing instabilities, limitations and risks of urban living, experienced by a whole range of people.

But rather than repelling people, the negative aspects of town and government have only underscored the need to obtain knowledge of the regulations and procedures that *might* offer security and protection, and turn threat into guarantee. This chapter explores both the reasons for the urban-rural moral dichotomy, and the complex urban-rural connections that it belies. It concentrates on the periods of urban expansion, particularly after the 1972 Addis Ababa peace agreement and in the first decade of the twenty-first century. The outskirts of the southern Sudanese towns have not simply marked the frontiers of an alien state power, but have continued to evolve as a centripetal frontier, towards which people have been recurrently impelled by the tensions or limitations of rural life and by the quest for new knowledge, experience and resources.

As the opportunities for employment, trade and town life have expanded, so too has the group of political and economic entrepreneurs on the urban frontier, from among whom chiefs are selected. An increasing number of people have participated in public, governmental institutions such as councils, courts and even churches, and have drawn bureaucratic ritual into the most local and intimate of contexts. Institutions of local government in southern Sudan have generally been criticised for their limited effectiveness or autonomy,[2] but from the 1970s they nevertheless generated a growing sense of participation

[1] As Giblin summarises in 'History, imagination', p. 189; e.g. Jeffrey Herbst, *States and Power in Africa: comparative lessons in authority and control* (Princeton, 2000); Thomas Bierschenk and Jean-Pierre Olivier de Sardan, 'Local powers and a distant state in rural Central African Republic', *Journal of Modern African Studies* 35:3 (1997), pp. 441–68.

[2] Howell, *Local Government*; Dennis A Rondinelli, 'Administrative decentralisation and economic development: the Sudan's experiment with devolution', *Journal of Modern African Studies* 19:4 (1981), pp. 595–624.

in the state. Increasingly local elites would describe themselves abstractly as 'members', a term derived from local council membership, but which has broadened to imply membership of the local state itself.

It is paradoxically through this process of acquiring knowledge of government that the discursive dichotomy between town and rural community has been reproduced. Many government employees and other literate townspeople – often experiencing the vulnerabilities and limitations of the money they earned – have asserted their distinct status as modern, urban intellectuals by constructing a contrasting rural world of tradition and kinship, supposedly the domain of chiefs. Chiefs in turn have defended their own niche of authority by criticising urban ways and the untrustworthiness of politicians. But whether the 'big people' have sought recognition as village 'elders', 'traditional' chiefs, savvy businesspeople, church leaders, or 'people of government', they have all been members of a porous but enduring local political elite, which has increasingly inhabited or traversed the urban frontier. Chiefs represent this elite, even as they have competed within it.

APPROPRIATING THE TOWNS? KNOWLEDGE AND AUTHORITY ON THE URBAN FRONTIER, 1960s–1980s

The increasing urban-rural interaction of the late-colonial period was brought to an abrupt halt when people fled the towns during the troubles of 1955. The subsequent government recriminations and continuing repressive security regime ensured that urban populations remained very small. There was some limited return to the towns under the government of General Abboud (1958–64) as government policy encouraged rather than prevented urban migration, and as people sought refuge from increasing insecurity. But schooling and employment were heavily restricted and regulated, provoking increasing frustration on the urban frontier; many students, soldiers, police and government employees joined the 'Anyanya' armed rebellion that commenced in earnest in 1963, or the political movements in exile.[3] In 1965, government forces killed hundreds of civilians in Juba and Wau, provoking a further exodus from the towns, as a headman of a village near Juba later recalled:

> In 1965 the Arabs surrounded the Malakiya and burnt houses down and shot people; they were shouting 'kill the slaves'. People were shocked and everyone left Juba for the villages; most went to Uganda and Kenya. The Arabs thought people were supporting the Anyanya, especially the educated people here in Juba... Many youth joined the Anyanya then; others went to school in Uganda and later came back to work in the offices here. They were put in a camp in Uganda and had to farm at the same time as studying.[4]

Hill suggests that the population of Juba might have subsequently dropped as low as 5,000 (and to only a few hundred or less in other Equatorian towns), at least until the ceasefires and amnesties of 1967 and 1969.[5] The government forced civilians into 'peace villages' around the towns in Equatoria, but these were heavily controlled and confined, and hundreds died from malnutrition and disease, according to Collins.[6]

[3] Øystein H Rolandsen, 'The making of the Anya-Nya insurgency in the Southern Sudan, 1961–64', *Journal of Eastern African Studies* 5:2 (2011), pp. 211–32.

[4] Interview 44R/JC.

[5] Roger L Hill, *Migration to Juba: a case study* (Juba, 1981); Rolandsen, 'A false start', p. 120.

[6] Collins, *A History*, p. 86.

Unlike the later SPLA, the Anyanya rebels did not succeed in holding any major towns during the war. If anything, the towns were instead captured after the 1972 Addis Ababa peace agreement, by people seizing the new employment, education and trade opportunities under the Southern Regional Government. People flooded back into the towns: the population of Juba only a year later had already reached almost 57,000, and by the end of the decade it was estimated by Hill at close to 100,000. As the new capital of the semi-autonomous Southern Region, Juba attracted migrants from across the south, particularly from the Equatorian provinces and Western Bahr el Ghazal, in search of government employment or business opportunities. Other towns like Rumbek and Yei also grew at this time, though less dramatically; the population of Yei had reportedly reached nearly 12,000 by 1973, and a decade later Rumbek's population was close to 20,000 according to a very dubious census.[7] By 1973 'the urban population (including all settlements of 5,000 inhabitants or more) of the south had risen from less than 50,000 to almost 300,000', representing over 10 per cent of the southern population.[8] All of these figures are unreliable, but there is little doubt that the population of the small towns, and particularly of the regional capital, Juba, increased rapidly in the 1970s.

The government was always the main source of formal waged employment, reinforcing the association of town and state. Studies of the occupations and livelihoods of Juba inhabitants by the late 1970s suggest that the vast majority of formally employed men and women were in government employment (including government companies and construction projects) – almost 90 per cent of female employees and more than 75 per cent of male employees. The population of recent in-migrants to Juba was disproportionally young, reflecting the appeal of urban education, employment, trade and life to youth or children. Not for the first time, returning refugees were able to deploy their schooling in Uganda or elsewhere to obtain jobs; there was a direct correlation between education levels and wages.[9]

While waged employment became increasingly significant for those living in and around the towns, business and trade, particularly in the informal sector, were always even more important. In 1970s Juba, almost half the adult male population and the majority of women were not counted as employed and must have relied upon the informal economy to make a living in the town.[10] The interaction of the surrounding Bari villagers with the town also resumed or increased further in this period; according to Huby, villages within easy walking distance of Juba had become 'completely dependent' on the town by the late 1970s – selling fruit, vegetables and alcohol, as well as undertaking waged labour, in order to purchase food and other goods in town.[11] Similarly around Rumbek by the early 1980s, the resources of the town had been added to the subsistence and accumulation strategies of households and families so that urban and rural economies were interconnected: town-dwellers remitted money to rural relatives and the latter sent them food; people variously sold produce, livestock, alcohol, tobacco and fish, usually for specific purposes such as to buy medicine, clothes and soap or to pay taxes or school fees.[12]

[7] Hill, *Migration to Juba*, pp. 77–9, 96, 172.

[8] LR Mills, 'The growth of Juba in southern Sudan', in John I Clarke, Mustafa Khogali and Leszek A Kosinski (eds), *Population and Development Projects in Africa* (Cambridge, 1985),p. 314.

[9] Hill, *Migration to Juba*, p. 90; WJ House, 'Labor market differentiation in a developing economy: an example from urban Juba, Southern Sudan', *World Development* 15:7 (1987), pp. 877–897.

[10] Hill, *Migration to Juba*, p. 89.

[11] Hill, *Migration to Juba*, p. 131; Huby, 'Big men', pp. 26–32, 36.

[12] Mawson, 'The Triumph of Life', pp. 90–1.

According to Mawson, Agar Dinka people believed that they had finally 'captured government' in the 1970s; for the first time the government offices in Rumbek were primarily staffed by local people. Education became valued as never before and was viewed by older people as a route by which their younger relatives might enter the state: careers in the army, police or prisons, justice system, politics and administration were particularly sought after as the principal 'channels through which the state exercised power'. As Mawson argues, the recent experience of civil war had only confirmed the dangerous unpredictability of the state. 'But what had changed, or for a while in the 1970s appeared to have changed, was that the expansion of employment possibilities had opened up new ways and opportunities of appropriating "government", and thereby protecting the interests of rural people.'[13]

As ever then, people sought access to the state in order to protect the property and interests of rural society. But in the process, the increasing participation in town and government institutions would also contribute to local state formation and to the institutionalisation of intermediary political elites. This was further encouraged in the 1970s by the establishment of new councils under the Numayri government's 1971 Local Government Act, which was supposed to replace the Native Administration with a new hierarchy of councils. This operated as a top-down, authoritarian system, concentrating power in the hands of Province Commissioners appointed and controlled by the regime, and leaving the councils with little autonomy, clear functions or funds; by the early 1980s many councils were insolvent.[14] It was also heavily controlled by Numayri's Sudan Socialist Union (SSU). Such analyses are confirmed by personal memories of this period. A headman just outside the town of Yei declared that he had been a 'member' in Yei before the SPLA war; when asked what this meant, he explained: 'the members were the ones who, if there is an election, they say vote this way, vote this way; they were members of SSU, in the reign of Numayri'.[15] An elderly man in Rumbek was particularly dismissive of the councils, saying that they were just a way for Numayri to get information from the people, 'like a telephone or radio'.[16]

Contemporaneous studies show that local elites, including the former Native Administration leaders, continued to dominate the local councils across Sudan.[17] This was not necessarily an entirely conservative sign, however; the councils did expand the membership and participation of these local political elites. One English-speaking elder in Yei had more positive memories of councils in the 1970s; both he and his father had been council members at different times:

> At first the British DC appointed members, but later in 1974 they started elections, with members elected from the different villages. Then problems from the village could be put on the agenda. The council was strong: if the DC was bad, the council could write to the [Province] Commissioner in Juba and he would be removed. Many of them [DCs] only lasted six months or a year. They caused complaints, for example if the council passed a resolution about road repairs and it became law but the DC failed to implement it.[18]

[13] Mawson, 'The Triumph of Life', pp. 87–8.

[14] Rondinelli, 'Administrative decentralisation'; Helge Rohn, Peter Adwok Nyaba and George Maker Benjamin, 'Report of the study on local administrative structures in Maridi, Mundri and Yei Counties – West Bank Equatoria, South Sudan', (Nairobi, 1997), p. 9.

[15] Interview 9R/YC.

[16] Interview 1bN/RC.

[17] Howell, 'The reform of local government, 1971', and 'Councils and councillors, 1969–1972'; Rondinelli, 'Administrative decentralisation'.

[18] Interview 48N/YC.

This ideal of a representative local government body that could hold even the powerful District Commissioners to account does not seem to match the perceptions of other people in this area or elsewhere. This man had considerable investment in such institutions, however, having been a member of successive councils and committees himself. His continuing use of the term 'DC' for local government officers is also indicative of the sense of institutional continuity that is frequently reflected in local terminology for officials and councils, despite changing formal government nomenclature.

Council members were not the only people gaining knowledge of government ways and helping to mediate the increasing urbanisation and urban-rural relations in the 1970s and early 1980s. A study of Yirrol District, neighbouring Rumbek, suggests that by the mid-1980s, local cattle traders and government employees were also playing such a role:

> Dinka attitudes have changed considerably as more and more visit towns and cities to work in petty trade or wage labour. Indeed, wage migrants and cattle traders have become agents of change in their communities. Cattle traders and wage earners now form an intermediate social category between the village and the town, the traditional economy and the market economy. They oscillate between both worlds.

The author, Mangor Ring, emphasised that while most cattle traders were illiterate, they gained invaluable experience of towns and of 'educated persons' through their participation in urban markets, and that this knowledge enabled them to act as channels of communication between government and 'the rural masses'. As ever it was those junior or marginal in kinship structures who were most 'open to change: they are the ones who join schools, seek wage employment and enter the cattle trade'.[19] Success enabled such men to transcend the usual obstacles of generational and lineage hierarchies to gain a voice in the management of family herds and to be appointed to court panels. Often they had migrated to work in Khartoum before returning to engage in trade; as Mading Deng also emphasises of the Ngok Dinka youth, 'the infiltration of youth into towns... is more and more viewed as a manly adventure'.[20]

The expertise, experience and position of these cattle traders was strikingly similar to that of chiefs since the nineteenth century: 'their mobility makes them knowledgeable... They acquire Arabic language and urban experience which is believed to make them more enlightened than the average villager.' Unsurprisingly then, the introduction of elections for chiefship in Yirrol in 1984 led to the election of several cattle traders as executive chiefs or court presidents.[21] Similarly around Juba in the 1970s, the ability to read and write and 'some knowledge of Arabic or English' gave younger men 'a chance to become "government chiefs" before they, strictly speaking, are old enough'.[22] It would remain common for chiefs to have previous experience of trade or urban employment: a chief of the town court in Yei in the 2000s had previously worked as a tailor in the town, and his father had been a soldier in the colonial army, indicative of continuing connections to the *malakiya*. A chief in the rural vicinity of Juba had worked as a university technician in Khartoum – which he described

19 Moses Mangor Ring, 'Dinka stock-trading and shifts in rights in cattle', in PTW Baxter and R Hogg (eds), *Property, Poverty and People: changing rights in property and problems of pastoral development* (Manchester, 1987), pp. 192–6.

20 Mading Deng, *Tradition and Modernization*, p. 60.

21 Mangor Ring, 'Dinka stock-trading', pp. 201–3.

22 Huby, 'Big Men', p. 199.

as 'government' work – until the outbreak of war in 1983 led him to become a trader in Juba instead.[23]

It is clear that these chiefs and many other individuals engaged in trade or employment on the urban frontier were breaching any boundary between town and rural community, acquiring knowledge and resources of value to those living outside the towns. As a study of another town, Kongor, asserted in 1979, 'the rural-urban imaginary dividing line does not hold'.[24] In the early 1980s, Huby argued that the Bari social world transcended any urban-rural divide, as the 'big people' – those able to earn a monetary income in Juba, including women – continued to defer to the moral and legal authority of the elders and male heads of households, despite the greater income and social status of the urban big people.

Contemporary accounts from the 1980s thus suggest that towns like Juba and Rumbek were increasingly encompassed within local social, economic and political worlds. Yet these accounts and more recent recollections of the period hint nevertheless at continuing tensions and moral ambiguities around the value and values of the towns, as revealed by an episode in Rumbek recorded by Mawson. In the 1970s, the most powerful spear-master, the master of the sacred *luak* or cattle-byre at Warnyang, Makuer Gol, became president of Rumbek Town Court. Mawson sees this as indicative of the general optimism towards the government at this time. But it aroused unease and opposition, articulated principally by other senior men from Makuer's own family and section, who argued that government chiefship and the spiritual authority of spear-masters were incompatible in one person. At the height of the resulting dispute, Makuer Gol succeeded in persuading the government to send drilling equipment to provide a borehole at Warnyang, enabling the ceremonial rebuilding of the *luak* to proceed. The value of his skill in mediating government as well as divinity was thus in one sense proven – indeed in some other Dinka areas these skills had long been complementary and integrated. In 2006, some people argued that it had been a good thing for Makuer to go to the town court, because 'it made some people know that town is a good place until some sent their children to school'.[25] A middle-aged woman from Makuer's family emphasised that Makuer's 'cleverness' and 'wisdom' equipped him to combine both responsibilities, and thus to prevent 'quarrels' among the people.[26]

But local political discourse also emphasised that forms of knowledge and power should be diversified rather than concentrated. According to an age-mate of Makuer Gol, the 'cloth' (government chiefship) had always been potentially harmful to the spear-masters, particularly if they deliberately sought it. He claimed that the famous spear-master of the colonial period, Makuer's father Gol Mayen, had become blind because he gave away cows in order to get the 'cloth'. Makuer ignored his father's subsequent warning not to repeat this mistake and 'insisted on having cloth at Maboric', the town court: 'He was advised not to do so by the community, telling him, "don't you remember what happened here with the blindness of your father?"'. But Makuer ignored the advice. 'It continued like that until war started [1983]... After a few years, he became sick in his throat, which he had used to speak to claim the cloth; that was the sickness that killed Makuer.'[27]

[23] Interview 41R/JC.

[24] Abdel Ghaffar M Ahmed and Mustafa Abdel Rahman, 'Small urban centres', p. 270.

[25] Interview 71R/RC.

[26] Interview 72R/RC. See also Johnson, *Nuer Prophets*, pp. 309–13: prophets were brought to Malakal town by the government in the 1970s.

[27] Interview 73R/RC.

This episode reveals the close association of government chiefship with the town, and the apparent separation of this sphere from that of the spear-masters. This separation is often explained in terms of the need to keep the moral authority and vital expertise of the *beny bith* away from the risks of the urban frontier. But this might also speak of concern at an over-accumulation of power by one person: the tensions centred on a dispute between Makuer and another powerful spiritual and political leader, indicating the political rivalries underlying the discourse around Makuer's position on the urban court. During this dispute, 'government' chiefs and other senior men became involved in debate and mediation, and the subsequent resolution appeared to re-unify a single moral community encompassing the government chiefs. This is very much the pattern of local political elite formation and reproduction, through tensions and rivalries that appear to divide the big people into distinct categories, but which actually unify them in a political community.

Over subsequent decades, chiefs have very often been rhetorically associated instead with rural communities, as the idea of 'traditional' authority has been revived. This was already emerging in 1984, when a series of peace conferences were held in the Rumbek area to try to resolve local conflicts. Chiefs were held responsible for the conflicts and made to sign 'bonds' of fifty cattle as a guarantee against further fighting. The Province Commissioner (himself an Agar Dinka) claimed that the 'Agar civilised citizens' he had spoken to in the provincial capital of Wau believed that chiefs were to blame for failing to prevent fighting. The chiefs conversely blamed the 'intellectuals' and 'advocates' (lawyers) for interfering in court cases without understanding the customary law, and one chief made a pointed reference to alleged instigation of recent conflict by a Prison Service brigadier:

> He blamed the police for not applying the law properly. He stated that people at the village level have no problem between themselves but they fight due to problems created by the town people.[28]

These discussions suggest that chiefs were positioning themselves in opposition to the 'intellectuals' and 'town people' and deploying discourses of tradition and custom. Yet the chiefs would be drawn ever more into the towns from the late 1990s. Why then has an urban-rural dichotomy continued to be reproduced, and by whom?

'SOMEWHERE IN THE MIDDLE': THE INSECURITIES OF THE URBAN FRONTIER SINCE THE 1980s

At least part of the answer lies in the very real experiences of the insecurities of town life, and of the continuing risks as well as opportunities presented by the urban frontier. The ambiguities and dangers of the town were intensifying at the time of Mawson's research in Rumbek, due to the increasing political tensions in Sudan in the early 1980s. Mounting southern resentments over too much political interference and too little funding from the central government in Khartoum were exacerbated by government plans to construct the Jonglei Canal and to control recently-discovered oil reserves in the south. While members of the Southern Regional Government were divided over proposals to break up the Region, southern military officers and soldiers began to join remnants of Anyanya One and new guerrilla forces, culminating in the mutiny of the Bor

[28] Minutes of the meeting between Gok and Agar sections on 20 August 1984, Rumbek; Minutes of the meeting of Commissioner Lakes Province with Aliamtoc Chiefs on 3 August 1984, both in Bahr el Ghazal Province Archive, Wau, LP 66.B.1.

garrison in May 1983, and the subsequent creation of the SPLM/A. Once again the rebellion originated on the urban frontier, among soldiers, police, students and government employees.

Initially the outbreak of war led some to take refuge in the towns, but the SPLA attacks on Rumbek (1986) and Yei (1990) confirmed the dangers of urban residence, and only a very small population remained in these government garrisons until both were captured by the SPLA in 1997. A much larger population remained in or took refuge in Juba, which remained in government hands, and where displaced communities were settled, mainly from Equatoria; by 2005, the population was estimated at approximately 250,000.[29] But the urban frontier was nevertheless constricted as the edges of town were policed more rigorously than ever before. The communities that had occupied the vicinity of the town suddenly found that a zone of opportunity and protection had become the frontline in the military struggle between the government garrison and the rebels all around. An elderly sub-chief of a village several miles north of Juba recalled the particular dangers of being caught travelling between town and village, which invited suspicion from both sides: 'Some of our people got lost in between the two groups; others were blown up with mines which were planted either by Anyanya [SPLA] or government soldiers'.[30] The early to mid-1990s are remembered as a particularly difficult time in Juba, with student protests and harsh repression by the security forces; many people fled after the unsuccessful SPLA assault on the town in 1992.

From 1997, people gradually returned to Yei and Rumbek as the SPLM/A established its administration of these areas; by the time of the Comprehensive Peace Agreement between the SPLM/A and the Sudan Government in 2005, both towns were thriving administrative and trading centres, and Rumbek was also the centre of UN and NGO activity. After 2005 these towns continuing to expand, with the greatest urban growth again occurring in Juba, as the capital of the new Government of Southern Sudan. The city's population was estimated as high as half a million by 2010. As in earlier periods, many of these people were employed by the government, and many more relied on the informal economy: most urban livelihoods in Juba after 2005 depended on multiple small-scale economic activities such as firewood and grass collection, charcoal production, petty trade, brick-making, stone-breaking, *tukl* (house) building and thatching, and alcohol production. The towns continued to act as a frontier of knowledge and enterprise: 'One emerging trend seems to be that of young, unskilled or semi-skilled males coming to Juba in search of better jobs and an urban lifestyle'.[31]

Yet this perception of opportunity was still accompanied by a sense of risk and exclusion, even during peacetime. The urban frontier had been recurrently pushed back to the edges of the towns, and to unstable, insecure sites within the town centres. The old colonial classification of urban residential areas had endured, ensuring that only middle- or higher-ranking government employees could afford to live in the second- or third-class residential areas in the town centres. The majority of townspeople were forced to live on smaller plots in fourth-class areas on the outskirts of the towns, or in squatter settlements. In early 2009, a massive demolition of squatter housing and informal markets and shops was carried out in areas of Juba, affecting tens of thousands of people.[32] Both in the first and second

29 Ellen Martin and Irina Mosel, *City Limits: urbanisation and vulnerability in Sudan – Juba case study* (London, 2011), p. 3.

30 Interview 43R/JC.

31 Martin and Mosel, *City Limits*, pp. 4, 13–14.

32 Martin and Mosel, *City Limits*, p. 21; Mills, 'The growth of Juba', p. 321; James Gatdet Dak, 'Squatters demolitions in Juba begins amidst tight security', *Sudan Tribune*, 27 January 2009, last accessed 24 January 2013: www.sudantribune.com/spip.php?iframe&page=imprimable&id_article=29975.

periods of civil war, some people had moved into the town during wartime and then were subsequently pushed back out to settlements just outside Juba like Gumbo and Lologo. This further blurred the town boundaries and expanded the urban frontier; by 2010 peri-urban settlements like Gumbo were 'slowly taking on the characteristics of a town'.[33] The advance of rural people towards the towns had repeatedly met with an exclusionary push from the government areas in the town centre, leading to a shifting frontier zone on the outskirts and immediate surroundings of the towns.

Insecure, informal settlement patterns were thus a feature of urban life for the majority of town inhabitants, particularly in Juba. People had also experienced the urban economy as arbitrary and expensive, due to recurrent inflation and hence rising food prices in the town markets. Few people were able to accumulate wealth from trade or employment; the overwhelming impression in accounts of Juba in the 1972–83 period is of urban poverty, and elsewhere townspeople relied heavily on the produce of their rural relatives. 'In the town there is money but no social security; in the rural communities, because of the continuing strength of kinship ties, there is social security but no money.'[34] Even better-off government employees might find themselves dependent on rural assistance when salaries went unpaid and grain imports collapsed in the early 1980s.[35] During the subsequent war most markets collapsed; even two years after the 1997 SPLA advances in Equatoria, a report on Yei and Maridi counties found that markets and buyers were still scarce and most people were unable to earn any money at all; military requisitions further discouraged the production of surpluses.[36]

As in other African towns and cities, urban residence is often explained as a temporary strategy, even if it lasts for decades. One chief in Juba, a long-term government employee and very successful townsperson, declared that 'we are standing on one leg here in Juba – when we return home we can put the other one down too'.[37] This sense of straddling different worlds also contributes to a sense of insecurity. A recent report on urbanisation in Juba cites youth who 'pointed out that many of their peers have dropped out of school or training and have thus ended up "somewhere in the middle" – with some skills but no proper certificates', and thus struggling to compete for skilled or semi-skilled jobs with more highly qualified peers.[38] In a broader sense, it is this 'somewhere in the middle' that the majority of people in and around the towns have occupied, relying on multiple – if incomplete – sets of knowledge and economic activity to survive.

But this frontier life has continued to present opportunity as well as risk. On the edge of Juba in 2006, for example, entrepreneurial young women were occupying a particular place 'in the middle', waiting by the roads and paths from the villages to intercept women coming to sell their produce, buying it from them and then taking it to the main urban markets to sell on at a profit. Although this meant they had to pay 'customs' taxes on the way to the market, their knowledge and contacts in the town put them in a privileged position in relation to the rural women, who were also in a hurry to return to the village. These

33 Martin and Mosel, *City Limits*, p. 5.

34 Mangor Ring, 'Dinka stock-trading', p. 201.

35 Mawson, 'The Triumph of Life', p. 90.

36 Lazarus Koech, Anne L Goinard and Olaf Willnat, 'Community participation in the primary health care programme and the new system of governance, West Bank, Equatoria Region, New Sudan' (Nairobi, 1999), pp. 37–9.

37 Interview 36R/JC.

38 Martin and Mosel, *City Limits*, p. 15.

young middle-women exuded the kind of savvy that brought success on the urban frontier. Women were even less likely to have educational qualifications or to obtain formal employment, and they played a particularly prominent part in the informal economy, usually in alcohol production or trade in produce between the rural areas and the town markets. Women were generally responsible for bringing household produce to the market. A recent report suggested that women in Juba were 'increasingly' providing for their families through petty market trade, but thirty years earlier Huby had emphasised that women were already more likely to bring the greatest income into their households, particularly through alcohol production and sale.[39]

Most people engaging in employment, enterprise and the informal economy in the towns have formed 'an intermediate social category', which transcends any urban-rural divide.[40] The discursive dichotomy between town and village has been perpetuated in part by the very real experience of the hardships and vulnerabilities of town life, ensuring a continuing need for rural subsistence activities to support townspeople and to act as a safety-net. Criticisms of the ills of town life thus act as warnings about life on the urban frontier:

> Town is good, but you must come to town for a particular purpose, like work or schooling. If you just come with money to stay here, then the money will just disappear. Those who build houses here, it is only for the children to go to school, and the others still stay in the village.[41]

Another town headman in Yei similarly explained that 'village people come here often to get salt and other necessities, and some even want to come to town, but there is not enough food here – they eat a lot there in the village, more than we do in the town'.[42] After 2005, as in earlier periods, there was rapid inflation of food prices: the price of flour in Juba reportedly doubled between 2005–6 and 2010, and continued to rise subsequently. It became more difficult than ever for townspeople to feed themselves and their immediate families, let alone to meet the expectations of wider family and social relations.[43] This naturally fed the perennial complaints of older people that young people living in the towns had become selfish and interested only in their own money, as an elderly widow on the outskirts of Rumbek declared: 'This is the generation of money: they don't listen to us elders, or plan for the future, or give anything to us... The educated people should bring us good things, but they just waste money.'[44]

Many people were expressing concern at the effects of rapid urbanisation, and continuing to associate the towns with crime, prostitution, youth delinquency, underage sex, divorce and other moral ills. They were also concerned at monetisation and monetary inflation, particularly of marital bridewealth, and associated these processes with the towns and government. An elderly lady living close to Yei town blamed the expansion of the town and spread of its cultures for the 'spoiling' of marriage: 'The land is all a town! A town is actually a place where there are a lot of bad acts. The bridewealth is too much to pay.'[45]

In cattle-keeping areas such as Rumbek or the Mundari settlements north of

[39] Martin and Mosel, *City Limits*, p. 14; Huby, 'Big men'.

[40] Mangor Ring, 'Dinka stock-trading'; Huby, 'Big men'. Cf. Trefon, 'Hinges and fringes'.

[41] Interview 30N/YC.

[42] Interviews 28N/YC; 29N/YC.

[43] Giblin similarly shows that inflation in Tanzania restricted the capacity of educated urban employees to provide for their older relatives: *History of the Excluded*, p. 278.

[44] Interview 31N/RC.

[45] Interview 29R/YC.

Juba, bridewealth was still being paid in the form of cattle, and people dismissed the idea of paying in money. But even here people complained that the 'dollar' earnings of the top military and government officials or remittances from abroad had driven up the prices of cattle in the market. In such areas, money was often contrasted directly with cattle, to explain the continued use of the latter for bridewealth. People particularly emphasised the insurance represented by cattle; even if disaster struck, they could move with their cattle and survive on milk, or exchange cattle for grain. Money, on the other hand, was said to run out more quickly; and people had of course experienced situations of war and rural displacement where it was impossible to purchase anything with money.[46]

The continuing primacy of the value of cattle – together perhaps with the effects of monetary inflation – had, according to a chief on the edge of Juba in 2006, continued to make marriage easier for rural people who could spend all their time cultivating, raiding and thus acquiring cattle for their bridewealth.

> But you, somebody from the town: you have been in school; while you are paying for school, where do you think you will find this money? And when will you have time for buying the cattle?... You cannot buy cattle with the little salary you have, which does not even satisfy the family's needs.[47]

This is striking for revealing the continuing relative poverty of townspeople in the enduring value-systems of livestock and marriage. It remained difficult or impossible for the majority of money-earners to accumulate wealth-in-cattle when a single cow cost hundreds of dollars in the auctions. Even in areas where the bridewealth was paid in cash, older people dismissed money as a source or measure of status and value and criticised the inflation of monetary bridewealth, declaring that even millions of pounds were 'worth' nothing.[48] Moral criticisms of money contributed to the depiction of townspeople as a distinct category, separated from the moral community by the individualising effects of town life and capitalist economy.

Despite – or indeed because of – the widespread discourse of selfish 'townese', townspeople actually worked hard to maintain kinship and wider relations and to invest in social capital, respectable marriages and recognition of their social status in networks and communities beyond the towns. Huby attributed this in the 1980s to an inherent social conservatism and gerontocratic authority. But instead it represented vital insurance and investment strategies in contexts where money incomes were generally limited and unreliable. 'If you don't distribute to the people in the village, they will say: what will you do if you end up without a job one day?'[49] A town headman in Yei explained the vital need to maintain urban-rural connections: 'Most people who come to stay here are bringing their children to school; they keep farms back in the villages and get relatives to cultivate them, or they provide food for other villagers so they will cultivate for them'.[50] For anyone to accumulate money alone would have been an immensely risky strategy, in a context where salaries, banks, markets and imports could be unstable or collapse altogether, and where military forces could once again endanger and displace people, not least in the towns. As this

[46] Interview 56R/RC.

[47] Interview 42R/JC. See Hutchinson on the continuing higher value of cattle in relation to money among Nuer: *Nuer Dilemmas*, p. 98.

[48] Interviews 28R/YC; 50R/JC.

[49] Interview 32N/YC.

[50] Interview 29N/YC.

woman argued, it was vital that becoming a 'town person' did not actually mean alienation from the village:

> You take your child to school in order to learn and to buy you clothes when he graduates. He will also buy medicines for you, or other good things of the town, and send it to you at home. People have not all gone to one side – there are people of the town [*koc peen*] and there are also people of the village [*koc bec*]. It is your child who is educated [*tueny*] who will bring you to town, if he has a good job. People will begin to speak well of him because of all the good things he brought. He may ask his parents to marry an uneducated wife from the village for him, and bring her to the town to bear children, and these children will be town people.[51]

The urban-rural – or *peen-bec* – dichotomy was thus above all a way of defining duties and obligations. *Koc peen* were expected to provide their relatives with access to town resources and money; in turn they could expect their rural relatives and dependents to help them when it came to marriage and subsistence. But towns were not simply an economic space, the site of markets and money. For as another interviewee from Rumbek declared, '*koc peen* are in the hand of government'.[52] The association of towns with the state also contributed to the simultaneous risk and opportunity of the urban frontier, and to its construction.

'COLLECTING REGULATIONS': CONSTITUTING THE LOCAL STATE

With good reason, people perceived the towns, markets and money to be connected with the state itself. Since the colonial period, education had been seen primarily as a route into waged employment, and even in 2006 going to school or joining the army could be expressed as 'going to the government'. Also, people tended to associate money and its use with the government, even if the informal economy was as or more important a source of monetary income as government employment. Towns remained the centres of state power; even after the 2005 Peace Agreement, the reach of state policing was still very limited in the rural areas.[53] People had always come to the towns not only in search of income and services but also to gain knowledge of the systems and workings of the government. Even Huby, with her focus on the conservative aspects of Bari society, acknowledged that the understanding that townspeople had gained of the government bureaucracy could be of even greater value for their families than their monetary income: they were 'an invaluable asset for their poorer relatives when it comes to arranging red-tape matters, getting jobs and education for themselves and their children'.[54] Even those not working directly for the government could thus claim a special knowledge and understanding of the ways of the town and state. A leading chief in Juba emphasised that people living in the town and nearby also knew more about the police and the laws:

> You know, when the distance between the town here and the village becomes fifty miles or more, then you find those people are less clever than the town people. The people close by are always collecting regulations from the police.

51 Interview 72R/RC.

52 Interview 71R/RC.

53 Abraham Sewonet Abatneh and Simon Monoja Lubang, 'Police reform and state formation in Southern Sudan', *Canadian Journal of Development Studies* 32:1 (2011), pp. 94–108.

 54 Huby, 'Big men', p. 39.

> People like to go and watch the judges settling cases, just to learn, so you find that people even know the right sections for their cases.[55]

'Collecting regulations' epitomises the acquisition of knowledge of the legal and judicial system in the towns. Even those who sought to avoid the state and to profit from the informal or illegal economies in the towns nevertheless needed to know how to evade problematic government attention and protect their assets.

Local government increasingly provided additional arenas in which people 'collected' regulations, institutions and practices. Councils or committees have remained part of the changing institutional landscape of local government, alongside or overlapping with chiefship. Many more people have therefore had the opportunity to participate in government as members of these formal, bureaucratic institutions. It is revealing however that my informants often claimed to be or to have been a '*memba*', without necessarily saying of *what* they were a member. For membership of various courts, councils and committees tended to remain relatively consistent even as the names of these bodies had changed, and so to be a 'member' was simply to be someone with experience of local government or justice in the village or town. An elderly sub-chief for one of the 'zones' in Yei town explained that he had been a 'member' before becoming a headman and eventually sub-chief:

> The people who help the headman are members. When there are issues in an area, the members forward the issues to the headman, who will forward to the sub-chief, who will then forward to the court... The members are: assistant, secretary and treasurer... Then there are nine members who report issues – the total is eleven.[56]

Recollections of local councils seem to be particularly strong in the Yei area, perhaps because many people here had also experienced councils in Uganda, where they migrated for work or schooling, or as refugees. This was also the area in which the SPLM administrative and political structures were first implemented after the SPLA capture of Yei in 1997, and its designation as the SPLM/A capital. In 1996, the SPLM had held its 'Conference on Civil Society and Civil Authority', which included representatives of churches, women's and youth groups, indigenous NGOs, traditional leaders and chiefs, and the armed forces. In 1998, as Rolandsen narrates, the SPLM launched a drive to establish and elect 'Liberation Councils', including at the village (or '*boma*') and county levels, in the areas under its administration, particularly around Yei.[57] By 2004–5, the councils at all levels were being increasingly criticised both by local people and outside analysts for their general ineffectiveness and the confusion and competition between structures at the local level. But they had nevertheless conveyed a sense of participation in the SPLM, now seen very much as the new *hakuma*. The councils enabled civilians to enact the formalities and procedures of bureaucratic government, and, increasingly, to engage with international agencies through these. Such procedures were being appropriated even into

55 Interview 34N/JC.

56 Interview 12R/YC.

57 Øystein H Rolandsen, *Guerrilla Government: political changes in the Southern Sudan during the 1990s* (Uppsala: Nordiska Afrikainstitutet, 2005), p. 163; Daniel Large, 'Local governance in South Sudan: context, condition and change' (Nairobi, 2004); Rohn et al, 'Report of the study on local administrative structures', pp. 7–8. The complexity of the structures on paper even at the *boma* level is illustrated in Herbert Herzog, 'Report: mission on governance to Western Equatoria, Southern Sudan' (Liebefeld, Switzerland, 1998), p. 22.

family settings: 'When a marriage is being negotiated, there is a chairman, a secretary who can write, and two members.'[58]

Other institutions and arenas have also provided opportunities for leadership and bureaucratic experience. The most important perhaps, particularly for women, have been the churches. Often during the research, the middle-aged and older women to whom I was directed were active in one of the churches. One such lady in Yei described herself as a spokesperson and elder 'both in the church and in the government'. She said that literate women had only recently been brought into government in the 'New Sudan' period, on the orders of the SPLM/A leader, Dr John Garang. But in the church, women had always been able to 'stand up' with the men.[59] Other women also explained that they were members of church 'committees' (the English word being commonly used) that would help to settle disputes and quarrels among church people, particularly marital problems.

Further opportunities for employment and participation were provided by NGOs and the refugee camp organisational structures, in which younger, educated men and women were often able to advance. From the 1990s the SPLM encouraged and supervised the formation of 'syndicated organisations' such as the New Sudan Women's Association.[60] The increasing presence of international agencies also institutionalised the 'workshop' as the latest manifestation of bureaucratic arenas like councils and committees.[61] Various initiatives created further organisational and institutional structures for widening participation; often these involved considerable performance of bureaucracy rather than significant autonomy or action.[62] Whether such initiatives were governmental or nongovernmental, people tended to see them all as part of the sphere of the *hakuma*, just as the 'UN' was.

The increasing sense of 'membership' of the local state was accompanied by increasing expectations of the state. People in and around Rumbek are particularly explicit about their recent 'discovery' of the benefits of the town.

> In the past the Arabs in the town used to make people carry out human waste and clean their houses. But we have found it to be something very good; life in the town is very good. If your son or daughter is educated, your life will not be bad again. Your bedding will not be missing and your sickness will easily be treated. Now that we have come to the town, our life will be very comfortable: no hunger, no bad bedding; you will not experience bad old age, like our ancestors. You will enjoy everything in the town.[63]

Within such narratives is the expectation that if people have come to town, they will be rewarded with a more 'comfortable' life. This discourse was a way to impose obligations on the 'children' working in the towns. But it went further in transferring some of this obligation to the government itself, as one woman emphasised:

> Now the town has become good, every child will be taken to school and this is why you find the town highly populated. Some have now reached America. Now the government should keep in mind also the problem of hunger; long

58 Interview 48N/YC.

59 Interview 28R/YC.

60 Herzog, 'Report: mission on governance', p. 37.

61 African Rights, 'Imposing empowerment: aid and civil institutions in southern Sudan' (London: African Rights Discussion Paper, 1995), p. 37.

62 Large, 'Local governance', p. 23.

63 Interview 71R/RC.

> ago people died in great numbers because of hunger. Now the government is present, it should maintain the hospitals well so that people survive, because town is not bad but very good.[64]

The very fact of people having come to town was thus presented as having established a claim upon the state to provide them with services. Some people suggested that communities had become reoriented from relying primarily on spiritual interlocution to bring protection from disease, infertility, drought and other calamities, to expecting the state to bring such protection. A group of women just outside Juba said they had no one to protect them from diseases; 'you just go to the government'.[65] In Yei and Maridi, a primary health care project in the 1990s failed to become seen as a community responsibility; people said it 'belongs to the "Hakuma" (government/authority) and hence do not feel responsible'. The report added, 'This is a "hangover" from the Old Sudan where the government provided health services'; it was certainly an enduring idea since the later colonial period.[66] In a number of areas, people suggested that the government had replaced former relations of dependency and clientage, such as the protection offered by big families to small or weak ones.[67] As some of the displaced Mundari living north of Juba explained, there were no longer any *'dupet* (people with client or 'slave' status): 'now if someone is orphaned the government looks after him'[68] and 'the government is supposed to feed people'.[69] The towns had always been particularly attractive for those of low social status or without family support, but this had evolved into the much broader expectation that the state should provide for people.

Such expectations were encouraged by administrative terminology. In Juba under the Sudan Government in the 1990s, 'Village Development Committees' were established, as one administrative officer explained in 2006: 'The Village Development Committees are alongside the chiefs, made up of the intellectuals, the educated elite of each village. They are supposed to enlighten and initiate development on a self-help basis.'[70] But this 'educated elite' could provoke considerable resentment. A group of middle-aged women in a village just outside Juba complained about trickery by literate women from the town, who participated in a development project in the village to raise goats and install water pumps: 'but the educated women took all the money saying it was to be put in the bank: the educated milked the udders while we held the horns!'.[71] Similarly women near Rumbek complained that they needed the government to bring services like a health centre, schools and water, and that the educated were 'tricky': 'they get relief and then only distribute a little to people and keep the rest for themselves, and then tell the foreigners that they have distributed it all'.[72]

Councils and committees widened the opportunities for individuals to participate in bureaucratic institutions and to appropriate regulatory orders into local and private contexts. But they tended in practice to cement small elites of

64 Interview 72R/RC.

65 Interview 35N/JC.

66 Koech et al, 'Community participation', p. 10.

67 Interview 63R/RC.

68 Interview 26N/JC.

69 Interview 36N/JC.

70 Interviews 37N/JC; 24N/JC.

71 Interview 27N/JC.

72 Interview 63R/RC.

(mainly) men who multiplied the intermediary skills and knowledge of chiefs – and indeed by and from among whom chiefs would often be selected. Yet this same group also continued to perpetuate the urban-rural dichotomies and to produce discursive distinctions between chiefs and 'town' people. Nostalgic, idealised visions of chiefship and rural community were usually expressed by elderly men, often also living in the town themselves. Such discourse served to produce and reinforce a particular version of chiefship as a rurally-rooted, socially-embedded form of authority or interlocution, distinct from the government employees living in the town. The educated townsmen even acknowledged the suspicions of rural people towards them, to underscore this distinction. A schoolteacher in Rumbek explained in 2006 that he could not succeed his father as a chief; the community would never allow it 'because I am an educated town person who might trick them'.[73]

The literate townspeople distanced themselves rhetorically from the rural communities and expressed a certain disdain for the politics of chiefship and for chiefs' courts, depicting themselves as above such matters. Some also claimed status as 'elders', knowledgeable in the history of the area and its chiefships, but from a position of social detachment, intellectual knowledge and foreign interlocution. Some denied having ever been in a chief's court, or ever taking part in village affairs or the selection of chiefs, and yet frequently their names appeared in chief's court records, and people in the village referred to their influence in chiefly politics. Their reticence about such activities might have reflected a presumption that a foreign researcher would interpret chiefship and village politics as backward and traditional, undermining the modern, urban and educated status they wished to cultivate. But these people of the town and government certainly contributed to their own status as a distinct category, and hence to the sense of an urban-rural divide that was perpetuated more widely. This in turn had led to chiefship appearing a more traditional and rurally-rooted institution, despite the close connections of chiefs and the big people of the towns.

In fact chiefship had become ever more town-based; the urban influx since the 1990s was accompanied by an increasing presence of chiefs and their courts in the towns. Some of these were specifically urban chiefs or headmen, appointed by either the SPLM administration or the preceding or parallel governments of Sudan, to be responsible for particular quarters or zones of the towns. Others were chiefs and headmen for war-displaced communities, particularly in Juba. But still others claimed to represent chiefdoms in the rural areas around the towns and in some cases even further afield, and yet were residing in the town and perhaps even holding their court there. This was particularly the case in Rumbek, where insecurity and armed conflicts outside the town were most often cited as the reason for chiefs to have moved their courts and homes into the town. But this trend was not entirely unique to Rumbek and nor was security the only attraction of the town for chiefs. As we have seen, individuals had often been selected to become chiefs or headmen precisely because they had experience of town life and hence of the ways of government, as one Yei sub-chief claimed: 'we who were once traders and have become chiefs: we know a lot of things'.[74]

There was increasing demand from many people for chiefs to be literate as well as to have experience such as government employment or trade. Such knowledge was seen to prepare chiefs to deal effectively with government, and so to bring the material benefits of development projects and services. Young

[73] Interview 38N/RC.

[74] Interview 12R/YC.

people and returnees from refugee camps in particular complained about illiterate chiefs and emphasised the need for chiefs to be able to speak English so that they could communicate with international organisations. In making such arguments, they were of course also elevating the value of their own kinds of knowledge and experience. But even an illiterate sub-chief also argued that people would increasingly demand educated chiefs, and that illiterate chiefs might well find themselves replaced by their own secretaries. In Juba, where chiefs already were literate, one IDP chief appointed in the 1990s argued for the value of his ability to write in Arabic during the war: 'when the UN bring food, the chief is the first person to come with a list of his people, and the chiefs also wrote passes for people to go outside Juba'.[75] A headman and schoolteacher on the edge of Juba argued that, while in the past chiefship had been given to the wealthiest men who could 'feed' people, now it was more important that they could read; even poor people were studying in school and 'learning laws', and such people were needed to become chiefs. 'As we have experienced that actually a man who could read provides better justice than one who was selected by the village people.'[76]

Knowledge acquired on the urban frontier was thus more important than ever to chiefship. But this was increasingly criticised or disguised by the ideal of rural chiefship. An elderly man, who had worked as a mechanic for the government in Wau and recently returned to his home area of Rumbek, criticised the residence of chiefs in the town, and complained about the wider effects of urbanisation:

> It is not good for chiefs to be in town. If we mix things in the town, there will be no difference between outside people and town people – we need to differentiate; this is one of the most important things now. The town is supposed to be only for soldiers, students, the educated, traders, technical people and government. Outside people are cattle keepers and cultivators. The town has become too congested and we don't know who is who anymore.[77]

It was such attempts to maintain the former exclusiveness of the towns that had preserved the discursive dichotomy between town and country. This man claimed to know how 'the system' in the town should work, unlike the rural people who came 'with primitive eyes' to the town. Yet he also saw rural life and cattle-keeping as a virtue, provided it remained separate from the town.

CONCLUSION

Such inventions of ideal town and rural communities served to mark off a sphere of specialist expertise, gained through education and/or urban experience, akin to the claims to knowledge of rain or other esoteric realms of epistemology. It also served to mask to outsiders the existence of the closely connected, if internally rivalrous, local political elites which held sway in both town and village. Members of this elite actually invested in multiple forms of knowledge – it was this eclecticism that in reality earned wealth and influence, rather than isolated specialisms. They could thus deploy a varying discursive repertoire, from custom, ancestry and autochthony to international ideologies.[78] The resulting

[75] Interview 33N/JC.

[76] Interview 46R/JC.

[77] Interviews 1aN/RC, 1cN/RC.

[78] Cf. Willis, 'Chieftaincy'; Hagmann and Péclard, 'Negotiating statehood', p. 547.

discourse of traditional authority fed into national South Sudanese ideologies and policies, which will be examined in more detail in Chapter 9. But ideals of chiefship were also being produced at the local level, particularly as people struggled to understand and explain the role of chiefs during the long periods of civil war.

8

Regulating depredation: chiefs and the military, 1963–2005

Chiefs are like the door to a chicken house: without it the chickens would not be safe.[1]

During periods of civil war, the urban frontier dramatically constricted around the government garrisons, and its inhabitants found themselves caught between two antagonistic '*hakumas*', the rebel government in the 'bush' and the government in the town. Both bush and town were ambiguous moral spaces, and the chiefs and their communities wrestled with how to gain protection from or in them, during both the first and second periods of war. The communities that had crystallised by the late-colonial period in the vicinity of the towns were frequently divided and scattered to different locations. The institution of chiefship had to be similarly mobile and capable of temporary splitting; yet in the process it became ever more entrenched in the political and social architecture, so that people could rarely imagine their world without chiefs. Yet chiefs in certain times and places are seen to have acted variously as agents and informants of brutal security forces, as executors of military requisitioning and conscription, as easily-bribed collaborators, as corrupt beneficiaries of commercial, development and relief projects, or as feeble victims of military power. Chiefs were killed by rebel forces, removed by their communities and imposed by governments. Chiefdoms became fragmented into ever smaller units, as the next chapter will discuss. The prevalent discourse in the twenty-first century was that chiefship had declined in power and value since the 'big chiefs' of the colonial period; that chiefship nowadays was either redundant or – more commonly – in need of restoration and re-empowerment.

In recent years, chiefs and their supporters contributed significantly to this latter rhetoric, harnessing perennial negative experiences of government and the widespread desire to protect local autonomy and culture to present 'traditional' authority as a champion of local interests in the face of centralising, corrupt government. But long before any discourse of 'traditional authority' had entered national political dialogue, chiefship was recognised by rebel forces and governments alike for more pragmatic reasons. This in turn forced chiefs and their supporters to justify their intermediary relations with military and security forces, which frequently appeared to contravene or exceed any basis for chiefly legitimacy in traditional political culture.

The result was local discourse in defence of chiefship which has also contributed to constituting the state itself. This chapter explores the nature of wartime chiefship and the way in which it has more recently been explained, firstly during the Anyanya One war of 1963–72, and then during the longer SPLA war from 1983. Experiences and accounts of the wars vary across the research areas of Yei, Juba and Rumbek and of course across the rest of South Sudan, according

[1] Payam Administrator, Raja County, 2 February 2005, quoted in Golooba-Mutebi and Mapuor, 'Traditional Authorities'.

to local relations with governments and rebel forces and the effects of wider political alliances and divisions. Broadly speaking, people in Central Equatoria have tended to contrast a positive depiction of the Anyanya One forces with a more critical account of later SPLA behaviour; whereas people around Rumbek tended to be more critical or ambivalent about the Anyanya One and more vociferously supportive of the SPLA. Such differences reflect the broader political divisions in the interim Southern Regional Government (1972–83), as well as the particular events of each war.[2] But beneath such highly politicised discourse, people everywhere recounted a more consistent experience of wartime hardships, including the fear of government surveillance and reprisals, and of rebel demands for supplies and recruits. It was in this context that chiefship held more than ever the potential for both threat and guarantee. Many individual chiefs have been criticised for collaborating with either government or rebel forces in ways that endangered or burdened their communities. But even such criticisms have fed a broader discourse of chiefship as the means – potential or real – to bring protection for people and property by dealing with military forces. Such protection is said to have been obtained through the regulatory orders of state law and even of military discipline. In turn, by providing such laws and orders, the rebel forces themselves – particularly the SPLM/A – were also being transformed into a new *hakuma* (government), even where civilian relations were most fraught and unstable. The history of the wars as told nowadays thus demonstrates not the destruction of the state, or of traditional authority or social fabric, but rather the remaking of the local state, and the appropriation of state laws and orders as a means of regulating the depredations of the state's own agents and forces.

BETWEEN TOWN AND BUSH IN THE FIRST CIVIL WAR, c. 1963–72

Source material on the role of the chiefs during the first civil war is limited; there are only occasional references to chiefs in the partisan reports of the government and its southern opponents, or in the contemporary accounts of journalists or researchers, particularly the doctoral thesis of John Howell.[3] What is clear from both the sparse documentary record and more recent oral accounts is the sense of the dangers of being caught between government and rebels, and the intensified threat of betrayal. The politics of knowledge discussed in Chapter 6 became ever more dangerous, as both sides demanded information and suspected people of knowing about or informing to the other side.[4] The knowledge of both government and people on which chiefship rested thus became as much a liability as an asset for individual chiefs. But secrecy and subterfuge are also used to explain the behaviour of chiefs who appeared to remain loyal collaborators with the Sudan Government, but who are said to have secretly supported the rebels.

South Sudanese tend to date the beginning of the first civil war to the 1955

[2] On political and military divisions and wartime relations, see Johnson, *Root Causes*, esp. pp. 85–7; Poggo, *The First Sudanese Civil War*, pp. 124, 141; Douglas H Johnson, and Gerard Prunier, 'The foundation and expansion of the Sudan People's Liberation Army', in MW Daly and AA Sikainga (eds), *Civil War in the Sudan* (London, 1993), pp. 117–141; Eisei Kurimoto, 'Civil war and regional conflicts: the Pari and their neighbours in south-eastern Sudan', in Fukui and Markakis, *Ethnicity & Conflict*, pp. 95–111; Jok Madut Jok and Sharon E Hutchinson, 'Sudan's prolonged second civil war and the militarization of Nuer and Dinka ethnic identities', *African Studies Review* 42:2 (1999), pp. 125–45.

[3] Howell, 'Political Leadership'.

[4] Hutchinson makes a similar point in *Nuer Dilemmas*, p. 135.

mutiny; with hindsight too, scholars can trace developments from that time in terms of the virtual counter-insurgency approach of military administrations in the south that helped to provoke eventual outright military rebellion. But it was not until 1963 that organised rebel military activities would really commence, when a meeting of exiled politicians in Kampala named the 'Anya-Nya' forces, and a formal declaration of war was issued around the same time.[5] The previous year, a growing number of southern politicians and former administrators living in exile in Uganda, Kenya or Congo formed the Sudan African Closed Districts National Union, which was renamed the Sudan African National Union (SANU) in 1963. Some of the men who had taken part or been implicated in the 1955 rising became leaders or members of this and other political movements; others took up arms to launch sporadic, small-scale rebel attacks within the south. This largely uncoordinated and 'loose-knit' political and military movement attracted school students and defecting soldiers, policemen and other government employees, impelled by the worsening repression in southern Sudan.[6]

From the beginning of the insurgency, chiefs were prominent in reports of both rebel attacks and government counter-insurgency. The first significant attacks took place in Equatoria in September 1963. SANU reported that chiefs around Yei bore the brunt of government recriminations in October 1963. Chief Nathana Bainja of Payawa was arrested and allegedly tortured after a rebel attack and sabotage of the bridge over the River Kembe on the Yei-Uganda road: 'the chief replied that he did not know that these people were there since they lived in the bush while he lived in his home'.[7] This is a telling expression of the new forces emerging from 'the bush' and outside the chiefs' domain – the chief may well not yet have had any links to the rebels. But the government was certainly making clear that chiefs would be punished for Anyanya activities in their area, reprising an older history of the risks of chiefship. In the same month, according to SANU, an Arab trader was killed by the Anyanya, and Chief Mursali of the Rwonyi clan on the outskirts of Yei was arrested and sentenced to two years in prison for supporting his killers. The people of this chiefdom remember Mursali being detained in Port Sudan, but not whether he actually had any relations with the Anyanya. There were also reprisals for an Anyanya attack on the Yei-Maridi road, and SANU reported the torture and death of Chief Stephen Lomugun in Kajo Keji after the Anyanya killed a northern policeman in his area.[8]

Operating in small bands, with limited technology and means of communication, the Anyanya relied heavily on messengers and 'scouts' – often young boys or girls – to pass information, and the government forces in turn employed many informants. The resulting suspicion and intrigue is one of the most remembered aspects of the war, leading to killings of suspected civilian spies and traitors by both sides. The term 'CID' (Criminal Investigation Department) has come to be widely used to mean 'informant': someone who reported rebel or subversive activity to the security forces.[9] An older chief near Juba in 2006 described the dangers of co-operating with the Anyanya at this 'critical time' for chiefs: 'A chief would be arrested and killed if a CID came to the government and accused him.'[10]

[5] Rolandsen, 'Civil War Society', pp. 159–62.

[6] Johnson, *Root Causes*, p. 32; Howell, 'Political Leadership', p. 192; Rolandsen, 'Civil War Society' and 'A false start'.

[7] SANU, *Memorandum presented to the Commission*, p. 11.

[8] SANU, *Memorandum presented to the Commission*, pp. 11, 24, 34.

[9] Cf. Johnson, *Nuer Prophets*, p. 337

[10] Interview 42R/JC.

In this tense situation, some chiefs were also criticised and attacked by the Anyanya for collaborating with government. The Bari officer who took the Anyanya alias of 'David Dada' is said to have blamed some chiefs in Juba District for acting as informants, including his own nephew, as a southern administrator later recalled:

> David Dada – you put in brackets 'Lobugu'– we called him this – 'hyena'... sent me a letter when I was in Juba saying he wanted all the chiefs to go out, so I informed the chiefs. So I wrote to David and said, 'May I come also with the chiefs?' But he said 'no, we don't like you to come because you are an administrator and the Government will know that you are dealing with us, with the Anyanya'. So these chiefs were sent to the eastern bank, to a place called Kit. So all these people when they went there, David arrested this chief, his nephew, and he was made to dig his own grave and then he shot him and buried him there. Then [Chief] Yosepa Sokiri was suspected to have killed an Anyanya man with poison. So when they arrested this Yosepa Sokiri he refused to be killed so he poisoned himself and died. That was 1963. So the Anyanya were brutal with the chiefs.[11]

A former Anyanya soldier thought that Chief Yosepa had been killed by Dada because he was an informant, a 'CID'.[12] In Meridi District, another chief's houses and court premises were burned down by the Anyanya forces during the 1965 ceasefire, because the chief refused to give them his guns. This led to a government attack on the suspected Anyanya camp, according to the local government officer who wrote to the Anyanya commander Ali Batala to explain this breach of the ceasefire.[13] Such government action no doubt only appeared to confirm the collaboration of this chief. A few months later the Southern Front political movement reported a number of incidents perpetrated by government military forces and chiefs, in breach of the ceasefire or the law, and particularly drew attention to 'the malice the authorities in the Country are employing to exploit the ignorance of some of the tribal chiefs'.[14]

The ceasefire soon broke down with the failure of the 1965 Roundtable Conference, followed by the army massacres of educated southerners in several towns, and the escalation of the war. Many civilians took refuge abroad, and there was increasing popular support for the rebels, including from the chiefs. Even in Rumbek, where the rebel activity had thus far been more limited than in Equatoria, August 1965 is remembered as the time when civil servants, police and politicians were killed in the town, including at least one chief.[15] A European visitor reported the burning of villages around Rumbek and seizure of cattle, as well as the imprisonment and torture of chiefs and suspected Anyanya.[16] Mawson suggests that the famine in the area resulting from destruction of crops and villages by army patrols in the late 1960s hit hardest the same sections that had been most affected by the Turco-Egyptian and British punitive patrols.[17]

11 Interview 1R/YC.

12 52R/JC; Equatoria Province Intelligence Report 21–28 September 1956, NRO UNP 1/20/168. David Dada (Vitorio Logungu) is mentioned in Rolandsen, 'Civil War Society', pp. 125, 129, 160.

13 Acting Local Government Inspector Maridi, Babikir el Nafie, to Ali Batala, CO Anyanya, 7 January 1965, SRO MD 32.A.1.

14 Report sent to Godfrey Lienhardt by Joshua Reiwal of the Southern Front, 14 May 1965, Pitt Rivers Museum, Oxford, Lienhardt Papers 8/9.

15 Interview 1bN/RC.

16 Dr Halvor Nordskog, 'Report from a safari to the Southern Sudan' (West-central Equatoria and Bahr el Ghazal), 1971, SAD 803/5/1–103.

17 Mawson, 'The Triumph of Life', p. 86.

Some people around Rumbek nowadays are critical of the Anyanya for having provoked such government reprisals and civilian suffering. But the killings of 1965 and subsequent army patrols also convinced many to support the rebels. One of the most prominent Agar Dinka chiefs around Rumbek, who would at other times hold his court in the town itself, took refuge in the rural areas:

> During Anyanya One, Manyiel Cindut was helping the Anyanya. In the end the Arabs sent soldiers to kill him, but his sister's son found out and warned us, so I ran with Manyiel to Ayen cattle camp. The news of our location reached the town, so we ran again to Poben cattle camp. They wanted to get Manyiel because his sons had all joined the Anyanya, so the Arabs said that he was 'the father of Anyanya', although really his sons just chose to join by themselves. He remained outside for two years without coming to the town, along with the whole of Nyaing... until the peace in 1972, when we heard that even Anyanya were walking around in the town and it was safe.[18]

Some chiefs went into refuge in Uganda from this time, some actively joined the Anyanya camps and others remained in their villages, where they are said to have secretly assisted the rebels with supplies and information. People are often sympathetic now in explaining even the continued government collaboration of some chiefs, suggesting that they had little choice. Chiefs were after all not the only ones trying to manage relations with both sides at this time; Dinka cattle traders had to be similarly pragmatic:

> Cattle trading involved a lot of risks. Either of the warring parties could accuse a cattle trader of collaboration. Cattle traders solved this problem by pledging loyalty to both warring parties. They obtained licenses from the Anyanya who controlled the rural areas and also obtained travel permits from army commanders who controlled the towns. The cattle traders also used to pay taxes to the Anyanya. As for the army, they bribed them with bulls for their consumption.[19]

As the war escalated and government authority became increasingly restricted to the main towns, the gap between town and bush became increasingly dangerous to cross.[20] A Rumbek elder said that chiefs were brought to the town at this time 'by the force of the Arab military'; if they were found outside, they would be killed.[21] Even the chiefs in the towns are said to have secretly assisted the Anyanya, such as Chief Andarea Farajalla in Juba, who, according to a former Anyanya soldier, used to send money and information to the rebels, even though he would be killed if discovered. His warnings are said to have helped the Anyanya to escape detection, to the fury of the 'CID'.[22]

An elderly teacher in Rumbek explained that chiefs did not join the Anyanya themselves, because they had to remain with their people. But if the rebels came from the bush, then 'the chief is an accommodator', a neat expression of how chiefship combined ideals of hospitality with the new demands to 'feed' armies.[23] Increasingly the chiefs were involved in organising supplies for the Anyanya, working together with young men known as 'Fronts' in the Yei area. A European who travelled with Anyanya forces in 1971 also reported positive

18 Interview 21N/RC.

19 Mangor Ring, 'Dinka stock-trading', p. 199.

20 Howell, 'Political Leadership', p. 247.

21 Interview 1aN/RC.

22 Interview 52R/JC.

23 Interview 14N/RC. Cf. Johnson, *Nuer Prophets*, p. 306.

relations with local chiefs and people, claiming that whenever they arrived in a village, they would be welcomed and fed, even if there were two hundred of them – the villagers called the Anyanya their sons, fighting to liberate them: 'Many chiefs said that they always cultivated much more than they needed themselves only because of "our boys".'[24] A former young Anyanya recruit from near Juba recalled a peaceful system of provisioning through the chiefs, sub-chiefs and 'scouts'. Some also claim that the Anyanya intervened to appoint their own chiefs, leading to a parallel system of chiefs, one 'in the bush' with the Anyanya, and one in the town or village still working with the government.[25]

Chiefship was thus an integral part of the constitution of a parallel administrative order by the rebel forces. Certain chiefs are also remembered to have acted as judges or arbitrators for the Anyanya, such as Lolik Lado of Lyria in Juba District.[26] A former rebel soldier claimed that Anyanya soldiers were not allowed to marry girls by force; if they tried to, they would be arrested and tried by a chief, and the soldier's commanding officer would have to pay bail to the chief while the soldier went to 'look for bridewealth': in this rather idealised depiction, 'the chief was very important'.[27] A European reporter also asserted that the Anyanya had a 'very effectively working civil administration' by 1971, with their own border customs posts, police, court houses, judges and lawyers, using the Laws of Sudan. He personally observed a court case of a soldier who stole from a civilian and was sentenced to twenty lashes and twenty days in prison.[28]

In 1967, a 'National Convention' of political and military leaders was held at Angudri in Western Equatoria to try to coordinate the factionalised politicians and fragmented Anyanya; it produced a formal administrative structure of provinces and districts under commissioners, and also 'counties' under chiefs. In 1970, civil administrators received training near the Uganda border and were dispatched to exercise police and magisterial powers and to coordinate with local Anyanya officers. In reality, even by 1972, Howell describes Anyanya civil administration as 'sparse', but it had established some localised form of authority over villages as well as receiving support from villagers, and the most positive descriptions suggest harmonious civil-military relations and the operation of courts and schools.[29] A former Anyanya soldier asserted the existence of this 'government':

> The Anyanya One had a Government; they were organised with offices, and they had courts; there were chiefs in the bush who were presidents of the court... They could try soldiers and even beat them; they were encouraged by the big men in the army, so they were able to discipline the soldiers. The chief stayed in his house but there were scouts who took messages from the army headquarters to the chiefs and from them back to the headquarters. Boys were selected from the community to be scouts.[30]

On the other hand another former Anyanya soldier, who later became a sub-chief during the SPLA war, emphasised the 'lack of learning' among the rebels,

[24] Dr Halvor Nordskog, 'Report from a safari to the Southern Sudan' (West-central Equatoria and Bahr el Ghazal), 1971, SAD 803/5/1–103.

[25] Interviews 2bN/YC; 42R/JC.

[26] Simonse, *Kings of Disaster*, p. 138.

[27] Interview 52R/JC.

[28] Dr Halvor Nordskog, 'Report from a safari to the Southern Sudan' (West-central Equatoria and Bahr el Ghazal), 1971, SAD 803/5/1–103.

[29] Howell, 'Political Leadership', pp. 251, 260, 269–70.

[30] Interview 20N/YC.

so that there were no literate people who could 'go out to bring us weapons or power'. Once again bureaucratic knowledge is presented as the means of accessing 'power'.[31]

There were reports of atrocities against civilians committed by the Anyanya, although it is very difficult to verify any of the sporadic and partisan reports from this period. Howell likens the Anyanya administration to the 'government by patrol' of early British colonial rule, and suggests that 'the Anya Nya was sometimes indiscriminately violent to recalcitrant villagers, and often notoriously indifferent to property, especially cattle'.[32] But the dependence of the Anyanya on support and provisions from the civilian population (particularly until the late stages of the war, when they began to receive outside support from Israel and Uganda) does seem to have led to some regularisation of relations between villagers and soldiers, mediated by chiefs, local officers and perhaps eventually even civil administrators.

The first civil war is remembered more for government repression and reprisals and as a time when many people therefore first fled to refuge in Uganda or elsewhere. It was also characterised by individual killings or punishments of suspected spies and traitors, prominent educated people and chiefs.[33] Yet while both government and Anyanya might blame and punish individual chiefs, it is significant that both sides continued to recognise the *institution* of chiefship itself, and sought to utilise and control it. On the government side, the 1960s saw a growing movement among modernising bureaucrats and politicians in northern Sudan to abolish the outdated colonial instruments of local governance, which would culminate in the abolition of Native Administration in 1971. It might be expected that the southern rebels – mostly young students and former police and soldiers, whose leaders were influenced by similarly modernising wider African nationalist movements – would also attack chiefship for collaboration with the 'enemy' government as well as its colonial predecessors. That such attacks were confined to individual instances is testament to the value that chiefship had gained in the minds of southerners and government alike, as well as to the skills and strategies employed by individual chiefs to negotiate the heightened dangers of their interstitial position. In relying on chiefs to 'feed' hungry soldiers, the Anyanya were both replicating long-standing patterns of chiefship and establishing a precedent for the role of chiefs during the second period of civil war.

BETWEEN GOVERNMENT AND REBELS, THREAT AND GUARANTEE: GARRISON TOWN CHIEFS

As we have seen, despite revived competition from civil servants and local politicians during the period of peace after 1972, chiefs continued to occupy a prominent position in the local government architecture of councils and courts. But the resumption of civil war in 1983 would pose fresh challenges for chiefs, and require new strategies for dealing with both the Sudan Government (and the various militia forces it supported) and the new SPLM/A forces. The SPLM/A succeeded in capturing many towns in the south, and in establishing more extensive and lasting administration of the 'liberated areas', especially in the later stages of the war. But despite a major assault in 1992, it never succeeded in capturing Juba, nor the other provincial capitals of Wau and

[31] Interview 24R/YC.

[32] Howell, 'Political Leadership', p. 260.

[33] Howell, 'Political Leadership', p. 245; Interview 52R/JD.

Malakal. As the previous chapter also showed, many people displaced by the fighting took refuge in Juba; the town thus maintained a much larger population than during the first civil war. In the 1990s, the NIF government's revival of Native Administration led to the recognition or appointment of many chiefs, sub-chiefs and headmen in the city, including for the various displaced communities. These appointments have generated some of the most critical discourse around chiefship, and a lasting ambivalence towards chiefs in Juba nowadays. The town inhabitants were subject to a particularly intense bureaucratic and technical regime of surveillance, repression and regulation, in which chiefs were intimately implicated. But in turn the dubious legitimacy of the garrison town chiefs has also stimulated some revealing arguments in their defence.

These chiefs were often quite open about their close relationship with the government security, but they presented this as a necessity in order to protect and rescue their people from detention, torture or death:

> If it were not for the chiefs, many people would have lost their lives. The government of Omar al-Bashir brought chiefs and made things better. If you were arrested, you were asked where you were from. Your chief would go to the Headquarters, and if he answered that this was his man, you would be released. You would be lost if you were arrested without it being known publicly. Chiefs were at risk during that period and in that work; some of them were killed... The situation was dangerous, yet people were also being saved.

This chief emphasised that as a chief 'you are just in between', and that chiefs were slandered or killed because they were tricked and trapped by corrupt officials or informants: 'those who were junior to Omar did not leave the chiefs to do as Omar had wanted'.[34] Other chiefs also referred very personally to 'Omar' or 'Bashir', reflecting the efficacy of the President's speeches and messages in support of chiefs. One particularly widely-criticised chief boasted of the tractor he was given by Bashir personally. Another leading chief in Juba claimed to have spoken out to the 'MI' (military intelligence) to demand the right to identify and bail people who had been arrested; he also asserted that such processes improved significantly 'during Bashir', when chiefs enjoyed better relations 'with good MI officers like *n* from Omdurman'.[35] A former policeman appointed to be chief in Juba for one of the displaced communities from Central Equatoria claimed that his community responded well to Bashir's order in 1991 to appoint chiefs and 'chose someone who could protect them'. He also stressed that when the chiefs were taken to conferences with the government, as most famously in Khartoum in 1995, 'we were frank that they should not appoint us as shields or as a whitewash to attract the people'; instead 'we gained recognition there from higher authorities and even the President, who empowered us to bail anyone caught and prevent his torture'.[36]

These Juba chiefs had by 2005 honed a more general discourse of chiefship, in which close relations with illegitimate and even predatory government forces were justified on the grounds that the chiefs were risking their own lives to negotiate protection for their people. They even showed off their relations with individual security or militia officers, and symbols like their ID cards from the MI, because they claimed that this knowledge had helped to regularise the dealings of government with their people. Their accounts also upheld the importance of belonging to a chief and being known by him; the personal social knowledge held by chiefs was emphasised as the primary means of protection for people. Yet in

[34] Interview 41R/JC.

[35] Interview 37R/JC.

[36] Interview 38R/JC.

the context of wartime suspicion, that same knowledge was feared as a means of informing on people to the security forces. Knowing the name of one's chief was said to have been the only hope for those arrested, to avoid being taken to the feared detention facilities like the 'white house'. Yet having one's name known also rendered one vulnerable to being reported. Even in 2005 in Juba, people were extremely reluctant to mention names of chiefs or other people to me, explaining that to do so during the war – especially to someone with a notebook and pen – was tantamount to informing on them: 'we don't like giving names here; you don't know what is in someone's heart when he asks for a name'.[37] Many people were critical and dismissive of the chiefs for having been agents of the security forces, claiming that often they were merely appointed by the government as IDP camp leaders:

> They were taken to Khartoum and given military training; some even wore police uniforms, and they were given handouts of grain from the army. So people said 'they are now with the system; instead of supporting us they are selling us'.[38]

Chiefs and headmen claimed of course that they only ever used their knowledge to protect people, and that they resisted manipulation by the government:

> Since 1983 when I became headman, there was a lot of suffering. We were treated like MI agents – they come and ask for information, like whether new people had come to the area. The Arabs thought they could treat chiefs now like those in 1947 who were deceived. But they couldn't, because now chiefs are intelligent.[39]

Badiey also found considerable sympathy among Juba inhabitants for the difficult position of chiefs, caught between conflicting pressures and in a dangerous position themselves: 'Though the discourse of "collaboration" is unforgiving, co-operation with northern government agents permitted leaders in Juba to safeguard a limited degree of local autonomy and to protect residents from hunger, beatings, arbitrary arrests, and even death.'[40] Though the situation in Juba was particularly extreme, this scenario also represents a recurrent pattern of chiefship since the nineteenth century.

Chiefs and headmen in the rural areas north of Juba also claimed to have 'bailed' people from the security forces in the town. Mundari civilians were displaced here from the Tali and Terekeka areas by fighting in 1986.[41] Their chiefs had to have close relations with both the pro-government Mundari militia of Clement Wani and the government security forces; some chiefs had military training or experience themselves. Even – or especially – in this militarised context, the capacity of chiefs to communicate effectively was vital, as one chief explained. He had been a trader in Tali and so had picked up Arabic, which is why, he claimed, he was chosen as chief.[42] This illiterate chief wanted to see papers stamped by 'MI' before being interviewed; when shown a letter from the Government of Southern Sudan's Relief and Rehabilitation Commission, read to him by my translator, he pointed to the stamp on it saying 'this is what I know', and agreed to be interviewed. The most frequent recollection of people who stayed

37 Interview 25N/JC.

38 Interview 24N/JC.

39 Interview 44R/JC.

40 Badiey, 'The State Within', p. 134.

41 Interview 26N/JC.

42 Interview 53R/JC.

in this area is of the difficulty of moving between town and village: 'Government was all along the road to Terekeka and we had to have permits to move or else we were considered to be SPLA'. Mundari and Bari alike also recalled the recruitment or forced conscription of young men into the government Sudan Armed Forces (SAF), the SPLA, Clement's militia or another government-aligned Bari militia, so that sometimes brothers ended up on opposing sides.[43]

The interstitial position of people living around Juba during the war was reflected in their ambivalence towards the SPLA; unsurprisingly both government and rebel forces were seen as a threat by these civilians. One elderly man complaining about the behaviour of the SPLA exclaimed, 'at least Bashir's soldiers stayed in their posts and didn't come to the village demanding food like the Anyanya Two [SPLA]'.[44] In sticking to the garrison, town and roads, the SAF behaved in more familiar expected ways of the government. The new rebel forces emerging from the bush were seen as a greater threat in the rural areas. Another chief of a displaced community from Central Equatoria, speaking in English, contrasted the government and SPLA-held areas: 'Unlike [my village in an SPLA-held area], law prevailed here in Juba; we were lawfully bound, despite hard security. The lawlessness here was political – unlawful confinements, assaults, repression.'[45] The phrase 'lawfully bound' is an apt expression of the ambiguity of government, with all its connotations of restraint, imprisonment and control discussed in previous chapters, and intensified in the 'repression' of wartime life in Juba. 'We had been locked in a gourd since 1983' as a woman declared on leaving the town for the first time in early 2006. But the chief's statement was equally revealing of the sense nevertheless that 'law prevailed' – the repressive security somehow operated in a more regularised way than his impression of the SPLA's administration of his home village. But in the SPLM/A areas too, regulatory orders brokered in part by chiefs had also become seen as the means by which to ameliorate the depredations of the war.

THE CHIEFSHIP OF FOOD: DEALING WITH THE SPLA

Before the SPLA attacks on the government garrisons in Rumbek in 1986 and Yei in 1990, the rebels warned the town population to leave; the exodus was negotiated and led by the Rumbek spear-master Makuer Gol and by church leaders in Yei. Many fled to IDP or refugee camps, but some also remained in the surrounding countryside, where they became a vital source of support for the rebels. The extent and nature of SPLM/A administration in these rural areas has generated some debate, as summarised by Rolandsen in his study of 'guerrilla government' in the 1990s.[46] The SPLM/A sought to establish a formal judiciary with its own legal codes from as early as the mid-1980s, and when its forces arrived in an area, people 'were told that the SPLA worked with somebody called a chief'.[47] As Johnson argues, the role of the chiefs was crucial to forging the relationship between SPLA and people, because by working with chiefs from the outset, the rebel government slotted into familiar historical patterns.[48]

43 Interviews 26N/JC; 27N/JC.

44 Interview 50R/JC.

45 Interview 38R/JC.

46 Rolandsen, *Guerrilla Government*, pp. 64–71.

47 Leonardi, 'Violence, sacrifice', p. 535.

48 Douglas H Johnson, 'The Sudan People's Liberation Army and the problem of factionalism', in Christopher Clapham (ed.), *African Guerrillas* (Oxford, 1998), pp. 53–72.

But there was variation in patterns of administration according to individual SPLA area commanders, who often enjoyed considerable autonomy in their areas. An NGO report on the Yei area in the late 1990s claimed that '[s]ome SPLA commanders assumed the role of the traditional chiefs, settling customary cases, marginalising the traditional authority and eroding their influence in their communities', and that this 'may have been the single most important reason for some tribes to form tribal militia and alliances with the enemy'.[49] Certainly some people later recalled having taken cases to military officers, even if such authorities were like 'fire' as one man in Rumbek put it.[50] An elderly lady living near Rumbek told of pursuing a case of seven stolen cows as far as the military court in the northern Agar area of Pakam, where she was told 'to see the big officer [*tueny-dit*] with stars on his shoulder, who will sit and tell someone to give this person their right.'[51] As the SPLM judge Monyluak Alor put it, 'A good number of commanders at the early stages of the war used to consider legal disputes when brought to them by the local citizens who would resort to the justice of any available high authority.'[52] From the outset though, the SPLM/A placed some emphasis on the establishment of formal courts and of its own judiciary. From 1985 it created special courts, made up of former police and prisons officers as well as chiefs. The 1994 National Convention established an independent judiciary and recognised the chiefs' courts as the lowest tier in a court hierarchy.[53] Johnson argues that in some areas, the chiefs' courts and justice provision had been at the core of SPLM/A administration since the 1980s.[54]

In both Yei and Rumbek, people were critical in their recollections of military rule and abuses by the SPLM/A throughout the 1990s, and indeed as an ongoing problem even by the time of the Peace Agreement in 2005. But it was around Yei that people were most vociferous in their accounts of SPLA demands and brutalities, reflecting more ambiguous political relations with the SPLM/A here, and more fraught military-civilian relations up to the early 1990s.[55] People here readily recounted stories of theft, torture and killings by SPLA soldiers, and particularly of the rape of young girls or of men's wives. The discursive retelling of brutal and humiliating incidents of rape – said to have been committed with the husband lying underneath – was the ultimate expression for these people of the terrifying disregard of the soldiers for any law or moral order.

But this was by no means the only story. Even in this area, the SPLM/A would become the '*gela* [government] of the bush': the rebel *hakuma*; becoming a government required it to take on some of the associated bureaucratic orders and the legalism of the state, even if its laws were initially military ones. One headman near Yei is said to have declared that he was 'too old to manage the laws of the SPLA' and handed over the duties to his younger relative, who explained that the SPLA demanded someone energetic to work with them, to attend 'meetings' punctually and to collect food and provide conscripts. These meetings were an opportunity to 'talk and bring out laws' to handle the problems of the war.[56] It was thus the bureaucratic arena of the 'meeting' that could produce the law to

49 Rohn et al, 'Report of the study on local administrative structures', p. 5.

50 Interview 19bN/RC.

51 Interview 64R/RC.

52 Monyluak Alor Kuol, 'The anthropology of law and issues of justice in the Southern Sudan today' (MPhil: University of Oxford, 2000), p. 19.

53 Monyluak Alor Kuol, *Administration of Justice*.

54 Johnson, 'The Sudan People's Liberation Army'; Rolandsen, *Guerrilla Government*.

55 Johnson, *Root Causes*, pp. 85–7.

56 Interview 19R/YC.

govern and regulate the soldiers. The priority was to keep the latter away from property, homes and women, as another headman explained: 'if they came to you for food, you quickly collected the food from the people and gave it to them while they were seated with you, because if they entered the village, they would cause damage and rape and rob.'[57] There was a common emphasis on the need for a chief to shield people from the soldiers: 'somebody who could confront the SPLA soldiers without fear, to prevent the civilians being flogged'.[58] The chief's own house often became the site of collection and even preparation of food for the soldiers: 'the soldiers will go and find the food in the house of the chief; then they don't do bad things in the area'.[59] People in Yei thus emphasised the risks of chiefship during the war and the beating and torture of chiefs and headmen, bearing the brunt of military recrimination to protect their people.[60] People also frequently told stories of the protective magic employed by certain rain or earth chiefs to punish or confuse soldiers who were trying to seize their property.

In the end though it was the SPLA's own laws and military orders that were seen to have most improved the capacity of the chiefs to bring about more routinised and regularised relations between soldiers and civilians. In 1992, chiefs around Yei were taken for six months' military training and given ranks; one of them later explained that as well as being 'drilled', they were also taught about 'laws like "manifesto", "customary laws" and "culture" [English words]', so they could use the same laws in their villages.[61] As trained officers of the 'hoe brigade', the chiefs 'rescued the people from the hands of the SPLA... If the SPLA wanted to mistreat the people then the trained chiefs could go to the commanders to inform them about the mistreatment by the SPLA.'[62]

Around Rumbek too, chiefs recalled improving relations and court powers in the 1990s once chiefs had been given 'one star' or 'two stars', i.e. ranks as first or second lieutenants in the SPLA. The son of a prominent Rumbek chief, who had been working in local government, claims to have been 'arrested' by the SPLA in 1985 and appointed as one of seven members from different sections to the new Appeal Court. He recalled the difficulties of imposing any authority over the soldiers at that time: 'the military would take money from people and then threaten and beat people and threaten the courts' to obstruct justice. Things improved when 'we were given ranks'; 'then soldiers respected us more because the officers were good and would punish them if they didn't show us respect'.[63] Military hierarchies thus became a vital means of regularising justice and relations with soldiers.

While the Yei area had seen some of the worst military-civilian relations, after 1997 it also became the site for the trial of the civil administration structures that helped to give people an increasing sense of membership and participation in the liberation 'Movement'. Liberation Councils were created at the level of *boma* (village), *payam* (sub-county) and county. The county councils established a large number of government 'departments' (education, agricul-

57 Interview 14R/YC.

58 Interview 20R/YC.

59 Interview 5R/YC.

60 Meeting of Yei chiefs, sub-chiefs, elders and court members, 5 February 2005, Yei, during research for Cherry Leonardi, Deng Biong Mijak and Eli Achol Deng Höt, 'Report on Traditional Authority in Western and Central Equatoria' (Nairobi: UNDP, unpublished report, 2005).

61 Interview 24R/YC. Cf. Johnson, 'The Sudan People's Liberation Army', pp. 67–8.

62 Interview 13R/YC.

 63 Interviews 17N/RC; 54R/RC.

ture, etc.), some with offices and type-writers, but with virtually no resources.[64] Immediately the county-level councils and committees began to complain about abuses and lawlessness of soldiers and the weakness of bureaucratic procedure, calling for more stationery, financial forms, keeping of office hours and general efficiency; bureaucratic regulation was clearly seen as a resource with the potential to regulate and limit the prevailing power of the military.[65] Another report found that people were referring to the SPLM Constitution as *ganun*, the local Arabic for 'laws'; they did not know the term 'constitution', but tellingly '[s]ome feel the document is law controlling the activities of the SPLA and stipulates the rights of the people'. Again the demand for law and regulation is apparent: 'As a result of people operating for a long time without any system of governance, it is a clear "felt need" that guidance should be provided on how to go about doing various things in different places' – such guidance and 'seminars' were particularly needed for the military, it was stressed.[66]

While the councils were important as bureaucratic and discursive arenas, chiefs nevertheless remained the primary interlocutors with the SPLM/A at the local level. As during the Anyanya One war, chiefs' intermediary role and possession of knowledge and information also became significant. One of the most frequent statements about the role of chiefs recorded in early 2005 in central and Western Equatoria was that 'the chief is the eye of the government', always a rather intriguing and ambiguous metaphor given the prevalent experience of government here. Yet chiefs themselves were quite proud to describe themselves in this way: 'I am the eye of the *hakuma* [government]; *hakuma* put me here to inform if there is anything wrong in the area'.[67] Another chief also asserted that chiefs were the eye and backbone of government, adding that 'the SPLA had to penetrate through the chiefs – it was the only way to spread the idea to people that they were not the enemy'. One chief in Yei declared that he had supported the SPLA ever since 1983, sending information about government convoys as well as donating supplies and uniforms, risking arrest by government.[68]

However, the appointment of new chiefs to work with the SPLA also created lingering disputes and resentments, with some claiming that these were not really chiefs, but were more like the 'Fronts' in Anyanya One. A headman complained that one chief had claimed the chiefship on the basis that he had 'fed the SPLA', even though he had no hereditary claim to it. The original chiefs were bypassed, and the new ones 'did not fit into their places'[69] – i.e. their appointment usurped the order of kinship descent. Others, however, argued that the chiefs had earned their position through their courage and their capacity to provide supplies for the new government of the bush – 'this chiefship is the chiefship of food'.[70]

Worse even than the demands of the SPLA for food was their need to recruit or conscript boys and young men into their ranks. A former headman explained that people ended up hating the headmen and chiefs for conscripting their children, especially if the latter were killed. Yet 'it was not the chief who took the

64 Rohn et al, 'Report of the study on local administrative structures'.

65 Herzog, 'Report: mission on governance', p. 19, 42.

66 Koech et al, 'Community participation', pp. 36–7, 46.

67 Meeting with sub-chiefs and elders in Mapoko sub-*boma,* Adio, near Yei, 8 February 2005, during research for Leonardi et al, 'Report on Traditional Authority'.

68 Meeting with Pojelu chiefs and elders, in Yei Chamber of Commerce, 10 February 2005, during research for Leonardi et al, 'Report on Traditional Authority'.

69 Interview 9R/YC.

70 Interview 12R/YC.

child; it was the government [SPLM/A] who wanted the child'.[71] Once again, however, regulatory orders are seen to have ameliorated the worst effects of conscription, but in this case the regulation was produced by indigenous as well as state orders. As with long-standing government demands for tax and labour, 'good' chiefs are said to have shared out the demands for conscripts fairly, according to the number of sons in any family. According to a senior SPLA officer, 'the chiefs knew each family and how many can be spared; chiefs would even protest and have soldiers brought back if too many have been taken from one family'.[72] A headman near Yei was beaten for his outright refusal to provide the required number of conscripts; he claimed to have told the soldiers they would have to 'grow boys like trees' if they wanted that many.[73] In the same area other people also described a process of consultation and discussion among headmen and elders as to which boys it was fairest to send: 'force is not to be used'.[74] Chiefs claim to have used their personal knowledge of the families under their protection to distribute the conscription as fairly and mercifully as possible. As ever, the ideal of chiefship was thus to articulate the regulatory orders of government *and* of lineage and kinship structures.

Rumbek County was one of the prime recruiting grounds for the SPLA in the 1980s and its inhabitants presented themselves as having contributed more to the 'struggle' than other regions. But relations between SPLA and civilians nevertheless deteriorated here in the 1990s, not least because the split of the SPLA in 1991 led to Nuer-Dinka fighting in the region.[75] Increasingly people were keen to keep the young warriors in the cattle camps to protect the cattle rather than have them recruited into the SPLA, and so conscription became more forced. In this context, one particular chief was remembered as having abused his link with the SPLA to use excessive force against his own people:

> When *n* was told to bring a certain number of conscripts, he did it harshly by calling soldiers to come from the barracks and just take anybody, without the usual method. *Gol* leaders know who is who, but he did not consult them. Panamacot was lucky because we are a big family, but the smaller families were really complaining. *N* told them it was the fault of their own fathers for not having more wives, which just made people more angry. Then with the tax collection [for the SPLA], he just demanded it without sitting with *gol* leaders and saying, 'the government wants this', and discussing how to collect it. The big bulls were just taken randomly instead of in turn. Lastly, when Amothnhom and Panyon [sections] fought, *n* told the soldiers to come and take all the guns from everybody in the cattle camp, and that was at the time when the Nuer were still coming to attack us.[76]

This account is from an interview with a *gol* leader from the Panamacot lineage, so it perhaps unsurprising that he should have emphasised the need to consult *gol* leaders over conscription and taxation. But the same story was told by many different people from Panamacot, and other people of the Amothnhom section. It is indicative of a fundamental discourse as to how chiefs should behave, which may have in turn reflected not only the views of *gol* leaders and family heads about autonomy and fairness, but also the arguments of chiefs themselves, deployed to justify their demands and actions. It suggests, for example,

71 Interview 12R/YC.

72 Interview 22N/RC.

73 Interview 20R/YC.

74 Interview 29R/YC.

75 See Johnson, *Root Causes*, pp. 111–9.

76 Interview 23N/RC.

that the established norm for tax collection had been for chiefs to explain it as a government demand which had to be met; the discussion would then be about how to achieve this, rather than anyone actually resisting the demand. The chiefs' role in tax collection was thus seen to mediate government extraction, rendering it more predictable and regularised by following a 'usual method', and at the same time enabling the actual collection to respect the internal structures of descent and kinship.

But this chief contravened the core ideal of fair distribution of both requisitions and rewards among relatives, families and *gols* according to lineage order and logics, which was vital to enabling the aggregation upon which chiefship relied. He made the mistake of ignoring or overriding the detailed knowledge of personal relations and situations that was supposed to distinguish the traditional leadership from the impersonal bureaucratic practices of government – a leader who knew his people would avoid conscripting too many boys from a small family, or requisitioning bulls without following the kind of rotational sequence that was also supposed to govern the payment and receipt of cattle in bridewealth or compensation. This chief made matters still worse by insulting the small families for not having enough children, rather than offering the kind of patronage and protection that 'big' families were supposed ideally to provide for poorer, weaker ones. Finally he failed in what was perhaps the most basic requirement of chiefship: to provide protection from the predatory force of government or enemy groups. Instead he allowed military forces to penetrate the refuge of the cattle camps and remove their means of protection. The combination of arbitrary behaviour and the failure to protect ensured that this chief was deposed and replaced in 1995, and continued to be referenced as the ultimate example of a bad chief.

His successful removal, however, was also attributed to bureaucratic efficacy, even during wartime, as a headman affirmed:

> To remove a chief, you write the complaint to the county secretary so that he can see the charges. Then he will order an election and someone can challenge the old chief and get a majority. Then we send a letter to the office with the result, and they confirm the new chief. It was the same way during the war.[77]

As this example shows so clearly, the intensified wartime pressures and suffering led not – as is now often supposed – to the decline or destruction of traditional authority, but rather to the intensification of debates and discourses around chiefly legitimacy. Chiefs – especially SPLA-appointed ones – and their supporters dug deep into their own history to justify the demands they had to make on people during the war, claiming through their knowledge to protect people, resources and land, and to ameliorate government depredations by placing their own lives and bodies in the frontline of encounters with military force.[78] Chiefs seemed to have succeeded once again in refracting their institutional character away from the military authorities with whom they worked so closely, so that people very often supported chiefs and their version of the history of the war as a means of criticising governments. But in the process popular discourse also reinforced the need for chiefs to distance themselves from the ways of government and armies: 'if a chief behaved like a soldier he would be removed after just two or three days!'[79]

Despite the dangers and humiliations of the war, it enabled the chiefs to

[77] Interview 23N/RC.

[78] On the 'continuous theme of self-sacrifice in the stories of chiefly families' in another area of South Sudan, see also Mading Deng, *Tradition and Modernization*, p. 47.

[79] Interview 1cN/RC.

re-establish themselves as brokers of protection and rights, and hence as focal points for otherwise vulnerable, scattered populations in the bush. One elderly lady near Yei defended the role of a chief who was appointed from outside the hereditary line of chiefs during the war because of his ability to deal with the SPLA, which was enhanced by his military training in 1992. While some people in the chiefdom argued that the chiefship should now return to the hereditary line, she instead argued that the current chief should continue to 'hold' the village or country, because he had protected the people during the war and taken care of them when they were 'scattered in the bush'.[80] As this reveals, the tension between chiefship and kinship structures also endured throughout the wars and if anything only intensified with the appointment of wartime chiefs or the behaviour of militarily-aligned chiefs. But the wartime chiefs were actually reprising a role with a much longer history, as they brokered relations with the dangerous military forces.

CONCLUSION

The extended and devastating periods of war in the last fifty years of South Sudanese history are frequently recounted in terms of the destruction not only of lives and property but of the 'social fabric' and norms of government and traditional authority. Indeed, new chiefs did emerge on the basis of their relationship with military forces; old chiefs were beaten, humiliated or killed; rights in women, property and person were at times brutally transgressed; the youth became soldiers, some recognising only the gun as their parent and their commander as authority. Yet paradoxically, the re-intensified threat to property and persons posed by multiple military forces during wartime only underscored the need for chiefs to ameliorate that threat and negotiate protection. The means by which chiefs brokered more regular and routinised relations with military and security forces was through the laws and regulatory orders of these forces themselves. In the process, the chiefs were helping to constitute the new *hakuma* of 'our boys', the SPLM/A, even through criticising those soldiers or officials who contravened such laws. In turn – partly in growing recognition of the wartime role of the chiefs – the SPLM would make traditional authority and customary law a central part of the ideology of the emerging new state of South Sudan.

[80] Interview 29R/YC.

9

Reprising 'tradition': the mutual production of community and state in the twenty-first century

> Question: Are chiefs part of the government or of the village?
> Response: Both: they go there to bring the laws and information from the government, and then they come to talk and be with the people here as well. At night if there is a fight they are the ones to come and stop it. Because they are the *nutu lo miri* [government people].[1]

As this response demonstrates, my original question to this young Mundari man near Juba was problematic because it assumed that the 'government' was a separate entity from the rural communities, when such a distinction was blurred or false. My question reflected the wider discourse that was increasingly manifest by 2005 at both local and national levels, of tradition and community as distinct from the state. Yet in practice, both traditional authority and definitions of 'community' were being produced in relation to, and in dialogue with, the state.

From the early 1990s the National Islamic Front government recognised and appointed chiefs in its garrison towns and in Khartoum to represent every part of the south, constituting a High Council of Chiefs with an office in Juba.[2] The SPLM/A also formally recognised chiefs as part of the local government structures for the liberated areas formulated at its 1994 National Convention. A decade later, the SPLM stepped up its rhetorical endorsement of chiefship, increasingly expressed in terms of 'traditional authority', customary law, cultural rights and ethnic 'nationalities', a discourse promoted by some international agencies, as well as by prominent SPLM leaders, judges and administrators. It was a rhetoric which reprised many aspects of colonial native administration policies, and it posed many of the same challenges and contradictions with which colonial administrators had wrestled: the old 'repugnancy clause' of indirect rule policy was replaced by concerns over human rights, gender equality, democracy and 'good governance'. This chapter is more concerned, however, with the ways in which the discussions and legislation on traditional authority in the twenty-first century contributed to the ongoing discursive, dialectical production of state and community, a dialectic embodied in the institution of chiefship.

In and after the Comprehensive Peace Agreement of 2005, communities and community rights were formally, if vaguely, constituted in legislation relating to land and local government, as well as in the transitional constitutions. Yet, of course, definitions of community remained extremely contested. Political tribalism and ideas of cultural rights were making ethnicity more prominent than ever in political discourse, but very few ethnic groups in South Sudan have had any consistent central leadership, and ordinary people did not see their tribe as their 'community' except perhaps in national political contexts. Chiefdoms were sub-ethnic and even multi-ethnic; as we have seen, these units had been produced

1 Interview 36N/JC.

2 Interview 37R/JC.

and reproduced through processes of settlement (and forced resettlement), the attractions of patronage and protection, and administrative amalgamation and sub-division. In recent years chiefdoms had fragmented and proliferated, while at the other extreme new institutions had produced new claims to paramount chiefship, usually of counties or states. The internal politics of chiefdoms remained often tense and highly contested; many versions of their history depict them as artificial units, or the chief as illegitimate. Certainly chiefdoms had not been units for the ownership of resources such as land or cattle.

Yet chiefship as a definer and signifier of community was in some senses stronger than ever, as Southern Sudan approached its independence, and its government sought to generate national identity and unity. Experiences of war, military government, displacement, aid, urbanisation and the policy and practice of local government and national politics had all contributed to simultaneously breaking down and yet hardening local identities. The popular desire for secession was huge, but people were also very critical of their new government. In this context, it is easy to see how tradition and custom had become a useful discourse through which to defend local autonomy against state intrusion, centralisation and homogenisation. Even senior government officials admitted their own authoritarian and centralising heritage.[3] The issue of land rights had already become a particular focus of struggle between the new government and the 'community' rights that it claimed to uphold.

But expectations of the state were nevertheless greater than ever. Ideas of a social contract between state and society became prominent in political arenas and media comment after 2005;[4] while this belied the continuing instabilities and uncertainties of relations with the state, nevertheless people were seeking to contract state power and resources in all kinds of quotidian contexts. In many – though by no means all – of these contexts, they found that their officially-recognised 'community' and its chiefs might be a lever by which to obtain the most favourable terms for dealing with the state.[5] Since the later 1990s, communities had been defined by both government and people as units for the provision of services and development projects. Much more in hope than in reality, people expected chiefs to access such resources and to ensure that their communities were known and recognised in government offices: 'the chief takes our voice to meetings'.[6]

This chapter examines the production of community and traditional authority since the 1990s, beginning with the effects of decentralisation policies on local administrative units and chiefdoms. It then explores the increasing prominence of tradition, custom and chiefship in the discourse of national and international actors and agencies, and at its intersection with local political discourse in internationally-sponsored chiefs' conferences and workshops. The Local Government Act of 2009 would bring together the rhetoric and recognition of traditional authority with the policies of decentralisation to enshrine the chiefs as sole executive and judicial authorities in the '*boma*', the lowest administrative unit. These units, and those above them, became the focus for intense expectation and often dispute, resulting in ever more and smaller units, and more exclusionary, territorialised and ethnicised definitions of locality and community. Yet at the

3 E.g. GoSS Vice-President, Dr Riek Machar, speaking at the Rift Valley Institute – US Institute of Peace launch of the report 'Local Justice in Southern Sudan' in the Home and Away Hotel, Juba, 22 October 2010: author's notes, and Mabior Philip, 'Decentralized justice is lucrative, says Machar', *The Citizen*, 23 October 2010, pp. 1–2.

4 Rolandsen, 'To mend the broken contract'.

5 Cf. Richard Fanthorpe, 'On the limits of liberal peace: chiefs and democratic decentralization in post-war Sierra Leone', *African Affairs* 105:418 (2006), pp. 27–49.

6 Leonardi et al, 'Report on Traditional Authority', p. 11.

same time, enduring local discursive ideals of chiefship coincided with political imperatives to promote strength in numbers, inclusivity and fairness. The ambiguities of chiefship as a definition of community and the perennial tensions between fission and fusion thus continued to play out; the chapter ends with an examination of how authority over land became an increasing focus of resulting dispute and debate, and yet also of claims upon the state.

DECENTRALISATION AND TRADITIONAL AUTHORITY

As previous chapters showed, long-term policies of decentralisation were given a new lease of life by both the NIF government and the SPLM in the 1990s. In northern Sudan, the ensuing division of old administrative units and creation of new states, localities and Native Administration units produced considerable controversy and conflict, particularly in the west, and has generally been attributed to political agendas.[7] Only more recently has the parallel fragmentation of such units under the SPLM in southern Sudan begun to be highlighted as a cause of tension and conflict over boundaries and administrative centres.[8] In the process, chiefdoms were gaining heightened significance, and becoming widely seen as the recipient units for services, relief and development, which of course also placed chiefship at the centre of local politics.

By the 1990s, disputes over administrative units were already erupting or reviving in the SPLM/A-held areas. For example, Mundri and Maridi were placed under a single SPLA Independent Area Command in 1992, but persistent agitation from Mundri led to its separation as a county after the 1994 SPLM Convention.[9] Such disputes would increase as the counties, *payams* and *bomas* became the focus for what limited services and relief were available after 1997, such as seed distributions. The primary responsibility of new Payam Administrators was 'receiving the NGOs coming from the SRRA (the SPLM's Sudan Relief and Rehabilitation Association) via the Commissioner and announcing the purpose of their visit to the community'. Not surprisingly, with rising expectations of relief and development, competition developed between chiefs, administrators and council chairmen. With nobody receiving salaries, the revenue from market and NGO taxes and customs, and any other perquisites of administrative officers, became a further source of competition.[10]

By 2004–5, people were expressing many complaints and criticisms about the changes in local government and chiefship, claiming in particular that the situation had become confused and complicated by the multiplication of authority. It was clear that the Boma Liberation Councils (BLCs) were not really functioning but that there was nevertheless often competition or confusion between the roles of the BLC Chairman, the Boma Administrator and the chief. The administrators were usually younger, literate men with links to the SPLM leadership in the area; the Chairmen saw their role as more overtly political, to support the 'Movement'. Chiefs complained that now if a letter came from the county government, the

[7] Musa A Abdul-Jalil, Adam Azzain Mohammed and Ahmed A Yousuf, 'Native administration and local governance in Darfur: past and future', in de Waal (ed.), *War in Darfur*, pp. 39–47; Douglas H Johnson, 'Decolonising the borders in Sudan: ethnic territories and national development', in M Duffield and V Hewitt (eds), *Empire, Development and Colonialism: the past in the present* (Woodbridge, 2009), pp. 176–87.

[8] Øystein H Rolandsen, *Land, Security and Peacebuilding in the Southern Sudan* (Oslo, 2009); Mareike Schomerus and Tim Allen, *Southern Sudan at Odds with Itself: dynamics of conflict and predicaments of peace* (London, 2010).

[9] Rohn et al, 'Report of the study on local administrative structures', p. 10.

[10] Herzog, 'Report: mission on governance', pp. 17, 23.

three would compete to get hold of it, revealing the continuing value of such bureaucratic resources and symbols. The chiefs successfully conveyed their resentments and criticisms of their new rivals to teams of SPLM administrators and judges and United Nations Development Programme (UNDP) consultants in 2005, feeding into local government policy with enduring effect.[11]

There was also growing concern at the fragmentation and multiplication of counties, *payams* and *bomas*, and corresponding chiefdoms. In some counties, the creation of the *bomas* led to the breakup of the old chiefdoms and the appointment or promotion of new '*boma* chiefs', often from among the former sub-chiefs or headmen, as one 'paramount' chief in Mundri County complained:

> [SPLM] Political Affairs came and established 28 *bomas* – this is going to destroy the chiefs' work. I used to control Kotobi and Kalaka – now there are independent chiefs in each of these. The problem now is that we can't do our traditional role – there is a chief who was just picked from among the ordinary people. In the past we chiefs used to talk to the rain-makers to make sure that there was rain, but now the Boma council chairmen prevent this and say that it is nonsense. So now the place is dry because we cannot play our traditional role.

An elder in Yambio to the west similarly claimed that there had been an increase of new diseases since the chiefs had lost power.[12] As chiefs faced the breakaway of their former sub-chiefs and increasing competition from literate administrators, they resorted to emphasising their 'traditional' role, claiming links to spiritual authority and the moral health of the community. They would find a ready source of support in developing national discourses around traditional authority and customary law.

In Juba, however, there had instead been a gradual shift since the 1980s towards education and elections – rather than heredity or history – as the basis for chiefship: 'Now the chiefs are very educated; we even have graduates... Most of them have at least senior secondary schooling, and some were educated in these seminaries, which is the equivalent of a PhD in English!'

> Here we have been shifting to an elected system of chieftainship, since the 1981 Local Government Act. The local government advertise the election and anyone can stand provided he has not committed a crime, he is from that village, he belongs to that ethnic group, and these days it should be someone a bit educated. The Commissioner organises an electoral committee to go to the area, and they will ask the people what method of voting they want. Usually it is by lining up – there is no question of free and fair – everyone can see the result![13]

The practice of elections may have disguised continuing internal selection of chiefs, however, according to another administrative official in 2006. He emphasised that the hereditary system of chiefship had become unpopular and that people wanted 'quality leadership' in the form of educated chiefs. But as he went through his file on Native Administration, he read out letters concerning the appointment of two chiefs the previous year, in which it was made clear that the 'community' had already selected a single candidate and it was impossible to

11 Leonardi et al, 'Report on Traditional Authority'; Golooba-Mutebi and Adak Costa, 'Traditional Authorities'; Simon Harrigin and Nikodemo Arou Man, 'Traditional Authority Study: report for Upper Nile team B', and Mark Aiken and Afaf Ismael, 'Traditional Authority Study: report on Southern Blue Nile and Eastern Equatoria' (all Nairobi: UNDP unpublished reports, 2005); SPLM Local Government Secretariat, 'Local Government Framework for Southern Sudan', Fourth Draft (Rumbek: SPLM, 2004).

12 Interviews with male Moru chief in Mundri County, 2 February 2005, and male Zande elder in Yambio town, 21 January 2005, cited in Leonardi et al, 'Report on traditional authority', p. 14.

13 Interview 24N/JC.

find other candidates to stand for election. Presented with this fait accompli, the administrator had agreed to the chosen chiefs. He also explained that since 1989 chiefs had been paid salaries by the government, since they no longer collected taxes and so had lost this source of remuneration.[14]

In Juba County under the Government of Sudan (and continuing after 2005 under the Government of Southern Sudan), the large chiefdoms of the colonial period had also been gradually split up. The old Tokiman chiefdom, for example, was broken into several new chiefdoms in the 1990s, due to disputes over the selection of chiefs: 'so came the scattering', as one of the new chiefs described it with some ambivalence or regret, despite his apparent benefit.[15] A chief from the southern part of the county complained that there were now 400 chiefs in Central Equatoria State where there used to once be only seventeen; he urged a restoration of the big chiefdoms so that chiefs had enough taxpayers to be paid from the taxes collected rather than receiving a salary from government like a civil servant.[16] He was the son of one of the 'big' colonial chiefs so it was not surprising he should argue for this, but his rationale reflected the long-standing ideology that chiefship depended on having many people – 'a chief does not exist without taxpayers'.[17] This statement is of course revealing not simply of chiefs' need for followers, but of the way in which chiefdoms had been defined principally by their bureaucratic relationship to the state, long represented by the chiefs' tax registers.

The creation of new chiefdoms and administrative units was accompanied by an increasing focus on territory and boundaries, but this revived the problems of the colonial period in terms of the incongruence of territory and ethnic or descent groups. A young man in Rumbek explained the confusion when the SPLM or GoSS sought to create territorial *payams* on such a basis: 'The government tried to create *payam* centres for each sub-tribe or clan but it doesn't work because it's based on territory, not people. People here live all mixed.'[18] But increasingly the government and international agency discourses were associating territorial units with chiefs, tradition, ethnicity and 'community'. As we shall see further in the discussion of land below, decentralisation was thus working to heighten the politicisation of autochthony and ethnic rights to territory.

These units gained such significance because people increasingly believed that they needed their own *boma* or *payam* to be recognised in order to receive services and resources from government or agencies. John Garang's oft-quoted call for decentralisation to 'take the towns to the people' was being rather negated by the reverse movement of people into the towns. But both Garang's ideal and the reality of urbanisation were driven by the notion that local government should mean service delivery, i.e. the provision of medical and educational facilities, water sources and development projects. The *boma* was therefore frequently seen primarily as a potential focus for services. In reality such resources rarely materialised, but popular expectations were high before and after the 2005 peace, and this also impacted on chiefship. Local government officers and local or international aid agencies emphasised the vital necessity of involving chiefs in relief distribution and project implementation. In turn, individuals were being selected as chiefs because they had past experience as

[14] Interview 37N/JC.

[15] Interview 41R/JC.

[16] Interview 12N/JC.

[17] Chief Mangar Maciek of Aliamtooc I, quoted in the minutes of the meeting of Commissioner Lakes Province with Aliamtoc Chiefs on 3 August 1984, Bahr el Ghazal Province Archive, Wau, LP 66.B.1.

[18] Interview 19cN/RC.

block leaders in the refugee camps or because they knew some English and could therefore communicate with international organisations.[19]

As the *bomas* were being established as units of service delivery then, they were being defined by both territory and chief. There are parallels with Le Meur's account of the production of villages as 'locality' in Benin, where the decentralised implementation of development projects built upon the colonial-era transformation of villages into 'entry-gates for state penetration'; the production of territorial locality as the site for interventions also set up enduring tensions with the realities of mobility and competing notions of community.[20] In southern Sudan, similar tensions were evident by 2004–5, but these were increasingly focused on the institution of chiefship itself and its effectiveness as a point of access to resources and services. An elderly former chief in a rural *payam* on the Yei–Congo road elaborated this, neatly turning the rhetoric of community self-help being preached by the government and NGOs into the basis for claiming state resources: 'We advise the people to join hands to help health and education services so that the government will also help. When we join hands like this, and the chief communicates this to government, and the government responds, then we know that there is a good link to the government.'[21] People hoped that by conveying loyalty to the government through their chiefs and by attending meetings and participating in 'self-help' activities, they would be rewarded with state resources. Chiefs were also likely to be the loci for the provision or distribution of services and resources, reinforcing the significance of locality and chiefship in defining community.[22]

This kind of discourse was being articulated in the proliferating meetings and workshops (English words that had entered the vernaculars) conducted by government and international agencies for the purposes of consultation, dissemination and training as part of a broader goal of state-making before and after the establishment of the Government of Southern Sudan. In 2004 and 2005 there was a drive by the SPLM Local Government Secretariat and Judiciary, supported principally by the UNDP, to draft a local government policy and ultimately an act. The vision of the individual SPLM actors involved intersected with an increasing international interest in traditional authorities and with the local-level discourse of chiefs and their supporters. The Local Government Framework – and the eventual GoSS Local Government Act 2009 – established the chiefs as the sole executive and judicial authorities at the *boma* level. The process of producing this act both fed into and was fed by developing discourses of traditional authority.

THE POLITICS OF TRADITION

The SPLM agenda of decentralisation was part of the broader political vision for a 'New Sudan' aimed at overturning the centralisation and concentration of political power and state resources in Khartoum. The 1994 Chukudum National Convention had formally committed the Movement to decentralisation, as

[19] Leonardi et al, 'Report on Traditional Authority'; Interview 7N/YC. See also an interesting Zambian case in Wolfgang Zeller, '"Now we are a town": chiefs, investors, and the state in Zambia's Western Province', in Lars Buur and Helene M Kyed (eds), *State Recognition and Democratization in Sub-Saharan Africa: a new dawn for traditional authorities?* (New York, 2007), pp. 209–31.

[20] Le Meur, 'State making'.

[21] Interview with male Kakwa elder and ex-chief, Lasu Payam, near Yei, 7 February 2005, for Leonardi et al, 'Report on Traditional Authority'.

[22] Cf. Achim von Oppen, 'The village as territory: enclosing locality in northwest Zambia, 1950s to 1990s', *Journal of African History* 47 (2006), p. 70.

reiterated in its 1998 *Vision*.[23] From 1994 the role of chiefs had also been recognised, and their relations with the SPLA on the ground had gradually become more regularised, as we saw in Chapter 8. The 1996 SPLM Conference on Civil Society noted that '"Traditional"/indigenous institutions' had 'thus far been overlooked or marginalized by the Movement and the authorities it has created'.[24] But it was not until 2004 that the SPLM really began to associate chiefs and traditional authority more explicitly and formally with its claim to be fighting for rights and freedoms of culture and custom.

Between 2000 and 2004, a vocal group of Southern leaders, academics and international advisors had developed the idea of a forum or institution to bring together representatives from all the ethnic groups in southern Sudan, to develop 'unity through diversity', and to gain greater recognition for cultural rights. Funding for associated meetings and workshops came primarily from the Swiss government. The most prominent supporter of this 'House of Nationalities' proposal was Riek Machar, who re-joined the SPLM in 2002. In 2004 he spoke in support of the idea at a youth workshop in Upper Nile.[25] A few months later the SPLM/A leader John Garang invited traditional leaders from across the south to a conference in Kamuto where he thanked them for their role in the war. The conference produced the 'Kamuto Declaration', which affirmed respect for 'cultures' and the 'role and responsibilities of Traditional Leaders and Chiefs in all aspects, particularly as regards the tenure and ownership of land and other resources belonging to their respective communities'.[26] The prominence of land in this declaration will be discussed further below. The chiefs from Western and Central Equatoria who attended the Kamuto conference were still wearing their name badges with pride in 2005 and the conference was held to have demonstrated Garang's personal recognition of the chiefs.

The Kamuto Declaration also called for forums of traditional leaders, including at the national level. However, despite the public appreciation of the chiefs at Kamuto, the SPLM leadership remained wary of the House of Nationalities proposal. Riek Machar and the House of Nationalities promotional website openly acknowledged and addressed concerns that the institution was designed to promote smaller ethnic groups at the expense of larger ones, or that it might become 'an obstacle for building a modern state' or a rival to the SPLM structures.[27] Unsurprisingly, the idea raised tensions over visions of the state: one supporter, Jacob Akol, declared a 'radical' goal of placing ethnicity at the 'centre of governance'.[28]

[23] SPLM, 'Vision and programme of the Sudan People's Liberation Movement (SPLM)', (Yei and New Cush, New Sudan, 1998). (At this time the SPLM/A referred to southern Sudan as 'New Sudan'.)

[24] Cited in Large, 'Local governance', p. 21.

[25] Dr. Riek Machar Teny, 'On the concept of the "House of Nationalities": Opening Speech at the Upper Nile Youth Association for Development (UNYAD) workshop', Panyagor, Upper Nile, 1 April, 2004, last accessed 6 February 2013 at: http://bit.ly/UY0V2k.

[26] 'Kamuto Declaration', Kamuto, Kapoeta County, New Sudan, 29 June – 10 July 2004, last accessed 4 February 2013 at: http://sudanarchive.net/cgi-bin/pagessoa?a=pdf&d=Dslpd184.1.1&dl=1&sim=Screen2Image.

[27] Dr. Riek Machar Teny, 'On the concept of the "House of Nationalities": Opening Speech at the Upper Nile Youth Association for Development (UNYAD) workshop', Panyagor, Upper Nile, 1 April, 2004, last accessed 4 February 2013 at: http://sudanarchive.net/cgi-bin/pagessoa?a=pdf&d=Dslpd181.1.1&dl=1&sim=Screen2Image; House of Nationalities website, archived and last accessed 4 February 2013 at: http://archive.is/OV0j.

[28] Jacob Akol, 'South Sudan "House of Nationalities" – an answer to "Burden of Nationality"', *Sudan Vision Daily* 15 July 2003: last accessed on 4 February 2013 at www.sudanvisiondaily.com/modules.php?name=News&file=article&sid=2120; Jacob Akol, 'Constitution and concept of "House of Nationalities" revisited', *Gurtong* 8 March 2012: last accessed on 4 February 2013 at www.gurtong.net/ECM/Editorial/tabid/124/ctl/ArticleView/mid/519/articleId/6592/categoryId/24/Constitution-and-Concept-of-House-of-Nationalities-Revisited.aspx.

The House of Nationalities did not materialise at the national level in South Sudan, but its proponents' advocacy of ethnic and cultural rights was indicative of the constitutional language and political debates of the interim period. The idea of forums for traditional leaders became focused at the federal state rather than GoSS level, still with support from the Swiss government. In 2007, a conference of Lakes State traditional leaders was held in Rumbek, which revealed the role of certain key chiefs in mediating the national and international discourse of traditional authority. The conference was led by Chief Dut Malual, from Rumbek East County, who was a former trader and a politician and SPLA officer as well as a chief. He told the conference that his participation in the chiefs' tour of South Africa, Botswana and Ghana in 2006 had given him 'fruitful knowledge about how our brothers and sisters govern traditionally in the modern world'. The Chairman of the GoSS Local Government Board then spoke nostalgically of the 'superb administration by the Chiefs' under British Indirect Rule, 'told the Chiefs that they were the GoSS representatives at the grassroots', and even charged them with 'achievement of the eight Millennium goals'. One of the chiefs responded that 'it was for such activities that people like Chief Dut Malual were selected to visit and see the world around us, and bring us better information such as we are about to hear'. As the conference proceeded, chiefs became rather more critical of 'you leaders who travel to Juba and Khartoum', and who had failed to fulfil all the promises and resolutions that had already been made at numerous previous 'conferences and workshops'.[29] But however limited their efficacy, such conferences were producing and disseminating an increasingly prevalent discourse of traditional authority, from the local to the national level.

Such discussions fed into the GoSS Local Government Act of 2009, which enshrined ethnic and cultural rights: 'Every ethnic and cultural community within a local government territory shall have the right to freely enjoy and develop its cultures and practice its own customs and traditions' (section 11.2). But it also defined a more official territorial administrative unit of 'community': 'The Community shall comprise of clans, neighbourhoods and families who reside within the territorial area of a Local Government Council' (section 107.2). Territory was thus to define community and administration. Yet as in the colonial period, kinship and descent were also recognised as the basis of community: 'The clan or neighbourhood shall be the family tree of all the families residing in the villages of a Boma or the residential areas of a Quarter Council'; 'The family is the fundamental and natural unit of a society which shall be protected' (sections 108.1 and 108.3). 'Traditional authorities' were to be 'semi-autonomous authorities', and were to exercise judicial and executive functions with 'deconcentrated powers' (section 112). Again, chiefdoms were to be territorial, but within these the 'traditional authorities are organized on the basis of lineages and clans'; their population should be between 6,250 and 9,000 (sections 113–116). The Act thus embodied contradictions that had endured since the colonial period as to the administrative definition of communities – whether on the basis of territory, residence, population numbers, or ethnicity and kinship.[30]

The Act also provided for the establishment of Councils of Traditional Authority Leaders (CoTALs) at both national and state levels, to 'provide a forum for dialogue with all levels of government on matters of customs and traditions of the people of Southern Sudan' and to help to resolve and prevent

[29] PASS, 'Traditional Leaders Conference, Lakes State, South Sudan, Rumbek, 12–15 March 2007', copy in author's possession.

[30] See also Markus V Hoehne, *Traditional Authorities and Local Government in Southern Sudan* (Washington DC, 2008), pp. 10–11; Laars Buur and Helene M Kyed, 'Traditional authority in Mozambique: the legible space between state and community', in Buur and Kyed, *State Recognition*, pp. 115–21.

conflict (sections 119–121). Towards the end of 2009, the state governments began formulating their own CoTAL bills. The CoTAL process continued to be influenced by the South African example, and by international discourses of cultural rights, ethnic identity and the compatibility of tradition and modernity.[31] But notably, the debates at the state level tended to move away from the idea of representing each tribe, since this led to disputes as to what constituted a tribe, and recurred instead to having representatives from each county.[32]

The CoTALs and the many other programmes and initiatives that increasingly demanded the participation of chiefs contributed to the emergence of a few prominent chiefs in each state, from whom leadership of the CoTALs tended to come. Some were calling themselves or being called 'paramount chiefs' and there were also ideas of creating paramount chiefs at the level of each county, as stipulated in the Local Government Act. Just as by the later colonial period certain chiefs had gained particular prominence and favour with government, so it was possible to discern this new elite of chiefs, who tended to be the most highly educated, politically well-connected, and experienced in government-related or military employment, like Chief Dut in Rumbek East. They were also more likely to speak some English, and to live in the towns. Such chiefs had been drawn into an increasing number of internationally-sponsored activities and institutions, as a Central Equatoria State 'Director of Native Administration' explained:

> We are trying to raise the standard of the traditional authorities. We are changing the names to *boma, payam,* and so on. And we take them to South Africa and other places. We want to raise their standard to be like such places. By 2011 we want them to be like South Africa; chiefs there are like a government.[33]

More so than with any other chiefs, it is evident that this new political elite claiming leadership of traditional authority had invested in and deployed multiple forms of knowledge in order to achieve their prominent position. They were also able to use this position to act as powerful brokers in deals over land or development projects. They aroused a lot of popular criticism and opposition, particularly if they were claiming unprecedented paramount chiefship. But often they were also grudgingly admired and valued because they were seen to stand up and speak strongly to or against the government, with a confidence and authority that most chiefs lacked in the 'big' offices.[34] Sometimes too their close relations with top political or military leaders were seen as a means of defence and protection for their county or chiefdom. The perennial tensions over the size of chiefdoms were thus raised again, as people squared the desire for autonomy and access to resources with the need for the kind of defence and status that 'big', political chiefs might appear to offer.

[31] E.g. Prof. Kwesi Kwaa Prah, of the Centre for Advanced Studies of African Society in Cape Town, spoke at the Swiss Government's CoTAL Workshop, South Sudan Hotel, Juba, 2–4 December 2009 (author notes).

[32] Martina Santschi, personal communication.

[33] Interview 39N/JC.

[34] E.g. Chief Denis Daramollo in Juba and Chief Madol Mathok in Rumbek each spoke challengingly to Vice-President Riek Machar over implementation of the Local Government Act and border disputes respectively: author notes on the Rift Valley Institute – US Institute of Peace launch of the report 'Local Justice in Southern Sudan', in the Home and Away Hotel, Juba, 22 October 2010; 'South Sudan VP receives cool reception in Lakes State over border dispute', *Sudan Tribune*, 4 July 2012, last accessed 25 January 2013 at: http://www.sudantribune.com/spip.php?iframe&page=imprimable&id_article=43139.

'CHIEFS HAVE THE PEOPLE': THE NUMBERS GAME

> In the past people were not aware of their own rights, but the NGOs came into the liberated areas and preached the rights of women, rights of the child, the right to rule themselves, to run their own affairs; so this contributed to the idea of having their own bomas and payams. Also there has been politicisation of government offices – in the past government officers could not engage in politics. Some counties are not financially viable – we say they should have a minimum of 100,000 population (and for a payam it is 25,000 and a boma is 5,000). Dr John [Garang] approved counties politically to get support, not because they were viable.[35]

As this senior officer in the GoSS Local Government Board made clear, the international and national discourses of cultural rights and decentralisation fed into more local-level political struggles over administrative units and control of population. As we saw in Chapter 5, by the later colonial period, government officials had been emphasising that the provision of services depended on population numbers, in the perennial administrative desire to cluster people in accessible centres of settlement. The fragmentation of chiefdoms since the 1990s undid many of the colonial amalgamations. At the same time, administrative units were being sub-divided into ever more counties and *payams*. Government officials justified these processes on the grounds that the population had increased. Sometimes people explicitly compared the administrative situation to that of a family that had become too large to sustain itself on existing resources, necessitating a split. In one sense then, the fragmenting of old chiefdoms and administrative units was presented as simply the natural result of perennial indigenous processes of segmentation. But it was also understood to result from political competition and ethnic or sectional divisions, exacerbated by the creation of electoral constituencies and by the idea of decentralised service provision. Population numbers became a resource with which to claim rights and resources.

Rather ironically, chiefs and headmen had in the past had reason to under- rather than over-estimate their population numbers, not least for taxation purposes. In Maridi County between 1995 and 1997, an SPLA conscription drive 'frightened many people from giving correct figures out of fear of being drafted into the army'.[36] Headmen around Rumbek in 2006 described their attempts to play the numbers game, reducing numbers for the purposes of tax registers, but then having to increase the numbers when relief food distribution occurred.[37]

In 2008, the fifth national Sudanese census was conducted, fuelling the focus on numbers. As Santschi reported, the census data was supposed to be used to determine resource allocation and service provision according to population size, as well as to be the basis for both political constituencies in the forthcoming elections and for adjusting administrative units.[38] It was widely acknowledged by administrators in preceding years that many of the new counties, *payams* and *bomas* were unlikely to reach the stipulated population requirements. The census therefore became highly politicised, with politicians, administrators and chiefs all concerned to maximise the returns of their units by ensuring that people living in the towns or elsewhere outside their supposed home areas returned to be counted. Santschi quotes an administrator in Yambio

[35] Interview 40N/JC. The challenges of enumeration in southern Sudan are discussed in African Rights, 'Imposing empowerment', pp. 13–4.

[36] Rohn et al, 'Report of the study on local administrative structures', p. 17.

[37] Interviews 23N/RC; 41N/RC.

 [38] Martina Santschi, 'Briefing: counting "New Sudan"', *African Affairs* 107:429 (2008), pp. 631–40.

who warned chiefs: 'Make sure that your people are being counted. If they are not counted, your *boma* or *payam* will not reach the numbers required and will be dissolved. Then you will not be a chief anymore.'[39] Conflicts erupted as to the affiliation of villages and chiefs to particular *payams*; one chief near Juba prevented enumeration because he claimed his people were being counted in the wrong *payam* and therefore under another chief. He explained to Santschi that 'The census shows everything, the location of the constituencies and the distribution of wealth. Development projects are given according to the number of people. That is why each *payam* is struggling for its own people.'[40]

The political game of numbers was also heightening tensions over the location of administrative boundaries, particularly when new counties or lower administrative units were created, necessitating new or newly significant boundary-making. A dispute over the boundary between Terekeka and Juba counties centring on Mongalla, north of Juba, was blamed for violent conflict between the Mundari and Bari in 2008. A longer-term dispute over whether Wonduruba should be removed from Juba County into Lainya County became increasingly bitter and led to an attack on a Lainya politician and senior SPLM official, who was widely accused of seeking to enlarge his own electoral constituency. In 2008, one Central Equatoria State government official blamed both of these border conflicts on politics: 'The politicians are spoiling the system of traditional authority – they go there and mobilise and tell the chiefs, "this is your place", all for the sake of politics.'[41]

A county official in Juba similarly complained at the fragmenting of the old colonial chiefships of Tokiman, Belinian and Gondokoro, claiming that it had not even been justified by a population increase, but was entirely a political affair:

> We have many more chiefs now, and yet the population is less, because of war and displacement. This is partly because of politics – our elder brothers in the North wanted to break people up so that they have less power or strength. Also it is our own politics – people think that having more chiefs will mean more support from the constituency, and they don't look at the actual demography. Our politicians and MPs will promise all kinds of development, schools, health centres, etc, and then once they are in office they never even visit the people.[42]

Chiefs and sub-chiefs of the Northern Bari, formerly under the Tokiman chiefship, claimed that new separate counties for Tokiman and the Northern Bari had been proposed by SPLM/A leaders from Tokiman, because they knew that the population of Tokiman was less than that of the northern area, and so they could not be confident of winning elections if the two areas remained a single constituency.[43] The 2010 elections further fuelled this political concern with numbers; the chiefs were repeatedly urged to support the SPLM in the elections.[44]

[39] Speech by Peter Lado at a conference in Yambio, 29 March 2008, cited in Santschi, 'Counting "New Sudan"', p. 637.

[40] Chief Benjamin Tonlado, Somba, 26 April 2008, interviewed and cited by Santschi, 'Counting "New Sudan"', pp. 637–8.

[41] Interviews 39N/JC; 40N/JC. See also Isaac Vuni, 'Community border row in Equatoria to be addressed by committee', *Sudan Tribune*, 10 March 2009, last accessed 25 January 2013 at: http://www.sudantribune.com/spip.php?page=imprimable&id_article=30444.

[42] Interview 24N/JC.

[43] Interview 42R/JC.

[44] E.g. Gurtong, 'Lakes State chiefs meet, Local Government head tells them to vote SPLM', *Gurtong* 13 March 2007, last accessed 25 January 2013 at: http://www.gurtong.net/ECM/Editorial/tabid/124/ctl/ArticleView/mid/519/articleId/1358/Lakes-State-Traditional-Leaders-Council-Meeting.aspx. Cf. Kjetil Tronvoll and Tobias Hagmann (eds), *Contested Power in Ethiopia: traditional authorities and multi-party elections* (Leiden, 2011).

Many people thus blamed politics and politicians for creating divisions and conflicts over units and boundaries. But there were multiple aspects to the territorialisation of community, administration and ethnicity. Chiefdoms as localities had also gradually – if partially and intermittently – become foci for the formation of communities of multiple lineages and origins, forged through everyday contact and relations with the state. As an administrator in Maridi claimed, people of multiple ethnicities came together in chiefdoms because 'they feel that they are under the protection of the chief's clan'.[45] This was not an entirely new basis for community – people had always come together in larger communities and negotiated inclusion and exclusion beyond immediate kin relations. But the territorial and institutional definition of chiefships had been novel, and it developed in distinctive ways over the twentieth and into the twenty-first century, through interaction with national and international policies and political discourse. New motives and means of exclusion and developing discourses of tribalism and autochthony might be seen as what von Oppen terms 'the dark side of the territorialisation of locality'.[46] But there were also still ideals of inclusion, of safety and strength in numbers, and of chiefship as a neutral, non-lineage institution through which people might access state protection and resources.

GATHERING PEOPLE: CHIEFDOMS AS COMMUNITY

> Even animals have leaders. They are led by the big animals. Without a leader, animals scatter. Even people would scatter if there were no chiefs. They would migrate to where there are chiefs.
> If you slaughter mother-chicken, the chicks will scatter.[47]

These statements, collected in 2005 in Raja County in Western Bahr el Ghazal, demonstrate the perceived danger of being scattered in the bush, which had of course been a very real experience for many during periods of war. But they also reflect a deeper sense in which chiefship had been a focus for community cohesion. One of the most frequently cited functions of chiefs in 2004–5 was their ability to gather the people – or in the current idiom, to 'mobilise' people – for meetings, communal labour, relief and aid distributions, and so on. A church preacher asserted that 'villages need meetings for development', reflecting the association of 'meetings' and 'committees' with accessing resources.[48] More so than ever, the chiefs' ability both to access state resources and ameliorate government requisitions and to allocate and distribute these fairly was seen as the most important factor in their capacity to 'hold' the community.[49] Community was thus being made through the fulcrum of chiefship as the point of articulation with the state.

A middle-aged woman, who was born into the most important spear-master lineage in the Amothnhom section of Agar Dinka around Rumbek, spoke at great length about the value of chiefship. She talked about how it brokered access to government services, market and land, and how good chiefs also brought protection for their people, both through military leadership like the war chiefs of the

45 Interview with Maridi County Executive Director, 26 January 2005, for Leonardi et al, 'Report on Traditional Authority'.

46 Von Oppen, 'The village as territory', p. 74.

47 Interviews with an 'elder' and 'youth', Raja County, 2 February 2005, cited in Golooba-Mutebi and Adak Costa, 'Traditional Authorities', pp. 7–8.

48 Interview 20N/YC.

49 Interviews 63R/RC; 69R/RC; 19bN/RC; 41N/RC.

past, but also through their strong words and knowledge of the government law. Moreover, good chiefs attracted large communities: 'keeping an area well multiplies the inhabitants'. But it was evident from her account that community and chiefship were also produced through the state bureaucracy:

> If you go to the hospital, you will be asked from which chief you come, and you will be registered against your chief. If you take any animal for auction, you will be registered the same to your chief. If it is a lady, the chief of her husband will be registered. If you want to get a plot also you will be asked and allotted a place according to your chief.[50]

A man from the same chiefdom claimed that the chief 'knows everything in the community, even every birth of a child'.[51] As in the colonial period, such bureaucratic regulation might imply a potentially unwelcome extent of control and restriction, but this woman was positively emphasising how belonging to a chief brought access to resources and services, as well as protection and security. An elderly woman in Yei similarly reminisced about the strength and protective capacity of a former chief, who had combined the rain and government chiefships from the colonial period until his death in the 1970s:

> He was brave, so much that he would even bang the table, right in the government official's face; he could silence people. He spoke straightforwardly. These teak trees that are now being cut: if he were there, they would not be cut like this... He was very able: if somebody argued with him, he could do a miracle or something wonderful by which people would know that he was the genuine owner of the place.[52]

Tables were a prominent symbol of government, making 'banging the table' a powerful expression of resistance and demand. As these testimonies suggest, ideals and nostalgic memories of chiefship tend to emphasise the benefits of protection, status and access to state resources that a strong, powerful chief brought to the people who could claim to belong to his chiefdom. But there was also a longer-term tension at work, between the desire for the protection and status of belonging to a large community, and the inevitable divisions and fissions produced within such a community. A chief's claim to be 'the genuine owner' of the land could easily provoke conflict, as we shall see.

Chiefship was on the one hand depicted as central to definitions of community and custom, and on the other hand as merely the work of a 'messenger', even by chiefs and their supporters.[53] Chiefs often described themselves, and were described, as poor, and yet they might have relatively large houses, many wives and other conspicuous signs of relative wealth, and their families had often become powerful in local, regional and even national politics and government. These paradoxes arose in part from continuing tensions between rival sources of wealth and power, ensuring that chiefly income did not necessarily translate into social status. Ambiguity was also produced by the interstitial position that chiefs were supposed to occupy, between government and people – sometimes the pressures of this position were explicitly presented as mysterious dangers attached to chiefship. These multiple discourses around chiefship acted both to restrict the status of chiefs, and to dilute envy and rivalry and disguise their income and influence.

[50] Interview 72R/RC. A senior GoSS official in Juba also stated in conversation on 6 March 2006 that the names of one's chief and sub-chief were needed in order to obtain a passport.

[51] Interview 42N/RC.

[52] Interview 29R/YC.

[53] Brief conversation with Kakwa sub-chief, Rwonyi, near Yei, 28 October 2005.

One elderly man in Rumbek summed up some of these ambiguities, in objecting to the common use of the word *beny* to refer to chiefs:

> '*Beny*' should actually mean a spear-master or a wealthy person; it should not be used for chiefs, because a chief is just there to give your right. He has to go every day to work and can't look after his household to become wealthy. I refused to be on any courts even though they asked me, because being a chief means being put there to suffer.[54]

It remained the case that the work of chiefs and headmen was often still seen to be suited to younger people who could 'run quickly'.[55] One clan rain chief also explained that he could not engage in 'government work' because it would heat or bake him and thus endanger the rain, which depended on an ideal state of coolness. He went on to say that he had refused to become a headman like his father, because the work of distributing labour demands and relief food was bound to provoke the suspicion and resentment of the people, 'and so they would curse us'.[56] In all the research areas, chiefship had often remained associated with the risk of illness or death, whether from deliberate use of poison or witchcraft by resentful opponents, or from a vaguer sense of an intrinsic danger or curse in the very nature of chiefship.[57] A chief just outside Juba claimed that some clans or individuals refused to claim the chiefship because they feared that it would bring illness and death due to jealousy and conflicts over it: 'chiefship is not something easy or cool; there will always be people who hate you'.[58] Such tensions within chiefdoms would be particularly apparent in the disputes over 'community land' that were proliferating in and around the towns by 2005.

'LAND BELONGS TO THE COMMUNITY'

Tensions over land in Central Equatoria were a culmination of long-term processes and enduring questions as well as the result of more recent political, economic, military and demographic factors.[59] During the SPLA war, much of the population of Central Equatoria had sought refuge in areas remote from the fighting or across the international borders. When they returned to Yei or other areas after 1997, they often found their former plots of land inhabited by soldiers or displaced civilians from other parts of South Sudan. After the 2005 Peace Agreement, accelerated returns and urbanisation exacerbated the resulting tensions, leading to fundamental debates over land and territory. Some people asserted territorial rights of national citizenship and claimed the right to settle anywhere in Southern Sudan. Some declared that their part in the liberation struggle had earned them the right to land in the liberated areas, evoking some of the themes of Kopytoff's internal frontier thesis – the war as a pivotal moment representing a kind of 'first-coming' and the conquest or erasure of prior rights.[60] But others seized upon the SPLM assertion that 'land belongs to the community' to argue that land rights were defined by autochthony or

54 Interview 1bN/RC.

55 Interview 43R/JC; cf. Badiey, 'The State Within', p. 126.

56 Interviews 32R/YC; 12R/YC; cf. Badiey, 'The State Within', p. 133.

57 Leonardi, 'Violence, sacrifice and chiefship', p. 546.

58 Interview 41R/JC. Huby, 'Big men', p. 70.

59 See Cherry Leonardi, 'Paying "buckets of blood" for the land: moral debates over economy, war and state in Southern Sudan', *Journal of Modern African Studies* 49:2 (2011), pp. 215–40.

60 Kopytoff, 'The internal African frontier'.

antecedent 'first-coming'.[61] Often in national political arenas and media this was expressed in ethnic terms, or in the even broader regional categories of 'Equatorians' and 'Nilotics'. But at a local level, these arguments were intersecting with the longer-term internal political debates over authority and community, territoriality and mobility.

Such debates were particularly fraught around the towns of Yei and Juba. The towns were expanding outwards, creating tensions over the appropriation of formerly rural land. But at the same time, the urban frontier was expanding from the other direction as people moved closer to the towns from the rural areas. The settlements within about a ten-mile radius of Yei, for example, had become part of a broad peri-urban frontier zone around the town with a population that was both heterogeneous and mobile – many people were returning refugees from Uganda and still had families there, others were soldiers who had often married locally, others displaced people or economic migrants.

The increasing congestion around the towns had the obvious effect of suddenly increasing pressure on the land and giving it unprecedented potential value. There did not yet seem to be a shortage of land for cultivation – many people had farms at a short distance from the town and roads. But there was something of a scramble to establish authority over land because an increasing number of organisations or individuals were seeking to acquire large plots on which to construct offices, houses or other enterprises. In promoting communal customary land rights, the chiefs and clan heads were careful to emphasise that the only payment required for such leases was to cover the necessary 'blessings' and 'rituals' that they would perform on the land. One man put the price of such a ceremony at US$1,500 however;[62] this effective commodification of spiritual authority over the land provoked intense debates over who should perform such blessings and receive the 'token' payments. The roles of individual landowning clan heads, land chiefs and even rain chiefs – who had so often remained largely offstage in the colonial period – were brought into much more public arenas, such as court cases, through disputes with one another and particularly with the government chiefs.

The chiefs were asserting their authority over all land transactions and attempting to enforce this through their courts. Some were even claiming to be spiritual land or earth chiefs. One elderly chief in Yei declared a special authority over the land, on the basis that he had remained in the county (though not in his chiefdom itself) during the war: 'I did not run. Some have remained as refugees; some have just returned. They found me here, which means that I am the guardian of the land of my grandfather.'[63] He claimed to have performed protective and cleansing rites during the wartime. Now he was claiming authority over all land transactions in his chiefdom or even in Yei town, where he was living and serving as a member of the town Boma Court. He was not from the hereditary line of chiefs, although he claimed maternal relation to it; his opponents emphasised that he was 'only a nephew'. The landowning clan heads were bitterly complaining that their rights were not being recognised. But a whole series of interconnected disputes were going on, including between different claimants to clan headship and between a prominent rain chief and the landowning clans. Clan members in Khartoum and Juba were writing or visiting to assert their land rights, revealing the kind of elite networks that linked urban, rural and even diaspora communities.

[61] On tensions over land elsewhere or more generally in South Sudan, see Rolandsen, *Land, Security*; Frode Sundnes and N. Shanmugaratnam, 'Socio-economic revival and emerging issues relating to land and customary institutions in Yirol, Southern Sudan', in N. Shanmugaratnam (ed.), *Between War & Peace in Sudan & Sri Lanka: deprivation & livelihood revival* (Oxford, 2008), pp. 59–76.

[62] Interview 43N/YC.

[63] Interview 2R/YC.

For a time everyone focused the blame on one elderly headman for transacting land with soldiers on the edge of Yei, and he was arrested and imprisoned. Multiple actors were vying for recognition as land authorities, including a town quarter sub-chief from the same chiefdom, who welcomed the recent prosecutions of individuals claiming the right to sell land:

> The person who purchases the land... is supposed to come to me here and then we go to the government and tell him the 'number' [amount] we want. We also take some money for blessing, if he wants to build a school or compound. And if you are from this area then we will not charge you highly.[64]

As this final sentence suggests, the internal disputes over land rights and authority could also be transcended in the desire to protect territory and exclude outsiders. This was often expressed in ethnic terms and in opposition to the continuing occupation of land by soldiers or people from other states. But it was also expressed through witchcraft accusations as a means of excluding and evicting individuals, and through attempts to define clans and their territories in more strictly patrilineal terms:

> Most people living now in Rwonyi are our sister's children, people from broken homes – some are not even Kakwa. So we have to say who has the right to exist there. We will get all the Rwonyi, even those who are abroad, and make a list. And it will be done [sub]clan by [sub]clan.[65]

Such maternal relations and the broader use of kinship as a means of assimilation had always been more significant than strict patrilineal orders. But in areas of dense population, the desire for wealth-in-people was being countered to some extent by newly exclusionary definitions of community and land rights.[66]

However, these exclusionary definitions continued to exist in tension with both the realities of relations and settlement patterns and the enduring sense that larger communities and more entrepreneurial chiefs might also be a means of access to state protection and resources. This tension was particularly apparent in Juba, where the most prominent Bari chief established a powerful and profitable role in land transactions. As Badiey shows, there was considerable competition here between different levels of government and various actors claiming to represent the local community. The Central Equatoria State government claimed to be protecting the Bari and their land from the GoSS. A group of politicians formed the Bari Community Association, and also claimed to be a better voice for the Bari in dealing with government than were the chiefs.[67] But there were divisions among the Bari too: some elders near Juba claimed that their land was being sold by the state government Director of Lands, who was from the southern Bari.[68] Others claimed that the politicians were complicating the issues and that the chiefs should handle specific land transactions on behalf of and in consultation with their communities, as indeed some chiefs were doing. In 2005, one administrative officer of a former quarter council, now a *payam*, asserted that in land matters (such as a recent request by the Haggar company for land on which to construct a hotel), 'We reach the people through the chiefs,

64 Interview 12R/YC.

65 Interview 43N/YC. See similar connections between control of land and accusations of witchcraft in Tim Allen and Laura Storm, 'Quests for therapy in northern Uganda: healing at Laropi revisited', *Journal of Eastern African Studies* 6:1 (2012), pp. 30–1.

66 Cf. Locatelli and Nugent, 'Introduction', to Locatelli and Nugent (eds), *African Cities*, pp. 4–5.

67 Badiey, 'The State Within', pp. 207, 226, 232–4, 239.

68 Interview 49R/JC.

not through the quarter councils, because the land belongs to them.'[69] Bari people in and around Juba expressed varied and conflicting opinions of the leading Bari chief in Juba: some saw him as a Khartoum-appointed chief exploiting his position to make personal profits from land transactions; but many others, sometimes grudgingly, admitted that he was a 'strong' spokesman for Bari land rights, and had the courage (or political connections) to speak out even to the most powerful government and military actors.

The competition and conflict over land was thus generating considerable political dispute over chiefship. But it also contributed significantly to the potential value of chiefship, to definitions of community, and to claims upon the state. Chiefs had to justify their residence in the towns, which contributed to the imagining of urban space by surrounding communities as the visible historical evidence of their special claim upon the state. In Rumbek, for example, most people said that the chiefs now lived and held their courts in the town because of insecurity in the rural areas; they needed to be close to the state forces that protected and enforced their authority. But one such chief instead declared: 'What made me to be in the town here is that it is our home starting from our ancestors coming down to us; this was our original place.'[70] Such claims were often supported by a sense of pride in a long history of local interaction with the town; people were claiming, as it were, to be the 'first-comers' to the urban frontier, not only in terms of owning the land, but also of having established first relations with government. In every town, people frequently drew attention to key sites and located these in their own lineage and family histories – the grave of a grandfather, the site of a sacrifice, the ancestral land on which the prison or the hospital had been constructed.[71] Even the town centres, the original *merkaz* sites from which the colonial government had sought to exclude people, had thus been appropriated into local historical geographies.

In seeking authority over the land around the towns of Juba and Yei, chiefs and the multiple other claimants to community representation were not seeking to exclude government from their territory, but rather to gain state recognition of their land rights, and consequent compensation and other benefits. Complaints and criticisms about government appropriation of land focused on corruption and lack of regulation, and people seized upon the idea of a law that 'land belongs to the community' to argue their rights. It was common for people to claim that Garang himself would have recognised their rights (for example, to compensation for the property his soldiers seized during the war), and so one elderly man near Juba declared that 'if Garang was here' the state government officials would not have been able to sell 'our land'.[72] An acting chief in the same area repeatedly emphasised the enduring debt of the government to the original inhabitants of Juba and asserted his resulting special rights to perform rituals for government events.[73] Similarly in Yei, people were increasingly articulating claims to the town itself, based on their pre-colonial ownership of the land: 'We have been the ones pushed out from the town, so we are pushing that our area should be demarcated' within the town.[74] Claims to land rights were thus part of a continuing quest for state recognition. In a sense the land transactions were

[69] Interview 44N/JC.

[70] Interview 54R/RC.

[71] Cf. Giblin, 'History, imagination', p. 190.

[72] Interviews 49R/JC; 2R/YC.

[73] Interview 41R/JC.

[74] Interview 43N/YC.

another opportunity to contract the state, but in a kind of reverse relationship, drawing the state into debts and obligations to landowning patrons.

This sense of ownership over the towns was being asserted with increasing confidence. In 2005 when the new Governor of Central Equatoria State visited Yei for the first time, the local chiefs, led by the town Boma Court chief, presented a 'memorandum' which was read out in English by a local NGO manager at the Governor's rally. It complained about the mistreatment of chiefs and civilians by soldiers and military police and the alienation of land and sale of teak by the military, before proposing that the army barracks should be moved further away from the town, a suggestion met with wry laughter and heartfelt applause from the crowd. Naturally the 'memo' concluded with requests for uniforms, salaries and training for the chiefs, a familiar refrain voiced at any opportunity. In both requesting and deploying the resources of bureaucratic formalities and convention, these chiefs were following a long history of chiefship, in which knowledge of government and town might be turned into claims to state protection and laws.

CONCLUSION

The disputes over land which escalated after 2004 are particularly revealing both of the tensions around chiefship as a definer of community, and of the way in which chiefship was nevertheless being used to claim rights and to access the state. The 'communities' in and around the towns represented diverse ethnic origins, and histories of migration and affiliation; now their elites were vying to construct more exclusive definitions of community in the discourse of patrilineal descent, often with an uneasy relationship to chiefship. But they were actually seeking legitimation and recognition of these communities 'in the ideological constructs of an emergent national metropole',[75] as the GoSS and SPLM promoted ideas of communal rights and traditions, with a long history in government discourse. Just as the state might have imagined communities into political and administrative existence, so people were imagining the state as a source of protection, justice, services and resources. Neither imaginary was entirely fulfilled: communities remained indistinct, incoherent, fragmented and porous, while the state was largely failing to meet popular expectations. But chiefship remained the primary means through which people sought to lever these ideals of state and community into existence. Government and international agencies believed that by working through the chiefs they were reaching and supporting 'communities', while ordinary people continued to hope that chiefs would channel state resources and bring development, and that belonging to a chiefdom would be a means of obtaining state recognition of their rights and entitlements. Such belonging was defined primarily by bureaucratic records and requirements, often belied by the shifting and uncertain composition of settlements and allegiances. Many people instead sought to appeal much more directly to the *hakuma* and its elusive ideals of law and order, to obtain recognition of individual rather than communal rights. But in seeking these rights, they once again turned to the chiefs and their courts, thus further institutionalising chiefship. State and community were being made through both their dialectical imagining, and their mutual recognition of chiefship.

[75] Igor Kopytoff, 'A contemporary "anomalous" society on the rural frontier', in Kopytoff, *The African Frontier*, p. 241.

10

Knowing the system: judicial pluralism and discursive legalism in the interim period, 2005–2010

> I have a case in the town chiefs' court concerning my brother's daughter's dowry. My brother died since the last court hearing, so the family asked me to re-open it because I am an intellectual and it needs someone who can read and write the papers...
> And my sister had a problem with her neighbour... She said she doesn't know the procedures for going to the police, so I went with her to the Attorney-General...
> In the courts you can spend the whole day going from office to office. It is just like in the market where village people will be charged more because they don't know the price...
> But if you know the system you can go step-by-step and you will get your right.[1]

People had long been drawn to the towns not only to obtain services and commodities but also to access the state and to acquire knowledge of its 'procedures'. This was always a risky strategy, because the urban frontier was subject to the unpredictable threat of repressive or exclusionary government force emanating from the town centres or military barracks. Unsurprisingly, the nodal, urban state has been characterised as dangerously capricious in the existing literature on South Sudan's history, in common with much analysis of post-colonial African states. Yet the *idea* that government works according to fixed, predictable rules and systems has nevertheless been taken up over the last century; by the 2005–11 interim period, people were asserting that by knowing 'the system', they could claim rights, resources and the protection of the state.

As South Sudan approached its independence, law and justice became an ever greater focus of its government and of international agencies, in tandem with the discourse of traditional authority discussed in the previous chapter. Having claimed to be fighting in part against the imposition of *shari'a* law, SPLM leaders, judges, lawyers and administrators promoted 'customary law' as the basis for an autonomous legal system and recognised the enduring role of chiefs' courts as vital to the provision of justice at a local level.[2] At the same time the legal and judicial branches of the SPLM government and later GoSS were also seeking to extend greater regulatory control over the local courts. International agencies often had more mixed and cautious views of the existing local justice system. But some of these too were calling for recognition and strengthening of customary law and justice. The following quotation by Mennen sums up some of the most prevalent views:

[1] Interview with Balanda Viri man, a recent returnee from Khartoum, Wau, 28 November 2009, cited in Cherry Leonardi, Leben Nelson Moro, Martina Santschi and Deborah H Isser, *Local Justice in Southern Sudan* (Washington DC: 2010), p. 29.

[2] See Francis Mading Deng, *Customary Law in the Cross-fire of Sudan's War of Identities* (Washington, 2005).

> Customary law exists in its unadulterated form in the rural mono-ethnic regions of the South... Questions of harmful cultural practices, draconian martial law, lack of professionalism and jurisdictional uncertainty plague the administration of justice... Customary law in southern Sudan largely embraces reconciliation and community harmony... restoring balance in the family unit and community. Traditional values and the community structure that reinforce them are under siege in post-conflict Sudan.[3]

This chapter contests almost all of these statements, and the wider scholarship and policy directions that they reflected. The justice system in southern Sudan was not one of legal pluralism – in which a separate 'unadulterated' customary law would exist separate and parallel to state law – but of *judicial* pluralism: a multiplicity of judicial institutions and actors which were seen to apply a unified set of laws, albeit subject to varying degrees of competence, corruption or capacity. 'The law is one', as many people said. From occasional courts of elders and headmen through to the county magistrates, there were indeed considerable commonalities in the amalgamation of forms of customary and tort law with selective use of penal codes to settle both civil and criminal cases. These outcomes were derived from both 'situational interpretations of state law' and a broader normative base comparable to Eckert's notions of 'common sense' judgments.[4] Over the last century, the local courts had recognised rights in property and persons based on an amalgamation of aspects of statutory and indigenous laws.

But while giving the impression of a unitary law, the composite basis and situational interpretation of legal norms actually gave room to contending interpretations and articulations of rights in the courts. It is in such contention that a further problem with the notion of customary law cited above is apparent. Twenty years ago, Sally Falk Moore critiqued the sentimental images of African justice as 'harmonious settlement', restoring 'social equilibrium'. As she argued, 'What appears to be equilibrium from the outside is often a temporary moment of agreement in which a dominant segment of the group has prevailed and everyone recognises that predominance and acquiesces in all public behaviour.'[5] Dispute resolution in southern Sudan at all levels was adversarial and adjudicative in both process and outcome, bearing little resemblance to sentimental notions of community harmony and reconciliation.

Moore's emphasis on the influence of social hierarchy and the inherently political nature of community justice is a vital counterweight to enduring misconceptions of consensual customary mediation. But it is nevertheless important to address the ubiquitous belief among South Sudanese in the *potential* of the law to guarantee individual rights and to transcend social inequalities. It is in this regard that the association of the local courts with the state was essential to their public recognition and use. Widening definitions of 'governance' have led to an increasing scholarly focus on 'non-state' actors and regulatory orders, particularly in political and legal anthropology.[6] But as one of the more perceptive recent reports on justice in southern Sudan argued, local justice systems were certainly not 'non-state'.[7] It was the very connection of the chiefs' courts to the state that litigants had always sought to use. Since

3 Mennen, *Adapting Restorative Justice Principles*, pp. 3–4.

4 Eckert, 'From subjects to citizens'.

5 Moore, 'Treating law as knowledge', p. 32.

6 See, for example, Alice Bellagamba and Georg Klute (eds), *Beside the State: emergent powers in contemporary Africa* (Cologne: 2008).

7 Eric Scheye and Bruce Baker, 'The multi-layered approach: supporting local justice and security systems in southern Sudan' (Juba: draft report for DFID Strategic Development Fund, 2007).

the 1970s, the broadening of the urban frontier and its bureaucratic cultures had only increased the understanding of court cases as a transaction with the state. As the opening quote asserted, litigants needed to 'know the price' as well as knowing the system. The chiefs' courts also became situated more than ever on the urban frontier itself, and played a central role in mediating the proliferating exchanges, conversions and contracts between the value-systems and forms of property and wealth that intersected on the site of the frontier. As the Comaroffs argue, 'legal instruments appear – we stress, *appear* – to offer a means of commensuration: a repertoire of standardized signs and practices that, like money in the realm of economics, permit the negotiation of values and interests across otherwise intransitive lines of difference' [original emphasis].[8]

This chapter will explore the signs and practices that litigants and judicial actors employed in their pursuit of rights and guarantees, particularly bureaucratic and legalistic resources. The *pursuit* of rights increasingly came to be articulated in a *discourse* of rights. In the process, the use of laws and institutions to gain recognition of rights was simultaneously signifying popular recognition of those institutions.[9] Even in criticising state practices and failures, people were thus participating in state formation by promoting the ideal of state law and regulatory orders.

MARKETPLACE COURTS AND MONETARY TRANSACTIONS

The association of colonial courts with towns, money and markets had continued and even intensified in subsequent decades. A description of Kongor town in Upper Nile in the 1970s elaborates the typical spatial and economic connections:

> [T]he residential area is arranged around the court building and other services' houses. Court activities are one of the two major functions that attract people to the centre, the other being the marketing facilities. The court through the system of payment of fines has introduced cash into the Dinka economy, normally not through direct sale by the individuals but through auction after an animal has been handed over by its owner to the court and its police... Market places of limited economic activity are to be found in most court centres in the area. They are focal points for social interaction where people of the same group meet to converse, attend court deliberations, and participate in social occasions and festivals.[10]

The return and influx of population to the SPLM-controlled towns after 1997 and the major growth of Juba, particularly from 2005, was accompanied by the immigration of chiefs into the towns. In the interim period, more courts than ever were therefore functioning in the towns, both new kinds of town court and relocated rural courts. Some of these were located right next to the market, as in Rumbek. Some chiefs and court members had formerly been traders, and ideas of exchange, transaction and monetisation permeated the procedures and cultures of the courts. But at the same time the courts dealt in ideas of tradition and custom, with court members and litigants alike appealing to historical and community-based notions of rights and obligations. The town-based courts

[8] John L Comaroff and Jean Comaroff, 'Reflections on the anthropology of law, governance and sovereignty', in F von Benda-Beckmann, K von Benda-Beckmann and J Eckert (eds), *Rules of Law and Laws of Ruling: on the governance of law* (Farnham: 2009), p. 37.

[9] Cf. Lund, 'Twilight institutions', p. 675.

[10] Abdel Ghaffar M Ahmed and Mustafa Abdel Rahman, 'Small urban centres', p. 267. See also Mading Deng, *Tradition and Modernization*, pp. 106–12.

had become ever more crowded arenas of debate between different versions of rights, duties and offences, responsive to arguments for both individual and collective rights. Marriage, cattle and land were particular foci of such debate and argument, because they involved the intersection of different kinds of property rights and of individual rights and duties with familial obligations. As a locus for these debates, the courts both revealed and encouraged the cultivation of multiple forms of moral knowledge and discursive resource.

The transactional nature of local justice was apparent in the language and procedures of the courts. 'Laws' or *ganun* were commonly said to come from the government, and tended to mean scales of fines and compensation payments for various offences. Penalties of prison terms or flogging were nearly always readily convertible into monetary payments. Money paid to bail people from prison was described in the Dinka language as 'exchange' money – 'he has exchanged himself with money' – which is the same terminology as that used for cattle exchanges in Rumbek. The courts were helping to enable exchange between different economies, by fixing an artificially low monetary bridewealth. Huby reported this in 1981: bridewealth as enforced by the court was twelve head of cattle or £120. 'It is only in this context that the price of one cow is fixed at £10. On the open market, a cow is worth at least £200.'[11] This pattern still applied, as one chief explained:

> If you are in need of marriage, you must look for bride price such as animals, but now there is an alternative: you can get money according to the value of a cow, which is about £100,000 as required by customary law. Now if you happen to marry at home or in the village, you pay £500,000 according to market price, so you buy cattle in the market. But according to law, it is £100,000.[12]

As in the colonial period, young men might therefore elope with a girl in order to achieve a marriage in court which they could afford in monetary terms.

The association of the courts with money naturally also led to criticisms and moral condemnations, however. In a sense courts were seen as another means of state extraction of resources, and also as indicative of the risks and immoralities of the money economy. During the war, court fees had been remitted directly to SPLA military officers or to the SPLM administration, and were '[t]he only fee of significance collected in cash in the villages'.[13] Court members and clerks referred to fees and fines formally as money 'for the government' or 'for the court', underscoring the notion of cases as transactions with the state. As one chief put it, 'money must be paid' for a court case to be heard.[14] And as others said, people went to court when and because they 'want money'.

> If the case is settled there in the village, little money is demanded, but if they come to the courts in town the money is much more. In my father's time people settled at home, but now they rush to get money, and can even appeal up to the judge. And they can bribe the courts to make sure they get their money.[15]

Courts had always been a way to use, lose or gain money. One man trading vegetables in a village market near Juba described quite literal 'shopping' for a

11 Huby, 'Big men', p. 78.

12 Interview 42R/JC.

13 Rohn et al, 'Report of the study on local administrative structures', p. 59; Regional Chiefs' Court records, Rumbek, consulted by the author in 2006; interview with male Moru chief in Mundri County, 2 February 2005, cited in Leonardi et al, 'Report on Traditional Authority', p. 14.

14 Interview 74R/RC.

15 Interview 45N/YC.

favourable judicial outcome: 'Some chiefs are good; others aren't. If you're not happy with the verdict, you save your money and go to another chief.'[16] But others used this association with money to advise against going to court; as one elderly woman in Juba declared, it was better to settle disputes at home than to give money to be 'eaten' by the court.[17] Even a litigant in the government County Court in Rumbek agreed, adding the common complaint that courts wasted time as well as money: 'If you can settle problems outside the court with relatives, it is better because it is quicker – the court takes a long time and you have to pay money.'[18]

Criticisms and caution around the use of courts further contributed to the construction of dichotomies between state and society, *hakuma* and 'home'. One elderly man in Rumbek declared that it was 'shameful' to take petty or family disputes to court. He elaborated this in terms of the public nature of the court, arguing that settling disputes at home, outside the courts, was 'like the night', whereas the court was 'like daytime, where you can see everything': 'The court will make you talk openly whatever is in your heart, but it is better to maintain community things secretly.'[19] There were thus strong social pressures to maintain privacy and respectability and avoid the 'shame' of being seen publicly in court. The courts themselves added to this by occasionally mocking and humiliating individuals, and more often by ordering cases to be sent back to families to resolve themselves. In Yei this was formalised in the sometime English-language court records as sending 'to Home Affairs'. In theory marriages were supposed to be settled outside the court, in terms of the specific details and distributions of bridewealth, as one sub-chief near Yei explained: 'It is for the parents to complete the marriage; we are not involved... Government cannot enter there.'[20] Marriage was thus depicted as the preserve of a kind of 'home' sphere, closed off from government penetration. Yet of course marriage was also the most common source of court cases across all the research areas. Particularly in Rumbek, where cattle bridewealth produced the most complicated disputes, even the detailed allocation of shares in the payment or receipt of marriage cattle was sometimes done in court, and certainly many subsequent disputes over individual shares of marriage cattle were being settled in the chiefs' courts.

Such a gap between discourse and practice regarding the courts reflected efforts to preserve the authority of elders and senior people within families and neighbourhoods. The advice and settlement of elders and relatives was still widely held up as the best and first means of resolution, drawing on long-standing indigenous means of mediation and arbitration, such as the role of neutral families or maternal relatives. One elderly man near Juba explained the social pressure that could reinforce such advice:

> If a man is very angry, a member of his own family should not try to talk to him; instead a man from a different family should approach him to talk to him. If a lot of people have begged you to accept something, and if you refuse to listen to them, then they will turn their backs on you. Even if you happen to meet some misfortune, they will treat you as a foreigner; they will not stand with you. If

[16] Conversation with middle-aged male Mundari vegetable stall-owner, translated from Mundari, in Kworijik market, near Juba, 25 January 2006.

[17] Conversation with elderly Bari woman, translated from Bari, Juba na Bari village, Juba, 21 March 2006.

[18] Interview 46N/RC.

[19] Interview 1bN/RC.

[20] Interview 7N/YC.

> elders are the ones to talk to you and you do not listen to them, they will curse you; you have to accept their words.[21]

Similarly a woman near Rumbek emphasised the dangers of failing to listen to the elders, declaring that such a person would be ignored and left out of the community, 'exposed to any danger'; if he had a problem, people would say it was his own doing because he ignored advice, and in the end people would 'forget' him altogether.[22]

Women were the most likely to criticise going to court as a sign of hot temper and greed for money, and they often referred to Christian ideals of forgiveness to urge more peaceful means of resolution. As this suggests, the courts were seen as highly adversarial and combative arenas, in which social relations could easily be damaged. Those who went to court were hot-tempered – with 'bitter hearts' – and willing to risk breaking relations or even bringing potential harm to their families by, for example, swearing dangerous oaths in the court. Litigants in the heat of the argument were often willing to swear an oath by licking a spear or other means, and it was their relatives who would stop them, claiming that it might bring harm to their children or the family in general. The perceived dangers of the courts reflect the way in which they encouraged the claiming of individual rights, potentially at the expense of familial and social relations.

The attachment of ideas of shame to the courts may have also reflected a desire on the part of court members and advisors to keep knowledge of the courts esoteric and privileged, like other forms of specialist expertise claimed by elders and spiritual leaders. A group of women in a village on the edge of Juba, for example, recalled how in the 1950s and 1960s, Chief Andarea Farajalla had discouraged young women or girls from taking cases to court 'because standing in court might make them learn to be stubborn'.[23] Learning to be stubborn might be interpreted as learning how to speak defiantly in court and claim one's rights. Several people complained that young women were now too quick to go to court with their own petty quarrels and fights, when in the past they would have feared to. This was described in terms of a loss of discipline, but it also revealed a growing permeability of the boundary of the state, and a banalisation of knowledge of its institutions, laws and procedures.

GETTING YOUR RIGHT

Recent international reports and articles on the justice and legal systems in South Sudan have often associated customary law with communal, patriarchal rights rather than with individual rights.[24] Yet the chiefs' courts have actually been principal sites for the negotiation of individual rights and obligations in relation to familial ones, and for the claiming of one's own 'right'. The chiefs' courts in the towns were closely associated with – and helped to regulate – the urban economy and the use of money. In doing so, they upheld principles of private property, commercial exchange and individual rights, which people appropriated and employed in other contexts. The colonial courts had provided a new opportunity to argue the illegality of certain acts of appropriation that the

[21] Interview 49R/JC.

[22] Interview 72R/RC.

[23] Group discussion, translated from Bari or Arabic, Nyaing village, near Juba, 28 February 2006.

[24] E.g. Jeffrey L Deal, 'Torture by *cieng*: ethical theory meets social practice among the Dinka Agaar of South Sudan', *American Anthropologist* 112:4 (2010), pp. 563–75; Sudan Human Security Baseline Assessment (HSBA), *Women's Security and the Law in South Sudan* (Geneva: Small Arms Survey, 2012); Mennen, *Adapting Restorative Justice Principles*.

perpetrators might defend as a duty or obligation. Such disputes continued to be argued in the courts, reflecting enduring tension between individual and collective property rights and between private ownership and kinship obligations – tensions which had if anything increased as the opportunities to purchase private property had also expanded. This is why it made sense that courts were located increasingly in the towns where such opportunities were found.

One elderly man near Rumbek explained that people took cases to the courts when something was taken from them which was 'needed for survival' and hence could not 'be given up easily to somebody':

> If it is not sold nor given in marriage, but is just taken from you, then you must claim it back at all costs, even through the court. Even if your brother is very rich and takes something of yours, you will say 'I shall get it back peacefully or through the court'.

Yet he added that a generous man might simply accept that his property had been taken, saying 'this is my brother; there is no need for us to quarrel for nothing: let him keep it'.[25] While both courses of action were entirely understandable and appropriate to this man, it is clear that going to the court was ultimately an individualistic act.

It was by no means predictable to an outside observer which or whose version of rights would actually be upheld in any individual court case. In general the courts promoted the institution of bridewealth and recognised the rights it conveyed, but this still left room for considerable debate, for example over marital duties and obligations. Failure to pay bridewealth could thus be cited by women to successfully argue the failure of their husbands to fulfil their wider duties to their wives – while women were likely to be criticised in such cases for having gone to a man without bridewealth, the real fault was commonly seen to lie with the husband. More generally, the courts were receptive to women's complaints against their husbands for failing to provide adequately for them or to handle their family responsibility and manage multiple wives fairly. In all the court records, there were many decisions ordering men to pay 'feeding money' to their wives. Women's property rights are commonly seen to be denied by customary law in South Sudan,[26] but women too were using the courts to debate issues of family and individual rights in property.

A woman might also claim the right to divorce her husband independently of her family's agreement if he had failed to pay bridewealth.[27] The courts had become established as the only source of legal divorce, even though the original marriages did not require such official registration. In Rumbek the Regional Town Court was known to be the source of divorce certificates.

> If there are marital problems, we first try to settle outside with both families. Then if necessary you can go to the Executive Chief, or if he fails, then to the Regional Court. The Regional Court has the right to make 'separation' with a 'document' [English words] and they will see how many children are there. Each child is equivalent to five cows, so not all of the dowry may be repaid. The relations between the families remain because of the children; the separation is only between the husband and wife.[28]

[25] Interview 71R/RC.

[26] E.g. Large, 'Local governance', p. 15; HSBA, *Women's Security*, p. 6.

[27] Court cases observed in Rumbek Regional Town Court, 13 November 2006.

[28] Interview 1bN/RC.

The court procedures in these and other cases encouraged the articulation of individual rights: a plaintiff and defendant had always to be recorded; case observation and court records suggested that there were rarely more than one or two plaintiffs and defendants. Other relatives and parties to a case might be present as witnesses, but someone had to be nominated to argue the case. The selection of such a person recognised their own ability and maturity and their knowledge of court procedures, but it was likely to also indicate their own particular interest in a case. For example one of my research assistants in Rumbek was pursuing a case concerning the bridewealth of his female cousin: he was proud that the family considered him 'responsible' enough to lead the litigation; at the same time it was clear that he had the most pressing interest in the case since his own capacity to marry depended on receiving his cousin's bridewealth.

Even in the most complicated cases involving different extended families, individual rights were recognised. A case in Rumbek involving elopement led to a dispute as to who should contribute to the court-enforced marriage payment; the family produced a detailed breakdown of individual contributors (in English), which was deposited in the chief's court records. Their document added that if anybody refused to pay, 'he should clarify before the court', but acknowledged his right to refuse because it was not the turn of the offending young man to marry yet: 'Anybody's cows should not be touched without any reason', underscoring individual property rights in the midst of a collective family liability.[29]

Debates over rights and obligations were particularly complex in the context of cattle-owning societies. Examples from the Rumbek courts in 2006 included a man whose relative committed adultery and then took a cow from him to pay the resulting compensation; the man went to the police 'because it is a criminal case', accusing his relative of theft because relatives are not obliged to contribute to adultery payments as they would to bridewealth or bloodwealth payments. No doubt his relative would have argued otherwise, perhaps by reference to some previous assistance he had given the plaintiff; certainly he would deny that taking the cow was theft. In another case, also at the County Court, a man working in the town had put fifteen cows in the care of someone else, probably a relative, in the cattle camp, a common practice of 'townese'. When he found out that some of these cows had been taken by the people who were supposed to be looking after them, he 'rushed to the police' and the case went to the Rumbek Town Payam Court: 'The accused denied it and we were all sent to Mapel to the spear-master there to take an oath: they were found guilty and told to return the cows and pay fine to court, but they have appealed to county court.'[30]

In another example of how multiple competing rights intersected in the courts, a divorce case was brought by a woman to the Rumbek Regional Town Court. She admitted committing adultery and her husband was willing to divorce her. But this time it was his mother who disputed the divorce, explaining that it was she who had married that wife for her dead husband, and arguing that they needed continuing procreation in the name of the deceased. Another case from the same court in 2006 concerned the elopement of a girl; as the plaintiff declared, 'girls are the source of wealth'. The defendant admitted taking the girl but being unable to marry her, and the case became a dispute within his family over his right to a share of family cattle for his own marriage. His paternal uncles claimed they couldn't help him, particularly as he was also trying to marry another girl from a wealthy family who needed high bridewealth. The

29 Enclosure in Amothnhom Regional Court register book, Rumbek, dated 24 April 2006.

30 Interview 46N/RC.

man's sister then spoke up for him, accusing their uncles of mistreatment because their father had died:

> What our uncle said is wrong, because their sons had expensive marriages and when it comes to my brother they want to have a lesser marriage. Now is it because of the death of our father? If not, let them marry these two girls for my brother. I and my sisters have been married by rich families whereby each of us brought one hundred cows as bridewealth, and they have consumed it all on their different businesses. So if possible, Court, let these two girls be married for my brother to be equivalent to their sons' marriages.[31]

The court ordered the family to go away and arrange the marriage of at least one of the girls for the defendant. As ever, young men who were junior in kinship structures used elopement and resulting court cases to assert their right to marry and compel relatives to pay for their marriage outside the normal order. Such people were making creative use of multiple resources and ideas of law to seek guarantees of their rights.

PAPER GUARANTEES: BUREAUCRATIC KNOWLEDGE AND THE COURTS

Signs of the bureaucratic and regulatory orders of the state had always been conspicuous in the chief's courts, demonstrating their close links to state justice and police power. But bureaucratic orders had often been unstable, so that it was difficult to predict whether official papers, letters and records, bureaucratic identifiers, monetary transactions and the offices of police and security forces represented 'threat or guarantee'.[32] Yet what was striking throughout the research for this book was the extent to which people nevertheless prevailed upon the state through the courts to guarantee their rights and property even though they had more often experienced the state as a threat to those rights. The means by which to claim the guarantee and avoid the threat was widely seen to be knowledge, in the form of literacy and experience of the ways of town and government. An elderly Dinka Malakiyan in Juba extolled the benefits of education, arguing that in his illiterate father's time, people could be tricked into putting their mark on papers that were actually 'making a noose for your own neck'.[33] Literacy was thus seen to mediate the line between threat and guarantee, enabling people to contract the perceived regulatory power of the state in protective ways.

Bureaucratic forms and records were prominent in all the courts in and around the towns, and, as we have seen, they helped to differentiate formal and public arenas of justice and dispute resolution from informal ones, although the written record was creeping into the latter too. Even if chiefs were not themselves literate, they had court clerks who recorded cases, processed police forms and letters and produced receipts, warrants and summonses. Many literate chiefs handled some or all of this paperwork themselves, and took considerable pride in keeping their court registers (*Fig. 10.1*). Often the greatest symbol of chiefs' status and link to the state was their court ink stamp. A chief in Juba held up his court stamp on more than one occasion to tell me that 'this is what makes you a chief', or 'this is what brings all the villages together under this court'. In Yei, when it was decided to remove one elderly SPLA-appointed sub-chief, the

[31] Court cases observed in Rumbek Regional Town Court, 21 and 23 November 2006.

[32] Cf. Poole, 'Between threat and guarantee'.

[33] Interview 11N/JC.

Fig. 10.1 Amothnhom Regional Court, Rumbek, 2006: Court President Chief Madol Mathok Agolder writing court records; other court members to the left, and advisory elder seated in front of bicycle. (Photograph © Cherry Leonardi)

boma chief emphasised the necessity of retrieving his court stamp from him. A common complaint or request by chiefs was for official forms on which to write summonses or warrants. The signs of bureaucratic officialdom were thus seen to be central to the authority of the courts.

Hutchinson's account of Nuer communities in the 1980s suggests that people generally felt a sense of vulnerability in relation to the 'hidden powers' of paper, from which most were excluded.[34] Twenty years later in different research areas, the Arabic word for paper, *waraga*, was certainly heard frequently in the courts. But it was used not simply to mean 'paper', but to mean specific official documents; it was the power of the producers and executors of these papers that mattered, not the medium in itself. While in any bureaucracy papers might be fetishised, court documents were also valued for very practical reasons, as one litigant in Rumbek explained:

> All courts record cases. It is good when things are written down because a case may be settled and then ten years later someone brings it up in a different court and denies the earlier agreement. So then you can bring the original receipt and the chiefs in the new court will bring the original court records to see if it is true. So writing cases prevents later problems.[35]

This is a clear illustration of the idea that written records brought lasting guarantees of rights: 'If a case is not written down, it is like it is not seen, because it has no number, so if there is any appeal later and the Appeal Court asks for the

[34] Hutchinson, *Nuer Dilemmas*, pp. 270–88.

[35] Interview 46N/RC.

papers, if they are not there, the case is not seen.'[36] Government bureaucracy and judicial proceedings had encouraged the idea that human witnesses might be less reliable or enduring than documentary evidence, which is why people often held up papers and records as more reliable guarantees. Yet the flimsiness and ephemerality of paper as a medium for such guarantees had also been only too evident, not least in the common stories of school books and court records being literally smoked by soldiers during the war. In many other contexts too, people were disappointed by the vagaries of bureaucratic orders. Court records might consist of mounds of loose papers mouldering and fluttering in corners of crumbling town court buildings. Often litigants waited in diminishing hope while clerks rifled through piles and pages in unsuccessful search of their case history. Yet at other times the chief was able to hold up a series of correspondence from other chiefs or from the police as decisive evidence in a case. Papers, forms and stamps could send people to prison, seize their property or sever their marriages, often without their subjects being able to read or understand their contents.

Litigants dealt with the unpredictability of bureaucratic officialdom by seeking the assistance of literate friends or relatives to help their case, and illiterate chiefs similarly turned to literate young men to assist in the absence of a clerk. But it was not just literacy that was seen as an asset; people also sought knowledge of systems, procedures and laws. Chiefs in the towns, to whose courts the police sent cases, referred constantly to the section numbers in penal codes, which had changed at least once in the last decade as new codes were introduced by the SPLM or GoSS. Litigants were often familiar with the penalties for particular offences, as well as with the official bridewealth amounts in the courts. Virtually everybody I spoke to also expressed a confident knowledge of the local court hierarchy, a sense of the corresponding scale of case types, and ideas of which 'criminal' cases should be reported directly to the police: 'You know which courts to go to according to how small or big the matter is, and because you know the courts for each section: the executive chief, paramount chief and *payam* judge.'[37] As one headman emphasised, 'Each person, chief, sub-chief, gives fines according to his powers. The chief is for the *payam* and the sub-chief works in the *boma*; it goes in stages, not randomly.'[38]

But certain courts also gained a reputation for particularly good judgments and attracted large numbers of cases, suggesting that forum shopping was subverting the official hierarchical and appellate court system. People might even go directly to higher courts like the county magistrates; there was something of a gambling mentality that the higher the court fee, the higher the potential reward, as well as a desire to conduct the case in the most prestigious or authoritative court. In the towns, especially the rapidly expanding capital, Juba, the chiefs' courts heard cases from a variety of ethnic groups; one lowly headman in an IDP camp, for example, gained a reputation for good judgment and frequent floggings in his court, and so attracted cases from other displaced and urban communities.

The popularity of flogging as a punishment for sexual offences or petty crimes in Juba might appear to reflect the impact of Sudanese penal codes in a town that remained in the hands of the Khartoum government. But people seemed to particularly welcome the public, visible exercise of disciplinary power in urban contexts where many also perceived property and marital conventions to be under greatest threat. After the death of the long-serving chief

36 Interview 14N/RC.

37 Interview 46N/RC.

38 Interview 20R/YC.

Fig. 10.2 Kator 'B' Chiefs' Court, Juba, 2006, held in the original late-colonial courthouse. (Photograph © Cherry Leonardi)

Andarea Farajalla in the late 1970s, Huby was told that the 'late chief was much respected by the Bari for his strict attempts to prevent adultery and pre-marital relations resulting in illegitimate children'.[39] The building in which his court was held has remained the most prominent chiefs' court in Juba, and retained the symbols of punitive justice on its walls (*Fig. 10.2*).

However, the chiefs continued to distance themselves personally from such punitive justice, reflecting an enduring desire to abstract and depersonalise the use of force. A recent report highlighted the deliberate recourse to a policeman to administer lashes in a Juba chiefs' courts: 'It was said that it was crucial that a police officer carried out the sentence and did so in uniform because then the execution of the sentence assumed legality, appeared impersonal, and looked "official".'[40] This demand for the 'officiality' and neutral detachment of state law and order was also apparent in the increasing recourse directly to the state police, despite parallel criticism and fear of police abuses and corruption.[41] People living in the towns in the interim period frequently asserted that they would take cases to the police in the first instance, and the police were working closely with the chiefs and bringing cases to their courts. One middle-aged woman near Rumbek declared that 'the police and the chief have co-existed since the world came into being', and emphasised the vital role of police force when there was any fighting: 'If the chief goes to the fighting place first, he may

[39] Huby, 'Big men', p. 78.

[40] Scheye and Baker, 'The multi-layered approach', p. 19.

[41] Leonardi et al, *Local Justice*; Alfred Sebit Lokuji, Abraham Sewonet Abatneh and Chaplain Kenyi Wani, *Police Reform in Southern Sudan* (Ottawa, Khartoum, 2009).

be beaten or killed immediately, but the police come with guns; if you insist on fighting when the police are there, they may shoot you.'[42]

The increasing involvement in police procedures also imposed or brought access (depending on one's perspective) to further resources of bureaucracy and officialdom. In particular any cases involving personal injury were sent to the hospital to have the police form 'No. 8' completed by a medical authority. This form had become crucial in obtaining compensation according to the number of days of treatment/rest awarded, and so even relatively minor injuries or bruises were reported to police and hospital, largely by people living within reach of these urban institutions. Some women in particular pursued this avenue if beaten by their husbands or other women. People complained about the cost of this and other police forms – these were further monetised transactions – and a recent report on gender-based violence criticised the practice as a potential deterrent and obstacle for women bringing cases against abusive husbands or rapists.[43] But other women seemed to see Form 8 as an additional bureaucratic resource with which to strengthen their case.

As well as resources of police and hospitals, people sought to demonstrate their knowledge of laws, rights and government in multiple ways. Women in particular drew on both old and new concepts of their rights, often to argue for divorce or to demand better treatment from their husbands. The testimonies they gave in court were often very long, and followed a standard narrative format, including the detailed background context for the dispute. As Moore puts it, '[t]he law used the performative power of words quite magically',[44] but this was something that litigants had appropriated and deployed. Even women who might appear shy and reticent until called upon to speak would launch into vociferous and articulate performances of their narratives.

The men and women who most often deployed in court their literacy, language and wider experiences were those who were town-dwelling, often young, and usually returnees from displacement or refugee camps. They were viewed with disapproval by others as being too quick to 'rush' to court to air in public minor quarrels, jealousies and fights that should be kept private, but they demonstrated that the courts were arenas for debate and for contesting values and logics. The rights-based campaigns by international and national organisations had provided further ammunition with which to criticise and challenge the judicial authorities.

Two letters to different courts illustrate the way in which people might articulate their rights and expectations in writing to strengthen their cases. One young woman had employed a friend or relative to write a letter which was passed from her headman to her sub-chief and eventually to Yei Payam Court, which sent the case to the Yei Boma Court. The letter was written in English, in neat handwriting with important phrases highlighted by quotation marks and underlining. She complained firstly that her husband was not working or providing for her and their children; for the past five months 'no assistance, even a coin for soap or salt'. Secondly, she complained of his dishonesty and his frequent threats and violence towards her, and she made explicit her demand for a 'guarantee': 'The 12 years up to now, I couldn't get his reality and Guarantee of handling a firmly and safe family with him'. Finally she drew attention to the man's failure to pay bridewealth: 'since 94 he didn't do something good to my parents'. She demanded a 'divorce letter', and ended her own letter with stylistic formalities strikingly similar to those employed in the appeal letters of colonial

42 Interview 72R/RC.

43 Mennen, *Adapting Restorative Justice Principles*, p. 45.

44 Moore, 'Treating law as knowledge', p. 39.

government employees: 'With sincerelity[*sic*], hornour[*sic*] and respect, your highly consideration will be highly approcaited [*sic*]. I don't want him, "To be my husband". Yours sincerely...'. The letter received the appropriate stamps from the various courts through which it was passed, and ultimately the Boma Court granted the divorce. With this confirmation of the efficacy of writing, the woman subsequently enrolled in the girls' school in Yei, where she was still studying in 2009.

The second letter was typed in English, this time with the support of someone in the county social welfare department, again from a woman demanding a divorce but this time addressed to the Central Equatoria State judiciary, as an appeal. It was even more formal, laying out the 'complainant' and 'accused', and then a numbered list of grounds for divorce in highly legalistic language: 'abandonment', 'false accusation based on suspicions', 'violent assault', 'confiscation of shared family assets and denial of my basic rights to ownership of assets that have been jointly acquired by both'. To strengthen these assertions of her rights, the letter listed items from the bill of rights in the state Interim Constitution of 2005,[45] including equality before the law and the rights of women to property and protection from violence, and even the rights of the child. It then listed in detail the 'properties or assets that we acquired together during our marriage life', down to plastic plates and cups, plus house rental income and cash deposited 'with a man called Mzee' in Moyo, across the border in Uganda. This woman had run a business with her husband, including a bar and accommodation, but had been denied any share in it when the marriage broke down. She went to a series of chiefs' and magistrate's courts but each tried to dismiss the case to be settled by the family; she claimed her husband was influencing a chief and a magistrate because he knew or was related to them. Eventually she was advised to appeal to the state high court, but she could not afford to travel to the state capital of Juba. It is not known if she ever pursued the case further, but in early 2010 she was hoping that she might get help from 'a new human rights organisation' that she had been told of by 'the person of gender in the county'.

The case reveals the obstacles and frustrations experienced by many people in the justice system. But it also shows how litigants seized on potential resources, particularly if they were as well-connected and experienced as this businesswoman. While most of her letter detailed her complaints in terms of legal codes and the bill of rights, she also complained of the failure of her husband's family to support the marriage, revealing the multiple sets of moral and legal principles to which such people appeal. Litigants with less bureaucratic and legal support than that received by this woman employed what signs and resources they could – another woman in the Yei Boma Court defending herself against a charge of assault and insult by her co-wife showed off her status as a businesswoman and independent earner, including by her dress style, by dropping frequent English words into her vernacular speeches and by trying to pay her case fees in US dollars. The chief ordered her to pay compensation for the injury since her co-wife had a Form 8 as evidence, but also criticised their husband for failing in his 'home administration'. Afterwards the chief complained about troublesome 'town women'. But in another case in this court involving an older, well-known and much-respected local businesswoman who had purchased land without permission of chiefs and local government, the same chief told her 'you are a town person and supposed to know better'. This is the paradox – urbanisation and the opening up of access to the state had enabled ever more people to claim or be seen to have knowledge of government laws, institutions and procedures, and yet the chiefs and other senior men who claimed special expertise in this area bemoaned this banalisation of such

[45] Last accessed 4 February 2013 at www.unhcr.org/refworld/docid/4ba74c4a2.html.

knowledge for undermining their control and discipline over 'townese'. Partly for this reason, chiefs and elders were constantly reasserting their claim to privileged knowledge of tradition, history and custom, alongside their knowledge of government, since the former was less easily claimed by the younger people of the towns.

However, a case in the Yei Boma Court in 2005 revealed the kind of debates that could also go on around tradition and innovation. The defendant had failed to agree and pay proper bridewealth to his wife's family, and her brother had opened the case. The court told the plaintiff, 'You want your rights but a court cannot facilitate payment of brideprice. The best place is at home: you need the two families to settle this.' The plaintiff and his relatives complained bitterly to the court that it was being too lenient on the defendant and not 'following Kakwa ways'. The chief responded that 'things have changed recently; we have gone back to the old ways', whereby a man was not to be punished immediately on his first failure to meet his in-laws and pay bridewealth – a neat summation of how tradition might be invoked to legitimate innovation. In arguing over rights and liabilities, people thus appealed variously to notions of tradition and established local practice, and to national or even international notions of legal rights.

DISCIPLINE AND ORDER: FAILING SYSTEMS?

When ordinary people analysed the courts, they tended to attribute their problems and failings to changes wrought by or during the second civil war. Both the SPLM/A and the Sudan Government made changes to the court system and legal codes, and under their wartime administrations the numbers and kinds of 'court' had often proliferated. The result was seen to be greater confusion and competition – the systems had become harder to discern and understand. Further, the broader effects of war were seen to have undermined the power of courts and increased the likelihood of conflict and transgression of laws of marriage and property. Yet the paradox was that the courts of chiefs and government judges and the police in the towns were also widely acknowledged to be frequented by more people than ever before. Most importantly, criticisms of corruption or of the breakdown of systems represented a powerful popular discourse in support of the regularising orders and bureaucratic ideals of the state.

There were frequent complaints that 'the system' was not working as it should or as it used to, and that it had been confused and corrupted by lack of enforcement of hierarchies, proper procedures and court orders, and by bribery, deliberate delays and favouritism. Even after 2005, the behaviour of soldiers and the limited capacity of any court to bring powerful officers to justice contributed to an enduring perception that the government no longer respected the property and other rights of civilians. This was actually a powerful normative discourse about the duty of government to recognise such rights. There were also complaints in Juba that the Khartoum government had imposed *shari'a* law in cases of adultery or defilement, resulting in fines but no compensation payments – again a perceived failure to recognise the rights of husbands and parents.

Chief and elders complained that the hierarchical court structure was no longer being followed, and associated this with a wider breakdown of order. They often looked back nostalgically to the colonial era as a time of regularity and order. One chief near Yei recalled how fighting between youth from different clans used to be handled:

> People used spears and arrows. Chief Jebedayo would come from the town in a car with police to bring the wounded and fighters. Then the police would take them to hospital (and get the medical forms from the doctor) or to prison, and then take them with their 'statement' [English word] and forms to the judge, who would either send them to the A or B [chiefs'] court, or handle the case himself. The headmen would also come to the court. Those who started the fight would be charged.

But now, he added, such systems had broken down: 'now someone just decides to go to any court'.[46] Elders often recounted the predictable, regularised ways in which the British administrators supposedly handled conflicts, by arresting people only when they fought for a second time, and then only punishing the aggressor.[47] One elder in Rumbek blamed the supposed breakdown of systems to protect property rights on previous 'Arab' governments:

> Since 1955 the problem has remained like this. If someone steals your cows, you have to decide whether to fight and die, or go to the government, but it has become more common to fight and die. The Arabs created more judges and demanded a lot of money. Before the Arabs, the chiefs were the ones responsible for the community and all the cows, and problems were to be settled outside by them rather than in government courts. But the Arabs came and put themselves directly over people, so that they have to go to government courts. The Arab courts caused complaints, but there was nowhere to complain because there were Arabs in all the offices. The British had proper procedures; there was a book called 'Sixty eight' with all the numbers and fines, and without it no one could make judgement. But the Arabs just created their own judgements without a book.[48]

The failings of the judicial system were particularly debated in areas like Rumbek, where local and regional conflicts between young men of different sections were continuing or intensifying after 2005. Such conflicts were frequently attributed to the proliferation of small arms in the region,[49] although local people elaborated this problem to blame politicians and military officers for allegedly interfering in the conflicts and supplying weapons for their own profit. But others also highlighted the failure to achieve conflict resolution through the courts, for a number of reasons. The judiciary courts that heard the homicide cases resulting from fighting were accused of corruption and deliberate delaying of hearings. They were also seen to prioritise the extractive aspect of court penalties, the fees and fines, rather than the execution of compensation awards, so that the value of the lives lost could only be reclaimed by revenge and further raiding. But above all, many people, including the chiefs themselves, were complaining that the chiefs had become ineffective in preventing or resolving fights because they were no longer effectively backed up by military and police power; instead the latter were said to release prisoners and to interfere in court cases.

The increasing appropriation of government office by South Sudanese, together with the effects of decentralisation policies, increased the likelihood of officials being employed in their home state or county, which made it more difficult for them to appear as neutral agents. Gordon and Meggit examine similar dynamics in their study of Papua New Guinea, where new indigenous

[46] Interview 47N/YC.

[47] Interview 65R/RC.

[48] Interview 1bN/RC.

[49] Richard Garfield, *Violence and Victimization in South Sudan: Lakes State in the post-CPA period* (Geneva, 2007).

officials in the 1970s tasked with preventing local conflicts lacked not only the arbitrary powers of their expatriate colonial predecessors, but also the latter's 'appearance of power and distance'. As Enga people sought to appropriate the government, it became drawn into local political competition and vulnerable to manipulation by their own 'Big Men'.[50] Similarly in interim-period Southern Sudan, there was concern that the state was no longer an impersonal, alien government, and this created ambiguity as well as a sense of victory at having 'captured' the state.[51] The capacity to enforce quick decisions and the power of 'officiality' was seen to have been eroded as the state had been permeated by local political interests. Of course, as earlier chapters showed, state agents had always interfered in local politics. But the nostalgia and idealisation of a neutral state abiding by laws and regulations represented the appropriation of the state's own legal norms – and increasingly also wider international legal norms – as a means of protesting arbitrary state practices.[52] People were under little illusion that the law could actually be enforced to combat extra-legal practices by state agents and military personnel. But even the discursive use of legalism was important in producing the idea of the state and in legitimising state law, state institutions and state regulation.

But it is also significant that people did not necessarily see the law as something derived or appropriated entirely from the state. The ideal of neutrality and detached mediation had been an aspect of indigenous political culture even before the arrival of the state, as Johnson argues.[53] The law was seen as the product of meetings and bureaucratised encounters between the state and the chiefs and elders. Laws were 'made', not imposed. Even when people protested certain laws employed by government judges, such as imprisonment for statutory rape, they were reinforcing the sense that there *should* be harmony and compatibility of legal norms between state and people. Many people also praised the flexibility of the oral proceedings in the chiefs' courts, and the attention to the detailed oral narratives of the litigants, which enabled the right judgments to be reached and the individual context of each case to be taken into account in sentencing.[54]

The demand for regulatory orders nevertheless led some people – particularly younger, literate townspeople – to promote the recording in written form of customary law, in order that chiefs' decisions might be bound more by regulations and that litigants might be able to know the laws themselves. This idea connected with the wider political debate over ethnicity, community and decentralisation.[55] But at the local level, it revealed the sense that bureaucratic regulation might be a means by which ordinary people, even the 'weak', might exert control over the powerful by knowing the law and the system – and indeed the price.

50 Gordon and Meggit, *Law and Order*, p. 11, as summarised by Sally E Merry, 'Law and Colonialism: review essay', *Law and Society Review* 25:4 (1991), p. 907.

51 Cf. Mawson, 'The Triumph of Life', for an earlier instance of this in the post-1972 period.

52 Cf. Eckert, 'From subjects to citizens'.

53 Johnson, 'Judicial regulation'.

54 Leonardi et al, *Local Justice*, pp. 73–82.

55 See Leonardi et al, *Local Justice*; and Cherry Leonardi, Deborah Isser, Leben Moro and Martina Santschi, 'The politics of customary law ascertainment in South Sudan', *Journal of Legal Pluralism and Unofficial Law* 63 (2011), pp. 111–42.

CONCLUSION

> There used to be centres like Rumbek Town from where laws were issued and checked out. That beautiful system was affected during the war.[56]

In the towns and surrounding areas by the time of the CPA, nearly everyone seemed to have a strong idea as to what the 'system' and the 'laws' were and should be. There was a great demand for state justice and bureaucratic guarantees. People were not under any illusions: everyone also knew that such guarantees were only ever as ephemeral as the paper they were written upon, and that papers could as easily be turned into the smoke of soldiers as into property rights and protection. But the courts were a particular interface with state power, in which there appeared to be more possibility than ever to appeal to regulation and order and to predict a positive outcome to bureaucratic and formal procedures.

People only approached this interface for specific purposes, when they were willing to gamble resources and relations for material gain and recognition of rights and status. Most social and economic life of course went on away from the courts, and many people still relied on alternative forms of guarantee and protection. Many people asserted that spiritual leaders remained more important than chiefs, who were needed only for specific functions: 'The chiefs are there to say who is right or not right; they are for if something is stolen, or someone is insulted, then you go to court.' This woman mimed writing with a pen while saying this, demonstrating the continuing association of the chiefs' courts with writing and bureaucracy.[57]

Yet it would be a mistake to dismiss the chiefs and their courts as irrelevant to a sense of community cohesion and health, as a leading Rumbek chief declared:

> Long ago we used to be together with the spear-master, and when the government came, we had a chief to put us together. These are the things that bring us together to be one. What brings us together is the *luak* [sacred cattle-byre of the spear-masters] and the court.[58]

A man from a related section reiterated the notion that chiefs and police were vital to the ordering of society:

> It would be bad if we had no chiefs because everything would be chaotic and police would not be able to manage. If there is fighting now, you can identify which section and chief a killer is from and so the police can trace them, but otherwise there would just be random fighting.[59]

Just as calves were tethered to keep them together, people needed to be tied to chiefs to prevent scattering and chaos. Such idealised visions of order and community were, as ever, both contested and ignored by people as they sought to make their livings, homes, families and communities in towns, villages and cattle camps, across state borders and ethnic boundaries, and by harnessing whatever means they could of securing safety and property from or against the state itself. But the idea of the state was nevertheless being produced through the appropriation of state legal norms and the demand for institutions and 'officiality' in the courts.

56 Recommendations of Group 3, in PASS, 'Traditional Leaders Conference, Lakes State, Southern Sudan, Rumbek, 12–15 March 2007'; copy in author's possession.

57 Interview 72R/RC.

58 Interview 54R/RC.

59 Interview 46N/RC.

Conclusion

In 1997, Charles Tripp remarked on the 'peculiar' resilience of Sudanese state structures, despite the crisis of the Sudanese state project and its fundamental imbalances between centre and periphery. His cautious prediction that the 'deep frustration' of 'those who have historically been excluded' would lead to the breakup of the territorial state has proven accurate.[1] The leaders of the new Republic of South Sudan – and many of their international supporters and donors – have presented the successful revolt of this former marginal region as a fundamental departure from the history of the 'Old Sudan', establishing a *tabula rasa* for new state-building efforts. But the South Sudanese government nevertheless remains deeply aware of its historical heritage. As its own Vice-President warned in 2010, the new government has emerged out of the very centralising, authoritarian political culture against which the liberation struggle was fought.[2]

The analyses of the structural inequalities in the Sudanese political economy on which Tripp was reflecting have been a vital corrective to simplistic assumptions of primordial racial or religious division as the cause of Sudan's conflicts.[3] But the spatial centre-periphery paradigm may in turn simplify and obscure the local patterns of state formation on which this book has focused. More widely, scholars have increasingly challenged any assumption that the margins of states are peripheral to state formation, as Reid has recently argued: the violent 'fault lines and frontier zones' of northeast Africa have instead 'defined the very nature of the states'.[4] This book has also argued for the 'fertility of the frontier' in South Sudan. But rather than focusing on broad frontier zones between states or peoples, the book has traced the formation of an internal frontier zone around the urban government centres. This is not simply a spatial, territorial zone, though it has centred on the towns; it is a multifaceted and mobile frontier, which has also been replicated and reproduced in institutions, practices, and discourse; in markets and courts, along the roads and in the centres of chiefdoms.

For those who are seeking to create a nation-state in contemporary South Sudan, this book perhaps offers encouragement, by demonstrating the roots and

1 Charles Tripp, 'Review – Sudan: state and elite', *Africa* 67, 1 (1997), p. 172.

2 Mabior Philip, 'Decentralized justice is lucrative, says Machar', *The Citizen* 23 October 2010, Juba, pp. 1–2.

3 Woodward, *Sudan 1898–1989*; Johnson, *Root Causes*; Tim Niblock, *Class and Power in Sudan: the dynamics of Sudanese politics, 1898–1985* (Basingstoke, 1987).

4 Richard J. Reid, *Frontiers of Violence in North-East Africa: genealogies of conflict since c. 1800* (Oxford, 2011), pp. 20, 22. See also Vaughan, 'Negotiating the State'; Das and Poole, *Anthropology in the Margins*; Dereje Feyissa and Markus V. Hoehne (eds), *Borders & Borderlands as Resources in the Horn of Africa* (Woodbridge, 2010); Lotje A. De Vries, 'Facing Frontiers: everyday practice of state-building in South Sudan' (PhD, Wageningen University, 2012); Anne Walraet, 'Governance, violence and the struggle for economic regulation in South Sudan: the case of Budi County (Eastern Equatoria)', *Afrika Focus* 21:2 (2008), pp. 53–70; Nugent, *Smugglers, Secessionists*; McGregor, *Crossing the Zambezi*.

resilience of the idea of the state (and its law) and of local state institutions. The urban frontier has been a fertile site of state formation. But there is a warning here too, for it is upon this frontier that frustration bred violent rebellion, even if the rebellion was then transported to the borderlands and bush.[5] If the margins have mounted an invasion of the centre,[6] this has not been an advance on Khartoum but a capture – by negotiated settlement as well as by military action – of the urban state nodes, and of the existing state institutions within South Sudan. As such, it is an invasion with a long history and with deep roots in local relations with the state. Frontiers have formed and fluctuated around these state nodes over a century and a half, representing myriad small-scale invasions of the 'centre' from the rural margins.

The individuals drawn to the urban state frontier did not immediately or necessarily capture the institutions of the central state. But they learned and appropriated its languages and laws. Oral histories narrated by people living in and around South Sudanese towns in the early twenty-first century place great emphasis on the idea of a unitary law, which they identify as both the product and the means of dealing with government since the colonial period. Comaroff argues that the discourse of legality is indeed the distinguishing feature of the modern state: that it was above all the language of the law that 'held colonial states together'. The state exists then at *both* metropole and margin 'as a narrated and enacted description of order'. 'Legalese' has provided

> an ostensibly neutral medium for people of different cultural worlds, different social endowments, different material circumstances to enter into contractual relations, to transact commodities and to deal with their conflicts. In so doing it forged the impression of consonance amidst contrast: of the existence of universal standards which, like money, facilitated the negotiation of incommensurables across otherwise intransitive boundaries.[7]

The evidence presented in this book certainly supports this analysis: the legal and judicial resources of the state were sought out by South Sudanese from the earliest encounters with state forces; chiefs' courts have proven the most resilient and vital of local state institutions; and it appears to many people that 'the law is one'. The courts have facilitated transactions across boundaries, and the language of the law has enabled people to contract with government. Yet as Comaroff goes on to argue, 'the law was also mobilized to delineate the moral frontiers of civil society', to control and exclude.[8] For Mitchell, the distinctiveness of the modern state lies in this capacity to constitute an appearance of boundaries: to produce difference.[9] In the African context, Mamdani, like Comaroff, has argued forcefully that the result has been an enduring distinction between citizens of the metropole with individual legal rights, and the rural subjects collectivised as communal units and excluded from such rights.[10]

What then are we to make of the adoption of a discourse of legality in South Sudan? Where is the line between citizen and subject? Does it correspond to

[5] A point made even during the first war by Mading Deng: *Tradition and Modernization*, pp. 60–8.

[6] As Reid argues of the modern Eritrean and Tigrayan insurgencies: *Frontiers of Violence*, p. 250.

[7] John Comaroff, 'Governmentality, materiality, legality, modernity: on the colonial state in Africa', in Jan-Georg Deutsch, Peter Probst and Heike Schmidt (eds), *African Modernities: entangled meanings in current debate* (Oxford, 2002), pp. 126–7. See also David Scott, 'Colonial governmentality', *Social Text* 43 (1995), p. 208.

[8] Comaroff, 'Governmentality, materiality', p. 127.

[9] Mitchell, 'The limits of the state'.

 [10] Mamdani, *Citizen and Subject*; Comaroff, 'Governmentality, materiality', p. 129.

an urban-rural divide? Or to the unpredictable 'slippage' between threat and guarantee, represented by the legal and official documents of government bureaucracy?[11] Does the discourse of people living in and around the towns signify the hegemony of legalist state ideologies; the epitome of 'governmentality' – are they complicit in the modern state project: a direct antithesis to the art of not being governed?[12]

To address these questions, this book has sought to move beyond 'the dichotomy of either resistance or hegemonic submission', as Eckert urges.[13] As Mitchell emphasises:

> [J]ust as we must abandon the image of the state as a free-standing agent issuing orders, we need to question the traditional figure of resistance as a subject who stands *outside* the state and refuses its demands. Political subjects and their modes of resistance are formed as much *within* the organizational terrain we call the state, rather than in some wholly exterior social space.[14]

This is evident in the history of armed rebellion in South Sudan, instigated by state officers, government employees, soldiers, police and students; the leaders of 'civil society' have frequently sought to enter or capture the state rather than to oppose it.[15] But more importantly, resistance is also evident in the quotidian attempts to obtain rights and protection through state laws and regulatory orders. Eckert argues that the pursuit of rights and guarantees in urban India may have led people to 'a more active engagement with domination': to the appropriation and creative interpretation of state legal norms. The repertoire of 'weapons of the weak' identified by Scott[16] might thus paradoxically include the state law itself, deployed as a 'means of resistance', a 'legalism from below', to protest transgressions of the law by state agents. While citizens might not themselves obey state laws in other contexts – or behave 'as they ought', in Bentham's formulation[17] – they nevertheless further the hegemony of state law and the very 'idea of the state' through such protests: 'State legal norms thus become hegemonic by being used as a form of resistance against modes of governance that run counter to these norms.' But this is an active, creative process, not a state imposition.[18]

While Eckert presumes democratisation to have enabled this Indian 'legalism from below', in South Sudan similar discourses of citizen rights and state duties have emerged instead from a history of violence and state coercion. The first chiefs dealt with dangerous imperial and commercial forces, their contracts sealed by the return of captured women, the blood of severed hands, gifts of guns and the staking of flagpoles. Colonial chiefs exchanged coerced labour and taxes for state recognition and rewards. Later chiefs traded security information for government protection, or dealt in conscripts and food for rebel armies. Little wonder that people around Yei claim that their chiefship has been 'bought with blood'. Yet it is through this very history of capture and coercion that chiefship acquired its value, because the unequal contracts, bargains and exchanges

[11] As argued by Poole: 'Between threat and guarantee'.

[12] This latter phrase is of course Scott's: *The Art of Not Being Governed.*

[13] Eckert, 'From subjects to citizens', p. 67; Nugent, *Smugglers, Secessionists*, p. 274; Alexander, *The Unsettled Land*, p. 9.

[14] Mitchell, 'The limits of the state', p. 93.

[15] As Alexander also argues of Mozambique: 'The local state', p. 3.

[16] James C. Scott, *Weapons of the Weak: everyday forms of peasant resistance* (New Haven, CT, 1985).

[17] Jeremy Bentham, *A Fragment on Government* (1776), as quoted in Scott, 'Colonial governmentality', pp. 202–3.

[18] Eckert, 'From subjects to citizens', pp. 67–9.

brokered by the chiefs represented a means of ameliorating depredation and regulating state force. The language in which these deals were struck was the language of the law, the shared terms of a contract or the disciplinary rules of the military. Just as the law and order of the colonial state held the double meaning of regulation and restraint, guarantee and threat, so the attempt to contract the state implied both 'regularising one's dealings with it' *and* 'circumscribing its reach'.[19] When chiefs came to meet the government on the DC's verandah or at the military camp, they were simultaneously securing deals and keeping the state at a distance from rural property and people.

The complication of course is that even as people welcomed the ability of chiefship to secure spaces where 'the soldiers never go' and to negotiate regulation and protection from the state, they were nevertheless resisting any attempt to restrain them in a rural order of chiefly rule and communal labour. Chiefship was acquired and produced on the urban state frontier, but chiefs were never the exclusive gatekeepers to the towns and government. Whether entrepreneurial and adventurous, or destitute and desperate, young men and women found pathways out of chiefdoms to the opportunities of town life, trade, waged employment, schooling or soldiery. The urban frontier fluctuated and expanded, endlessly criss-crossed by these pathways, blurring any attempts to constitute clear boundaries between urban and rural, state and society. When the frontier was constricted – by periodic government efforts to police the edges of town, to evict 'squatters' and 'vagrants', or to repress political activism and educational opportunity – those who were excluded would forge new frontiers, whether of armed rebellion or migration abroad. But they have tended to take the state frontier with them, remaking its institutions in the bush or the camp.

Chiefs have been central to that remaking of the local state, not because they are, or have ever been, the sole interlocutors or authorities, but because chiefship is above all the institutionalised expression of the frontier itself. However much chiefdoms have been imagined by successive governments as the spheres of rural community and conservative traditional authority, in reality chiefship has been reinforced, paradoxically, by the very strategies people might have pursued to avoid its demands on their labour or its threat to their property. For the more that people sought the opportunities of the urban frontier, the more they also turned to the chiefs' courts to manage relations, exchanges and transactions across the overlapping, shifting frontiers between commodity and non-commodity status, between money and other forms of value, and between individual rights and property and the duties, debts and obligations of kinship and community. Chiefship has been constituted and has acquired its value primarily in a context of authoritarian government and very limited decentralisation of state resources or real power. It does not command age-old, automatic communal identification – far from it. But it originates on, and represents, the frontier of engagement with the state, the risky threshold on which people have sought to use state law and regulatory orders to protect their own rights and property. Chiefs are not a distinct category of spiritual or landowning authority; they are individuals, usually men, who claim that they or their bloodlines embody the art of knowing how to deal with government: knowledge acquired principally on the urban frontier.

I have described the urban and peri-urban research areas as a form of 'frontier', not because they mark the limits of state penetration, but because they have been the most productive site of new institutions and regulatory orders, forged out of the meeting of indigenous and state orders, and characterised by both replication and innovation. People came to the towns in a quest for knowledge and to 'collect regulations', as well as in pursuit of money and material resources; they were seeking new institutions of education, justice, employment and authority. Such new institutions have continued to emerge on the

[19] Rafael, *Contracting Colonialism*, p. 121.

urban frontier: youth associations, courts and committees of market traders, church councils, NGO offices and committees, and proliferating urban courts and town headmanships. The frontier is increasingly international, both in terms of its inhabitants and investors, and in terms of its expansion through refugee migrations into a global diasporic frontier, connected by internet, phones, international money transfers and air travel to the South Sudanese towns.

But as well as representing a zone of intense innovation and interaction, the urban frontier has also been characterised by 'replication', and it has been incorporated into local histories and geographies. 'Government found us here', as people nowadays like to emphasise – the towns were founded on the 'gift' of land by the existing inhabitants, cementing a contract in the very foundations of the government buildings. Local narratives in the research areas thus depict this as a 'conquest-by-invitation',[20] as key local interlocutors recognised the potential benefits of government and struck deals with the state forces to institute a new order of property rights and protection. When such people were appointed as chiefs, they were slotted alongside other kinds of authority: the chief of the government was labelled in parallel with the chief of the rain or the master of the fishing spear or the lord of the land. The *hakuma* was of course a very different phenomenon to the divinity that spiritual leaders mediated; government chiefs never acquired the moral authority of the latter. But people have nevertheless drawn parallels between these various 'offices', in terms of how their holders communicate with an abstract, external, potentially dangerous force, and make claims upon it through the exchange of resources for protection and aid.[21] All such mediation depends on claims to specialist expertise, in a continuing political economy of knowledge.

If the language of 'legalese' was the 'vernacular' of the colonial state, as Comaroff argues,[22] then it met with often complementary vernaculars on the ground in South Sudan. The chiefs' courts did not simply speak the language of the state, but rather a creolisation of state and vernacular discourses of law and order.[23] Indigenous judicial practices and cultures had already recognised the need for abstract, neutral and/or collective sources of arbitration and sanction, and individuals had approached foreign forces from the outset to seek settlement or aid in their disputes. The idea of the state as an external source of justice and enforcement is not then understood by my informants as an alien imposition, but as an important addition to pre-existing means of 'uncovering' individual rights and rightness. Perhaps we might discern a 'statism from below' equivalent to the 'folk nationalism' or 'folk socialism' described by Scott.[24] The law is not imposed by government, according to my informants, but 'brought out' or 'made' in meetings between government and chiefs: laws and institutions are thus seen to have been produced in *dialogue*.

Such dialogue was intensified in and around the towns. This book has not claimed that the research areas around three of the largest towns in South Sudan are typical of life and livelihoods across the country. But they represent one end

[20] Kopytoff, 'The internal African frontier', pp. 65–6.

[21] Chief Wol Athiang of the Pakkam Agar Dinka reportedly compared government to god [*miri ku nyalic*]: *Mamur* Rumbek, Ibrahim Bedri, to Governor Equatoria, 1 May 1936, SRO EP 66.E.1; while the widow of the Rumbek spear-master Makuer Gol, Ajuot Alok, was quoted as saying, 'the administrative chief is the tax-gatherer for Government, while the Beny bith is the tax-gatherer for God': Rumbek District Monthly Report February 1940, SRO EP 57.D.10.

[22] Comaroff, 'Governmentality, materiality', p. 126.

[23] Mading Deng makes similar arguments in *Tradition and Modernization*, pp. 69–116. The term 'creolisation' is also used by Willis in '*Hukm*: the creolisation'; and Peter Pels, 'Creolisation in secret: the birth of nationalism in late colonial Uluguru, Tanzania', *Africa* 72:1 (2002), pp. 1–28.

[24] Scott, *Weapons of the Weak*, p. 319.

of a spectrum of strategies for dealing with government and for pursuing rights and resources; and it is important to recognise that this is a spectrum, and not a dichotomy between citizens and subjects or urban and rural, let alone between modern and traditional. Media reports frequently depict South Sudanese as inherently conservative, wedded to an outdated cattle economy and age-old cultures.[25] Yet even in areas much further from the towns, individuals and community representatives have been engaging with government in multiple ways, just as they or their relatives have been pursuing varied careers and livelihoods away from the rural 'home'. Individuals from the pastoralist societies labelled by early political anthropologists as stateless anarchies now dominate the government of the new South Sudanese state. Hutchinson recorded the attempts of 'rural' Nuer in the 1980s to access the powers of government, and their negotiation of increasingly complex conversions between money and cattle, markets and marriage.[26] Recent inter-communal conflicts in supposedly 'remote' areas have revealed the webs of connections from internet commentators in the diaspora to the chiefs whose letters of grievance and complaint to the President are published online.[27] The historic 'shatter zones' and borderlands where people might have sought refuge from the state have become some of the most contested areas of contemporary Sudan and South Sudan, their populations frequently forced to flee armed conflict to refugee camps where state forms of regimentation and categorisation are more intense than anywhere.[28] As Scott emphasised, escaping the state has become virtually impossible in the context of modern technologies and economies.[29]

Yet this book has shown that technological and territorial factors alone do not explain the patterns of state formation or penetration in South Sudan. Formal or visible state control and service provision may have been largely restricted to urban nodes and largely failed so far to 'take the towns to the people', as John Garang had urged.[30] But the people have come to the towns, and they have then transported the state frontiers back with them into rural, local and familial settings. State penetration is not then simply a matter of the territorial reach of formal policing or infrastructural capacity; rather, as Boone argues, it is determined by local power relations and processes of institutionalisation.[31] Certain South Sudanese have been willing to cover long distances to 'come in to government'; the region has after all been characterised by high levels of mobility even before the displacement of recent wars.[32] Such people have appropriated the idea of the state and used state materials to rebuild institutions and reform regulatory orders, even while fighting and dismantling the state in the liberation struggle.[33]

[25] E.g. *The Economist*, 'On your tractor, if you can', 6 May 2010, Bor, *The Economist*, last accessed 26 January 2013 at: www.economist.com/node/16068960?story_id=16068960&reason=0.

[26] Hutchinson, *Nuer Dilemmas*.

[27] E.g. an 'Open letter from Lakes Chiefs to President Kiir', 5 Aug 2006, posted on *Gurtong* by Maker Costa in the USA on 20 Aug 2006, last accessed on 26 January 2013 at: www.gurtong.net/Forum/tabid/81/forumid/91/postid/46894/scope/posts/Default.aspx.

[28] James, *War and Survival*; Guma Kunda Komey, *Land, Governance, Conflict & the Nuba of Sudan* (Woodbridge, 2010). See also Dereje Feyissa, 'More state than the state? The Anywaa's call for the rigidification of the Ethio-Sudanese border', in Dereje and Hoehne, *Borders & Borderlands*, pp. 27–44.

[29] Scott, *The Art of Not Being Governed*, pp. 10–11.

[30] Quoted in Dean Diyan, 'In the South – all want pie but not enough to go around', *The Nation*, 27 April 2007.

[31] Boone, *Political Topographies*.

[32] In the 1955–56 national census, over 70 per cent of southerners were enumerated in localities other than those of their birth: Mills, 'The growth of Juba', p. 311.

[33] Scott also acknowledges the wide travel and appropriation of the 'symbolic commodities' of the state, far beyond the reach of 'hard' state power: *The Art of Not Being Governed*, p. 35.

The blurring and mobility of the urban frontier and the appropriation of state orders has not, however, been a straightforward story of positive relations or progress, either from the perspective of ordinary people or in the view of state agents. The uncertainty of any state-society boundary produces insecurities and confusions. Just as successive governments have longed to contain the masses in legible rural units of administration and community, so many ordinary people have wanted to restrict the state to its offices, barracks and roads, even if at other times they appeal to its laws and force. The formation of a new state 'in the bush' during the last war disturbed the pattern of town-based government, bringing state forces into village settings. The wartime governments also accelerated the multiplication of authority and administrative units, most apparent in the proliferation of courts and security forces with unclear state regulation or sanction.[34] Throughout the history of the state in South Sudan, individuals have claimed or impersonated government authority to demand and command.[35] Nowadays the waters are further muddied by the diffusion and banalisation of armed force: when so many have fought, or claim to have fought, in various armies, even uniforms and guns no longer demonstrate the clear 'link to the government' that colonial officials had once intended.

Such uncertainties produce a common urge to define and demarcate the line between state and non-state, which is often translated into attempts to police territorial boundaries around the 'nation-state' and its urban nodes. One manifestation of this is the intense dispute over land rights in the peri-urban areas, as the towns have expanded territorially in recent years. Such disputes bring to a head the broader, perennial tensions over individual citizenship and rights versus community recognition and rights; as Comaroff also argues, 'these two images of nationhood and political order are arraigned against each other more than ever'.[36] Autochthony or 'first-coming' is an increasingly exclusionary discourse of local history and genealogy, and an increasingly lucrative commodity for those using it to claim land rights and customary dues. The contractual and patrimonial idioms in which the history of chiefship is told exist in uneasy relationship to these patrilineal genealogies, ensuring that chiefs often retain a kind of 'junior' status in kinship structures.

Yet the uncertain authority of chiefs has always been a resource in itself for both chiefs and people, endlessly frustrating government officials who sought to use chiefs to execute orders. In recent years this is also apparent in government attempts to hold chiefs to account for sectional fighting; on the one hand chiefs claim to be the means of achieving peace and security, and distance themselves rhetorically from the 'government' and 'town' people whom they accuse of provoking the conflicts. But at the same time chiefs complain at their lack of authority over the militant 'youth', and their need for the backing of state force.[37] The uncertainty of chiefly authority thus leaves room for manoeuvre and for a gap between rhetoric and reality, just as does the lack of any clear line between state and society or town and country. Reports nowadays are frequently undecided as to whether chiefs are 'the sole authority' in the village, or whether their authority has been destroyed by wartime militarisation, just

[34] See e.g. Manyang Mayom, 'Lakes State caretaker closes down all illegal courts in Sudan's Rumbek state', *Sudan Tribune* 7 March 2010, last accessed 26 January 2013 at: www.sudantribune.com/Lakes-state-caretaker-closes-down,34344.

[35] E.g. Stigand, *Equatoria*, p. 88; Gessi, *Seven Years*, pp. 51–4.

[36] Comaroff, 'Governmentality, materiality', p. 131.

[37] E.g. Minutes of the meeting between Gok and Agar sections on 20 August 1984, Rumbek, and the meeting of Commissioner Lakes Province with Aliamtoc Chiefs on 3 August 1984, Bahr el Ghazal Province Archive, Wau, LP 66.B.1.

as colonial officials struggled to 'know where the power lies' among southern Sudanese communities. Even longer ago, an exasperated Samuel Baker realised the potential value in such uncertainties: 'This is the regular African diplomacy when work is required. The people say, "We must receive orders from our sheik". The sheik says, "I am willing, but my people will not obey me". It is this passive resistance that may ruin an expedition.'[38] This might appear to demonstrate the value of chiefship as an intermediary institution and as a means of resistance to the state. But this book has argued against the idea that chiefs are simply the intermediaries between distinct, antagonistic entities of state and society. For what is clear in this archetypal conversation is the power of *discourse*, and Baker's own uncertainty and scepticism as to the reality it perhaps belied. In many other contexts 'the people' would approach the state directly; there were myriad other conversations taking place between government and individuals, even in the 1870s. But in the context of dealing with state demands and requisitions, individuals realised the advantage in being categorised as 'the people', with a chief as broker. As an elder in Raja told a UNDP team in 2005, 'Without chiefs there would be no people; without people there would be no government.'[39] Of course, to complete the circle, without government there would be no chiefs of the government. But it is this claim to 'have the people' that gives the chiefs power in negotiating contracts with the state, while the uncertainty of their power simultaneously leaves room for manoeuvre and dissembling; there is no moral duty to obey the governmental demands imposed by chiefs, but there might be practical advantages in allowing the chiefs to negotiate these demands. For such reasons, people have colluded in imagining state and community dialectically, despite a simultaneous emphasis on the dialogical production of the law.

Chiefship has been the lens through which these imaginaries have most often been refracted, producing images of state and community that are at once distorted and yet useful. Administrators and external agents might choose to believe that 'the chief is the eye of the government', through which society can be seen by the state.[40] And people might view their chief as a 'person of government', whose table is a site on which to stake their claims to state resources and recognition of their rights. Of course everyone also knows that the lens distorts and blinkers, and that these visions fragment and fail. But like the 'African diplomacy' that Baker bemoaned and admired, there have always been contexts in which a dark glass, a partial recognition, is an advantage; and in which there is value in distancing 'state' from 'society'. Yet this imagined distance is simultaneously traversed and broken down by the multiple claims to 'membership' of the local state, and to knowledge of how the right system, 'the good order',[41] is supposed to work. Through such claims and ideals, and the local institutions in which they are voiced and recorded, the idea of the state continues to be constituted and shaped by South Sudanese. State structures may still be in the making, but the pioneers and inhabitants of the urban frontier recognise deep foundations in the ground which their ancestors gave to government, and upon which they have staked their claims on the state.

38 Baker, *Ismailia*, Vol. 2, p. 23.

39 Interview with an 'elder', Raja County, 2 February 2005, cited in Golooba-Mutebi and Adak Costa, 'Traditional Authorities', p. 8.

40 On the attempt to make society 'legible' to the state, see James Scott, *Seeing like a State: how certain schemes to improve the human condition have failed* (New Haven, 1998); Buur and Kyed, 'Traditional authority in Mozambique'.

 41 Eckert, 'From subjects to citizens', p. 45.

Interviews

NOTE ON INTERVIEW CITATIONS

Interviews are referenced with abbreviated codes in the footnotes.

Abbreviations take the following form:

E.g. Interview 23bR/JC:
23 = individual number of informant; b = second interview with same informant
R = recorded and transcribed interview; or N = interview notes, without recording
JC = location of interview: Juba County; RC = Rumbek County; YC = Yei County;
K = Khartoum

INTERVIEW ACKNOWLEDGEMENTS

It would be impossible to name everybody who contributed to this research, but I would like to thank the following for their most helpful interviews and conversations:

In Khartoum (2001–2), Barnaba Dumo Wani, Festo Limi Sominda, Francis Bassan, Gajuk Wurnyang Lupaya, Margaret Keji Loro, Paulino Wadn Lado, Peter Cirillo, Philip Yona Jambi, Rubena Lumaya Wani, Serefino Wani Swaka, Severino Mati, Simon Wani Ramba, and Venanzio Loro Lado; (2008) Jaafar K Juma and other members of the South Sudanese Malakiya/Nubi community in Khartoum.

In Yei (2004–7), Nimaya Guya, Peter Said, Molly Dudu, Lubari Ramba, James Remasu, Peter Aringu, Ismael Luate, Isaac Joja, Aggrey Wata, Elizabeth Lajiji, Lewe Aligo Mursale, Alemi Charles, Gordon Sworo, Morris Luate, Edward Wani, Monica Ide, Ananea Lawea, Alison Wani, Arkanjelo Soroba, Andarea Joja, Oliver Gala, Philip Lasuba, Santino Lasu, John Gale, Joyce Jamboro, Justin Joja, Joseph Kepa, Wilson Loruba, Alfred Lasuba, Eliaba Lumaya, Philip Aligo, James Yosea Ramadalla, Eunice Keji Oliver Geriwa, Stephen Milla, Gaytano Aligo, Amosa Ladu, Wilson Joja, Kalistu Kujo, Dickson Lenga Surur, Charles Lugala Beshir, Charles Taban Lupai, Justin Diko, Justin Modi, Moses Lubang, Joseph Wani Ida, Joshua Nyalimo Lomuyu, Alfred Kenyi, Moses Leju, Alex Aligo, and many others in Yei town and in Gimunu and Rwonyi clan areas, up to Mile 10 Juba road and Mile 6 Kaya road.

In Juba (2005–8), Hilary Tombe, Alfons Legge, Desiderio Tongun, Terenzio Wani, Joseph Aligo, Paul Lado Boreng, Paul Lako, Onesimus Ladu, Denis Daramollo, Lasu Eresto, Michael Nyarsuk, Yohana Gumbiri, Morbe Pitya, Martha Duki, Dario Loro, Angelo Wani, William Wani, Lino Wani, Joseph Abuk, Hamdan Jubara, Alfred Keri Yokwe, Daniel Sokiri Yokwe, Tongun Lado Rombe, Peter

Tongun Swaka, Martin Wani, Emmanuel Constantino, Nikodemo Aru Man, Aqualino Ladu, James Wani, Gore Lado Gideon, Gordon Lado, Pantronio Pitya, and many others in Juba and in Juba na Bari, Nyaing and Kworijik Luri.

In Rumbek (2005–7), Dhalbeny Makuer, Madol Mathok Agolder, Agok Macot, Kuc Adhil, Lueth Marial Buoc, Them Apac, Kau Anyar, Makal Buolkuec, Aggrey Miit Maguet, Wade Manyiel, Maker Mathiang, Mamer Makur, Ding Mayath, Makur Akec, Marial Kodi, Paul Awan Gol, Wetnhiak Manyiel, Aluk Bol, Mangok Marol, Marial Aborok, Maguen Alom, Matoc Lak, Akon and Ding Majak, Makur Arop, Moses Muordar, Padier Cindut, Malual Manyiel, Bongo Maker, Marial Ater Gol, James Mayom Rok, Ater Maker, Malek Chol, and many other people in Rumbek town, Timic and Abinajok, and of Amothnhom, Monytik and Nyaing sections.

INTERVIEWS CITED IN TEXT

Yei County interviews, translated from digital recordings in Kakwa language, unless otherwise stated:

1R/YC, 16 Aug 2005, Yei, in English: Elderly retired male local government officer, originally from Rokon in Central Equatoria State and a CMS teacher before 1954.
2R/YC, 23 Aug 2005, Yei and;
4R/YC, 30 Aug 2005, Yei: Elderly male chief and town chiefs' court member living in Yei, from Gimunu, near Yei.
3R/YC, 27 Aug 2005, Yei: Elderly male sub-chief and town chiefs' court member living in Yei, from Atende in Gimunu, near Yei.
5R/YC, 30 Aug 2005, Yei, in Arabic and Kakwa: Male chief, Yei town.
6R/YC, 5 Sept 2005, Yei: Elderly male sub-chief living in Yei town, from Rwonyi, near Yei.
7R/YC, 7 Sept 2005, Rwonyi: Elderly male rain chief, Rwonyi.
8R/YC, 9 Sept 2005, Atende: Male elder and male headman, Atende.
9R/YC, 10 Sept 2005, Mahat: Headman and elderly male clan rain chief, Mahat, near Yei.
10R/YC, 12 Sept 2005, Lutaya: Female elder, originally from Rwonyi.
11R/YC, 13 Sept 2005, Yei: Male clan elder, Atende.
12R/YC, 14 Sept 2005, Yei: Male town zonal sub-chief, Yei, from Gimunu, near Yei.
13R/YC, 16 Sept 2005, Rwonyi: Male elder and town chiefs' court member, Rwonyi.
14R/YC, 17 Sept 2005, Rwonyi: Clan headman, Rwonyi.
15R/YC, 21 Sept 2005, Yei: Town quarter headman, Yei, originally from Maridi road.
16R/YC, 22 Sept 2005, Yei: Female town chiefs' court member, Yei.
17R/YC, 30 Sept 2005, Kimbe: Clan headman and male clan rain chief, Kimbe, in Gimunu.
18R/YC, 3 Oct 2005, Atende: Clan headman and male elder, Atende.
19R/YC, 4 Oct 2005, Marakonye: Clan headman, Marakonye, near Yei.
20R/YC, 6 Oct 2005, Gimunu: Elderly clan headman, Gimunu.
21R/YC, 8 Oct 2005, Gimunu: Male sub-chief, Gimunu.
22R/YC, 10 Oct 2005, Rwonyi and;
29R/YC, 26 Oct 2005, Rwonyi: Female church elder, Rwonyi.
23R/YC, 11 Oct 2005, Rwonyi: Clan headman and male clan rain chief, Rwonyi.
24R/YC, 12 Oct 2005, Rwonyi: Male acting sub-chief, Rwonyi.
25R/YC, 13 Oct 2005, Sanja Siri: Male church pastor, Sanja Siri, Yei.

26R/YC, 14 Oct, 2005, Rwonyi: Clan headman, Rwonyi.
27R/YC, 15 Oct 2005, Yei, in English: Elderly male Pojelu county court magistrate: chief's son.
28R/YC, 17 Oct 2005, Yei, in Kakwa/Pojelu: Female Kakwa church elder and her elderly Pojelu aunt, Yei.
30R/YC, 27 Oct 2005, Gimunu: Clan headman, Gimunu.
31R/YC, 28 Oct 2005, Rwonyi: Clan headman, Rwonyi.
32R/YC, 28 Oct 2005, Rwonyi: Clan rain chief, Rwonyi.
33R/YC, 31 Oct 2005, Atende: Male clan elder, Atende.
34R/YC, 1 Nov 2005, Atende: Landowning clan head, Atende.

Juba County interviews, translated from digital recordings in Bari language, unless otherwise stated:

35R/JC, 24 Nov 2005, Juba: Elderly male market trader and former town chiefs' court member in Juba.
36R/JC, 28 Nov 2005, Juba: Elderly male chief for Kuku displaced community in Juba.
37R/JC, 30 Nov 2005, Juba, in English: Male Bari chief, president of town chiefs' court; former police officer.
38R/JC, 1 Dec 2005, Juba, in English: Male chief for Pojelu and Kakwa displaced community in Juba.
39R/JC, 2 Dec 2005, Juba: Male chief for Bari displaced community.
40R/JC, 5 Dec 2005, Juba: Male market trader and sub-chief for Mundari in Juba town; also working for radio station in Juba.
41R/JC, 26 Jan 2006, Dongoda, and;
42R/JC, 30 Jan 2006, Dongoda, in Bari and English: Male acting chief, Juba na Bari village, near Juba; also acting as *payam* chiefs' court president.
43R/JC, 1 Feb 2006, Kworojik Luri: Elderly male sub-chief.
44R/JC, 2 Feb 2006, Juba na Bari: Male headman and male elder.
45R/JC, 4 Feb 2006, Juba na Bari: Elderly male former teacher and church elder.
46R/JC, 6 Feb, 2006, Dongoda: Headman in Dongoda, working as school headmaster in Juba.
47R/JC, 9 Feb 2006, Juba: Elderly male sub-chief in Juba, originally from Gudele.
48R/JC, 11 Feb 2006, Walawalang: Male government employee and his wife, living in Walawalang, near Juba.
49R/JC, 2 March 2006, Nyaing: Male elder, retired hotel worker, brother of one of the first South Sudanese political leaders.
50R/JC, 4 March 2006, Juba: Elderly male court watchman in Juba, originally from Loggo, near Rejaf.
51R/JC, 7 March 2006, Dongoda: Elderly male former government employee and cook, originally from Jebel Lado.
52R/JC, 15 March 2006, Dongoda: Elderly male former driver and Anyanya One veteran.
53R/JC, 25 March 2006, Lopepe: Male chief of Mundari community, Kworijik, near Juba.

Rumbek County interviews, translated from digital recordings in Dinka language, unless otherwise stated:

54R/RC, 4 May 2006, Rumbek: Male chief, Amothnhom section of Dinka Agar Kuei.
55R/RC, 8 May 2006, Rumbek: Male chief, Monytik section of Dinka Agar Kuei.
56R/RC, 10 May 2006, Rumbek: Two male elders, Amothnhom section.

57R/RC, 11 May 2006, Rumbek: Male spear-master, Amothnhom section.
58R/RC, 13 May 2006, Rumbek: Male town court chief, Amothnhom section.
59R/RC, 17 May 2006, Rumbek: Two male chiefs, Amothnhom section.
60R/RC, 22 May 2006, Abinajok: Group of male elders and spiritual leaders, gathered to perform a sacrifice to bring rain.
61R/RC, 23 May 2006, Rumbek: Male chief, Nyaing section of Dinka Agar Kuei.
62R/RC, 24 May 2006, Rumbek: Young male song-maker and cattle-camp leader, Nyaing section.
63R/RC, 25 May 2006, Timic: Elderly male *gol* leader, Amothnhom section, and his wives and female relatives.
64R/RC, 26 May 2006, Rumbek: Female elder, Amothnhom section.
65R/RC, 29 May 2006, Timic and;
73R/RC, 14 June 2006, Timic: Male elder and spiritual leader, Amothnhom section.
66R/RC, 30 May 2006, Ronga: Male elder and chiefs' court member, Amothnhom section.
67R/RC, 1 June 2006, Timic: Two male elders, Amothnhom section.
68R/RC, 2 June 2006, Timic: Two elderly sisters, Panyon section, originally from Amothnhom.
69R/RC, 3 June 2006, Makoi: Male elder, Amothnhom section.
70R/RC, 5 June 2006, Rumbek: Male town chief, Amothnhom section.
71R/RC, 7 June 2006, Pulcum: Three male elders, Amothnhom section, one the former assistant to a spear-master.
72R/RC, 9 June 2006, Adol: Senior woman, Amothnhom section.
74R/RC, 31 Oct 2006, Rumbek: Male town court chief in Rumbek, originally from Athoi section.

Tape-recorded interview transcriptions, Khartoum, in English:

1R/K, 17 Feb 2003: Elderly male retired engineer, Kuku, from Wonkijo, Kajo Keji County.
2aR/K, 20 Oct 2002 and;
2bR/K, 23 Feb 2003: Elderly male retired engineer, Bari, from Tokiman, Juba County.
3R/K, 11 Feb 2003: Elderly male retired teacher, Bari, from Loggo East, Juba County.
4R/K, 10 Jan 2003: Male police brigadier and government minister, Pojelu, from Lainya.
5R/K, 28 Nov 2002: Elderly male retired government official and politician, Mundari, from Tali.
6R/K, 27 Jan 2003: Elderly male university professor, Lokoya, from Langabu, Juba County.
7R/K, 18 Feb 2003: Elderly female retired teacher, Bari, from Rejaf East, Juba County.
8R/K, 11 Nov 2002: Elderly male retired local government officer, Bari, from Tokiman, Juba County.
9R/K, 27 Oct 2002: Elderly male retired major-general and Anyanya One veteran, Bari, from Rejaf East, Juba County.
10R/K, 19 Feb 2003: Elderly male university professor, from Amadi, Mundri West County.

Interviews and conversations, transcribed as notes;
in English unless otherwise stated:

1aN/RC 15 Nov 2006, Rumbek;
1bN/RC, 18 Nov 2006, Rumbek;

1cN/RC, 28 Nov 2006, Rumbek, all in Dinka: Elderly male mechanic, Nyaing section of Agar Dinka, recently returned from long-term government employment in Wau.
2aN/YC, 31 Aug 2004, Mitika, near Yei, and;
2bN/YC, 23 Aug 2005, Yei: Elderly male retired government official and politician, Kakwa, from Mitika, near Yei.
3N/YC, 31 Aug 2004, Yei: Elderly male county court magistrate and son of a chief, Pojelu, from Mukaya Payam, Lainya County.
4N/YC: 19 Feb 2005, Rumbek: Male SPLA officer, Kakwa, from Mugwo, Yei County.
5N/YC: 15 Jan 2007, Yei: Male former chief, Pojelu, from Mukaya Payam, Lainya County; now working as journalist in Yei.
6N/YC: 5 Sept 2004, Yei: Male agricultural officer, Pojelu, son of a former chief in Limbe, Lainya County.
7N/YC: 22 Jan 2007, Rwonyi, near Yei: Male sub-chief and teacher; former refugee camp councillor; adopted dependant or nephew of chiefly family, Kakwa, Rwonyi.
8N/JC: 22 Aug 2008, Juba: Elderly male university professor, Lokoya, from Langabu, Juba County (as Interview 6R/K).
9N/JC: 26 Aug 2008, Juba: Elderly male retired engineer, Bari, from Tokiman, Juba County (as Interviews 2aR/K and 2bR/K).
10N/JC: 29 Aug 2008, Juba: Male university professor, Bari, from chiefly family in Tokiman, Juba County.
11N/JC: 17 Aug 2008, Juba, in Arabic: Male elder in Juba Malakiya community; father was soldier originally from Bor Dinka.
12N/JC: 23 Aug 2008, Juba: Two brothers: both former government officials; one now a chief; Bari, from Kogi, southern Juba County.
13N/JC: 28 Aug 2008, Juba: Male elder and state MP; former prison brigadier, Bari, from Luri, northern Juba County.
14N/RC: 17 Nov 2006, Rumbek: Elderly male retired schoolteacher, Nyaing section of Agar Dinka.
15N/JC: 19 Aug 2008, Juba, in Bari and Arabic: Elderly male market trader and former town chiefs' court member in Juba (as Interview 35R/JC).
16N/RC: 13 June 2006, Rumbek: Male church translator, Agar Dinka.
17N/RC: 4 Nov 2006, Rumbek: Male county magistrate from prominent chiefly family, Nyaing section of Agar Dinka.
18N/RC: 31 May 2006, Abinajok, near Rumbek: Son of a prominent spear-master, Amothnhom section of Agar Dinka.
19aN/RC: 18 June 2006, Rumbek;
19bN/RC: 12 Nov 2006, Rumbek, and;
19cN/RC: 17 May 2006, Rumbek: Young male schoolteacher in Rumbek, from a prominent spear-master family, Amothnhom section of Agar Dinka.
20N/YC: 19 Sept 2005, Yei, in Kakwa: Male church preacher, Kakwa, from Rwonyi.
21N/RC: 23 Nov 2006, Rumbek, in Dinka: Elderly male chief and court president, Nyaing section of Agar Dinka, Rumbek.
22N/RC: 7 Sept 2004, Yei: Male SPLA major-general, Bor Dinka.
23N/RC: 16 Nov 2006, Timic, near Rumbek, in Dinka: Elderly *gol* leader (headman), Amothnhom section of Agar Dinka (as Interview 63R/RC).
24N/JC: 3 Jan 2007, Juba: Male local government officer, Bari, from Gondokoro, Juba.
25N/JC: 14 March 2006, Kworojik, near Juba, in Mundari: Group of Mundari men and women of mixed ages, most originally from Terakeka and displaced during the war.
26N/JC: 8 March 2006, Kworojik, near Juba, in Mundari: Group of Mundari men and women of mixed ages, originally from Tali and displaced during the war.

27N/JC: 9 March 2006, Nyaing, near Juba, in Bari: Elderly man and three elderly women, Bari, Nyaing.
28N/YC: 15 Aug 2005, Yei, in Kakwa: Male headman of town area (*Hai*), Kakwa.
29N/YC: 23 Aug 2005, Yei, in Kakwa: Male headman of town area (*Hai*), Kakwa.
30N/YC: 20 Aug 2005, Yei, in Kakwa: Male timber trader, Kakwa, from Ombasi, Yei County.
31N/RC: 26 May 2006, Rumbek, in Dinka: Elderly widow of a policeman, Amothnhom section of Agar Dinka.
32N/YC: 12 May 2006, Rumbek: Male NGO employee, Pojelu from Lainya County.
33N/JC: 2 Dec 2005, Juba: Male chief for Pojelu displaced community in Juba.
34N/JC: 19 Dec 2006, Juba: Male Bari chief, president of town chiefs' court; former police officer (as Interview 37R/JC).
35N/JC: 21 March 2006, Juba na Bari, near Juba, in Bari: Women of mixed ages.
36N/JC: 24 March 2006, Kworijik, near Juba, in Mundari: Group of young and middle-aged men and women, displaced Mundari from Dari.
37N/JC: 3 Dec 2006, Juba: Male local government officer, Lulubo, Juba County.
38N/RC: 6 June 2006, Rumbek: Young male schoolteacher and church leader in Rumbek, from chiefly family of Agar Dinka in Rumbek East County.
39N/JC: 28 Aug 2008, Juba: Male local government officer, Bari, from Juba County.
40N/JC: 20 Aug 2008, Juba: Elderly male senior local government officer, Dinka.
41N/RC: 17 Nov 2006, Timic, near Rumbek, in Dinka: Male *gol* leader (headman) and male elder, both Amothnhom section of Agar Dinka.
42N/RC: 4 Nov 2006, Rumbek, in Dinka: Male trader, Rumbek market, from Amothnhom section of Agar Dinka.
43N/YC: 25 Aug 2008, Juba: Male journalist and state MP, Kakwa, from Rwonyi, Yei.
44N/JC: 26 Nov 2005, Juba: Male local government officer for a Juba town *payam*.
45N/YC: 20 Jan 2007, Yei, in Kakwa: Elderly male sub-chief living in Yei town, Kakwa, from Rwonyi (as Interview 6R/YC).
46N/RC: 6 Nov 2006, Rumbek, in Dinka: Two male litigants from Nyaing section of Agar Dinka at the Rumbek County Court .
47N/YC: 25 Jan 2007, Mahad, Yei, in Kakwa: Male chief and sub-chief, both Kakwa from Gimunu, near Yei (chief as Interview 21R/YC).
48N/YC: 25 Jan 2007, Yei: Male businessman, county council member and elder, Kakwa from Maridi road, Yei County.

Bibliography

ARCHIVAL SOURCES

National Records Office, Khartoum (NRO)

BGP	Bahr el Ghazal Province
Civsec	Civil Secretary
Dakhlia	Dakhlia (Ministry of Interior)
EP	Equatoria Province
INTEL	Intelligence
JD	Juba District
MP	Mongalla Province
UNP	Upper Nile Province

The National Archives, London (TNA)
Sudan Monthly Intelligence Reports (*SIR*) 1899–1925, located in Egypt and the Sudan files, FO series 78 and 371; WO series 106 and 33

FO 2/164, 2/201, 2/299: Uganda files, 1898–1900
FO 371/1027 17–57; FO 371/1136 19: files on Southern question, 1953–55

Southern Records Office, Juba (SRO)

CEOE	Chief Election Officer Equatoria
EP	Equatoria Province
MD	Moru District
TD	Torit District
UNP	Upper Nile Province
ZD	Zande District

Bahr el Ghazal Province Archive, Wau

LP	Lakes Province

The Sudan Archive, Durham (SAD)
53/1/1–536: G. R Storrar papers
428/1/1–29: G. M. Culwick papers
541/7/1–32: John Winder papers
600/7/1–49: B. A. Lewis papers
748/10/1–71: J. H. Dick papers
753/5/1–69, 753/3/1–129: H. Ferguson papers
761/7/1–56: J C. N. Donald papers
777/3/1–40, 777/8/1–20: T. H. B. Mynors papers
777/10/1–52: H. A. Nicholson papers

802/9/1–13, 804/10/1–136, 813/2/1–64: O. C. Allison papers
815/5/1–17: C. W. North papers
817/2/1–118, 817/3/1–88, 817/6/1–118, 817/7/1–154, 817/8/1–119: M. W. Parr papers
864/2/1–38: H. B. Bullen papers
865/2/1–52: L. W. C. Sharland papers
890/1/1–80: Misc. papers (Hilary Paul Logali, 'Autobiography')

Church Missionary Society Archive, Birmingham (CMS)
G3 AL (1917–39), AF AL (1940–49): Annual Letters
G3S Station Reports
G3SO: Original Papers
AFg AD1, AFE AD3: Tours
Acc. 18: Gwynne Papers
Acc. 21 and 28: Baring-Gould Papers
Acc. 111: Shaw Papers
Acc. 168: Fraser Papers
Acc. 300: Gelsthorpe Papers
Acc. 409: Hadow Journal
Acc. 469: Parr Papers

Pitt Rivers Museum, Oxford
Godfrey Lienhardt Papers

Rhodes House Library, Oxford
MSS Perham, files 542, 548–9

Shetland Archive, Lerwick (SAL)
D12/200–203, 206: letters of B. H. H. Spence

BOOKS, ARTICLES, THESES, DISSERTATIONS AND SPEECHES

'Abd al-Rahim, Muddathir. *Imperialism and Nationalism in the Sudan: a study in constitutional and political development 1899–1956*. Oxford: Clarendon, 1969.

Abdul-Jalil, Musa Adam, Adam Azzain Mohammed and Ahmed A Yousuf. 'Native administration and local governance in Darfur: past and future'. In Alex de Waal (ed.), *War in Darfur and the Search for Peace*. London: Justice in Africa, 2007, pp. 39–47.

African Rights, 'Imposing empowerment: aid and civil institutions in southern Sudan'. London: African Rights Discussion Paper, 1995.

Ahmed, Abdel Ghaffar M and Abdel Rahman, Mustafa. 'Small urban centres: vanguards of exploitation. Two cases from Sudan'. *Africa* 49:3 (1979), pp. 258–71.

Aiken, Mark and Afaf Ismael. 'Traditional Authority Study: report on Southern Blue Nile and Eastern Equatoria'. Nairobi: UNDP unpublished report, 2005.

Aleu Akechak Jok, Leitch, Robert A and Vandewint, Carrie. *A Study of Customary Law in Contemporary Southern Sudan*. Monrovia, CA: World Vision International and the South Sudan Secretariat of Legal and Constitutional Affairs, 2004.

Alexander, Jocelyn. 'The local state in post-war Mozambique: political practice and ideas about authority'. *Africa* 67:1 (1997), pp. 1–26.

Alexander, Jocelyn. *The Unsettled Land: state-making & the politics of land in Zimbabwe 1893–2003*. Oxford: James Currey, 2006.

Allen, Tim. 'Ethnicity & tribalism on the Sudan-Uganda Border'. In Katsuyoshi Fukui and John Markakis (eds), *Ethnicity & Conflict in the Horn of Africa.* London: James Currey, 1994, pp. 112–39.

Allen, Tim and Storm, Laura. 'Quests for therapy in northern Uganda: healing at Laropi revisited'. *Journal of Eastern African Studies* 6:1 (2012), pp. 22–46.

Ambler, Charles H. *Kenyan Communities in the Age of Imperialism: the central region in the late nineteenth century.* New Haven, CT: Yale University Press, 1988.

Anderson, David M. 'Cultivating pastoralists: ecology and economy among the Il Chamus of Baringo, 1840–1980'. In Johnson and Anderson, *The Ecology of Survival*, pp. 241–60.

Andersson, Jens A. 'Administrators' knowledge and state control in colonial Zimbabwe: the invention of the rural-urban divide in Buhera District, 1912–80'. *Journal of African History* 43 (2002), pp. 119–43.

Arens, W. 'Mto wa Mbu: a rural polyethnic community in Tanzania'. In Kopytoff, *The African Frontier*, pp. 242–54.

Badiey, Naseem. 'The State Within: the local dynamics of "post-conflict reconstruction" in Juba, Southern Sudan (2005–2008)'. DPhil, University of Oxford, 2010.

Baker, Samuel White. *The Albert N'yanza: great basin of the Nile.* London: Macmillan, 1867.

Baker, Samuel W. *Ismailia: a narrative of the expedition to Central Africa for the suppression of the slave trade, organized by Ismail, Khedive of Egypt.* 2 vols. London: Macmillan, 1874.

Barber, James. 'The moving frontier of British imperialism in northern Uganda, 1898–1919'. *Uganda Journal* 29:1 (1965), pp. 27–43.

Barnes, Sandra T. 'The urban frontier in West Africa: Mushin, Nigeria'. In Kopytoff, *The African Frontier*, pp. 261–2.

Bayart, Jean-François (tr. Rendall, S, Roitman, J and Derrick, J). *The Illusion of Cultural Identity.* London: Hurst, 2005; originally Paris: Librairie Arthème Fayard, 1996.

Bayart, Jean-François. *The State in Africa: the politics of the belly.* London: Longman, 1993.

Beaton, AC. 'A Chapter in Bari History: the history of Sindiru, Bilinian and Mogiri'. *Sudan Notes and Records* 17:2 (1934), pp. 169–200.

Beaton, AC. *Equatoria Province Handbook*, Vol. 2. Khartoum: McCorquodale, 1949.

Beaton, AC. 'The Bari: clan and age-class systems'. *Sudan Notes and Records* 19:1 (1936), pp. 109–45.

Beaton, AC. 'Report on the effects of the Anglo-Egyptian agreement on the Southern Sudan', 17 March 1953. In Johnson, *British Documents*, Part II, no. 302, pp. 228–33.

Beck, Kurt. 'Tribesmen, townsmen and the struggle over a proper lifestyle in northern Kordofan'. In Stiansen, Endre and Kevane, Michael (eds). *Kordofan Invaded: peripheral incorporation and social transformation in Islamic Africa.* Leiden: Brill, 1998, pp. 254–79.

Bell, Heather. *Frontiers of Medicine in the Anglo-Egyptian Sudan, 1899–1940.* Oxford: Clarendon, 1999.

Bellagamba, Alice and Klute, Georg (eds). *Beside the State: emergent powers in contemporary Africa.* Cologne: Rüdiger Köppe, 2008.

Berman, Bruce. 'Structure & process in the bureaucratic states of colonial Africa'. In Berman and Lonsdale, *Unhappy Valley*, Vol. 1, p. 140–176.

Berman, Bruce and Lonsdale, John. *Unhappy Valley: conflict in Kenya & Africa.* 2 vols. London: James Currey, 1992.

Berman, Bruce and Lonsdale, John. 'Coping with the contradictions: the development of the colonial state 1895–1914'. In Berman and Lonsdale, *Unhappy Valley*. Vol. 1, pp. 77–100.
Berry, Sara. *Chiefs Know their Boundaries: essays on property, power and the past in Asante, 1896–1996*. Oxford: James Currey, 2001.
Berry, Sara. *No Condition is Permanent: the social dynamics of agrarian change in Sub-Saharan Africa*. Madison: University of Wisconsin Press, 1993.
Berry, Sara. 'Social institutions and access to resources'. *Africa* 59:1 (1989), pp. 41–55.
Bierschenk, Thomas and de Sardan, Jean-Pierre Olivier. 'Local powers and a distant state in rural Central African Republic'. *Journal of Modern African Studies* 35:3 (1997), pp. 441–68.
Bjorkelo, Anders. *Prelude to the Mahdiyya: peasants and traders in the Shendi Region, 1821–1885*. Cambridge: Cambridge University Press, 1989.
Boone, Catherine. *Political Topographies of the African State: territorial authority and institutional choice*. Cambridge: Cambridge University Press, 2003.
Bravman, Bill. *Making Ethnic Ways: communities and their transformations in Taita, Kenya, 1800–1950*. Portsmouth, NH: Heinemann, 1998.
Burton, John W. 'When the north winds blow: a note on small towns and social transformation in the Nilotic Sudan'. *African Studies Review* 31:3 (1988), pp. 49–60.
Buur, Lars and Kyed, Helene M (eds), *State Recognition and Democratization in Sub-Saharan Africa: a new dawn for traditional authorities?* New York: Palgrave Macmillan, 2007.
Buur, Laars and Kyed, Helene M. 'Traditional authority in Mozambique: the legible space between state and community'. In Buur and Kyed, *State Recognition and Democratization in Sub-Saharan Africa*, pp. 105–27.
Buxton, Jean. *Chiefs and Strangers: a study of political assimilation among the Mandari*. Oxford: Clarendon, 1963.
Carless, TFG. 'Malakal Town'. In Johnson, *Upper Nile Province Handbook*, pp. 319–20.
Casati, Gaetano (Tr. Clay, JR). *Ten Years in Equatoria*. London and New York: Warne, 1898.
Chabal, Patrick and Daloz, Jean-Pascal. *Africa Works: disorder as political instrument*. Oxford: James Currey, 1999.
Chanock, Martin. 'A peculiar sharpness: an essay on property in the history of customary law in colonial Africa'. *Journal of African History* 32 (1991), pp. 65–88.
Chanock, Martin. *Law, Custom and Social Order: the colonial experience in Malawi and Zambia*. Portsmouth, NH: Heinemann, 1998.
Chrétien, Jean-Pierre (Tr. Strauss, S). *The Great Lakes of Africa: two thousand years of history*. New York: Zone, 2003.
Clapham, Christopher (ed.). *African Guerrillas*. Oxford: James Currey, 1998.
Collins, Robert O. *A History of Modern Sudan*. Cambridge: Cambridge University Press, 2008.
Collins, Robert O. *King Leopold, England and the Upper Nile, 1899–1909*. New Haven, CT and London: Yale University Press, 1968.
Collins, Robert O. *Land Beyond the Rivers: the Southern Sudan, 1898–1918*. New Haven, CT and London: Yale University Press, 1971.
Collins, Robert O. *Shadows in the Grass: Britain in the Southern Sudan, 1918–1956*. New Haven, CT: Yale University Press, 1983.
Collins, Robert O. *The Southern Sudan, 1883–1898: a struggle for control*. New Haven, CT: Yale University Press, 1962.

Comaroff, John. 'Governmentality, materiality, legality, modernity: on the colonial state in Africa'. In Jan-Georg Deutsch, Peter Probst and Heike Schmidt (eds), *African Modernities: entangled meanings in current debate*. Oxford: James Currey, 2002, pp. 126–7.

Comaroff, John L and Comaroff, Jean. *Of Revelation and Revolution*, Vol. 2: *The dialectics of modernity on a South African frontier*. Chicago: University of Chicago Press, 1997.

Comaroff, John L and Comaroff, Jean. 'Reflections on the anthropology of law, governance and sovereignty'. In F von Benda-Beckmann, K von Benda-Beckmann and J Eckert (eds), *Rules of Law and Laws of Ruling: on the governance of law*. Farnham: Ashgate, 2009, pp. 31–59.

Cooper, Frederick. *Decolonization and African Society: the labor question in French and British Africa*. Cambridge University Press, 1996.

Cotran, TS. *Report of the Commission of Inquiry into the Disturbances in the Southern Sudan during August, 1955*. Khartoum: McCorquodale, 1956.

Crowder, Michael and Ikime, Obaro (eds). *West African Chiefs: their changing status under colonial rule and independence*. Ife-Ife: University of Ife Press, 1970.

Daly, Martin W. *Empire on the Nile: the Anglo-Egyptian Sudan, 1898–1934*. Cambridge: Cambridge University Press, 1986.

Daly, Martin W. *Imperial Sudan: the Anglo-Egyptian Condominium 1934–1956*. Cambridge: Cambridge University Press, 1991.

Das, Veena and Poole, Deborah (eds). *Anthropology in the Margins of the State*. Oxford: Oxford University Press and James Currey, 2004.

Deal, Jeffrey L. 'Torture by *cieng*: ethical theory meets social practice among the Dinka Agaar of South Sudan'. *American Anthropologist* 112:4 (2010), pp. 563–75.

Dellagiacoma, Fr V (ed.). *How a Slave became a Minister: autobiography of Sayyed Stanislaus Abdallahi Paysama*. Khartoum, 1990.

Dereje Feyissa, 'More state than the state? The Anywaa's call for the rigidification of the Ethio-Sudanese border'. In Dereje and Hoehne, *Borders & Borderlands*, pp. 27–44.

Dereje Feyissa and Hoehne, Markus V (eds). *Borders & Borderlands as Resources in the Horn of Africa*. Woodbridge: James Currey, 2010.

Eckert, Julia. 'From subjects to citizens: legalism from below and the homogenisation of the legal sphere'. *Journal of Legal Pluralism and Unofficial Law* 53:4 (2006), pp. 45–76.

Emin Pasha (ed. Georg Schweinfurth; tr. RW Felkin), *Emin Pasha in Central Africa: being a collection of his letters and journals*. London: G. Philip, 1888.

Englebert, Pierre. *State Legitimacy and Development in Africa*. Boulder, CO: Lynne Rienner, 2000.

Evans-Pritchard, EE. *Nuer Religion*. Oxford: Clarendon, 1956.

Evans-Pritchard, EE. *The Nuer: a description of the modes of livelihood and political institutions of a Nilotic people*. Oxford: Oxford University Press, 1940.

Evans-Pritchard, EE. *Witchcraft, Oracles and Magic among the Azande*. Oxford: Clarendon, 1937.

Ewald, Janet. *Soldiers, Traders, and Slaves: state formation and economic transformation in the Greater Nile Valley, 1700–1885*. Madison: University of Wisconsin Press, 1990.

Ewald, Janet. 'A moment in the middle: fieldwork in the Nuba hills'. In Carolyn Keyes Adenaike and Jan Vansina (eds), *In Pursuit of History: fieldwork in Africa*. Oxford: James Currey, 1997, pp. 94–103.

Fanthorpe, Richard. 'Neither citizen nor subject? 'Lumpen' agency and the legacy of native administration in Sierra Leone'. *African Affairs* 100:400 (2001), pp. 363–386.

Fanthorpe, Richard. 'On the limits of liberal peace: chiefs and democratic decen-

tralization in post-war Sierra Leone'. *African Affairs* 105:418 (2006), pp. 27–49.
Feierman, Steven. *Peasant Intellectuals: anthropology and history in Tanzania.* Madison: University of Wisconsin Press, 1990.
Feierman, Steven. *The Shambaa Kingdom: a history*. Madison: University of Wisconsin Press, 1974.
Feierman, Steven. 'A century of ironies in East Africa (c. 1780–1890)'. In P Curtin, S Feierman, L Thompson and J Vansina (eds), *African History: from earliest times to independence.* London: Longman, 1995, pp. 352–76.
Fields, Karen Elise. *Revival and Rebellion in Colonial Central Africa.* Portsmouth, NH: Heinemann, 1996.
Fukui, Katsuyoshi and Markakis, John (eds). *Ethnicity & Conflict in the Horn of Africa*. London: James Currey, 1994.
Fund for Peace. *Failed States Index 2012*. Washington DC: Fund for Peace, 2012.
Garfield, Richard. *Violence and Victimization in South Sudan: Lakes State in the post-CPA period.* Geneva: Small Arms Survey, 2007.
Garretson, Peter P. 'The Southern Sudan Welfare Committee and the 1947 strike in the southern Sudan'. *Northeast African Studies* 8:2–3 (1986), pp. 181–91.
Geschiere, Peter. 'Chiefs and colonial rule in Cameroon: inventing chieftaincy, French and British Style'. *Africa* 63:2 (1993), pp. 151–75.
Gessi, Romolo. *Seven Years in the Soudan: being a record of explorations, adventures, and campaigns against the Arab slave hunters*. London: Sampson Low, Marston & Co, 1892.
Gewald, Jan-Bart. 'Making tribes: social engineering in the Western Province of British administered Eritrea, 1941–1952'. *Journal of Colonialism and Colonial History* (online version) 1:2 (2000).
Giblin, James L. *A History of the Excluded: making family a refuge from state in twentieth-century Tanzania*. Oxford: James Currey, 2005.
Giblin, James. 'History, imagination and remapping space in a small urban centre: Makambako, Iringa Region, Tanzania'. In Burton, Andrew (ed.). *The Urban Experience in Eastern Africa c. 1750–2000*. Nairobi: BIEA, 2002, pp. 187–203.
Gifoon, Ali Effendi. 'Memoirs of a Soudanese soldier'. Dictated in Arabic to and translated by Captain Percy Machell. *Cornhill Magazine* 1:2 (August 1896), pp. 175–87.
Glassman, Jonathon. *Feasts and Riot: revelry, rebellion and popular consciousness on the Swahili coast, 1856–1888*. Portsmouth, NH and London: Heinemann / James Currey, 1995.
Golooba-Mutebi, Frederick and Adak Costa Mapuor. 'Traditional Authorities in South Sudan: chieftainship in the Bahr el Ghazal region'. Nairobi: UNDP unpublished report, 2005.
Gordon, David. 'Owners of the land and Lunda lords: colonial chiefs in the borderlands of Northern Rhodesia and the Belgian Congo'. *International Journal of African Historical Studies* 34:2 (2001), pp. 315–38.
Gordon, Robert J, and Meggitt, Mervyn J. *Law and Order in the New Guinea Highlands: encounters with Enga.* Hanover, NH: University Press of New England, 1985.
Governor-General of the Sudan, *Report on the Finances, Administration and Condition of the Sudan*. London: HMSO, 1906–26.
Gray, Richard. *A History of the Southern Sudan 1839–1889*. Oxford: Oxford University Press, 1961.
Guma Kunda Komey. *Land, Governance, Conflict & the Nuba of Sudan*. Woodbridge: James Currey, 2010.
 Guyer, Jane I and Belinga, Samuel ME. 'Wealth in people as wealth in knowl-

edge: accumulation and composition in Equatorial Africa'. *Journal of African History* 36 (1995), pp. 91–120.
Haddon, Ernest B. 'System of chieftainship amongst the Bari of Uganda'. *Journal of the Royal African Society* 10:40 (1911), pp. 467–72.
Hagmann, Tobias and Péclard, Didier. 'Negotiating statehood: dynamics of power and domination in Africa'. *Development and Change* 41:4 (2010), pp. 539–562.
Hanson, Holly E. *Landed Obligation: the practice of power in Buganda*. Portsmouth, NH: Heinemann, 2003.
Harrigin, Simon and Nikodemo Arou Man. 'Traditional Authority Study: report for Upper Nile team B'. Nairobi: UNDP unpublished report, 2005.
Herbst, Jeffrey. *States and Power in Africa: comparative lessons in authority and control*. Princeton, NJ: Princeton University Press, 2000.
Herzog, Herbert. 'Report: mission on governance to Western Equatoria, Southern Sudan'. Liebefeld, Switzerland: Herzog Consult, 1998.
Hill, Richard. *Egypt and the Sudan 1820–1881*. London: Oxford University Press, 1959.
Hill, Roger L. *Migration to Juba: a case study*. Juba: University of Juba Population and Manpower Unit, 1981.
Hobsbawm, Eric and Ranger, Terence (eds). *The Invention of Tradition* (Cambridge: Cambridge University Press, 1983.
Hødnebø, Kjell. *Cattle and Flies: a study of cattle keeping in Equatoria Province, the southern Sudan, 1850–1950*. Bergen: Universitetet i Bergen, 1981.
Hoehne, Markus V. *Traditional Authorities and Local Government in Southern Sudan*. Washington DC: World Bank, 2008.
Holt, Peter M and Daly, Martin W. *A History of the Sudan: from the coming of Islam to the present day*. Harlow: Longman, 2000.
House, WJ. 'Labor market differentiation in a developing economy: an example from urban Juba, Southern Sudan'. *World Development* 15:7 (1987), pp. 877–897.
Howell, John (ed.). *Local Government and Politics in the Sudan*. Khartoum: Khartoum University Press, 1974.
Howell, John. 'Political Leadership and Organization in the Southern Sudan'. PhD, University of Reading,1978.
Huby, GO. 'Big men and old men – and women: social organization and urban adaptation of the Bari, Southern Sudan'. Magistergrad thesis, University of Trondheim, 1981.
Huntingford, George WB. *The Northern Nilo-Hamites*. Ethnographic Survey of Africa: East Central Africa; Daryll Forde (Series Ed.). London: International African Institute, 1953.
Hutchinson, Sharon. *Nuer Dilemmas: coping with money, war and the state*. Berkeley: University of California Press, 1996.
Iliffe, John. *Africans: history of a continent*. Cambridge: Cambridge University Press, 1995.
James, Wendy. *'Kwanim Pa, The Making of the Uduk People: an ethnographic study of survival in the Sudan-Ethiopian borderlands*. Oxford: Clarendon, 1979.
James, Wendy. *The Listening Ebony: moral knowledge, religion, and power among the Uduk of Sudan*. Oxford: Clarendon, 1988.
James, Wendy. *War and Survival in Sudan's Frontierlands: voices from the Blue Nile*. Oxford: Oxford University Press, 2007.
Jeppie, Shamil. 'Constructing a Colony on the Nile, c. 1820–1870'. PhD, Princeton University, 1996.
Johnson, Douglas H. (ed.). *British Documents on the End of Empire Project*. Series B, Vol. 5, *Sudan*. London: Stationery Office, 1998.

Johnson, Douglas H. 'Criminal secrecy: the case of the Zande "secret societies"'. *Past and Present* 130 (1991), pp. 170–200.
Johnson, Douglas H. 'Colonial policy and prophets: the "Nuer settlement", 1929–1930'. *Journal of the Anthropological Society of Oxford* 10:1 (1979), pp. 1–20.
Johnson, Douglas H. 'Decolonising the borders in Sudan: ethnic territories and national development'. In M Duffield and V Hewitt (eds), *Empire, Development & Colonialism: the past in the present*. Woodbridge: James Currey, 2009, pp. 176–87.
Johnson, Douglas H. 'From military to tribal police: policing the Upper Nile Province of the Sudan'. In David M Anderson and David Killingray (eds), *Policing the Empire: government, authority and control, 1830–1940*. Manchester: Manchester University Press, 1991, pp. 151–67.
Johnson, Douglas H. 'Judicial regulation and administrative control: customary law and the Nuer, 1898–1954'. *Journal of African History* 27 (1986), pp. 59–78.
Johnson, Douglas H. *Nuer Prophets: a history of prophecy from the Upper Nile in the nineteenth and twentieth centuries*. Oxford: Clarendon, 1994.
Johnson, Douglas H. 'Prophecy and Mahdism in the Upper Nile: an examination of local experiences of the Mahdiyya in the southern Sudan'. *British Journal of Middle Eastern Studies* 20:1 (1993), pp. 42–56.
Johnson, Douglas H. 'Recruitment and entrapment in private slave armies: the structure of the *zara'ib* in the southern Sudan'. In Elizabeth Savage (ed.), *The Human Commodity: perspectives on the trans-Saharan slave trade*. London: Frank Cass, 1992, pp.162–73.
Johnson, Douglas H. *The Root Causes of Sudan's Civil Wars*. Oxford: James Currey, 2003.
Johnson, Douglas H. 'The Structure of a legacy: military slavery in northeast Africa'. *Ethnohistory* 36:1 (1989), pp. 72–88.
Johnson, Douglas H. 'The Sudan People's Liberation Army and the problem of factionalism'. In Christopher Clapham (ed.), *African Guerrillas*. Oxford: James Currey, 1998, pp. 53–72.
Johnson, Douglas H. (ed.). *The Upper Nile Province Handbook: a report on peoples and government in the southern Sudan, 1931*. Compiled by CA Willis. Oxford: Oxford University Press for the British Academy, 1995.
Johnson, Douglas H. 'Tribal boundaries and border wars: Nuer-Dinka relations in the Sobat and Zaraf valleys, c. 1860–1976'. *Journal of African History* 23:2 (1982), pp. 183–203.
Johnson, Douglas H and Anderson, David M (eds). *The Ecology of Survival: case studies from northeast African history*. London: IB Tauris, 1988.
Johnson, Douglas H and Prunier, Gerard. 'The foundation and expansion of the Sudan People's Liberation Army'. in MW Daly and AA Sikainga (eds), *Civil War in the Sudan*. London: British Academic Press, 1993, pp. 117–141.
Jok Madut Jok and Hutchinson, Sharon E. 'Sudan's prolonged second civil war and the militarization of Nuer and Dinka ethnic identities'. *African Studies Review* 42:2 (1999), pp. 125–45.
Junker, Wilhelm (Tr. Keane, AH). *Travels in Africa During the Years 1875–1878*. London: Chapman and Hall, 1890.
Kasfir, Nelson. 'Southern Sudanese politics since the Addis Ababa Agreement'. *African Affairs* 76:303 (1977), pp. 143–66.
Kaufmann, A. 'The White Nile Valley and its inhabitants'. In Toniolo and Hill, *The Opening of the Nile Basin*, pp. 140–95.
Kimambo, Isaria N. *Penetration and Protest in Tanzania: the impact of the world economy on the Pare 1860–1960*. London: James Currey, 1991.
Knoblecher, Ignaz. 'The official journal of the missionary expedition, 1849–1850'. In Toniolo and Hill, *The Opening of the Nile Basin*, pp. 47–54.

Koech, Lazarus, Goinard, Anne L and Willnat, Olaf. 'Community participation in the primary health care programme and the new system of governance, West Bank, Equatoria Region, New Sudan'. Nairobi: Aktion Afrika Hilfe and the Konrad Adenauer Foundation report, 1999.

Komma, Toru. 'Peacemakers, prophets, chiefs and warriors: age-set antagonism as a factor of political change among the Kipsigis of Kenya'. In Eisei Kurimoto and Simon Simonse (eds), *Conflict, Age & Power in North East Africa: age systems in transition*. Oxford: James Currey, 1998, pp. 186–205.

Kopytoff, Igor (ed.). *The African Frontier: the reproduction of traditional African societies*. Bloomington: Indiana University Press, 1987.

Kopytoff, Igor. 'The internal African frontier: the making of African political culture'. In Kopytoff, *The African Frontier*, pp. 3–84.

Igor Kopytoff, 'The political dynamics of the urban frontier'. In Kopytoff, *The African Frontier*, pp. 255–6.

Kurimoto, Eisei. 'Civil war and regional conflicts: the Pari and their neighbours in south-eastern Sudan'. In Katsuyoshi Fukui and John Markakis (eds), *Ethnicity & Conflict in the Horn of Africa*. London: James Currey, 1994, pp. 95–111.

Kurita, Yoshiko. 'The role of "negroid but detribalized" people in modern Sudanese history'. *Nilo-Ethiopian Studies* 8–9 (2003), pp. 1–11.

Lacher, Wolfram. *South Sudan: international state-building and its limits*. Berlin: Stiftung Wissenschaft und Politik, 2012.

Lane, Paul J and Johnson, Douglas. 'The archaeology and history of slavery in South Sudan in the nineteenth century'. In Andrew CS Peacock (ed.) *The* Frontiers of the Ottoman World. Oxford: Oxford University Press, 2009, pp. 502–37.

Langley, Michael. *No Woman's Country: travels in the Anglo-Egyptian Sudan*. London: Jarrolds, 1950.

Large, Daniel. 'Local governance in South Sudan: context, condition and change'. Nairobi: UNDP unpublished thematic paper, 2004.

Larick, Roy. 'Warriors and blacksmiths: mediating ethnicity in East African spears'. *Journal of Anthropological Archaeology* 10 (1991), pp. 299–331.

Le Meur, Pierre-Yves. 'State making and the politics of the frontier in Central Benin'. *Development and Change* 37:4 (2006), pp. 871–900.

Leonardi, Cherry. 'Paying "buckets of blood" for the land: moral debates over economy, war and state in Southern Sudan'. *Journal of Modern African Studies* 49:2 (2011), pp. 215–40.

Leonardi, Cherry. 'Violence, sacrifice and chiefship in Central Equatoria, Southern Sudan'. *Africa* 77:4 (2007), pp. 535–558.

Leonardi, Cherry, Deng Biong Miajak and Eli Achol Deng Höt. 'Report on Traditional Authority in Western and Central Equatoria, South Sudan'. Nairobi: UNDP, unpublished report, 2005.

Leonardi, Cherry; Isser, Deborah; Moro, Leben and Santschi, Martina. 'The politics of customary law ascertainment in South Sudan'. *Journal of Legal Pluralism and Unofficial Law* 63 (2011), pp. 111–42.

Leonardi, Cherry; Moro, Leben Nelson; Santschi, Martina and Isser, Deborah H. *Local Justice in Southern Sudan*. Washington DC: US Institute of Peace, 2010.

Leopold, Mark. *Inside West Nile: violence, history & representation on an African frontier*. Oxford: James Currey, 2005.

Lienhardt, Godfrey. 'Dinka clans, tribes and tribal sections', in AC Beaton, *Equatoria Province Handbook*, Vol. 2 pp. 45–7.

Lienhardt, Godfrey. *Divinity and Experience: the religion of the Dinka*. Oxford: Clarendon, 1961, pp. 171–206.

Lienhardt, Godfrey. 'Getting your own back: themes in Nilotic myth'. In John

HM Beattie and Godfrey Lienhardt, *Studies in Social Anthropology: essays in memory of E. E. Evans-Pritchard*. Oxford: Clarendon, 1975, pp. 213–37.
Lienhardt, Godfrey. 'Nilotic kings and their mother's kin'. *Africa* 25:1 (1955), pp. 29–42.
Lienhardt, Godfrey. 'The Sudan: aspects of the south government among some of the Nilotic peoples, 1947–52'. *British Journal of Middle Eastern Studies* 9:1 (1982), pp. 22–34.
Lienhardt, Godfrey. 'The Western Dinka', in John Middleton and David Tait (eds), *Tribes Without Rulers: studies in African segmentary systems* (London, 1958), pp. 97–135.
Logan, Carolyn. 'Selected chiefs, elected councillors and hybrid democrats: popular perspectives on the co-existence of democracy and traditional authority'. *Journal of Modern African Studies* 47 (2009), pp. 101–128.
Lokuji, Alfred Sebit, Abraham Sewonet Abatneh and Kenyi Wani, Chaplain. *Police Reform in Southern Sudan*. Ottawa; Khartoum: North-South Institute; Centre for Peace and Development Studies, University of Juba, 2009.
Lonsdale, John. 'The conquest state of Kenya, 1895–1905'. In Berman and Lonsdale, *Unhappy Valley*, Vol. 1.
Lonsdale, John. 'The moral economy of Mau Mau: wealth, poverty and civic virtue in Kikuyu political thought'. In Berman and Lonsdale, *Unhappy Valley*. Vol. 2, pp. 315–504.
Lonsdale, John. 'The politics of conquest: the British in Western Kenya, 1894–1908'. In Berman and Lonsdale, *Unhappy Valley*. Vol. 1, pp. 45–74.
Lund, Christian. *Local Politics and the Dynamics of Property in Africa*. Cambridge: Cambridge University Press, 2008.
Lund, Christian. 'Twilight institutions: an introduction'. *Development and Change* 37:4 (2006), pp. 673–684.
Mabior Philip, 'Decentralized justice is lucrative, says Machar', *The Citizen* (Juba), 23 October 2010.
McGregor, JoAnn. *Crossing the Zambezi: the politics of landscape on a Central African frontier*. Woodbridge: James Currey, 2009.
McKinnon, Susan. 'Domestic exceptions: Evans-Pritchard and the creation of Nuer patrilineality and equality'. *Cultural Anthropology* 15:1 (2000), pp. 35–83.
MacMichael, Harold. 'Memorandum on Southern Policy', enclosed in Civil Secretary to Southern Governors, 25 January 1930, appended in Muddathir 'Abd al-Rahim, *Imperialism and Nationalism in the Sudan*, pp. 244–9
Mading Deng, Francis. *Customary Law in the Cross-fire of Sudan's War of Identities*. Washington: US Institute of Peace, 2005.
Mading Deng, Francis. *Tradition and Modernization: a challenge for law among the Dinka of the Sudan*. New Haven, CT and London: Yale University Press, 1971.
Mahmud, Ushari A. *Arabic in the Southern Sudan: history and spread of a pidgin-creole*. Khartoum: FAL Advertising and Printing, 1983.
Mamdani, Mahmood. *Citizen and Subject: contemporary Africa and the legacy of late colonialism*. Princeton NJ: Princeton University Press, 1996.
Mamdani, Mahmood. *Saviors and Survivors: Darfur, politics and the war on terror*. New York: Pantheon, 2009.
Mangor Ring, Moses. 'Dinka stock-trading and shifts in rights in cattle'. In PTW Baxter and R Hogg (eds), *Property, Poverty and People: changing rights in property and problems of pastoral development*. Manchester: Manchester University Press, 1987, pp. 192–205.
Mann, Kristin and Roberts, Richard (eds). *Law in Colonial Africa*. London: James Currey, 1991.

Marshall, AH. *Report on Local Government in the Sudan*. Khartoum: Sudan Government, 1949.
Martin, Ellen and Mosel, Irina. *City Limits: urbanisation and vulnerability in Sudan – Juba case study*. London: Overseas Development Institute, 2011.
Mawson, Andrew NM. 'The Triumph of Life: political dispute and religious ceremonial among the Agar Dinka of the Southern Sudan'. PhD, Cambridge, 1989.
Maxwell, David. *Christians and Chiefs in Zimbabwe: a social history of the Hwesa people c. 1870s–1990s*. Edinburgh: Edinburgh University Press, 1999.
Mennen, Tiernan. *Adapting Restorative Justice Principles to Reform Customary Courts in Dealing with Gender-Based Violence in Southern Sudan*. Report for UNFPA. San Francisco, CA: DPK Consulting, 2008.
Merry, Sally E. 'Law and Colonialism: review essay'. *Law and Society Review* 25:4 (1991), pp. 889–922.
Middleton, John and Tait, David (eds). *Tribes Without Rulers: studies in African segmentary systems*. London: Routledge and Kegan Paul, 1958.
Miers, Suzanne and Kopytoff, Igor (eds). *Slavery in Africa: historical and anthropological perspectives*. Madison: University of Wisconsin Press, 1977.
Mills, LR. 'The growth of Juba in southern Sudan'. In John I Clarke, Mustafa Khogali and Leszek A Kosinski (eds), *Population and Development Projects in Africa*. Cambridge: Cambridge University Press, 1985, pp. 310–23.
Mitchell, Timothy. 'The limits of the state: beyond statist approaches and their critics'. *American Political Science Review* 85:1 (1991), pp. 77–96.
Monyluak Alor Kuol. *Administration of Justice in the (SPLA/M) Liberated Areas: court cases in war-torn Southern Sudan*. Oxford: Refugee Studies Programme, 1997.
Monyluak Alor Kuol. 'The anthropology of law and issues of justice in the Southern Sudan today'. MPhil: University of Oxford, 2000.
Moore, Sally Falk. 'Treating law as knowledge: telling colonial officers what to say to Africans about running "their own" native courts'. *Law and Society Review* 26:1 (1992), pp. 11–46.
Morlang, Franz. 'The journeys of Franz Morlang east and west of Gondokoro in 1859'. In Toniolo and Hill, *The Opening of the Nile Basin*, pp. 109–28.
Myers, Garth Andrew. *Verandahs of Power: colonialism and space in urban Africa*. Syracuse: NY: Syracuse University Press, 2003.
Nalder, LF (ed.). *A Tribal Survey of Mongalla Province, by members of the Province staff and Church Missionary Society*. London: Oxford University Press, 1937.
Nalder, LF. *Equatorial Province Handbook*, Vol. 1: *Mongalla*. Khartoum: McCorquodale, 1936.
Niblock, Tim. *Class and Power in Sudan: the dynamics of Sudanese politics, 1898–1985*. Basingstoke: Macmillan, 1987.
Nugent, Paul. *Smugglers, Secessionists & Loyal Citizens on the Ghana-Togo Frontier*. Oxford: James Currey, 2002.
Nugent, Paul. 'States and social contracts in Africa'. *New Left Review* 63 (2010), pp. 35–68.
Oomen, Barbara. *Chiefs in South Africa: law, power & culture in the post-apartheid era*. Oxford: James Currey, 2005.
von Oppen, Achim. 'The village as territory: enclosing locality in northwest Zambia, 1950s to 1990s'. *Journal of African History* 47 (2006), pp 57–75.
Pact Sudan. 'Sudan Peace Fund (SPF): Final Report, October 2002 – December 2005'. PACT/USAID, 2006.
Pedemonte, E. 'A report on the voyage of 1849–50'. In Toniolo and Hill, *The Opening of the Nile Basin*, pp. 55–73.
Pels, Peter. 'Creolisation in secret: the birth of nationalism in late colonial Uluguru, Tanzania'. *Africa* 72:1 (2002), pp. 1–28.

Pels, Peter. 'The pidginization of Luguru politics: administrative ethnography and the paradoxes of Indirect Rule'. *American Ethnologist* 23:4 (1996), pp. 738–61.

Peterson, Derek R. *Creative Writing: translation, bookkeeping, and the work of imagination in colonial Kenya*. Portsmouth, NH: Heinemann, 2004.

Peterson, Derek R. 'Morality plays: marriage, church courts and colonial agency in colonial Tanganyika, c. 1876–1928'. *American Historical Review* 111:4 (2006), pp. 983–1010.

Petherick, John and Petherick, Katherine. *Travels in Central Africa, and explorations of the western Nile tributaries*. London: Tinsley Brothers, 1869.

Poggo, Scopas S. *The First Sudanese Civil War*. New York: Palgrave Macmillan, 2009.

Poggo, Scopas. 'The origins and culture of blacksmiths in Kuku society of the Sudan, 1797–1955'. *Journal of African Cultural Studies*, 18:2 (2006), pp. 169–186.

Poole, Deborah. 'Between threat and guarantee: justice and community in the margins of the Peruvian state'. In Veena Das and Deborah Poole (eds), *Anthropology in the Margins of the State.* Oxford: Oxford University Press, 2007, pp. 35–65.

Raeymakers, Timothy. 'Protection for sale? War and the transformation of regulation on the Congo-Ugandan border'. *Development and Change* 41:4 (2010), pp. 563–587.

Rafael, Vicente L. *Contracting Colonialism: translation and Christian conversion in Tagalog society under early Spanish rule*. Ithaca: Cornell University Press, 1988.

Ranger, Terence. 'The invention of tradition in Colonial Africa', in E. Hobsbawm and Terence Ranger (eds), *The Invention of Tradition* (Cambridge, 1983), pp. 211–62.

Reid, Richard J. *Frontiers of Violence in North-East Africa: genealogies of conflict since c. 1800*. Oxford: Oxford University Press, 2011.

Reid, Richard J. *Political Power in Pre-Colonial Buganda: economy, society & warfare in the nineteenth century*. Oxford: James Currey, 2002.

Reining, Conrad C. *The Zande Scheme: an anthropological case study of economic development in Africa*. Evanston, IL: Northwestern University Press, 1966.

Richards, Paul. 'To fight or to farm? Agrarian dimensions of the Mano River conflicts (Liberia and Sierra Leone)'. *African Affairs* 104:417 (2005), pp. 571–590.

Riek Machar, GoSS Vice-President, speaking at the Rift Valley Institute – US Institute of Peace launch of the report 'Local Justice in Southern Sudan' in the Home and Away Hotel, Juba, 22 October 2010.

Robertson, Claire C. 'Gender and trade relations in central Kenya in the late nineteenth century'. *International Journal of African Historical Studies* 30:1 (1997), pp. 23–47.

Rohn, Helge; Adwok Nyaba, Peter and Maker Benjamin, George. 'Report of the study on local administrative structures in Maridi, Mundri and Yei Counties – West Bank Equatoria, South Sudan'. Nairobi: Aktion Afrika Hilfe, 1997.

Rolandsen, Øystein H. 'A false start: between war and peace in the Southern Sudan, 1956–62'. *Journal of African History* 52, 1 (2011), pp. 105–123.

Rolandsen, Øystein H. 'Civil War Society? Political processes, social groups and conflict intensity in the Southern Sudan, 1955–2005'. PhD, University of Oslo, 2010.

Rolandsen, Øystein H. *Guerrilla Government: political changes in the Southern Sudan during the 1990s*. Uppsala: Nordiska Afrikainstitutet, 2005.

Rolandsen, Øystein. 'In search of the peace dividend: the Southern Sudan one year after the signatures'. Paper presented at the 7th International Sudan Studies Conference, Bergen, 7 April 2006. Oslo: PRIO, accessed 21 January 2013, www.prio.no/Publications/Publication/?x=3417

Rolandsen, Øystein H. *Land, Security and Peacebuilding in the Southern Sudan.* Oslo: PRIO, 2009.

Rolandsen, Øystein H. 'The making of the Anya-Nya insurgency in the Southern Sudan, 1961–64'. *Journal of Eastern African Studies* 5:2 (2011), pp. 211–32.

Rolandsen, Øystein. 'To mend the broken contract: legitimacy and local government in South Sudan during the CPA-period'. Paper presented at the Symposium on Government and Governance in South Sudan, Oxford University, 9 June 2011, and at the ECAS4 Conference, Uppsala, 17 June 2011.

Rondinelli, Dennis A. 'Administrative decentralisation and economic development: the Sudan's experiment with devolution'. *Journal of Modern African Studies* 19:4 (1981), pp. 595–624.

van Rouveroy van Nieuwaal, E. Adriaan B., and van Dijk, Rijk (eds). *African Chieftaincy in a New Socio-Political Landscape.* Leiden: African Studies Centre, 1999.

Salva Kiir Mayardit, President of the Government of Southern Sudan. Speech to the conference of kings, queens, paramount chiefs and traditional leaders, Bentiu, Unity State, 17 May. Juba: Office of the President, GoSS, 2009.

Sanderson, Lillian Passmore. 'Education in the Southern Sudan: the impact of government-missionary-southern Sudanese relationships upon the development of education during the Condominium period, 1898–1956'. *African Affairs* 79:315 (1980), pp. 157–69.

Santschi, Martina. 'Briefing: counting "New Sudan"'. *African Affairs* 107:429 (2008), pp. 631–40.

Scheye, Eric and Baker, Bruce. 'The multi-layered approach: supporting local justice and security systems in southern Sudan'. Juba: draft report for DFID Strategic Development Fund, 2007.

Schilling, Donald G. 'Local Native Councils and the politics of education in Kenya, 1925–1939'. *International Journal of African Historical Studies* 9:2 (1976), pp. 218–47.

Schomerus, Mareike and Allen, Tim. *Southern Sudan at Odds with Itself: dynamics of conflict and predicaments of peace.* London: Development Studies Institute, LSE, 2010.

Schweinfurth, Georg. *The Heart of Africa: three years' travels and adventures in the unexplored regions of Central Africa. From 1868 to 1871,* Vols 1 and 2. Translated by EE Frewer. New York: Harper, 1874.

Scott, David. 'Colonial governmentality'. *Social Text* 43 (1995), pp. 191–220.

Scott, James. *The Art of Not Being Governed: an anarchist history of upland Southeast Asia.* New Haven (CT): Yale University Press, 2009.

Scott, James. *Seeing like a State: how certain schemes to improve the human condition have failed.* New Haven: Yale University Press, 1998.

Scott, James. *Weapons of the Weak: everyday forms of peasant resistance.* New Haven, CT: Yale University Press, 1985.

Sewonet Abatneh, Abraham and Monoja Lubang, Simon. 'Police reform and state formation in Southern Sudan'. *Canadian Journal of Development Studies* 32:1 (2011), pp. 94–108.

Shadle, Brett. 'Bridewealth and female consent: marriage disputes in African courts, Gusiiland, Kenya'. *Journal of African History* 44 (2003), pp. 241–62.

Shadle, Brett. '"Changing traditions to meet current altering conditions": customary law, African courts and the rejection of codification in Kenya, 1930–60'. *Journal of African History* 40 (1999), pp. 411–31.

Simonse, Simon. *Kings of Disaster: dualism, centralism, and the scapegoat king in southeastern Sudan.* Leiden: Brill, 1992.

Southall, AW. 'Stateless Societies'. In *International Encyclopedia of the Social Sciences*, Vol. 15. New York: Macmillan, 1968.
Spear, Thomas. 'Neo-traditionalism and the limits of invention in British colonial Africa'. *Journal of African History* 44 (2003), pp. 3–27.
Spear, Thomas and Waller, Richard (eds). *Being Maasai: ethnicity & identity in East Africa*. Oxford: James Currey, 1993.
Spire, F. 'Rain-making in Equatorial Africa'. *Journal of the Royal African Society* 5:17 (1905), pp. 15–21.
SPLM. 'Vision and programme of the Sudan People's Liberation Movement (SPLM)'. SPLM Political Secretariat, Yei and New Cush, New Sudan (1998).
SPLM Local Government Secretariat. 'Local Government Framework for Southern Sudan', Fourth Draft. Rumbek: SPLM, 2004.
Stigand, Chauncey H. *Equatoria: the Lado Enclave*. London, 1923.
Sudan African National Union. *Memorandum presented to the Commission of the Organisation of African Unity for Refugees*. Kampala: SANU, November 1964.
Sudan Government Intelligence Department. *The Bahr el Ghazal Province*. London: HMSO, 1911.
Sudan Human Security Baseline Assessment. *Women's Security and the Law in South Sudan*. Geneva: Small Arms Survey, 2012.
Sundnes, Frode and Shanmugaratnam, N. 'Socio-economic revival and emerging issues relating to land and customary institutions in Yirol, Southern Sudan'. In N. Shanmugaratnam (ed.), *Between War & Peace in Sudan & Sri Lanka: deprivation & livelihood revival*. Oxford: James Currey, 2008, pp. 59–76.
Thomas, Edward. *The Kafia Kingi Enclave: people, politics and history in the north–south boundary zone of western Sudan*. London: Rift Valley Institute, 2010.
Toniolo, Elias and Hill, Richard (eds). *The Opening of the Nile Basin: writings by members of the Catholic Mission to Central Africa on the geography and ethnography of the Sudan, 1842–1881*. New York: Barnes and Noble, 1975.
Tosh, John. *Clan Leaders and Colonial Chiefs in Lango: the political history of an East African stateless society c.1800–1939*. Oxford: Clarendon, 1978.
Tosh, John. 'Lango agriculture during the early colonial period: land and labour in a cash-crop economy'. *Journal of African History* 19:3 (1978), pp. 415–39.
Trefon, Theodore. 'Hinges and fringes: conceptualising the peri-urban in central Africa'. In Francesca Locatelli and Paul Nugent (eds), *African Cities: competing claims on urban spaces*. Leiden: Brill, 2009, pp. 15–35.
Tripp, Charles. 'Review – Sudan: state and elite'. *Africa* 67:1 (1997), pp. 159–73.
Tronvoll, Kjetil and Hagmann, Tobias (eds). *Contested Power in Ethiopia: traditional authorities and multi-party elections*. Leiden: Brill, 2011.
von Trotha, Trutz. 'From administrative to civil chieftaincy: some problems and prospects of African chieftaincy'. *Journal of Legal Pluralism and Unofficial Law* 37–38 (1996), pp. 79–107.
Udal, John O. *The Nile in Darkness* Vol. 1*: conquest and exploration 1504–1862*. Norwich: Michael Russell, 1998.
Udal, John O. *The Nile in Darkness* Vol. 2*: a flawed unity 1863–1899*. Norwich: Michael Russell, 2005.
Vansina, Jan. *Paths in the Rainforests: towards a history of political tradition in equatorial Africa*. Madison: The University of Wisconsin Press, 1990.
Vaughan, Chris. '"Demonstrating the machine guns": rebellion, violence and state formation in early colonial Darfur'. *Journal of Imperial and Commonwealth History* (forthcoming, 2013).
Vaughan, Chris. 'Negotiating the State at its Margins: colonial authority in Condominium Darfur, 1916–1956'. PhD, Durham University, 2011.
Vaughan, Megan. 'Food production and family labour in southern Malawi: the

Shire highlands and upper Shire valley in the early colonial period'. *Journal of African History* 23:3 (1982), pp. 351–64.

Vaughan, Olufemi. *Nigerian Chiefs: traditional power in modern politics 1890s–1990s*. Rochester, NY: University of Rochester Press, 2000.

Vinco, Angelo. 'First Christian to live among the Bari: his journeys 1851–1852'. In Toniolo and Hill, *The Opening of the Nile Basin*, pp. 74–105.

de Vries, Lotje A. 'Facing Frontiers: everyday practise of state-building in South Sudan'. PhD thesis, Wageningen University, 2012.

de Waal, Alex. 'Sudan: the turbulent state'. In Alex de Waal (ed.). *War in Darfur and the Search for Peace*. London: Justice in Africa, 2007, pp. 1–38.

Wai, Dunstan M. (ed.). *The Southern Sudan: the problem of national integration.* London: Frank Cass, 1973.

Walraet, Anne. 'Governance, violence and the struggle for economic regulation in South Sudan: the case of Budi County (Eastern Equatoria)'. *Afrika Focus* 21:2 (2008), pp. 53–70.

Watson, Ruth. *'Civil Disorder is the Disease of Ibadan': chieftaincy & civic culture in a Yoruba city*. Oxford: James Currey, 2003.

Werne, Ferdinand (Tr. CW O'Reilly). *Expedition to Discover the Sources of the White Nile, in the Years 1840, 1841,* Vol. 2. London: Richard Bentley, 1849 [British Library, 2010].

West, Harry G and Kloeck-Jenson, Scott. 'Betwixt and between: 'traditional authority' and democratic decentralisation in post-war Mozambique'. *African Affairs* 98:393 (1999), pp. 455–484.

Whitehead, GO. 'Crops and cattle among the Bari and Bari-Speaking tribes'. *Sudan Notes and Records* 43 (1962), pp. 131–42.

Whitehead, GO. 'Property and inheritance among the Bari'. *Sudan Notes and Records* 31:1 (1950), pp. 143–7.

Whitehead, GO. 'Social change among the Bari'. *Sudan Notes and Records* 12:1 (1929), pp. 91–97.

Whitehead, GO. 'Suppressed Classes among the Bari and Bari-speaking Tribes'. *Sudan Notes and Records* 34:2 (1953), pp. 265–80.

Williams, J Michael. 'Leading from behind: democratic consolidation and the chieftaincy in South Africa'. *Journal of Modern African Studies* 42 (2004), pp. 113–136.

Willis, Justin. 'Chieftaincy'. In John Parker and Richard Reid (eds), *Oxford Handbook of Modern African History*. Oxford University Press, forthcoming.

Willis, Justin. 'Clan and history in western Uganda: a new perspective on the origins of pastoral dominance'. *International Journal of African Historical Studies* 30:3 (1997), pp. 583–600.

Willis, Justin. '*Hukm*: the creolization of authority in Condominium Sudan'. *Journal of African History* 46 (2005), pp. 29–50.

Willis, Justin. '"The Nyamang are hard to touch": mission evangelism and tradition in the Nuba Mountains, Sudan, 1933–1952'. *Journal of Religion in Africa* 33:1 (2003), pp. 32–62.

Willis, Justin. 'Violence, authority and the state in the Nuba Mountains of Condominium Sudan'. *The Historical Journal* 46:1 (2003), pp. 89–114.

Wilson, Charles T and Felkin, Robert W. *Uganda and the Egyptian Soudan*, Vol. 2. London: S. Low, Marston, Searle & Rivington, 1882.

Woodward, Peter. *Sudan 1898–1989: the unstable state*. Boulder, CO: Rienner, 1990.

Young, Crawford. *The African Colonial State in Comparative Perspective*. New Haven, CT: Yale University Press, 1994.

Zanen, SM and van den Hoek, AW. 'Dinka dualism and the Nilotic hierarchy of values'. In PE de Josselin de Jong, R de Ridder and Jan AJ Karremans, *The Leiden Tradition in Structural Anthropology*. Brill: Leiden, 1987, pp. 170–97.

Zeller, Wolfgang. '"Now we are a town": chiefs, investors, and the state in Zambia's Western Province'. In Buur and Kyed, *State Recognition and Democratization in Sub-Saharan Africa*, pp. 209–31.

Index

EASTERN AFRICAN STUDIES

These titles published in the United States and Canada by Ohio University Press

Revealing Prophets
Edited by DAVID M. ANDERSON & DOUGLAS H. JOHNSON

East African Expressions of Chistianity
Edited by THOMAS SPEAR & ISARIA N. KIMAMBO

The Poor Are Not Us
Edited by DAVID M. ANDERSON & VIGDIS BROCH-DUE

Potent Brews
JUSTIN WILLIS

Swahili Origins
JAMES DE VERE ALLEN

Being Maasai
Edited by THOMAS SPEAR & RICHARD WALLER

Jua Kali Kerya
KENNETH KING

Control & Crisis in Colonial Kenya
BRUCE BERMAN

Unhappy Valley
Book One: State & Class
Book Two: Violence & Ethnicity
BRUCE BERMAN & JOHN LONSDALE

Mau Mau from Below
GREET KERSHAW

The Mau Mau War in Perspective
FRANK FUREDI

Squatters & the Roots of Mau Mau 1905-63
TABITHA KANOGO

Economic & Social Origins of Mau Mau 1945-53
DAVID W. THROUP

Multi-Party Politics in Kenya
DAVID W. THROUP & CHARLES HORNSBY

Empire State-Building
JOANNA LEWIS

Decolonization & Independence in Kenya 1940-93
Edited by B.A. OGOT & WILLIAM R. OCHIENG'

Eroding the Commons
DAVID ANDERSON

Penetration & Protest in Tanzania
ISARIA N. KIMAMBO

Custodians of the Land
Edited by GREGORY MADDOX, JAMES L. GIBLIN & ISARIA N. KIMAMBO

Education in the Development of Tanzania 1919-1990
LENE BUCHERT

The Second Economy in Tanzania
T.L. MALIYAMKONO & M.S.D. BAGACHWA

Ecology Control & Economic Development in East African History
HELGE KJEKSHUS

Siaya
DAVID WILLIAM COHEN & E.S. ATIENO ODHIAMBO

Uganda Now • Changing Uganda Developing Uganda • From Chaos to Order • Religion & Politics in East Africa
Edited by HOLGER BERNT HANSEN & MICHAEL TWADDLE

Kakungulu & the Creation of Uganda 1868-1928
MICHAEL TWADDLE

Controlling Anger
SUZETTE HEALD

Kampala Women Getting By
SANDRA WALLMAN

Political Power in Pre-Colonial Buganda
RICHARD J. REID

Alice Lakwena & the Holy Spirits
HEIKE BEHREND

Slaves, Spices & Ivory in Zanzibar
ABDUL SHERIFF

Zanzibar Under Colonial Rule
Edited by ABDUL SHERIFF & ED FERGUSON

The History & Conservation of Zanzibar Stone Town
Edited by ABDUL SHERIFF

Pastimes & Politics
LAURA FAIR

Ethnicity & Conflict in the Horn of Africa
Edited by KATSUYOSHI FUKUI & JOHN MARKAKIS

Conflict, Age & Power in North East Africa
Edited by EISEI KURIMOTO & SIMON SIMONSE

Propery Rights & Political Development in Ethiopia & Eritrea
SANDRA FULLERTON JOIREMAN

Revolution & Religion in Ethiopia
ØYVIND M. EIDE

Brothers at War
TEKESTE NEGASH & KJETIL TRONVOLL

From Guerrillas to Government
DAVID POOL

Mau Mau & Nationhood
Edited by E.S. ATIENO ODHIAMBO & JOHN LONSDALE

A History of Modern Ethiopia, 1855-1991(2nd edn)
BAHRU ZEWDE

Pioneers of Change in Ethiopia
BAHRU ZEWDE

Remapping Ethiopia
Edited by W. JAMES, D. DONHAM, E. KURIMOTO & A. TRIULZI

Southern Marches of Imperial Ethiopia
Edited by DONALD L. DONHAM & WENDY JAMES

A Modern History of the Somali (4th edn)
I.M. LEWIS

Islands of Intensive Agriculture in East Africa
Edited by MATS WIDGREN & JOHN E.G. SUTTON

Leaf of Allah
EZEKIEL GEBISSA

Dhows & the Colonial Economy of Zanzibar 1860-1970
ERIK GILBERT

African Womanhood in Colonial Kerya
TABITHA KANOGO

African Underclass
ANDREW BURTON

In Search of a Nation
Edited by GREGORY H. MADDOX & JAMES L. GIBLIN

A History of the Excluded
JAMES L. GIBLIN

Black Poachers, White Hunters
EDWARD I. STEINHART

Ethnic Federalism
DAVID TURTON

Crisis & Decline in Bunyoro
SHANE DOYLE

Emancipation without Abolition in German East Africa
JAN-GEORG DEUTSCH

Women, Work & Domestic Virtue in Uganda 1900-2003
GRACE BANTEBYA KYOMUHENDO & MARJORIE KENISTON McINTOSH

Cultivating Success in Uganda
GRACE CARSWELL

War *in Pre-Colonial Eastern Africa*
RICHARD REID

Slavery in the Great Lakes Region of East Africa
Edited by HENRI MÉDARD & SHANE DOYLE

The Benefits of Famine
DAVID KEEN

Lightning Source UK Ltd.
Milton Keynes UK
UKHW022047210919
350164UK00006B/288/P

9 781847 011145